Bodies of Violence

Oxford Studies in Gender and International Relations

Series editors: J. Ann Tickner, University of Southern California, and Laura Sjoberg, University of Florida

Enlisting Masculinity:
The Construction of Gender in U.S. Military Recruiting Advertising during the All-Volunteer Force
Melissa T. Brown

Cosmopolitan Sex Workers:
Women and Migration in a Global City
Christine B. N. Chin

Intelligent Compassion:
Feminist Critical Methodology in the Women's International League for Peace and Freedom
Catia Cecilia Confortini

Gender, Sex, and the Postnational Defense:
Militarism and Peacekeeping
Annica Kronsell

The Beauty Trade:
Youth, Gender, and Fashion Globalization
Angela B. McCracken

From Global To Grassroots:
The European Union, Transnational Advocacy, and Combating Violence against Women
Celeste Montoya

A Feminist Voyage through International Relations
J. Ann Tickner

The Political Economy of Violence against Women
Jacqui True

BODIES OF VIOLENCE
*Theorizing Embodied Subjects
in International Relations*

Lauren B. Wilcox

OXFORD
UNIVERSITY PRESS

Oxford University Press is a department of the University of Oxford.
It furthers the University's objective of excellence in research, scholarship,
and education by publishing worldwide.

Oxford   New York
Auckland   Cape Town   Dar es Salaam   Hong Kong   Karachi
Kuala Lumpur   Madrid   Melbourne   Mexico City   Nairobi
New Delhi   Shanghai   Taipei   Toronto

With offices in
Argentina   Austria   Brazil   Chile   Czech Republic   France   Greece
Guatemala   Hungary   Italy   Japan   Poland   Portugal   Singapore
South Korea   Switzerland   Thailand   Turkey   Ukraine   Vietnam

Oxford is a registered trademark of Oxford University Press
in the UK and certain other countries.

Published in the United States of America by
Oxford University Press
198 Madison Avenue, New York, NY 10016

© Oxford University Press 2015

All rights reserved. No part of this publication may be reproduced, stored in a
retrieval system, or transmitted, in any form or by any means, without the prior
permission in writing of Oxford University Press, or as expressly permitted by law,
by license, or under terms agreed with the appropriate reproduction rights organization.
Inquiries concerning reproduction outside the scope of the above should be sent to the
Rights Department, Oxford University Press, at the address above.

You must not circulate this work in any other form
and you must impose this same condition on any acquirer.

Library of Congress Cataloging-in-Publication Data
Wilcox, Lauren B.
Bodies of violence : theorizing embodied subjects in international relations/Lauren B. Wilcox.
   pages cm.—(Oxford Studies in gender and international relations)
Includes bibliographical references and index.
ISBN 978–0–19–938448–8 (hardcover)   1. International relations—Sociological aspects.
2. International relations—Philosophy.   3. Violence—Political aspects.   4. Human body—
Political aspects.   5. Human body—Social aspects.   I. Title.
JZ1251.W55 2014
327.1'17—dc23
2014016536

For my family

The body implies mortality, vulnerability, agency: the skin and the flesh expose us to the gaze of others but also to touch and to violence . . .
—Judith Butler (2004a, 26)

CONTENTS

Introduction   1

1. Bodies, Subjects, and Violence in International Relations   17

2. Dying Is Not Permitted: Guantánamo Bay and the Liberal Subject of International Relations   49

3. Explosive Bodies: Suicide Bombing as an Embodied Practice and the Politics of Abjection   80

4. Crossing Borders, Securing Bodies: Airport Security Assemblages and Bodies of Information   104

5. Body Counts: The Politics of Embodiment in Precision Warfare   131

6. Vulnerable Bodies and the "Responsibility to Protect"   166

Conclusion   190

Acknowledgments   205
Notes   207
Bibliography   213
Index   235

Bodies of Violence

Introduction

Theorizing Bodies, Subjects, and Violence in International Relations

Between 70 and 100 people died in one airstrike in northern Afghanistan in September 2009 when NATO targeted two fuel tankers that the Taliban had hijacked. Having gotten them stuck in a riverbed, the Taliban decided to give them to impoverished villagers who were struggling to stockpile fuel for the winter. The bodies were mangled and scorched beyond recognition; because the bodies were unidentifiable, village elders asked grieving relatives how many family members they had lost, and distributed one body to match each one lost so they could be buried and grieved. When bodies had run out, the elders gave body parts to families still missing relatives. One man said, "I couldn't find my son, so I took a piece of flesh with me . . . and I called it my son" (Abdul-Ahad 2009).

Bodies have long been outside the frame of International Relations (IR)—unrecognizable even as the modes of violence that use, target, and construct bodies in complex ways have proliferated. Drones make it possible to both watch people and bomb them, often killing dozens of civilians as well, while the pilots operating these machines remain thousands of miles away, immune from bodily harm. Suicide bombers seek certain death by turning their bodies into weapons that seem to attack at random. Images of tortured bodies from Guantánamo Bay and Abu Ghraib provoke shock and outrage, and prisoners on hunger strikes to protest their treatment are force-fed. Meanwhile, the management of violence increasingly entails the scrutiny of persons as bodies through biometric technologies and "body scanners." In each of these instances, the body becomes the focal point, central to practices of security and International Relations—the body brought into excruciating pain, the body as weapon, or the body as that which is *not* to be targeted and hence is hit only accidentally or collaterally. Such bodily focus is quite distinct from prevailing international security practices and the disciplinary ways of addressing those practices in IR. Convention has it that states or groups make war and, in doing so, kill and injure people that other states are charged with protecting. The strategic deployment of force in the language of rational control and risk management that dominates security studies presents a disembodied view of subjects as reasoning actors. However, as objects of security studies, the people who are protected from violence or are killed are understood as *only* bodies: they are ahistorical, biopolitical aggregations whose individual members breathe, suffer, and die. In both cases, the politics and sociality of bodies are erased.

One of the deep ironies of security studies is that while war is actually inflicted on bodies, bodily violence and vulnerability, as the flip side of security, are largely ignored. By contrast, feminist theory is at its most powerful when it denaturalizes accounts of individual subjectivity so as to analyze the relations of force, violence, and language that compose our profoundly unnatural bodies. Security studies lacks the reflexivity necessary to see its contribution to the very context it seeks to domesticate. It has largely ignored work in feminist theory that opens up the forces that have come to compose and constitute the body: by and large, security studies has an unarticulated, yet implicit, conception of bodies as individual organisms whose protection from damage constitutes the provision of security. In IR, human bodies are implicitly theorized as organisms that are exogenously determined—they are relevant to politics only as they live or die. Such bodies are inert objects: they exist to be manipulated, possess no agency, and are only driven by the motivations of agents. Attentive to the relations provoked by both discourse and political forces, feminist theory redirects attention to how both of these compose and produce bodies on terms often alien and unstable. Contemporary feminist theorizing about embodiment provides a provocative challenge to the stability and viability of several key concepts such as sovereignty, security, violence, and vulnerability in IR. In this book, I draw on recent work in feminist theory that offers a challenge to the deliberate maintenance and policing of boundaries and the delineation of human bodies from the broader political context.

Challenging this theorization of bodies as natural organisms is a key step in not only exposing how bodies have been implicitly theorized in

IR, but in developing a reading of IR that is attentive to the ways in which bodies are both produced and productive. In conceptualizing the subject of IR as essentially disembodied, IR theory impoverishes itself. An explicit focus on the subject as *embodied* makes two contributions to IR. First, I address the question vexing the humanities and social sciences of how to account for the subject by showing that IR is wrong in its uncomplicated way of thinking about the subject in relation to its embodiment. In its rationalist variants, IR theory comprehends bodies only as inert objects animated by the minds of individuals. Constructivist theory argues that subjects are formed through social relations, but leaves the bodies of subjects outside politics as "brute facts" (Wendt 2001, 110), while many variants of critical theory understand the body as a medium of social power, rather than also a force in its own right. In contrast, feminist theory offers a challenge to the delineation of human bodies from subjects and the broader political context. My central argument is that the bodies that the practices of violence take as their object are deeply political bodies, constituted in reference to historical political conditions while at the same time acting upon our world. The second contribution of this work is to argue that because of the way it theorizes subjects in relation to their embodiment, IR is also lacking in one of its primary purposes: theorizing international political violence. This project argues that violence is more than a strategic action of rational actors (as in rationalist theories) or a destructive violation of community laws and norms (as in liberal and constructivist theories). Because IR conventionally theorizes bodies as outside politics and irrelevant to subjectivity, it cannot see how violence can be understood as a creative force for shaping the limits of how we understand ourselves as political subjects, as well as forming the boundaries of our bodies and political communities. Understanding how "war is a generative force like no other" (Barkawi and Brighton 2011, 126) requires us to pay attention to how bodies are killed and injured, but also formed, re-formed, gendered, and racialized through the bodily relations of war; it also requires that we consider how bodies are enabling and generative of war and practices of political violence more broadly.

Security studies, the subfield of IR that focuses on violence, has defined its topic of study as "the study of the threat, use, and control of military force" (Walt 1991, 212), with emphasis on the causes of war and the conditions for peace. Despite the traditional focus on military force, security studies has by and large ignored the bodies that are the intended or inevitable targets of the use of such force. One classic work in the field, Schelling's *Arms and Influence* (1966), specifically addresses coercion as the threat to cause pain and to hurt human bodies in order to manipulate a certain outcome. Few works are so explicit—that force involves the threat or use of military power to hurt and kill human bodies is usually implicit in security studies. Furthermore, when the violence to human bodies is made explicit, as in Schelling, such bodies are implicitly theorized precisely as organisms that can be hurt or killed. Contributing to the neglect of theorizing bodies has been the emphasis placed on *national* security. National security has long been the center of analysis in security studies, but in recent decades, the field has broadened to consider the referent object of security to be the individual, as "people represent, in one sense, the irreducible basic unit to which the concept of security can be applied" (Buzan 1991, 18). The concept of "human security" posits the question of violence against human bodies as a central issue in security studies, yet this theorization accepts the individual as an exogenous unit of analysis. The relationship between bodies, subjects, and violence still remains under-theorized, a matter at least partly related to the ways in which the conduct of war and political violence, as violent social practices, have been written out of the field of IR and, in particular, out of security studies as a subfield (Barkawi 2011). This lacuna has been noted, if rarely explored in depth: "the absence of bodies in the discourses of a discipline that was borne of a concern with war and hence violence against bodies, itself raises curiosity as to the conditions of possibility that enabled this absence" (Jabri 2006b, 825). This work addresses this absence and aims to show what taking bodies seriously would mean to the study of violence in IR.

The four forms of contemporary political violence and its management that I address in depth in this work—torture/force-feeding, suicide bombing, airport security procedures, and precision warfare—all engage the human body in a fundamental ways that are ignored or obscured by the dominant framing of these issues in the literature. The IR literature has asked, for example, whether suicide bombing can be considered a rational practice and what strategic functions it serves (Pape 2005; Gambetta 2005; Crenshaw 2007; Moghadam 2009), and has asked what meanings this practice has for its practitioners and the audience for this type of violence (Hafez 2006; Dingley and Mollica 2007; Roberts 2007; Fierke 2009, 2013). Theorizing the body allows us to ask questions that have not, and cannot, be asked, given prevailing implicit conceptions of the body in IR. The literature has not asked what effects suicide bombing might have that are not reducible to the motivations of individual actors; that is, what does the use of the body in this particular way entail politically that is absent in other forms of political violence? Understanding the political dynamics of the construction and deconstruction of the body (and more specifically, the subject as embodied) opens a window into the symbolic power of bodily integrity and can help us to understand why suicide bombing is a particularly feared yet captivating form of violence. Taking bodies seriously as political not only serves an explanatory role in thinking about how subjects are constituted and how violent practices are enabled in IR, but also becomes a critical project for opening up space for thinking about politics and resistance in ways previously overlooked.

A focus on the bodies of prisoners at Guantánamo Bay reveals the workings of power in ways that have been overlooked by IR scholars seeking to theorizing torture and the "war on terror." The IR literature asks why states torture and how state identity and international laws and norms serve to constrain states in this regard (Foot 2006; Blakely 2007; McKeown 2009). Ethical perspectives in IR have also discussed when, if ever, torture may be permissible (Shue 1978; Bellamy 2006). Torture is generally regarded as impermissible, as a remnant of a pre-modern past, and as behavior that "civilized" states do not engage in. Seeing this kind of violent intervention on the body as something to be avoided misses how violence is often *productive*. We miss, for example, how torture and pain not only harm the body, but also produce particular subjects that can be tortured. Opponents to the force-feeding of hunger strikers argue that it is an unwarranted bodily intrusion, while proponents frame it as a necessary, lifesaving procedure, as well as an important tactic in the "war on terror"; both of these positions, however, miss the way in which this practice constitutes the bodies of the hunger-strikers as dependents and makes such techniques more acceptable to concerned audiences. By theorizing bodies as subject to human malleability rather than as fixed, we can see how violence constitutes differently embodied subjects, as well as some of the ways in which bodies can resist their constitution in the social order.

Extending our political analysis to bodies offers explanatory value into the constitutive conditions for violence in International Relations. By assuming that bodies are individuated biological entities, traditional IR theory has been unable to conceptualize bodies as constituted in relation to one another. As I argue in Chapter 5, this relational constitution of bodies is a condition of possibility for the violence of precision warfare. On the topic of precision bombing, traditional strategic studies debates have centered on whether or not the use of precision guided munitions substantially adds to the coercive effects of air power, and whether the reliance on such weapons is in the short- and long-term interests of the United States (Pape 1996; Press 2001). The causes and conditions that engender the targeting of civilians in bombing campaigns are still a matter of great debate in IR, even though the liberal humanitarian wars in the post–Cold War era, as well as the "war on terror," have focused on the use of precision bombing (Milliken and Sylvan 1996; Thomas 2001; Downes 2009). Scholars have probed how the choice to develop and use precision air strikes and drones affects how bodies are viewed as potential targets, but less well understood is how precision warfare constitutes a political adaptation of bodies themselves, of the pilots and drone operators as well as those of the targets and those at risk from aerial warfare. Scholars and critics of precision warfare have argued that physical distance and psychological distance between the bomber and victim is a crucial condition of possibility for this type of violence (Grossman 1995, 97–113; Gregory 2004, 197–217). This type of warfare once involved targeting coordinates or grids in which individual people could not be seen. However, in today's precision warfare, the bombers and drone pilots can often see the targets of their missiles quite clearly. We must therefore search beyond the issue of sight and distance for the roots of this mode of violence, for mere visual representation of bodies is not sufficient to make killing in this way psychologically and politically untenable. By theorizing precision warfare as enabled by a conceptualization of human bodies as information processors that are an integral part of a human/technology assemblage, we can better understand the conditions for producing certain bodies as "killable" as well as how this form of warfare comes to be perceived as legitimate in ways that are occluded by theorizing this form of violence as "disembodied."

Besides opening up interpretive space and offering a constitutive analysis of violence in IR, there are important normative implications for explicitly theorizing the subject as embodied in International Relations. One aim of this book is to help create space for new kinds of theorizing in IR by denaturalizing the body. By casting the body as a material, "brute" fact that can largely be ignored, or as only the medium through which power works, we limit our understanding of the political possibilities for different kinds of bodily politics. Making bodies central to theorizing in IR allows us to rethink the dynamics of global politics in ways that open new avenues for politics. In particular, we can theorize the body as an effect of practices of IR, rather than taking the body for granted as an apolitical object. For example, as I discuss in Chapter 3, the body of the "Israeli Jew" is constituted, in part, by practices of recovery organizations in the wake of suicide bombings. Understanding the body not only as something that is acted upon in instances of violence, but also as something that is constituted in and through violence, can open up the body as a space for engaging in politics. Thinking about the "sex" of bodies as something constituted not by nature, but by the state and society, as the experiences of transgender persons reveal, suggests that efforts to locate truth in the materiality of bodies—as biometric security procedures do—is not a neutral act of providing security for all travelers, but rather reinforces certain normative ways of living in a body as safe and others as risky or dangerous. The instability of the category of "sex" draws attention to the ways in which "the body" as a referent of security is also unstable. Bodies, then, can be thought of not only as objects to be defended from injury or as signifiers or ultimate truth, but as sites of tension and paradox that call into question the operations of security itself.

In this book, the normative aspects of theorizing the subject as embodied are also informed by feminist theory: feminists have been at the forefront of questioning the relationships between embodiment, power, and violence in order to challenge the legitimization of women's subordination through social and scientific discourses which contend that female physiology is the source of women's inferior social, economic, and political status. Through their analysis of the concepts of gender and sexuality, feminists have challenged the too-easy equation of subjectivity with physical embodiment. Feminists have interrogated issues of embodiment as political in order to expose how conceptions of the seemingly natural body normalize certain forms of political oppression and exclusion for those whose bodies are considered non-standard, deviant, or "other," including women, queer people, transgender people, racial and ethnic minorities, and people with disabilities. Denaturalizing the body and theorizing its political constitution in and through practices of political violence, as well as the ways in which bodies productively contribute to the character of that violence, is thus a crucial component of a project to undermine various forms of marginalization and subordination in International Relations. Much as "opening the black box of the state" allowed IR theorists to critically examine a much broader range of actors, issues, and practices relevant to IR, opening up the body to political analysis allows us to critically interrogate the body as something with a history whose story is continually being written. Feminist scholars have played a leading role in theorizing embodiment, yet feminist scholars in IR have yet to fully explore the implications of the political constitution of the body, and the body as a kind of political agent.

RETHINKING VIOLENCE, SUBJECTIVITY, AND BODIES

While feminists and other critical IR scholars have decried the "disembodiment" of theorizing about international security and have sought to center the broken, bleeding, and starving body produced by political violence in our political imaginaries, such efforts at pointing out the cruelty of the violent practices of war do not necessarily change the underlying conceptualization of the body as an object of manipulation. It is here that feminist theory is most incisive, for feminists have struggled with the problems of how to theorize embodiment as a necessary but not exclusive aspect of subjectivity in their own terms—terms that can help us to "think the body" in IR in such a way as to provide new purchase on central concepts such as power, security, vulnerability, and violence. For example, violence can be re-thought as something that is productive and not only destructive; vulnerability is not just a condition to be overcome but a constitutive feature of the embodied subject. This project is also significant in that it extends and adapts feminist theorizing about embodiment, and in particular the work of Judith Butler, to the realm of international political violence. The implication of feminist theory's emphasis on the co-constitution of bodies and political structures is to give IR a new starting point, as theorists can no longer begin with political communities populated by actors whose bodies are undifferentiated and can be transcended.

I turn to feminist insights in thinking about bodies not only to talk about how gender discourses produce particular bodies, but how bodies are performatively produced more generally. The concept of performativity is central to how I theorize the relationship between bodies, subjects, and violence. By "performative," I mean "that aspect of discourse that has the capacity to produce what it names" (Butler 1994, 33). Discourses can be termed performative because they do not provide a neutral reflection of an underlying reality, but rather create that very reality. To say that bodies are performative is to be concerned with the production of material realities, and thus, in feminist theory, to challenge the assumption that the sex of bodies as a material fact lies outside the realm of politics. Feminist thought teaches us that the body cannot be taken for granted as stable or pre-political. The apparent materiality of the body is due to "*a process of materialization that stabilizes over time to produce the effect of boundary, fixity, and surface we call matter*" (Butler 1993, 9). In other words, materiality has a history and a politics. The biological or "natural" body, stripped of its political history, is itself founded on a set of violent exclusions. The erasure of this process of materialization that makes it seem as if intelligible bodies are natural phenomena constitutes another moment of violence. Butler writes, "Gender is the repeated stylization of the body, a set of repeated acts within a highly rigid regulatory frame that congeals over time to produce the appearance of substance, of a natural sort of being" (1990, 33). The discourse of our bodies as outside politics is an effect, not of a single foundational moment, but of ongoing practices with the potential for alteration and resistance.

Butler refers to these violent exclusions—which not only form the body that appears to be material and complete (a "body that matters") but also obscure this very process—as normative violence. Butler's concept of normative violence names a form of violence that preexists the subject, as bodily norms produce certain bodies that fall outside the norm. "Normative schemes of intelligibility establish what will and will not be human, what will be a livable life, what will be a grievable death" (Butler 2004a, 146). The subject is an inherently embodied subject—it is not exogenous, but rather is produced through compliance with various bodily norms. In the subject's process of becoming, it must attempt to delineate its body from others, and to create clear boundaries between the self's inside and outside. To do this, it expels the abject or "constitutive outside" that nonetheless shows up to haunt the self, as this founding repudiation is still included *by* its exclusion. The subject is not reducible to the body, nor is the body reducible to the subject. Neither the body nor the subject is ever complete; they are vulnerable to each other and to others in ways that cannot be fully escaped and that are often violent relations.

Butler's concept of normative violence contributes to a distinctively feminist take on theorizing the subject in relation to embodiment and violence, but this approach is not confined to questions of gender or sexual difference.[1] Bodies that have already been subject to normative violence are often then subjected to the forms of violence that International Relations is more comfortable theorizing. Torture can be seen not as a matter of strategic calculation but as an attempt to maximize bodily pain on one who is already "unreal" as an embodied subject. Transgender people are often made insecure by being subject to extra scrutiny at airports because their bodies do not match gendered expectations of the security scanners. The posthuman bodies of precision warfare make it possible for individuals and civilians to be killed by drones. In establishing which lives will be livable, normative violence acts as a precursor to the violence we are more familiar with, making certain lives, certain bodies subject to violence that is not considered a wounding or a violation. Violence as we usually think of it—the violence that injures and kills preexisting bodies—is also performative in producing certain embodied subjects, as violence is also a practice that constitutes certain embodied subjects. For example, as I argue in Chapter 2, the force-feeding of hunger-striking prisoners produces these prisoners as "dependent" subjects by a citational reference to the practice of force-feeding unconscious and mentally unstable patients. Violence as something that can be rationally managed and controlled is undercut by this view of violence as productive of bodies and relations (see also Barkawi 2011).

My aim in this book is to challenge scholars of security studies and IR more broadly to rethink subjects in terms of their embodiment. Bodies are not natural or pre-political objects that are only acted upon, but are inherently unstable. They are produced in multiple ways through practices of international war and security, which are also productive of certain subjects and political possibilities. Warfare and political violence function to both make, and remake, bodies, not only in the sense of harming and killing them, but in making them into knowable types. Because suicide bombing, for example, obliterates the boundaries of the individual body and the boundaries between bodies—thereby destabilizing the political continuity of the state—and it expresses the political work that is necessary to make bodies appear as whole and complete and unquestionably belonging (or not) to a political community, work that is attempted in the recovery and burial effects following bombing. Because traditional IR theorizes the body of the subject as existing outside politics, it cannot see how violence can be understood as a creative force for shaping the limits of how we understand ourselves as political subjects, as well as forming the boundaries of our bodies and political communities. Torture, as I argue, expresses the instability of the role of prisoners relative to American identity in the "war on terror," as the prisoners are made into "enemy combatants" through their torture, and "dependents" through their force-feeding. In the practice of precision warfare, violence expresses the instability of bodies by its ability to transform certain bodies into virtually invulnerable "posthuman warriors" while simultaneously making other bodies "killable" as accidental collateral damage or as marked for death. These practices of warfare express the instability of bodies by making and remaking the terms on which these bodies are constituted in their respective political communities.

I engage critically with Judith Butler's work on various aspects of embodiment as an important grounding for rethinking bodies in IR, while acknowledging that her approach is not without several limitations. My argument of the expressivity of violence differs from Butler's in that her account of gender performativity describes a relationship between the structure of gender and an individual's performance of his or her assigned role in that structure. Individuals can undermine the power of the gender norm through parody (Butler 1990, 142–145). My claim about bodies is somewhat broader than Butler's. In discussing warfare and political violence, there is not necessarily a structure, like that of gender and heteronormativity, that regulates the behavior of individuals; rather, the political interactions that produce bodies and subjects take place in different power dynamics, including dynamics between two or more individuals, between individuals and the state, or between groups of individuals drawing on larger dynamics of gender, race, and nation. In other words, the power to produce bodies as political subjects is more diffuse. Butler is mainly concerned with the regulatory effects of gender, whereas I am concerned with the constitution of bodies as political subjects more generally. Gender is an important productive discourse, but it is not the only one. Bodies are produced by a variety of practices, including political violence, but they are also produced by discourses of race, religion, sexuality, and civilization that—most important for the argument I advance in this project—constitute the bodies of certain subjects as torturable or killable, lives that must be protected or lives that are expendable.

Butler's model of gender performativity also does not go far enough to account for the ways in which bodies matter; that is, it theorizes bodies, in effect, as only blank forms to be molded by discourse. In recent years, feminists have articulated a vision of embodiment in which bodies have a form of agency; bodies can be productive, as well as produced (Barad 2007; Coole and Frost 2010). The materiality of bodies is not only an effect of political practices, but such practices are formed in relation to bodies as well. The "culture" of discourse and politics and the "materiality" of the body are intimately entangled in a chiasmic relationship. Bodies are both constraining (insofar as they are imposed upon by relations of power) and enabling (as they possess creative or generative capacities to affect the political field). I argue that a dynamic model of embodiment is needed in order to theorize the body in International Relations: bodies must be understood as both material *and* cultural, both produced by practices of International Relations *and* productive themselves. Bodies are thus not fixed entities, but are always unstable and in the process of becoming. They are ontologically precarious, existing only in virtue of certain material/political conditions that allow them to be intelligible to others.

DESIGN OF THE BOOK

In this book, I engage concrete international events to think about the embodiment of the subject in practices of security and violence. In order to show what is at stake in thinking about bodies in IR, the first chapter provides a reading of how the subject has been theorized in relation to bodies and violence in both conventional and critical IR theories. I argue that, in conventional International Relations, bodies have implicitly and problematically been understood in liberal humanist terms as individual, material objects, preexisting the political entities that house sovereign subjects. However, contemporary practices of violence are constituted not only in reference to sovereign power, as most IR theory assumes, but biopower as well. Biopolitical violence takes bodies as not only objects of protection, but objects of active intervention; bodies are constituted as individuals and as populations that must be killed, or must be made to live (Foucault 2003). As such, biopolitical practices of violence call our attention to the question of *how* bodies are constituted as objects and what the parameters and possibilities for embodied subjectivity are. Feminist theory in IR has been at the forefront of thinking about embodiment as both a constitutive feature of the subject and as inescapably political, but such scholarship sometimes falls short of a political understanding of the constitution of bodies as opposed to an interpretation of a preexisting body. This poses a limitation for feminist thinking about violence.

The remaining chapters are each oriented toward a specific set of violent practices or the management of violence: torture, suicide bombing, airport security assemblages, and precision warfare. These chapters show how contemporary practices of violence undermine IR's implicit assumptions about bodies while contributing to an alternative theorization of bodies, subjects, and violence though readings of contemporary feminist theory, especially the work of Judith Butler. These chapters develop my argument of the productivity of violence—that violent practices in International Relations express the instability of bodies through their production of embodied subjects, and that violent bodies express the excess of the subject and are also productive of International Relations. I argue that understanding bodies as both produced by, and productive of, International Relations is crucial to understanding aspects of political violence that go untheorized when we assume that violence only befalls bodies constituted outside the dynamic relations that form bodies in the first place. The bulk of the book is separated into discussions of different yet interrelated practices of violence; as such, these arguments are woven together, rather than presented linearly.

Chapters 2 through 5 each critique prevailing theorizations of bodies in IR through an analysis of specific modes of contemporary political violence. Each of these chapters builds upon the theoretical work of prior chapters to dislodge traditional IR's view of the body: the body as individual organism driven by the will of subjects. Chapter 2 critiques IR's assumption of the subject as a self-preserving, speaking subject of consent to a social contract through a discussion of the embodied politics of torture, hunger striking, and force-feeding at Guantánamo Bay. Torture in this case cannot be explained solely as an act meant to establish the presence of the sovereign state, given that is it denied, done in secret, and purposefully deployed so as not to leave visible marks on the body. If the prisoners at Guantánamo Bay can be considered neither rationally self-preserving nor "speaking" in the terms offered to us by liberal and social contract theory, we must seek other grounds for theorizing this violence. The limits of torture, precluding the death of inmates and their force-feeding, suggest that torture in this context operates under a logic that prisoners can be harmed, but that their lives must also be forcibly sustained by the state. Such a logic needs bodies to be not only objects of manipulations, but able to be produced through violence as certain types of bodies (in this case, "torturable" enemy combatants and "dependents" who can be force-fed). I argue that the practices of violence in Guantánamo Bay suggest that bodies are not "natural" objects, as conventional IR theory would assume, rather that they are produced by practices of international security. Furthermore, the hunger striking of the prisoners suggests that bodies are not only objects of manipulation, but are a kind of agent in their own right.

Having set the stage for the need to think about bodies as politically constituted as well as *constituting*, I turn to suicide bombing in Chapter 3 as a form of violence that not only forces us to confront these themes, but also presents a challenge to the assumption of the body as individual and self-contained. The literature on this issue has been preoccupied with questions of the motivations of the bomber and has not probed the implications of suicide bombing as an embodied practice caught up in contemporary discourses of life and security. In this chapter, I ask not what this practice means to various parties, but what the body *does*—that is, what political work does the body do as it is destroyed in order to transform into a weapon to kill others? Likewise, what are the political effects of efforts at recovering and reconstructing the bodies of bomber and victims? I argue that suicide bombing, understood as an embodied practice, is not only a destructive act of killing oneself in order to kill others, but also can be understood as a productive act as well. The bodies produced in this moment as lifeless flesh, as corpses, are a source of horror and disgust. They are, in feminist psychoanalyst Julia Kristeva's concept, *abject*: that which defies borders and is expelled to create the self. As "abject bodies," suicide bombers frustrate attempts at calculation and rational control of security risks, and, in their mutilated flesh, expose as unstable the idea of the body as a whole with clearly defined boundaries between inside and outside. Female suicide bombers, whose bodies are already considered "abject," produce a politics of the body that exceeds narratives of victimhood, and whose very monstrosity symbolically threatens the foundations of the nation-state. I also turn to attempts at reconstructing the bodies of victims and perpetrators of suicide bombings to ask what is at stake in these attempts to construct subjects out of mutilated bodily remains, arguing that the "resubjectification" of these bodies is a key practice in the production of the state and gendered subjects. Suicide bombing thus becomes a site that reveals how power molds, shapes, and constitutes the borders of the body and the state simultaneously. The explosive body of the suicide bomber thus has destabilizing effects beyond the motivations of its perpetrators and exposes the political work necessary to maintain the illusion of secure, bounded bodies and states.

Chapter 4 continues to build the argument that our bodies are deeply unnatural by discussing their production in airport security assemblages as simultaneously *only* material as abject flesh and dematerialized as bodies of information. The airport security assemblages manage the threat of violence by transforming embodied subjects into suspicious flesh that can be dissected digitally in a search for the truth of a person's riskiness or trustworthiness. I begin by describing airport security assemblages in terms of how travelers are treated as informational patterns, and then as abject flesh in the process of locating dangerous or risky bodies. At the same moment that travelers are transformed into abject bodies by "body scanners," these bodies are dematerialized, made into information to be analyzed for evidence of risk. I argue that the lived experiences of travelers in airport security assemblages are situated at the nexus of the material and symbolic, and reveal how these categories are intertwined in the production of biometric bodies as ultimate truth. Transgender people and other bodies that do not conform to gender expectations reveal the problematic location of "the material" (and thus "securable") in the bodies of humans. I theorize airport security assemblages as a site of struggle over the meaning of materiality and "the real" and as a contested site of the production of both safe and unruly bodies in the name of protecting populations.

While previous chapters have theorized bodies as only precariously contained and both material *and* symbolic, Chapter 5 builds on this theorization to argue that bodies are formed in relation to other bodies, both human and non-human. In contemporary precision warfare, including the use of drones, the relationship between bombers and bombed is much more than strategic and adversarial; it is a deeply asymmetrical form of violence in which the bombers are virtually risk-free. In this chapter, I investigate the co-arising formation of the bodies of bombers and the bodies of those targeted for assassination, as well as the bodies of bystanders, to ask about the conditions of possibility for this kind of violence. The use of drones pushes our thinking about agency and subjectivity in terms of the posthuman, or the human bodies as an assemblage of organic and technological, cultural, and natural materials and forces. I argue that the attempted (but ultimately incomplete) transformation of the human body into an information processor enables a certain moral and political calculus of which bodies "count." The posthuman bodies of pilots and drone operators are constitutive components of a regime that carefully seeks out individual bodies to kill, yet cannot provide an accurate count of the number of civilians killed.

These four chapters are linked by a demonstration that bodies are not outside social relations, but instead are produced in various incarnations by practices of security. Violence is not only something that is done to an already established body—rather, various forms of violence are part and parcel of the production of the various bodies that are subjected to violence. These chapters demonstrate the inadequacies of the ways in which bodies have been conceptualized in security studies, whether security is understood in terms of the protection of discrete, separate human beings or the guarding of aggregations of bodies in populations. These four chapters, each in their own right, demonstrate the disaggregation of bodies and subjects and reveal the bodies of IR as profoundly *unnatural* bodies produced through practices of violence. I argue that bodies are neither stable in themselves nor in relations to other bodies, but rather are produced through their relations to other bodies.

In Chapter 6, I show how the theorization of embodied subjects that this work has enabled can be applied to critique an emerging framework for understanding and addressing contemporary mass violence: the doctrine of "Responsibility to Protect" (RtoP). If we theorize bodies as I have argued we should—as both produced by and productive of politics and not contained in themselves nor in their relations to others—we can now think about embodied subjects in connection to RtoP in such a way that challenges the terms of "responsibility" by considering not only harm done to existing bodies, but the production of certain bodies as those that can be harmed and certain bodies as invulnerable. Specifically, I attempt to think through the paradigm of RtoP from Judith Butler's theorization of bodies as constitutively vulnerable. I show that thinking through the ethical implications of RtoP from an ontology of vulnerability has broader implications for the way in which we think about agency in relation to practices of violence.

In the conclusion, I seek to rearticulate the nexus of bodies/subjects/violence through feminist theory, particularly engaging with the work of

Judith Butler. Placing her work in conversation with other feminist theorists, I provide a conceptualization of a body politics that understands bodies as produced by, and productive of, social and political relations. In reading feminist theories of embodiment, I seek to recapture a sense of the vulnerability that is always present in theories of power and violence, not only in the sense of bodily vulnerability to violence and death, but also in terms of the political forces that constitute bodies as we know them. Such a reading of subjects as constitutively embodied prompts a different understanding of the relationship among subjects, bodies, and violence that has implications for both constitutive theory and critical theory in IR. I also suggest a research agenda for the future study of embodied subjectivity in International Relations.

CHAPTER 1

Bodies, Subjects, and Violence in International Relations

In order to demonstrate the stakes of theorizing bodies and embodiment in International Relations (IR), this chapter describes how theories of International Relations have conceptualized human bodies in relation to subjectivity and violence. I argue that, in conventional IR, bodies have been problematically understood in liberal humanist terms as individual, material objects preexisting politics and housing sovereign subjects, even if such a theorization is often more implicit than explicit, with the embodiment of the subject serving as an "absent presence." Yet, contemporary practices of violence are constituted not only in reference to sovereign power, as most IR theory assumes, but to biopower as well. Biopolitical violence takes bodies as not only objects of protection, but objects of active intervention; bodies are constituted as individuals and as populations that must be killed, or must be made to live. As such, biopolitical practices of violence call our attention to the question of how bodies are constituted as objects and what the parameters and possibilities for embodied subjectivity are. Though disagreements exist within feminist theory about the constitution of "the body" and its role in politics, feminists have made questions of embodiment central to their deconstructive and emancipatory projects. Theorizing the subject as embodied demonstrates the stakes of rethinking IR's approach to violence and the subject. By understanding contemporary security practices as constituted in relation to biopower as well as the more familiar terms of sovereign power, I call attention to the ways in which the body must be interrogated in its contingent manifestations as a crucial means for apprehending contemporary global politics.

SUBJECTS OF INTERNATIONAL RELATIONS

Conventional IR tells two broad stories about violence, rooted in traditions of political theory. In both of these stories, violence is the *ultima ratio* of modern politics, and the subject's vulnerability to violence is foundational to understandings of subjectivity and politics (see *inter alia* Campbell and Dillon 1993), yet the human body is a natural organism whose integrity is to be protected from violence as the prerequisite for politics. The first is a realist story, in which violence is primarily about self-preservation. The second story is the liberal tradition, in which violence is a violation of the law. In both the realist and liberal traditions, the focus is on sovereign power: the power to kill or to let live, in which the body is a biological organism to be protected against death and deprivation.

Hobbesian Bodies

In realism, violence is natural and inevitable, and violence also marks the boundary between nature and human communities. Violence is sometimes necessary to maintain the political community from external and internal threats. Realism draws a sharp distinction between domestic and international politics, and maintains that states must be able to use or threaten violence in order to maintain the state's status and survival in the world. The iconic figure in the realist tradition is Hobbes, who is read as telling a relatively simple story of the establishment of the political community that excludes violence from the domestic realm. Realist theories of IR extend Hobbes's state of nature from individual "natural men" to relations between states. Violence in the form of interstate war is sometimes necessary because states provide protection for citizens not only from other states, but from anarchy and civil war, which could threaten individuals' lives in the absence of state authority. The objects that are to be defended by the state are, first and foremost, the living, breathing bodies of humans as organisms. Sovereign power, in the artificial man of the Leviathan, is constituted precisely to protect the "natural man" (Hobbes 1996 [1651], 9). It is their safety and bodily integrity that is to be protected. In order to foster life, to prevent the life that is "nasty, brutish and short," the state must be convened. In this logic, the survival of the state's citizens is dependent upon the survival of the state itself. As Dan Deudney insists, "Security from political violence is the first freedom, the minimum vital task of all primary political associations, and achieving security requires restraint of the application of violent power upon individual bodies" (2007, 14).

To the extent that Hobbes's work can be said to contribute to theories of embodiment, it is in considering human community on the organic terms of the body politic. This is not an entirely original insight in itself—after all, it makes use of the ancient and medieval philosophy of the great chain of being that orders God and the sovereign king above human subjects. In setting up the figure of the sovereign state as a body politic, Hobbes naturalizes the boundaries of the political community in the boundaries of the human body. The metaphor of the state as body allows for security threats being represented as bodily illnesses, contagions, or cancers, existential threats that threaten the "life" of the state (Sontag 1990 [1978], 72–87; Waldby 1996; Campbell 2000 [1992], 59). The body that is protected by the state as well as the body that is a representation of the state is not only a natural body, but also one that is self-contained and self-governed, internally organized, and bound by concrete borders. Security thus means establishing and protecting this self-governed body as an organism.[1]

Furthermore, the representation of the state as a body stresses the unity of the body politic. As an individual, the sovereign is not required to recognize any form of difference among his subjects—the body politic has one body and speaks with a single voice (Gatens 1996, 23). Sovereign power, invested in the "artificial body" of the state, is constituted on the basis of a metaphor of the body as indivisible, a singular totality that Rousseau characterizes as the "general will." As in Hobbes, the sovereign state is constituted in analogy to a human body. "As nature gives each man absolute power over all his members, the social compact gives the body politic absolute power over all its members also; and it is this power which, under the direction of the general will, bears, as I have said, the name of Sovereignty" (Rousseau 1997 [1762], 61). In naturalizing the state as a human body, Hobbes and other social contract theorists further naturalize the human body itself as a singular, indivisible entity whose freedom from violent death is paramount.

Hobbes's story of the foundations of the state calls our attention to the naturalization of political violence in a way that expressly relies upon analogy to a particular conception of the human body. As this body is considered natural, so too is the constitution of the state as body writ large. Just as threats to the human body's integrity are seen as contamination, so too are border incursions and infiltrations that breach the state's control over its territory and people. Whereas in realism, sovereign power is constituted in order to protect life, in liberalism, sovereign power is also recognized to be a threat to human life.

Violence and Liberal Subjects

Liberal political thought takes us away from Hobbes's preoccupation with self-preservation to a concern with the cultivation of conditions for human achievement and flourishing. Self-preservation is not the primary purpose of political community, but rather is a necessary condition for human flourishing. The subject of liberalism is not only dependent upon a protected, healthy, and naturalized body, but is also a subject with exogenous interests and desires—a willing, speaking subject who can pursue his or her own interests in the public sphere.

This liberal subject is not only a body that is threatened by violence from outside the sovereign state, but is always at least potentially threatened by the state itself. This is a central fear driving the liberal political tradition. Defining "cruelty" as "the willful inflicting of physical pain on a weaker being in order to cause anguish and fear" (Shklar 1984, 8), Judith Shklar writes, "liberalism's deepest grounding is in place from the first, in the conviction of the earliest defenders of toleration, born in horror, that cruelty is an absolute evil, an offense against God or humanity" (1998, 5). It is this fear of cruelty that not only legitimizes the sovereign state and the rule of law, as in Hobbes, but limits governmental power to prevent the government from cruelty toward its citizens. State-sponsored torture, for example, reveals a tension between the state's imperative to provide security for its citizens and its duty to respect the moral status of individuals as subjects with a moral right over their own bodies. In liberal societies, "pain is not mere negativeness. It is, literally, a scandal" (Asad 2003, 107).

In the social contract, violence is disqualified from the public, domestic realm. The subjects of liberalism are motivated by a fear of violence and cruelty, but as such, they solve problems in the domestic realm by deliberation and the creation of a sphere of tolerance. They are subjects of reason, who do not resort to violence except in self-defense. For Hobbes, it is an inalienable right to defend oneself, even against the sovereign (1996 [1651], 93). This is a right that cannot be contracted away, for it has to do with man's safety and security and so renders subjects as predominantly defined by a constitutive anxiety to preserve themselves. Violence in liberalism is figured differently. The possibility of violence provides the motive for founding a community that rejects it entirely and seeks to define humans in terms of their capacity for flourishing, as evidenced in their abilities to deliberate and reason. The result is that violence is thought of as a violation not only of community standards but also of inalienable rights. Sovereign power is not the means to security but rather a key threat to security.

Liberal norms of human rights are meant to provide the same protections for individuals against states as the sovereign provides against other citizens. Human rights are a statement of the limitations of government interference. The human rights that are considered *jus cogens*, or "non-derogable," even in times of emergency or martial law, are prohibitions against summary execution, torture, and slavery. Even in a state of emergency or "state of exception," the human rights regime stipulates the limits of sovereign power in killing, torturing, or enslaving the bodies of citizens. These non-derogable rights instantiate the body of the citizen as sacrosanct, as that which must be protected. The "liberalism of fear" may therefore be understood as a political theory built upon the same concept of security for individual bodies as for the national state. While the concept of human rights is understood to entail many more freedoms than the absence of state-sponsored violence against the body, these basic "non-derogable" rights form the basis without which no other rights or liberties could be enjoyed.

In contemporary international politics, the concept of human security is an attempt to articulate this combination of state and individual security in which states are not only the protectors of citizens, but also a major source of insecurity for citizens. This concept, first developed by the United Nations Development Programme in 1994, attempts to shift the referent of security from the state to the individual, and brings with it issues of health and welfare as well as the traditional freedom from violence. Security is re-theorized to encompass threats to the well-being of people, adding what had been considered development or economic issues to the security agenda. The doctrine of "responsibility to protect" has emerged as a simultaneous challenge to, and reinforcement of, state sovereignty. This doctrine stresses that sovereignty is not absolute; states have a "responsibility to protect" their own citizens against wide-scale violence and genocide. At the same time, the doctrine emphasizes that such human rights abuses are the state's responsibility to resolve before international actors may be involved (Bellamy 2009).

Human rights and human security are not only seen as foundational of the liberal state, but also serve as pre-conditions for the exercise of freedom. Ultimately, the liberal emphasis on the protection of human rights against the violence and cruelty of governments is founded on a similar conception of the subject as the subject of security, a subject whose political subjectivity is dependent upon the elimination of violence. The body, in liberalism, is a body whose natural functioning is protected and whose needs are met so that the subject can transcend such concerns to thrive and prosper according to his interests and desires. As violence is disqualified within the political community, the subject is able to exercise his exogenously given preferences, which he is entitled to pursue up until the point that he interferes with the same rights that others enjoy. The subject of liberalism is a rational, autonomous individual who is entitled to a sphere of freedom from government interference. "Over himself, over his own body and mind, the individual is sovereign" (Mill [1859] 1989, 13). Similarly, Locke's liberal subject is the owner of his body. In the liberal political tradition in general, the body is a mechanical feature that is animated by the conscious mind, a Cartesian view of the relationship between mind and body. The body of the citizen (and the citizen's property, as an extension of his body) is an instrument for putting the mind's desires into action. The sovereignty of the subject means that the subject is a self-governed and willing subject; the mind of the subject is in control of his body and can freely interact in the world to pursue its own direction.

However, in order to be a sovereign, self-governing subject, the liberal individual must possess reason, defined as freedom from bodily passions and other such impediments. Mill's canonical account on liberty, for example, excludes children, those in a state of dependency, barbarians, and those in "backwards states" (1989 [1859], 13). Feminists have also noted how women were excluded from liberal subjectivity because they were believed to lack reason and judgment. Those whose bodies are outside the standard set by white, bourgeois, heterosexual men are considered to be improperly embodied, and thus to be incapable of the reason required for full participation in public life. In short, only those inhabiting "proper" bodies are considered to be full subjects. Bodies of workers, the colonized, the enslaved, and women were marked as "other" by constructions of class, race, and gender, in contrast to the "unmarked" body of the rational, white, upper-class man (Young 1990, 128; Campbell 2000 [1992], 87).

There are several key similarities between the ways in which realism and liberalism theorize the relationship between bodies, subjects, and violence. As modern theories, the subject is figured as autonomous and rational. Both of these strains of modern theories of violence presume that bodies preexist politics; that is, the bodies that must be protected from war, from government violence or interference, or from obstructing the subject's reason and exercise of freedom, are natural objects. There is a radical disjunction between subjects and bodies; bodies are the necessary condition, the *sine qua non* of politics, but are outside politics itself, as their use is to fulfill the aims of subjects. They must be protected from violence that would harm or kill these bodies to avoid coercion of the subject in the interest of freedom; this subject's interests and propensities are also logically prior to political interaction. In recent decades, critical theorists across the social sciences and humanities have contested this vision of the subject, describing it as an effect of certain political discourses rather than an ontological certainty.

BIOPOLITICS, SECURITY, AND INTERNATIONAL RELATIONS

Sovereign violence, as the form of the power to take life, is disqualified from the public realm as a breach of the rights of (some) citizens to bodily integrity. While both realism and liberalism recognize the importance of sovereign power for providing protection to naturalized human bodies, liberalism also recognizes unchecked sovereign power as a threat to the security of the individual. Biopolitical practices of security, on the other hand, do not just protect humans as individual biological organisms, but promote the lives of the entire population by producing bodies as objects of knowledge. Biopolitical perspectives also challenge liberalism's presumption of the prohibition of violence by noting that the naturalization of a realm of non-violence enables a realm of active intervention elsewhere. Against the social contract theories of sovereignty and the creation of an internal space free from violence (under the sovereign, or in the private sphere), biopolitical perspectives argue that political order is not founded and governed by a social contract, but through the production of "bare life"—life that can be killed without constituting a murder (Agamben 1998), or by the "break between what must live and what must die" (Foucault 2003, 254).[2]

Realist and liberal conceptions of violence and bodies theorize security as protection from sovereign power, that is, the power to take life or let live. Security is understood primarily in terms of protecting bodies from this violent power, whether the sovereign power to kill comes from other people, other states, or the state itself. Such approaches theorize security as if sovereign power were the only threat to human life—in other words, as if security practices are not also biopolitical, that is, having to do with the contemporary politics of life. Modern theories of violence assume not only that bodies are insecure (see Dillon 1996), but also that they constitute discourses that produce the bodies they purport to secure. As such, biopolitical theories employ a productive definition of power, as well as the coercive power of violence. Rather than working on bodies as sovereign power, power works through bodies to shape subjects. Foucault suggests that we think of power relations rather than power itself; an analysis of power must include attention to resistance as "there are no relations of power without resistances . . . formed right at the point where relations of power are exercised" (Foucault 1980, 142; see also Edkins and Pin-Fat

2004, 2). If Foucault is at least partially right that sovereign power is complicated by practices of biopower, it means that we must interrogate how the human to be protected is defined in terms of the body first, as well as how bodies are implicated in practices of resistance.

Biopower, in Foucault's work, comes to supplement and permeate sovereign power. Biopower's purpose is to supervise the health and promote life of the population as a subject. Foucault argues that biopolitics works through discourses of security, through the provision of security measures that are meant to eliminate the risk of violent death to citizens and to secure the life of populations from random elements. Rather than the right to take life or let live, biopower is the power to make live or let die (Foucault 2003, 241). Foucault considers biopower to be the power "to designate what brought life and its mechanisms into the realm of explicit calculation and made knowledge-power an agent of transformation of human life" (1978, 143). Biopolitics is thus the management of life itself and works through making human life, "the basic biopolitical features of the human species" (Foucault 2007, 1), the object of expert discourses that enable certain interventions on bodies and populations. Biopower must first make the human into a species, into bodies that are amenable to management, before it can intervene.

Foucault argues that biopolitics emerged in the context of liberalism. Biopolitics works through the category of populations, which emerged when the ideal of the nation-state became prominent and the state became territorialized. The power of the state became tied to the economic capacities of its population (Foucault 2007). Liberal politics work through biopower, through the creation of a realm of non-interference through which society, its economy, and its population can circulate and function according to their natural tendencies, according to such mechanisms as the "invisible hand." Accordingly, liberal rationalities rely upon the properties of bodies. Liberal rationalities are new forms of rule in which humans are not divinely endowed, but are biological beings. While liberalism designates new forms of freedom, it is also invested in new forms of control and coercion though disciplinary and surveillance methods (Rose 1999). Foucault decisively links these economic rationalities with certain investments in bodies: "[s]ociety's control over individuals was accomplished not only through consciousness or ideology but also in the body and with the body. For capitalist society, it was biopolitics, the biological, the corporal, that mattered more than anything else. The body is a biopolitical reality; medicine is a biopolitical reality" (2000, 137).

Security, in both realist and liberal understandings, requires the subject's sovereignty over his own body. Discourses of security and rights are both constituted on the basis of protecting the body as a precursor for the establishment and enjoyment of rights and freedoms. Both of these understandings of violence have difficulty in grappling with the contemporary world. One might pursue the lines of inquiry into the subject's relation to the political community and the meaning of violence in a variety of ways. One contemporary scholar—Giorgio Agamben—has focused on the impossibility of stabilizing the meaning of violence. Agamben shows us that the meaning of violence is inherently political, and that both the realist and liberal conceptions of violence cannot be sustained. Agamben reminds us that our existence as full-fledged political subjects depends upon the designation of others as "bare life," the quintessential political figure that offers a startling contrast to the nominal equality of the subjects of liberalism as well as the protections of the social contract (1998).

In the logic of the national security state, life is de-politicized, reduced to survival. Security in this sense is concerned with the sovereign's duty to protect life from external threats and to make law that enables the sovereign to kill people for disobeying. "Security" works to de-politicize life, rendering it a biological proposition of avoiding death. Thus, at the moment of the founding of modern politics, a biopolitical notion of life, or "bare life," is inserted. While in Foucault's work, liberalism may be synonymous with the exercise of biopower, we need not locate biopower exclusively with liberalism. Agamben has argued that, rather than being a recent invention, biopolitics is an original effect of the political, most notably in the figure of *homo sacer* in Roman law. The *homo sacer* is stripped of his political subjectivity, reduced to "bare life." This figure of "bare life," or *homo sacer*, is an object created by sovereign power (Agamben 1998, 6). Bare life is not the same as biological life, *zoē*, or "the body"; rather, Agamben argues that, given that in contemporary politics we are now all potentially *homines sacri*, the distinction between biological life and political qualified life is irrelevant (1998, 187). Bare life is not a condition belonging to some individuals and not to others; it is rather the "hidden inner ground" of our political subjectivity (Agamben 1998, 9; Ziarek 2008). At this point we are quite distant from standard IR conceptions of individual subjects and sovereign states. If sovereign power is the power to designate "bare life," that is, species life, biopower is necessarily implicated because it is what makes it possible to define the human in terms of its raw life, its living, breathing body (Dillon 2004).

If security works through biopolitical mechanisms, we must be attentive to bodies in at least two moments. The first is the production of the subject of security as a discrete, separate human body. Foucault locates the individualization of human bodies as a historical production rather than a natural, ontological fact, as liberal discourses suggest. Bodies have become isolated, independent objects subject to intervention as a result of certain medical discourse (Foucault 1994 [1973]). Taking this seriously requires us to be attentive to the social and political conditions under which certain bodies are made into objects that can be intervened upon to promote life in certain populations, such as through torture, force-feeding, and security screenings, to name but a few examples.

The second moment that thinking about security as a set of practices of life points us toward is the emphasis that biopower places on populations rather than individuals. Biopolitics does not deal with bodies at the individual level, but as populations, in which bodies are general and universalized. While an individual might face a particular threat, the population as a whole can be protected by the minimization of certain risky elements. Security, in its biopolitical constitution, means optimizing life by working to forestall risks, not just to individuals, but to the population as species—its continuation as a biological element that reproduces itself. In this schema, bodies are naturalized, constituted as biological entities whose functioning can be enhanced, and death postponed. Security, in liberal states, is meant to actively intervene in order to promote these "natural" functions. Security is thus not confined to the territory of the nation-state, but may operate in a broader milieu.

Biopower is, first and foremost, a moral framework that structures the practice of violence and the narratives of justification of that violence. Biopolitics explains why liberal societies, despite their desire to preserve human bodies from war and violence, build massive capacities for dealing death and destruction and are engaged in a war without end in the "war on terror". Crucial to understanding the role of biopolitics in the contemporary world order is its dual nature: that in order to foster life, it has to kill. Foucault writes:

> Wars are no longer waged in the name of the sovereign who must be defended, they are waged on behalf of the existence of everyone; entire populations are mobilized for the purpose of wholesale slaughter in the name of life necessity; massacres have become vital. It is as managers of life and survival, of bodies and the race, that so many regimes have been able to wage so many wars. (1978, 137)

Biopolitical practices of security take a naturalized body as their object to be protected, while a deeply "unnatural" body is constituted as threatening. Such bodies are constituted as unreasonable, excessive bodies that cannot be dealt with through normal politics, but only through violence. In this way, contemporary practices of security produce certain bodies as normal and others as aberrant and unmanageable. Violence against these deviant bodies is made necessary in order to preserve these naturalized bodies. Violence is framed as a technical problem to be managed using expert knowledge, rather than as an existential threat or a violation of norms. The indefinite detention and torture of prisoners at Guantánamo Bay is one such example of "deviant" bodies being eliminated to promote life in others (although the prisoners are also being made to live); the killing of suspected terrorists by drone attacks in Afghanistan and Pakistan is another example of threatening bodies being eliminated in the name of promoting the life of certain populations. Foucault's work on power and modernity articulates two poles of the power over life, discipline, and biopower, with discipline aimed as "man as body" and biopower as "man-as-species" at the multiple bodies of a population (2003, 242). While Foucault's work provides us with an understanding of how bodies are formed by power, his work in this regard is limited by the assumption of individual bodies with clear, identifiable borders—something later readers of biopolitics, such as Donna Haraway and Judith Butler, will countermand.

When security is practiced through the biopolitical logic of risk-management, the subjects of security are not the juridical subjects of sovereignty, as in realism, or rights-bearing subjects, as in liberal conceptions of the security *problématique*, but biopolitical subjects—human life to be managed by various forms of technical expertise as an object of knowledge. Risk is a theme characterizing all four sets of violent practices discussed in depth in this project. The very nature of precision bombing is one of calculated risk, in which specialized technologies are deployed to overcome the political problem of waging war while avoiding casualties of both soldiers and civilians. Likewise, torture and suicide bombing function under logics of risk. Torturers are virtually invulnerable to violence. Torture in the "war on terror" is justified by the logic that the infliction of pain will make tortured prisoners provide information that will be used to prevent terrorist attacks that may place ordinary citizens at risk of a violent death. Medical expertise is used to minimize the risk that the prisoner/patient will die of his treatment. Suicide bombing, on the other hand, is a mode of violence in which the perpetrator makes him- or herself what we may consider infinitely vulnerable. The suicide bomber accepts not the risk of death, but the certainty of death, in order to inflict death and injury upon random people, as well as a sense of vulnerability upon many more in the knowledge of possible future attacks. Airport security assemblages manage violence through identifying risky travelers and use technology to discover such risks. In each of these cases, expert knowledge is deployed in order to manage risks, from the technical and legal calculations of precision warfare, to the medical knowledge perversely deployed to ensure the health of torture victims, and to the contemporary industries of counterterrorist experts and technologies made to detect suicide bombers. Importantly, none of these strategies to shore up vulnerability are ever completely successful: suicide bombers and other terrorists find ways to circumvent security protocols, tortured prisoners die, and civilians are regularly killed by precision bombs. The political technologies of risk are an attempt to assert sovereignty and control, an effort that can never be entirely successful, as sovereignty itself is never absolute, but is a political practice that is always incomplete.

What this detour through Foucault and the evolution of risk allows us to see is the proliferation of technologies whose violence comes not through overt acts of aggression but through the perpetuation of the very vulnerabilities and instabilities they purport to suppress. These developments in the field of International Relations suggest the need for an understanding of violence that exceeds narratives of self-preservation, violation of social norms, or risk to be managed. I argue that violent practices of International Relations produce the bodies that they affect; violence is not merely harmful but is constitutive of the embodied subjects of IR.

The four modes of violence I deal with in depth in this work are all implicated in what Jabri refers to as a "matrix of war" in which the presence of certain "others"—certain bodies—are seen not only as a danger but as an existential threat. These relations involve, and in fact constitute, global spaces that far exceed the modern liberal polity as complex interactions across different sectors that take global population as the object for technologies of control (Jabri 2006a). Torture and force-feeding are practiced at Guantánamo Bay and elsewhere with justification along such biopolitical lines; and precision warfare is correctly described as a biopolitical practice by its management of risks for some through increasing risks for others. Both of these practices deal with calculating risks to populations. They also naturalize the subject as a body that can be manipulated and intervened upon: torture by the use of medical knowledge to not only cause pain and disorientation but also to limit the stresses on the body to prevent death; and precision warfare by its logic of risk calculation of civilian casualties. Suicide bombing also expresses a relationship to the biopolitical by eschewing its logic. I theorize suicide bombing as a practice that disrupts both liberalism's assumption of an individualized, self-contained body and the logic of protection, as the bomber refuses protection, making him- or herself infinitely vulnerable in order to kill and increase the vulnerability of others. The security assemblage at airports and other border sites transforms the embodied subject into a body of information, a body that can be read by knowing experts with the explicit purpose of separating threatening or dangerous bodies. Finally, the practice of precision warfare integrates "bodies-as-information" into a posthuman form of embodiment, in which the human is transformed into part of an information network that enables "targeted killing" practices from afar. In such biopolitical scenes, the bodies that are the effects and targets of violent practices are far removed from the ways in which violence is theorized in International Relations, a fact that has been increasingly noted in the field (see Jabri 2006b; Masters 2005).

While International Relations has neglected theoretical engagement with the body, feminist theorists have struggled with the question of subjects and bodies as a central problem in theorizing the roots of women's subordination and the possibilities of change. Perhaps the most influential formulation of the relationship between subjectivity and embodiment to come out of feminist theorizing is the sex/gender distinction in which one's sexed embodiment as male or female is irrelevant to one subjectivity; it is gender as a social and cultural phenomenon that determines subjectivities and composes power relations that differentially expose bodies to violence. While enormously important politically, the move to cast bodies as pre-sexed and thus irrelevant to questions of gender and power has limited this strand of feminist theorizing, especially in confronting the nature of biopolitical power.

FEMINISTS THEORIZE VIOLENCE IN INTERNATIONAL RELATIONS

If we think of security as not something that can be absolutely obtained, but as a set of practices that produces embodied subjects, we are called upon to think about violence not as only an act of self-preservation or something that happens at the margins beyond the boundaries of the social contract, but as performative, that is, producing and sustaining embodied subjects within a broader social order. Feminist theorists in IR have been at the forefront of efforts to bring bodies back into the study of International Relations. To understand their contributions, as well as some of the potential pitfalls of feminist work, requires some understanding of the multiplicity of feminist positions on the relations among bodies, subjects, and violence, and the tensions between different positions. These tensions can be both productive and problematic.

While International Relations has by and large accepted an ontology of bodies as "natural" beings to be protected by state apparatuses, feminists have questioned the "naturalness" of this body to be protected and what politics are enabled by this protection. The question of the ontological status of the body is of particular concern for feminists, who have had to battle scientific and medical discourses of women's natural bodily inferiority, as well as the erasure of the potential of their intellectual achievements, due to the bodily influences of hormones, reproductive processes, and muscular frailty. Feminist thought has challenged discourses of women's nature, which considered women nurturing and motherly, and incapable of the abstract political, economic, or scientific thought that characterizes the full subject of liberalism. Discourses of women's natural vulnerability and weakness have constituted women as inherently in need of protection by the state. While men could partake in the provision of this protective state apparatus, not the least of which includes serving in militaries, women's exclusion from such institutions perpetuated their social, political, and economic marginalization and dependency. Feminists also critique liberalism's presumption of women's bodies as weak and inadequate, in which women are seen as embodied subjects unfit for participation in the public realm. The feminist critique of liberal theories of politics and International Relations is based on liberalism's presumption of a rational, universal, and disembodied subject.

Crucial to the subject of liberalism is the distinction between public and private spheres (Pateman 1988, 1989; Okin 1989; Ackelsberg and Shanley 1996). The private sphere serves as a protected realm of government non-interference; one's body, one's family, and one's home and possessions are considered to be in the private sphere, where one can be materially and emotionally sustained without government intrusion. The subject of politics, therefore, is the subject of the public sphere: this subject is the subject of reason, liberty, and autonomy. First, as a subject of reason, the subject has left behind his own particularities of embodiment or social relations and has learned to think from a universal perspective. As such, the reasoning subject is much like the modern subject that is the creator of knowledge from a disembodied perspective.

Second, the liberal subject of politics is a subject of liberty. The free subjects of liberalism are self-directed and unfettered; they possess power, rather than being effects of power (as in Foucauldian models of subjectification). The free subject of liberalism is a subject unencumbered by necessity or duty. The liberal subject is thus free from responsibilities for family members and of the necessities of the body; these make the subject unable to exercise freedom. However, the distinction between the public and private sphere means that family burdens and caring labor are not barriers to freedom that the government should abolish. Caring labor is privatized and feminized. Such duties, and the caring labor that goes with them (including the care for bodily needs), are necessary functions of the private sphere that the existence of the public sphere, and the free citizens who inhabit it, is built upon, and these roles of caring have been filled by women in almost any sexual division of labor (Tronto 1993; Fineman 2008). From a feminist perspective, liberalism is not strictly opposed to necessity or the body, but is dependent upon the relegation of these concerns to the private sphere of the family, and women's labor inside it, in order to produce liberated subjects in the public sphere (Young 1989).

The subject of liberalism is also an autonomous subject, defined in opposition to the dependent subject. The autonomous subject can care for himself without making claims on others for survival or protection. The autonomous subject is presented as prior to social relations: he is always an adult who can enter into contracts and decide which social relations to pursue. This view is not confined to liberal discourses: Hobbes's famous description of men springing up like mushrooms, with neither father nor mother, is a classic example of an autonomous model of the subject (DiStefano 1991, 83–90). Of course, this view of the subject radically understates the degree to which humans are constituted by social relations; they are born into families (through women's bodies) and dependent upon adults (usually mothers) for material needs and the development of language and other social capacities. The representation of the subject as autonomous understates not only the importance of women's labor in the private sphere but the degree to which adults are entangled in webs of social relationships, as well as larger webs such as those of the economy. Like the free subject, the autonomous subject is dependent upon non-autonomous subjects based in familial relationships for emotional and physical support. In Locke's state of nature, for example, only men are always autonomous; women are always attached to men and children (Brown 1995, 148).

The autonomous subject is contrasted with the vulnerable subject. Vulnerability is linked to discourses of dependence, victimhood, and pathology, all viewed in negative terms. Vulnerability is also linked to certain subjects such as women, children, the elderly, and the infirm. These are stigmatized subjects who are designated as "populations" (Fineman 2008). Vulnerability in liberal discourses is the opposite of freedom. We can also relate the designation of vulnerable populations to Foucault's concept of biopower: if vulnerability is a characteristic of certain populations (rather than a generalized condition), the government is enabled to intervene "for their own good." Feminists have engaged with the nature of biopolitical rule insofar as it is based on the management of bodies and populations. For example, feminists have critiqued natalist politics encouraging certain women of certain races, ethnicities, nationality, or classes to bear children, while women of "less desirable" groups are discouraged from reproducing, sometimes to the point of being forcibly sterilized (Yuval-Davis 1997). Discourses of the natural vulnerability of women as a population are primary topics for feminists seeking to provide critiques of political theories that justify women's subordination.

Feminist critiques of the liberal distinction between public and private spheres are also based upon women's experiences with violence. The issue of domestic violence illuminates some of the inadequacies of the liberal approach to individual rights and violence, as liberalism's best intentions can have the worst effects. Liberal subjects of reason are generic subjects, as "humans" or "persons." Such unsexed individuals can deliberate in the public sphere. In liberalism, men and women are equal in their inborn capacities to reason—sexed embodiment is irrelevant to a subject's rationality, autonomy, and self-awareness as a political subject. Feminists have argued that, contra liberalism's fears of state violence and oppression, the principal threats to women's liberty and flourishing belong to the private, rather than public, sphere. Patriarchal norms and internalized, socially constructed gender roles limit women's choices and agency more than governmental power.

While liberalism and its discourses of rights and equality are useful in overcoming some forms of women's oppression, the paradigm of liberalism is not sufficient for addressing all forms of violence and inequality. Furthermore, domestic violence, when read in the liberal tradition, is a failure to meet one's legal obligation to obey the law and refrain from violence. The liberal tradition focuses on the perpetrator's transgression of the law, a transgression that is difficult to prosecute without the cooperation of the victim. Treating people as neutral, equal subjects assumes that they are, in an important sense, the same. Feminists such as MacKinnon (1989) have pointed out that in liberalism's emphasis on sameness there is an inherent tension with the concept of gender as a constitutive difference between human subjects.

The liberal interpretation of violence ignores the role of violence in maintaining power relations between individuals and in society more broadly. The establishment of a private sphere, including family life, combined with the liberal presupposition of a rational subject whose specific embodiment is irrelevant makes the political and legal system incapable of addressing the issue of domestic violence. Just as feminist political theorists have critiqued liberalism for being unable to adequately address violence in the private sphere of the family, feminist theorists in International Relations have critiqued traditional IR theory for not being able to "see" certain forms of violence, including violence that takes place far away from the high-level decision-making of heads of state, generals, and so forth. While these types of violent politics in IR overwhelmingly involve men, the violence that affects women—such as wartime rape, civilian victimization, the disproportionate effects on women of sanctions, infrastructural damage, refugee crises, famine, and the broader destruction of the social order—often takes place "off the radar" of IR theory (Buck, Gallant, and Nossal 1998; Koo 2002; Plumber and Neumayer 2006; Sjoberg 2006). The international arena is the public sphere writ large, with war in particular being a separate and exceptional activity that takes place far from "the home front." When women do appear in stories of violence in IR, they are in roles that we would expect of mothers, wives, nurses, victims, and "beautiful souls" (Elshtain 1995 [1987]). Focusing on women's lived experiences of violence challenges the supposed objectivity of International Relations as a discipline in its neglect of women. Recognizing how women have been neglected in conflict, security, and peace building, the United Nations passed Resolution 1325 in 2000, extolling member governments and nongovernmental organizations (NGOs) to pay special attention to the ways in which women and girls are specifically affected by war.

However, the mere addition of women to studies of war and security is unsatisfactory to most feminists. While focusing on women's experiences of violence adds considerably to our understanding of war, conflict, and militarization, there is considerable slippage between a focus on "gender violence" and "violence that affects women and girls." This slippage ignores the fact that, as stated in Terrell Carver's excellent title, "gender is not a synonym for women" (1996). The focus on women and girls as victims of "gender violence" also erases the possibility that women could perpetrate "gender violence" (Richter-Montpetit 2007; Sjoberg and Gentry 2007) or that men could be victims of gender violence. It is also assumes that the category of "women" is coherent, fixed, and knowable (Shepherd 2007). In light of these issues, feminists also theorize violence as a means of producing gendered identities.

"Gender" is a key concept in feminist theorizations of violence. "Gender" serves as a way to denaturalize "sex" as the source of unequal power relations between men and women and replaces it with related accounts of socialization and power that impose meanings on the bodies of men and women. Many IR feminists have taken Joan Scott's influential definition of gender to heart in describing gender as a category of analysis, including Tickner (1992, 1997, 2001), Weber (2001), and Youngs (2004). Gender consists of two related but analytically distinct propositions: first, that "gender is a constitutive element of social relations based on perceived differences between the sexes"; and second, that "gender is a primary way of signifying relationships of power" and that "gender is a primary field within which or by means of which power is articulated" (J. W. Scott 1986, 1067, 1069). As such, the inclusion of women's lived experiences is not enough to interrogate the power relations at stake in gendered social life; what is needed is a gender analysis that examines how gender constitutes social relations and operates as a field of power. Such an analysis in IR involves thinking through the relationship between sexed bodies, gender identities, gender discourses, and contemporary practices of violence.

While much scholarship across the social sciences and humanities takes Foucault as a founding father of the investigations of the body in culture and society in recent decades, feminists have developed an independent analysis of the "politics of the body," albeit one that finds Foucauldian concepts of productive power, biopolitics, and discourse to be useful. Because of the use of discourses of women's bodily inferiority to justify subordinate political positions for women, it has been crucial for feminists to deny an ahistorical or essential subject based on an uncritical story of bodily morphology or composition, such as arguments that men are naturally more violent and women more peaceful because of differing hormone levels, or that women should be excluded from participating in militaries because of inferior strength. The use of discourses of the body in figuring women as less than human in terms of civic participation and intellectual ability means that feminists have been at the forefront of exposing the political roots and implications of discourses of the "natural" body. From this problem stems the "sex/gender system," first coined by Gayle Rubin (1975), a concept that feminist have used to differentiate between the nature/biology source of sex and the social/cultural source of gender as both an aspect of subjectivity and code for political power. Feminist theories of "sex/gender" conceptualize "gender" as a social and cultural phenomenon distinct from the natural, biological fact of "sex." From this vantage point, women and men may be marked by biological differences, but these differences are largely irrelevant: social factors are what determine the relevant differences between men and women. The bodies of men and women have no meaning outside the meanings given to them. As Christine Sylvester writes, "men and women are the stories that have been told about 'men' and 'women,'" and "'men' and 'women' [are] socially constructed subject statuses that emerge from a politicization of slightly different anatomies in ways that support grand divisions of labor, traits, places and power" (1994b, 4).

Closely associated with the work of Simone de Beauvoir, the relegation of biology, or "nature," to the realm of "sex," while social roles and individual personality characteristics are described as "gender," has been a central tenet of feminist political thought for decades. Beauvoir's famous statement, "One is not born, but rather becomes, a Woman" (1989 [1952], 267), is a denial of an eternal, biological essence of what it is to be a woman. Beauvoir accepts certain biological discourses about women as a category—their smaller size and reproductive abilities—but she challenges the idea that women's biology is what makes them inferior socially, economically, and politically. Becoming a woman, for Beauvoir, is a matter of the cultural portrayals of women and ideologies of womanhood that have created a romanticized view of femininity that women are compelled to emulate. Because of the culture they are raised in, women are denied subjectivity—she is "other" to man, made into an object. While "man" stands for what is universally human, women are particular, outside the progress of human history and defined by their role in the eternal process of human reproduction. Gender is a signifier of status within a social system, rather than a function of biology.

Insofar as feminists understand gender as a constitutive element of social relations, feminists have much in common with constructivist theories in IR. Constructivists have brought a deeper understanding to the study of International Relations by focusing on the social and political constitution of subjects, rather than assuming a rational actor with a pre-given set of interests, as do liberal and realist theories. Constructivism has challenged the rational subject with exogenous interests and has argued that a subject's interests are a function of that person's identity, which is formed by social processes. While constructivists insist that subjects are not pre-political, constructivist scholarship still maintains the existence of a human body that precedes politics, just as the concept of "gender" distinguishes the social identity of an individual from his or her sexed embodiment. Scholars sharing the broad label of constructivism have been influenced by a wide variety of different, often conflicting, schools of thought, yet constructivists generally do not understand the body as politically constituted rather than biologically given. Rather, the constitution of bodies falls outside the domain of politics. Alexander Wendt, in drawing the line between the constitutive role of "ideas" in terms of norms, culture, and identities, leaves the human body outside the realm of politics as stable and material. His defense of "rump materialism" is admittedly a Cartesian separation between mind and body (Wendt 1999, 112). The body, in Wendt's constructivism, serves as a "brute fact" that is analogous to a state's territory. It thus has an independent material existence and is not constituted by ideas or discourses. Fearon and Wendt suggest that the internal structure of the body, along with its ability to move and act, serves as a "platform on which actorhood is constructed" (2002, 63). Fearon and Wendt write that while the meaning and social position of bodies vary, prior to the process of meaning-making, bodies must be structured by an internal organization in order to acquire meaning. For individuals, this is the body's biological structure, which is shaped by survival needs. For states, the collective action of biologically given people is shaped by the structure of the state (2002, 63). As such, Wendtian constructivism parallels Hobbes's acceptance and reinscription of the existence of a natural body and the state's internal structure as analogous to a body.

While most feminists believe that gender is a social construct, they differ from Wendtian constructivism in insisting that gender is also a signifier of power (Tickner 2001, 16; Locher and Prügl 2002, 116). Here, feminists are frequently aligned with poststructuralists in theorizing identity as an effect of the productive power of discourse, and discourses structuring reality. Feminists, like critical theorists more broadly, take these social constructions to create and reproduce social hierarchies through the production of ideologies and identities. IR feminists understand power as productive; that is, power is implicated in the formation of identities through the creation of a self through the denigration of an "other." Influenced by poststructuralist thought, this is a significant departure from constructivist understandings of social construction, as gender is not imposed from outside but is integral to the formation of the subject (Barnett and Duvall 2005, 41). In her influential introduction to *Gendered States*, V. Spike Peterson insists that feminist scholarship "takes seriously the following two insights: first, that gender is socially constructed, producing subjective identities though which we see and know the world; and second, that the world is pervasively shaped by gendered meanings" (1992b, 9). Gender is a discourse that produces the subject positions of "men" and "women," and discourses of gender are also constitutive of contemporary life in that they underpin and shape other discourses as well.

Gendering Violence

The concept of gender as a social construction that is distinct from sex, and that is a form of power (whether structural or productive), has allowed feminists to theorize violence as productive of certain subjects—namely, making war a privileged site in constructing masculinities (as it is primarily men who fight in wars and perpetrate other forms of political violence), as well as femininities for both women who fight and women who provide material and ideological support while not partaking in the violence directly. Moreover, feminists argue that such violence cannot simply be "added" to existing IR theories because such theories are constituted by masculine concepts such as the public sphere, the state, and rationality. The exclusion of violence in the lives of women is dependent upon the exclusion of feminine concepts such as the family, the body, and emotion. Because gender is constitutive of IR, taking the experiences of women seriously requires rethinking how IR is implicated in reproducing masculinities and femininities as hierarchical power relations that intersect with nationalism, race, colonialism, sexuality, and class. Feminists in IR have argued that war, political violence, and the militarization of societies more generally both rely upon and reproduce gendered relations of power. In other words, the relationship goes both ways: war and violence as institutions produce masculinities and femininities, and gender roles, norms, and institutions underpin and shape practices of violence. Wars are a place where men learn to be men, and war also produces a series of discourses of the ideal feminine role as well (Goldstein 2001; Hooper 2001; Whitworth 2008). Militaries have needed men to act "like men," but they also need women to behave as the gender "woman" as well (Enloe 1983, 212). War and the institutions that enable it are invested in reproducing gender relations in myriad ways, from the encouragement and regulation of military base prostitution (Moon 1997; Enloe 2000) to the mobilization of discourses of gender to foster recruitment (Enloe 2000; Goldstein 2001). The gendered protector/protected dichotomy is not only about prescribing proper activities and attributes for sexed individuals, it is also about justifying violence more broadly; certain feminist projects encouraged or were co-opted into supporting the US-led wars in Afghanistan with the rationale of "saving Afghan women." Similar discourses have also been used to justify other uses of military force in the performance of masculine heroic narratives of the rescue of helpless, feminized populations (Orford 1999; Abu-Lughod 2002; Young 2003; Nayak 2006; Shepherd 2006; Sjoberg 2006).

Feminists have analyzed the formation of gender subjectivities and the broader influence of gender discourses across the social and scientific worlds. Although Foucault notoriously evades the question of gender, even though some of his most famous work is on sexuality, feminists have found Foucauldian (and Derridean) conceptual frameworks useful in thinking about the production of seemingly natural categories of "men" and "women," including the productive power of discourse and how power targets bodies to produce subjects (McNay 1992; Butler 1990, 1993; Bordo 1993; Grosz 1994; Bartky 1998). Foucault writes that discourse analysis "consists of not—of no longer—treating discourses as groups of signs (signifying elements referring to contents of representations) but as practices that systematically form the objects of which they speak"

(1972, 54). Theorizing discourse as sets of practices means, for IR feminists, looking at how discourses of IR reproduce the categories of "men" and "women," as well as how discourses of gender constitute International Relations. Poststructural feminists theorize gender as relational (there is no masculinity without femininity) and as historically variable rather than fixed. Poststructural feminist analysis also theorizes the formation of the subject of "women" through practices of linking and differentiation. "Woman" is constituted as a subject position through the linking of emotion, motherhood, simplicity, dependence, and the body. These attributes are differentiated from those that constituted "man": rationality, intellect, complexity, independence, and the mind (Hooper 2001; Hansen 2006, 19–22). "Woman" exists as supplement to "man"; she is a necessary part of society, but remains inferior and devalued.

"Gender" is a discourse that determines meanings and values as well as a constitutive feature of human subjectivity. Gender not only perpetuates the subordination of women but acts as a signifier of power such that values ascribed to masculinity are attributed to dominant groups, while values ascribed to femininity are ascribed to subordinate groups (see also Locher and Prügl 2001; Tickner 2001, 15; Sjoberg 2006, 34). Feminists also conceive of gender as a discursive structure that links the historical devaluing of women to the categories associated with women through binary relations, pairs in which the devalued term is associated with femininity and serves as a foil to the valued, masculine term. Culture/nature, mind/body, order/anarchy, public/private, agency/dependency, active/passive, rational/irrational, and objective/subjective are all gendered dichotomies that have political significance beyond male and female relationships; gender structures modern thought and naturalizes dichotomized thinking and the privileging of masculinity (Peterson 1992a; Hooper 2001; Peterson and Runyan 2010). Feminist poststructuralists also critique practices of knowledge that reproduce distinctions between knower and known, subject and object, fact and value, that presume that knowledge itself can represent a "view from nowhere," that the producer of knowledge is essentially disembodied (Bordo 1990; Haraway 1991b). These dichotomies are ultimately unstable and untenable. Because the terms rely on one another such that "masculinity" will always rely on "femininity" (for example) for its definition, femininity is the "constitutive outside" of masculinity. These terms, and their associated dichotomies, are thus not opposites but are mutually contaminated (Pin-Fat and Stern 2005, 29). Feminist scholars have examined how gender discourses produce the illusion of seemingly obvious and stable objects in International Relations, such as the civilian and the combatant, and show how such categories are dependent upon gender discourses of the naturalness of women's weakness and peaceable nature (Kinsella 2005, 2011). These discourses may structure meaning, but they are not stable or set in stone: as social constructions, they are subject to political contestation. Feminists working from this perspective examine how discourses of the "naturalness" of gender and sexed embodiment reproduce these dichotomies over time.

From this perspective, violence both relies upon and reproduces constructions of gender. War is legitimized by gender discourses that intersect with discourses of race, ethnicity, class, nationality, and heterosexism to produce images of "innocent women" that must be protected from "bad men" by the violence of "good men" (Elshtain 1995 [1987]; Tickner 2001; Young 2003; Sjoberg 2006). Feminists have described the national security state as a gendered and heterosexist "protection racket," in which the "natural" sex of women stabilizes both domestic and international orders as the patriarchal family is projected outward to states (Carver 2008, 83). Specifically, the state is gendered masculine, while those who are "protected" assume a feminine role, regardless of their sexed embodiment. There is thus an unequal power relationship between the protector and the protected, with the security of the protected bought by their subordination to the protectors. Gender as a signifier of power is delinked from the sexed bodies of men and women, so that some women can occupy the powerful status of "man," while some men (often racial or sexual "others") are feminized. "Man" in this sense is the abstract citizen or human, unmarked by sex, whose violence is legitimized by its use against a body marked by race, gender, or civilizational status, on behalf of another population whose bodies are not "neutral" but marked, primarily by gender. As Iris Marion Young puts it, "Their protector position puts us, the citizens and residents who depend on their strength and vigilance for our security, in the position of women and children under the charge of the male protector" (2003, 226–227). The bodies of the feminized, "protected" by practices of national security, are a political liability as their bodies are seen as vulnerable, weak, and inadequate. The association of women and femininity with peace serves as the constitutive "other" against which "real" men are created in and through war (Pin-Fat and Stern 2005).

These feminist stories critique and rewrite the traditional stories that IR tells of violence, in both its realist and liberal variants. It is, first and foremost, a critique of the sovereign as protector from violence against a neutral subject; feminists argue that the subject of violence is not neutral in regard to gender. "Gender" as a story of the inherent weakness of women and the need for men to protect them from "outside" enemies supports the patriarchal power of men over women, as well as racial superiority in the image of the "bad man" against whom the "just warrior" fights. The story told of a sovereign who protects our "natural life"—either from a violent death, or from violation of the private sphere of government interference—is predicated upon gendered relations of power: the "natural" weakness of women and their caretaking labor in the private sphere is a political effect of gender discourses that support the existence of hierarchical political institutions and practices of violence, rather than an innate feature of human life.

Following Foucault's use of military training techniques as examples of disciplinary power (1979, 135–141), feminists in IR have focused on the military as a particularly important site of the production of not only masculine subjects, but masculine bodies (Hooper 2001; Belkin 2012). Military bodies are also linked to rational-bureaucratic masculinity (Hooper 2001, 64). This form of masculinity merges with the traditional warrior protector masculinity in Western high-tech militaries (Masters 2005; Carver 2008). Masters argues that, in such militaries, the cyborg is constituted at the expense of fleshy body, a "living, laughing, loving body." The human body of the soldier is weak and vulnerable, while information systems and high-tech weapons are the strong protectors of this vulnerable body. As it is the technology, then, that embodies masculinity, the male body of the soldier has been feminized. Fleshy bodies have been effaced so that the masculine dream of disembodiment and absolute knowledge and power can be realized.

Bodies, Sex, and Violence

Some of the most profound contributions to interrogating bodies as an absent presence in IR have come from feminists who perceive the lack of attention to bodies and embodiment as a sign of the devaluing of the feminine: while IR attempts to provide abstract forms of knowledge in order to provide a measure of control or management of international violence, it disengages with the bodily nature of war. Feminists have tried to correct theories of violence and war that work to obscure the reality of bodily violence while focusing on political, strategic, and tactical maneuverings. No one has demonstrated how strategic thought in IR ignores and, in fact, necessarily obscures the gruesome realities of war and its impact on the human body more powerfully than Carol Cohn.

Cohn's work is a valuable deconstruction of the abstract discourses of war and violence that are so prevalent in IR. In her landmark essay, "Sex and Death in the Rational World of Defense Intellectuals" (1987), Carol

Cohn insists that this neglect of bodily harm is not an oversight, but rather is a pre-condition for the existence of the theory and the strategic apparatus underpinning it. The language of the nuclear defense specialists in her participant-observation not only euphemized the violent potential of nuclear weapons in terms of "collateral damage," "clean bombs," and assorted acronyms, but served to limit what could be thought and said. In the discourse of nuclear strategists, human suffering and death were invisible; rather, the survival of the weapons themselves was the focus. "Technostrategic" discourse has no room for imagining oneself as vulnerable to violence. Cohn's work is an example of feminist theorizing about violence: violence in its bodily, all-too-real manifestation cannot be seen in certain types of theorizing about international war and security. Not only is bodily violence invisible, but it is necessarily invisible if such theorizing is to proceed. Cohn does more than expose the erasure of injured and destroyed bodies in discourses of nuclear strategy. Her work is a powerful explanation of how such bodies come to be erased in the practices of nuclear strategy, and how this erasure makes it possible for the field of nuclear strategy to function as it does.

Feminists have also demonstrated their commitment to taking embodiment seriously by focusing on the specificities of sexed embodiment in particular institutions. These contributions to theorizing gendered subjectivity and violence have posed challenges to the story of the military as an unparalleled site of the production of masculine subjects and have contributed to the poststructuralist argument that dichotomous terms such as "masculine" and "feminine" are not strictly opposed but mutually implicated. Precisely by taking the issue of sexed embodiment seriously, feminists have shown that the presence of sexed bodies (more precisely, the bodies of women, which are marked as sexed, while men's bodies are seen as neutral or universally human) has the ability to disrupt or contaminate certain gendered spaces such as government or the military (Sylvester 2002; Pin-Fat and Stern 2005). Their presence drives a wedge in the argument that the military (or war, or International Relations) is constituted as a masculine sphere, not through showing how women can be accommodated in such sphere, and perform just as well (as in liberal feminist arguments), but that women or "the feminine" show up as the "constitutive outside," that which is included by its exclusion. The body can also be an ambiguous site of the differentiation between masculine and feminine/queer. The military as a site of the production of masculine bodies is solely a site of the rejection of all things feminine, rather, "the production of masculine warriors has required those who embody masculinity to enter into intimate relationships with femininity, queerness, and other unmasculine foils, not just to disavow them" (Belkin 2012, 4).

Deconstructive work showing the mutual implication of the masculine and feminine/queer (Sylvester 2002; Pin-Fat and Stern 2005; Belkin 2012) has important implications for theorizing violence from a biopolitical understanding of power and sovereignty. Agamben's neglect of the gendered, colonial, and racist logic of biopolitics has perhaps contributed to the relative lack of engagement of feminists with his concept of *homo sacer*, or "bare life." Bare life, as produced by sovereign power as an act that strips one of all political subjectivities, including those of gender, race, nationality, and class, produces a form of life that is still dependent upon these social categories, if only in the negative (Ziarek 2008). Even as "bare life," bodies are still constituted in relation to gender. Furthermore, the military itself can be understood as a zone of exception, in which people kill or are killed without a murder being commissioned, and soldiers exist as *homines sacri*. The protector/protected dichotomy that legitimizes military violence as sacrifice requires that women cannot be sacrificed by the state without undermining the gendered rationale for war. If soldiers cannot be "just warriors," and die to protect the feminine "homeland," they will be revealed as *homines sacri* rather than heroes (Pin-Fat and Stern 2005). The gendered protector/protected dichotomy is a sovereign script that makes it appear as if the deaths of soldiers are meaningful sacrifices, rather than the deaths of ultimately expendable subjects in a biopolitical zone of indistinction.

While feminists have sought to foreground bodies, and embodied subjects, in IR, there is a tension between some of intertwined feminist "moves" to see women, to theorize international violence from the lived experiences of women, and the focus on the productive power of discourse in forming subjects. First, lesbians, women of color, postcolonial or "Third World" women, and working-class women have insisted that there is no essential or singular "woman's experience" and that gendered subjectivity is always constituted in relation to other axes of difference, such as sexuality, race, class, and nationality. Representations of "women" that attempt to speak for all women universalize the experiences of particular women and reproduce hierarchical power relations. As such, the use of "gender" to refer to socially constructed differences between men and women has no essential meaning. Second, theorizing "gender" as if it were completely separate from "sex" leaves unanswered the question of why there are not many genders that could be attributed to each sex, and why gender is still dichotomous in masculine and feminine. Why are gendered subjectivities and sexed bodies so closely tethered together? Furthermore, despite their concern with the power of social constructions to determine reality, the insistence of feminist IR scholars on a gender analysis that marks only the social construction of gender as politically relevant is a move that naturalizes bodily sex differences and, ultimately, is susceptible to the same reproduction of culture/nature and mind/body dichotomies as constructivist scholarship (Butler 1990, 1993; Gatens 1996). Analyzing the power of gender discourses to shape international politics and differentially affect the lives of men and women is a crucial aspect in explaining the dynamics of International Relations, but the theorization of gender in these strains of feminist theorizing leaves the constitution of the body outside the realm of politics.

Feminist IR contributions to theorizing violence then, exist in a tension between theorizing women's lived experiences of violence, theorizing violence as produced gender identities of sexed individuals, and deconstructing the categories of gender. Sylvester quotes Ferguson's identification of this problem: "how can we simultaneously put women at the center and decenter everything including women?" (Ferguson 1993, 3; Sylvester 1994b, 12). Noting the diversity of experiences of war as well as the many divisions of gender, class, race, occupation, language, and more, Sylvester notes, "[w]hat unites them all is the human body, a sensing physical entity that can touch war, and an emotional and thinking body that is touched by it in innumerable ways" (2011, 1). Calling attention to the norms that influence bodily life and its relationship to experience, Sylvester cautions, "the body emerges as a key receptacle of experience; but it does not operate on its own" (2012, 498).

Women's experiences cannot be considered a reliable ground for knowledge claims, because the structures of gender encourage women to speak in socially acceptable ways (Tickner 2001, 17). Because of the power of gender norms in producing women as the subject "women," the inclusion of women's lived experiences can have the effect of reproducing gender as a meaningful category (Scott 1991). Discourses of gender produce the reality they purport to represent. In representing the lived experiences of women, feminist IR ends up reproducing the categories of "women" and "men," even as it means to challenge the meaningfulness of these categories. Maria Stern and Marysia Zalewski describe this problem as the "performative sex/gender predicament" (2009). By representing women or "the feminine," IR feminism as a discourse participates in the reproduction of the subject "woman." In particular, references to women as victims or women as "protected" has the effect of reproducing the category of "women" as linked to victimhood or protection. The move from men and women to masculinities and femininities does not solve this problem, because in stories about violence, "gender" is something that provides roles for sexed bodies. The stories told by feminists about war (with few exceptions) presume that boys and girls, men and women, exist as sexed bodies that are biologically given and ontologically prior to politics. "Sex" has disappeared, to be replaced by gender, which is a cultural and institutional force that ultimately harms both men and women. We still have to know who "men" are, and the question is what type of masculinity they will embody. If women and men (but especially men) could be taught how to "do" gender differently, wars and militarization might be ended. In such stories, gender is real, "as a disease or afflicted accessory to the body that could be cured" (Stern and Zalewski 2009, 622).

Similarly, if we are to focus only on theorizing bodies as the neglected part of the mind/body dichotomy, or as the concrete effect of wars that privilege abstract strategic thought, we run the risk of reproducing bodies precisely as they are considered in both modern security discourse and in biomedical discourses: as apolitical objects that breathe, suffer, and die. While such projects attempt to "humanize" war (to varying degrees of success), the "human" that they show is an injured body, a corpse, a body defined by its relationship to physiological harm or death. This kind of attempt to re-value bodies in opposition to strategic thought does not fundamentally challenge the reduction of the human to biological being, and thus erases the sociality of the body as it lives or dies. The representation of the injured or killed body is not enough for us to incorporate such persons as fully human in our ethical awareness; the representation of bodies fails to fully "capture" the human subject, as such bodies are not necessarily viewed as anything other than bodies (see Butler 2004a, 142–147). We need a fuller account of human bodies in their sociality and materiality to begin to account for bodies in their complex relationship to violence. Masters's (2005) call for a re-engagement with the "fleshy" body that is effaced in contemporary high-tech warfare is an excellent starting point, but runs the risk of reifying "the body" as precisely that which is the effect of biopolitics, rather than a natural object that has been left behind by political analyses. Here, Sylvester's discussion of sex, gender, power, and bodies is highly suggestive of the ways in which bodies can have power in ways that do not conform to the gendered expectations of them (2002, 53). It is precisely this possibility of bodily upheaval, of bodies that are not natural objects to be interpreted or even inscribed by gender, but are both constituted and constituting, that is a hallmark of the last several decades of feminist theorizing about embodiment.

Feminists and other political theorists have in recent years been concerned in ways to challenge the Foucauldian model of the body as passively inscribed through language or discourse, which they see as excessive weight granted to cultural or linguistic modes of explanation in previous feminist work in theorizing the embodied subject. Such theories, recently collected under the heading of "new materialisms" or "material feminisms" (see recent volumes edited by Alaimo and Hekman 2008, and Coole and Frost 2010) do not reject discursive and linguistic theories such as Butlerian performativity, but rather seek to build on them to more radically undermine culture/nature dichotomies. Such theories are important in their attempts to formulate a space of agency for bodies and materiality more broadly, without falling into the trap of biological determinism. A key argument of this movement is that nature "punches back" in ways that humans and their technologies cannot predict (Alaimo and Hekman 2008, 7). Materiality is re-theorized not as a limit to, or foundation for, cultural inscription, but as agentic in such a way that it cannot be ontologically separated from cultural or discursive forces. Diana Coole's work on the phenomenology of the body, for example, argues that that body has "agentic capacities" that are not reducible to the will of subjects nor to the interpretive frameworks of discourse (2005, 2007). N. Katherine Hayles uses the example of learning to type to illustrate what might be thought of as the agentic capacities of bodies. Learning to type does not require reading or cognitively mapping the keys but repeating performing actions so that the keys seem like extensions of the fingers. These capacities are distinct from discourse, and produce discursive formations (Hayles 1999, 199). From the vantage point of "new materialist" perspectives, bodies have a capacity to push back against their inscription and formation in discursive practices. In other words, human bodies can be productive as well as produced. They have a history, but are also historicizing.[3] This is one way in which feminist accounts of embodiment diverge from Foucault, Agamben and theories of discipline and biopower, in which before the imposition of power, bodies are always already docile. These critiques of Foucault from feminist perspectives are not novel to the "new materialist" turn: feminist work on corporeality has stressed the body as a set of potentialities rather than externally imposed norms in order to account for the possibility (and actuality) of resistance and change in gendered norms and subjectivities. Twenty years ago, Elizabeth Grosz insisted that the category of "nature" has a residue in the cultural. In theories of bodily inscription that take the body as the raw materials for the process of subject construction, an account of the body as pliable is necessary for this story to be plausible (Grosz 1994, 21). Lois McNay stresses the creative dimensions of bodily practice and the possibilities of new social configurations that stem from the generative capacities of bodies (McNay 2000). Revaluing "fleshy bodies" outside an analysis of precisely how these bodies are made to appear as "raw bodies" or "just bodies" risks reproducing culture/nature dichotomies that posit the passivity of bodies as a resource to be formed and molded. This logic reproduces the subordination and exploitation of women, racialized people, and other non-normative bodies in International Relations, as those marked by their embodiment, rather than as figures of neutral humanity.

While some work in this vein of material feminism critiques Butler among others (see, for example, Barad 2007), it is not clear that the critique of an overly deterministic, or overly linguistic, conception of the body or embodiment is entirely fair to Butler. Butler's concept of performativity as a way of embodying norms gives more room for agency (however, not in a voluntaristic sense) as well as a generative, or constituting, role of bodies.[4] The necessity of repetition, of repeated performance, underscores the insufficiency of the regulative norms or individual performances to "capture" or contain all the possibilities for action or experience. This failure refers to a realm of bodily experience that is not captured by discourse—or at least not yet. In the very instability of bodies, which necessitates the citational practices of materialization, there are openings for challenge. "The iterability of performativity is a theory of agency, one that cannot disavow power as the condition of its possibility" (Butler 1999 [1990], xxiv). Butler's emphasis on the need for norms to be repeated throughout the body sets her approach to agency and discourse apart from Foucault; whereas Foucault emphasized the productive effects of discourse in constituting subject positions, Butler's performativity thesis suggests that embodied life consists of iterations of norms (that we may or may not be aware of), which are subject to subversion and alteration through bodily performances. Butler specifies the body as "that which can occupy the norm in myriad ways, exceed the norm, rework the norm, and expose realities to which we thought we were confined as open to transformation" (2004b, 217). Butler's insistence that "language and materiality are fully embedded in each other, chiasmic in their interdependency, but never fully collapsed into one other, i.e., reduced to one another and yet neither fully ever exceeds the other" (1993, 69) is useful for thinking about the overlapping yet distinct contours of materiality and social production in theorizing embodiment. Because discourses are not closed, they overlap and come into conflict with one another; the body can be a site for transformation.[5] Regardless of whether Butler's work is fully capable of providing a non-dualistic account of agency and embodiment, the insistence on the generative abilities or "agentic capacities" of bodies is a welcome modification of Butler's performativity thesis in order to theorize violence and embodied subjects, as it allows us to theorize bodies and subjects as neither wholly determined nor fixed by discursive practices, including various practices of violence.

In her works *Precarious Life* and *Frames of War*, Butler has explicitly outlined what was implicit in her previous work: that our bodies are ontological vulnerable. Butler's articulation of precarious life, that is, of a constitutively vulnerable embodied subject, ties together her arguments of gender and sexuality, subject formation and normative violence, and makes clear that the issue of normative violence is not only a theory relevant to issues of gender and sexuality. Bodily vulnerability is not only a function of the body's materiality, that is, its fragility and susceptibility to injury and death in biological terms. Whether one is subject to such harm and physical coercion is a social matter—whether one's life is survivable is dependent upon how the body is socially constituted. Vulnerability is thus ontological rather than historical: the body is vulnerable both to physical violence and neglect as well as to normative violence (Butler 2004a, 2009). Because the body can be injured, it is a target for sovereign power. Because the body has material needs, it is the target for biopolitical interventions.

Bodies in their precariousness are not quite as autonomous as they are in liberalism. Butler points explicitly to violence as a reason that we cannot consider bodies as fully autonomous individuals. Precisely because one's body can be injured and killed, we are bound to others in our vulnerability. Butler does not deny the importance of political struggles to articulate and defend a space of bodily autonomy for those who have been denied control over their bodies. Rather, here Butler emphasizes a body that is not conceived of as the autonomous enclosure of the self, but rather is the medium of relations with others—its boundaries are porous, as it can be violated, but it can also violate. It is from this discussion of Butler's work that I take this work's epigraph "the body implies mortality, vulnerability, agency: the skin and the flesh expose us to the gaze of others but also to touch and to violence" (2004a, 26). The precarity thesis insists that the boundedness, certainty, and security of modernist thought have always been illusions (Ettlinger 2007). Butler's theorization of bodily life as fundamentally precarious is expressly concerned with the political and ethical implications of bodies as socially produced, marked by difference, yet also material and marked by material needs.

Butler has developed her argument of precarity or constitutive vulnerability in her more overtly political writing of recent years, addressing such contemporary issues involving state-sponsored violence such as Abu Ghraib, Guantánamo Bay, and the question of Israel and anti-Semitism. Her relevance to IR scholars is not only in her specific contributions to theorizing these and other issues, but more broadly in her theorization of the subject as embodied and thus necessarily vulnerable. Butler's theorization of the embodied subject as constitutively vulnerable is attuned to the ways in which relations with others, both in primary attachments such as the family and in broader political associations, are formative of the self. This constitutive vulnerability suggests a very different politics for Butler than it does for social contract theorists like Hobbes and liberals for whom the possibility of bodily harm and death requires protection by a sovereign.[6] For Butler, our vulnerability to violence is not only to death at the hands of others but is a constitutive condition of subjectivity. Her concern with precarity is not to empower the weak and the vulnerable, but to deny the more powerful their refuge in sovereignty and security. Her politics are not of sovereignty, but of responsiveness or responsibility outside sovereign states or sovereign subjectivity that accompanies recognition of this vulnerability.

Butler's work points us forward, simultaneously theorizing embodiment not as incidental to the subject, but as an effect of political relations. Furthermore, Butler's work theorizes bodies and embodiment as matters not of facticity, foundations, or limitations, but rather as a *question* central to understanding the operations of power and violence. In her various navigations of conceptualizing the subject as embodied, and specifically embodied in relation to power and violence, Butler's work serves as an inspiration for thinking about how International Relations theory might better address some of its core issues of violence and security if it were to take the embodiment of the subject seriously. Putting Butler's work in conversation with that of Donna Haraway, Julia Kristeva, and N. Katherine Hayles, among others, this book builds upon feminist and biopolitical perspectives that make questions of embodiment central to interrogating power and violence.

CHAPTER 2

Dying Is Not Permitted

Guantánamo Bay and the Liberal Subject of International Relations

At the US naval base at Guantánamo Bay, Cuba, prisoners captured in Afghanistan and elsewhere around the world are held in indefinite detention without a juridical decision as to their guilt or innocence.[1] Since the time the detention center opened in July 2002, 775 prisoners have been brought to Guantánamo Bay, and 149 remain as of June 2014. They have been subjected to techniques that the George W. Bush administration referred to as "enhanced interrogation techniques" but that fit the legal definition of torture. While the Obama administration has disallowed torture, it has also refused to close the prison at Guantánamo or give prisoners trials under civilian law. As a protest against their treatment and detention, as many as 200 prisoners have undertaken hunger strikes. One hunger striker, Binyam Mohamed, said to his lawyer, "I do not plan to stop until I die or we are respected" (Leonnig 2005). In response, military officials have opted to force-feed these prisoners by inserting tubes into their stomachs through their nasal passages while restraining them. Defending this practice, military physician John Edmonson asserted, "I will not allow them to do harm to themselves" (Miles 2006, 110).

Hunger strikes have occurred at Guantánamo from the time the detention center opened. In June 2005, hunger strikes reached a peak, when between 130 to 200 out of approximately 500 prisoners at Guantánamo Bay began refusing food. The *New York Times* has reported that at least 12 prisoners have been subjected to force-feeding, while lawyers say the prisoners have reported 40 or more (Golden 2007). In January 2009, the *Times* of London reported that 44 out of the 248 inmates were refusing food (though visiting lawyers reported that more than 70 were on hunger strikes) (Reid 2009). During the Bush administration, these strikes took place in the context of practices that are widely considered to constitute torture, such as sleep deprivation, humiliation, and the use of stress positions. In response to worsening treatment and the ongoing uncertainty of their status, up to 130 of the remaining 166 prisoners engaged in another hunger strike in the spring and summer of 2013. The Obama administration has not, as of June 2014, followed through on its promise to close Guantánamo Bay and has abandoned plans to try Khalid Shaikh Mohammad in a federal court in New York (Shane and Landler 2011).

The story of torture, hunger striking, and force-feeding at Guantánamo Bay as part of the US-led "war on terror" is the first of four chapters in this book that address a contemporary practice of violence. Having outlined how the field of International Relations traditionally conceptualizes bodies as organisms to be preserved as the basis for the flourishing of the subject, this chapter demonstrates the inadequacy of these assumptions about bodies, subject, and violence. The subjects of torture, hunger strikes, and force-feeding are not the self-preserving subjects of realism, nor are they the rational, individual, speaking subjects of liberalism. As such, these practices show the need to think about security *biopolitically*, in terms of the politics of life itself. Guantánamo Bay, one of the most controversial sites of violence in contemporary International Relations, is an example of the tensions between sovereign and biopolitical forms of the exercise of power in and through bodies. Guantánamo Bay is a state of exception, a spatialization of a politics of exceptionality in which the sovereign declaration of the detainees as "enemy combatants"—a new category outside both domestic and international law—makes this a site defined by its lawlessness, and makes its prisoners *homines sacri* (Agamben 2005, 3). These tensions reveal the inadequacy of IR's implicit theorization of bodies as strictly material organisms. The violence of Guantánamo Bay shows that violence not only harms (or "makes live") preexisting bodies, but also produces bodies as legible in a variety of ways. The bodily practices of torture, hunger striking, and force-feeding show, *contra* understandings of bodies as organisms, that the bodies that are the objects of various security practices are not natural and independently existing entities; rather, they exist in virtue of their instantiation in political relations.

The simultaneous torture and force-feeding of hunger-striking prisoners points to the ambiguous role of "the body" in contemporary security practices: the body occupies an intermediary role between subject and object. By referring to the body as object, I mean that the body is acted upon, injured, or treated in a direct way, but also that the body is produced, made into an object of knowledge by social and political forces that constitute the body as we know it. This is a more indirect way of making the body into an object. The body can also be considered a subject; that is, it has a sort of political agency in its own right that is not reducible to the will of the mind occupying it, as in a Cartesian model of embodiment. The use of feminist theory to think about the embodiment of subjects in Guantánamo Bay does not seem like an obvious choice, especially since all of the prisoners are male. However, as the last chapter discussed, feminist thought has been at the forefront of thinking through the dynamics of the body as both an object of power and a source of generative or agentic capacities. The complex dynamics of violence, subjection, and resistance in and through the body that forms a central problematic for feminist thought are brought into stark relief in the ongoing drama at Guantánamo Bay; moreover, this scene of violence usefully demonstrates the necessity of abandoning realist and liberal conceptions of the subject in IR.

While the liberal subject is supposed to transcend embodiment, the body haunts the liberal subject as its constitutive "other"—that which must be excluded. The subject of liberalism, as discussed in the previous chapter, is a subject that is unconstrained by bodily impediments; the free subject of liberalism is a subject whose body is unmarked. The normative body is an adult, young, healthy, male, cisgendered, and non-racially marked body. Butler's critique of the naturalness of sex as an effect of discourse ties "realness" and intelligibility as effects of norms. Bodies that do not conform to the normative standard, or which defy the model of the singular sovereign individual living in a singular body—bodies which are marked by excess, lack, or disfigurement—challenge and threaten the normative model of the body. Butler's emphasis on the need for norms to be repeated throughout the body sets her approach to agency and discourse apart from Foucault; whereas Foucault emphasized the productive effects of discourse in constituting subject positions, Butler's performativity thesis suggests that embodied life consists of iterations of norms (that we may or may not be aware of), which are subject to subversion and alteration through bodily performances.

While Butler's work is influenced by Foucault, she is also critical of Foucault's model of bodily inscription, pointing out that his concept of genealogy exempts the idea of a pre-discursive body from genealogical analysis, as it takes a historically imprinted body as its starting place (Butler 1989b). In taking up this paradox of Foucault's work, Butler's theory of gender performativity also challenges the sex/gender theory in feminism, which separates "gender" as social interpretation and cultural inscription from "sex," which is biological and natural. Her work is an anti-foundationalist critique of the liberal model of the self, a speaking, self-conscious willing subject; her critique is thus also relevant to our understanding of the embodied subject of Guantánamo Bay.

The political dynamics of the violence of torture and force-feeding in this context are not well captured through traditional IR theory. Rather, the violence of Guantánamo Bay compels us to pay attention to the ways in which the body as we know it is the product of social and political forces as well as being itself an agent of politics. The simultaneous torture and force-feeding of hunger-striking prisoners point to the exercise of two distinct logics of power: sovereign power and biopower. By being tortured, the prisoners are objects of the sovereign's ability to act directly on their bodies or, in Michel Foucault's terms, to "take life or let live." However, the deaths of the detainees pose a limit for the exercise of sovereign power—simply put, they cannot be killed. Rather, the health of prisoners is closely monitored by medical professionals, and hunger-striking prisoners are force-fed in order to prevent their deaths, evidence of what Foucault calls the exercise of "biopower"—a technology of power that can, in Foucault's terms, "let die" and "make live" (2003, 247) through the management of biological life and populations. This entwinement of military and medical discourses forces the prisoners to live as a particular type of subject. In other words, through the conjunction of torture and force-feeding, the prisoners' bodies are made into not only "useful bodies" for providing intelligence but also "dependent bodies" that are not autonomous agents but recipients of care that must be efficiently managed. The practices of torture, hunger striking, and force-feeding do more than demonstrate the inadequacy of IR's assumptions of bodies as organisms existing outside politics; these practices also reveal the ambiguous nature of bodies as produced by politics (as torturable "terrorists" or feminized, infirm patients that can be force-fed), as well as bodies that can affect politics as well, as in the bodies of hunger strikers.

In the context of the "war on terror", torture has been assessed in terms of its usefulness in providing citizens with short-term as well as long-term protection (Shue 1978; Dershowitz 2002; Hannah 2006; Brecher 2007). Torture is also justified by the crimes and identities of the terrorists—they are, in Rumsfeld's words, the "worst of the worst" (Seelye 2002). These two logics are contradictory, because the security rationale for torturing prisoners does not require the prisoner to be guilty of any crimes, only to have knowledge that could be used to save lives. In academic as well as policy debates, the hypothetical ticking-time-bomb scenario has structured the ethical question of torture in the "war on terror"; assuming that the guilty captive has the necessary knowledge, this scenario asks whether torture should be authorized in order to prevent the deaths of dozens or hundreds of civilians (people who are presumed innocent, just as the captive is presumed guilty). The ticking-time-bomb scenario also assumes that the torture will work, that causing the captive bodily pain will yield "actionable intelligence." As an instrument of information gathering, torture is dissociated from liberalism's anathemas of tyranny and cruelty, and can even be viewed as heroic, as it is meant to prevent future suffering (Luban 2005). The discourse of torture in the "war on terror" produces the body of the prisoner as a site of information to be gleaned in the most efficient way possible, as well as a site for the exercise of sovereign power, the power to punish. But while the bodies of prisoners may be subject to violence for the extraction of information, they are also objects of care for the preservation of their useful lives.

Forcing hunger-striking prisoners to live does more than breach the state's moral obligation not to torture: torture and force-feeding serve to enact US sovereign power while displacing vulnerability onto the individual subjectivity of the prisoners. Held in a legal and territorial gap and subject to torture for an indefinite period of time, the prisoners' existence is defined by an array of political technologies that refuse them even the choice to die in order to end their imprisonment. The exercise of torture at Guantánamo Bay and elsewhere by US officials is not an instance of sovereign power exercised on a juridical subject, as exemplified by the torture of Damiens in Foucault's *Discipline and Punish*, but is rather a moment in the exercise of sovereign power though biopolitics on subjects produced not as liberal subjects of consent, nor economic subjects of rationality, but as a quasi-population of dependents who must be managed. In these cases, violence is best understood as performative: the violence serves to create and reinforce subjectivities and relations of power between the US military and the prisoners through the exercise of sovereign power on the bodies of prisoners. These uses of violence are performative precisely because they enact and express US sovereignty while undoing the individual subjectivity of prisoners who are held indefinitely. The use of torture and force-feeding expresses the troubled, uneasy relationship of sovereign power and biopower and highlights the sociality of violence as effecting the production of "worlds" or the possibilities of existence as a human subject.

In developing this argument, I first discuss the motivations for the use of torture in terms of Foucault's categories of sovereign power, discipline, and biopower in order to articulate the paradox of applying violence through torture while maintaining the health of prisoners, including force-feeding hunger strikers. I then demonstrate how the exercise of sovereign power through torture meets with anxieties over injuring and killing the human body. I show how the use of hunger striking as a protest against torture and force-feeding makes use of the materiality of the body and its relationship to other bodies in a way that challenges liberal and biopolitical assumptions about bodies. In the final section, I discuss how anxieties that constitute the paradox of sovereign power and biopower are manifested in the force-feeding of hunger-striking prisoners, an exercise of power that transforms prisoners from dangerous "enemy combatants" to a biopolitical subjectivity as recipients of care.

TORTURE AS SOVEREIGNTY, DISCIPLINE, AND BIOPOWER

Why has the United States resorted to torture in its "war on terror"? Torture is something that liberal political communities are supposed to have left behind in their pre-modern pasts, rejected as a tyrannical abuse of state power against vulnerable people. For Foucault, torture exemplifies sovereign power in the classical period. Torture was used ritually to extract confessions and punish criminals. If sovereign power is the power to "take life or let live" (Foucault 1979, 48), then the sovereign uses torture to punish in self-defense, and as such, the tortured body represents an enemy of the sovereign rather than a citizen. Torture marked the body directly and thus performatively established the power of the sovereign.

But in the "war on terror", torture and indefinite detention in Guantánamo Bay take place not as part of a juridical discourse of truth and guilt but rather as a means for gathering ostensibly lifesaving information and to quarantine dangerous subjects apart from the US population. While the use of torture in the detention camps at Guantánamo Bay at first glance appears to resemble the tactics of disciplinary power, torture in this context is more consistent with the exercise of sovereign power through biopolitics. The bodies of the prisoners at Guantánamo Bay, though subject to torture, cannot legitimately be killed.[2] Torture demonstrates a contradiction in the exercise of biopower and sovereign power: while sovereign power names the power to "take life or let live," and biopower names the power to "make live and let die" (Foucault 2003, 241), the simultaneous exercise of torture and force-feeding at Guantánamo Bay indicates the exercise of power that not only injures the body but refuses to kill or allow the death of the tortured body. In order to explain the contradictions of sovereign power and biopower in the exercise of torture at Guantánamo Bay, I first argue that discipline, while seemingly apparent in the prison setting, is not the primary logic of the operation of power. Rather, the logic of torture is biopolitical, meant to protect one population at the expense of a "risky" population. However, this explanation, too, is insufficient to account for the operation of Guantánamo Bay. Torture in this case is a practice of sovereign power, exercised through biopolitical techniques.

Insofar as Guantánamo Bay is a detention camp, with daily life managed and controlled, it would seem to exemplify disciplinary power—a mode of power in which people are not dominated directly, as in sovereign power, but are turned into docile subjects, their bodies micromanaged so that they will be useful and compliant. Unlike biopower, which works on populations, disciplinary power is centered on molding individuals. Several key techniques of disciplinary power described by Foucault are used at Guantánamo Bay, from the division of space into cells, the control of activities by timetables, and the organization of men by categories and ranks (Foucault 1979, 138–149). Prisoners are kept to a precise schedule of eating, drinking, washing, and saying prayers, with these activities denied to prisoners who engage in "bad behavior." These details of the regulation of prisoners' movements and activities in order to compel cooperation with interrogators are contained in a 263-page document on standard operating procedures at Guantánamo Bay (Joint Task Force–Guantánamo 2003). The prisoners are subject to the documentation of every deviation from what is considered acceptable behavior in order to produce specific knowledge about each detainee in order to better manage all of them. Minute details about a prisoner's behavior are noticed and reported, an example of how disciplinary power "allows nothing to escape" (Foucault 2007, 45) in its quest to create docile subjects.

Sovereign power and disciplinary power produce the subject the sovereign purports to regulate, rather than reflecting a preexisting subject. Through torture, the body of the prisoner is made to signify the guilt of the prisoner, to make him into the social type of "terrorist," a dangerous subject outside of the bounds of civilization. Vulnerability is also located in the bodies of the prisoners through the practice of torture. Read as a performative practice as well as a violent injuring, torture works to make the torturer invulnerable and the torture victim into a vulnerable subject. As Judith Butler writes, "one locates injurability with the other by injuring the other and then taking the sign of injury as the truth of the other" (2009, 178). Torture not only attempts to shift bodily vulnerability onto the prisoner, but produces the body of the prisoner as a body of information. The nominal purpose of torture at Guantánamo is to produce a docile, productive subject who will give information to interrogators. The information that the prisoner supposedly possesses can be released through causing pain and discomfort. The "stress and duress" torture techniques, such as being kept in solitary confinement for days and lowering the temperature in their cells, are specific disciplinary technologies used to make prisoners submissive and useful to interrogators (Danner 2009).

However, the fact that Guantánamo Bay is to be kept out of the public eye suggests that something other than disciplinary power is at work. Both sovereign power and disciplinary power are meant to be visible: the former through spectacles that make the power of the sovereign present to the citizenry and the latter through the creation of a morality tale about a dangerous person being reformed and becoming an obedient person. The ambiguous legal place that the prisoners of Guantánamo Bay occupy points to difficulties in considering them strictly objects of disciplinary power. Peremptorily declared guilty by the United States, they have not been convicted and also are not subject to rehabilitation. Unlike a prisoner who breaks a social contract, the "terrorist" is a decidedly foreign subject, as evidenced by the difficulty in assigning the label "terrorist" to domestic perpetrators of political violence.[3] Even though international law is clear that everyone must have some status under the law (a disarmed person is either a prisoner of war or a civilian), the United States has claimed the special, extralegal status of "enemy combatants" for prisoners at Guantánamo Bay. Many prisoners at Guantánamo have been held for more than seven years without charge or trial. The Bush administration denied that even Common Article 3 of the Geneva Conventions applies to Al Qaeda detainees because the conflict between the United States and Al Qaeda is neither between states nor a domestic civil war (Yoo 2005, 49). Even though the US Supreme Court ruled in the 2006 case of *Hamdan v. Rumsfeld* that the prisoners at Guantánamo Bay must be given fair trials, only a few military commissions have occurred by 2014, and the Obama administration has de facto given up on trying the prisoners in civilian courts.[4] As the prisoners are not domestic subjects, the intended audience for detention and torture seems obscure. However, there is a way in which torture and indefinite detention play to a US domestic audience—Americans are made to feel safe not only from terrorists but from the techniques of biopower. The torture of Guantánamo Bay prisoners, who are bodies of information, is consistent with the instrumental logic of biopower and the management of populations.

While the lack of juridical guilt and the indefinite detention of the prisoners at Guantánamo Bay indicate that disciplinary power is not the only, or even primary, technique of power, these very characteristics signal that techniques of biopower are being exercised. Biopolitics is a moral discourse that moves away from the political realm of the rights and obligations of individuals and toward a model of familial care in which the main justification of sovereign power is to provide for the health and welfare of its people. Biopower concerns itself with risk and chance events that affect populations, such as diseases, famines, and the seemingly random violence of terrorist attacks. As the prisoners are detained on the basis of their assumed dangerousness to the United States if they were to be released, what they present is not an established danger but a risk of future danger. They are presumed to have the capacity to commit random, violent acts: in other words, the risk is that they will carry out violence that is itself constituted by chance and uncertainty in the form of a terrorist attack. The Justice Department has declared that the United States may detain prisoners not only if they are known or suspected of being agents of Al Qaeda or affiliated organizations but also if they are deemed to "constitute a clear and continuing threat to the USA or its allies" (Bradbury 2005b). Thus, aside from any evidence of involvement in a terrorist organization or the planning of terrorist acts, a person may be detained indefinitely on the declaration that he or she is dangerous to the United States. The prisoners have been described as "the most dangerous, best-trained, vicious killers on the face of the earth" by US Secretary of Defense Donald Rumsfeld (Washington 2002). The "terrorists" are constructed as unfathomable in their mental states, as "killing machines" in a discourse of savagery in opposition to civilization (Butler 2004a; Howell 2007). These subjects of biopower are not necessarily the villains and enemies of society who break the law out of malice; rather, they are aberrations, whose threat to society is more diffuse and amorphous (Foucault 2007, 7). They are not necessarily immoral subjects; they are amoral, as they cannot be rehabilitated into obedient domestic subjects.

Techniques of security are intended to minimize risk, and, to this end, torture has been deployed as a means of quickly obtaining information intended to prevent terrorist attacks. Thus the use of torture is made consistent with the exercise of biopower. Yet torture is known to be ineffective as a tool for information gathering. In the United States, interrogation experts have long recognized that the victims of torture frequently provide inaccurate information, as tortured people often say whatever they believe their torturers want to hear (Glanz 2004; Thomas 2006; Rejali 2007). There is evidence that official documents cautioning against the utility of torture, even if it were deemed to be legal, were suppressed (Finn and Warrick 2009b). Prisoners at Guantánamo Bay have made false confessions under torture, and those false confessions have provided the basis for the ongoing torture of the original prisoner as well as others (Worthington 2007, 2009; Finn and Warrick 2009a). The capture of failed airplane bomber

Umar Farouk Abdulmutallab in late December 2009 led to renewed calls for torture to be used to gather information from terrorist suspects, despite Abdulmutallab's willingness to cooperate with authorities. Likewise, the killing of Osama bin Laden in May 2011 has also reignited the debate over torture; however, there is no evidence that torture produced any information that helped to locate bin Laden. Furthermore, interrogators involved in the case and even the head of the CIA, Leon Panetta, have denied that information gathered by torture led to the capture of bin Laden (Shane and Savage 2011). Torture is known to be ineffectual at gathering accurate, useful information; and even if it were effectual, these doubts suggest that there are other logics at play than a strictly strategic rationale.

The rationale for torture does not fit with the experience of the body being tortured. Torture relies on a calculation of pain, such that the precise amount can be applied that will make the target "break," a logic of information based on biopolitical concepts of rationality and utility. While practices of torture make use of medical knowledge about bodies, the subjective experience of pain is not quantifiable. Humans vary greatly in their ability to endure pain. Pain is also not a singular, measurable experience but can take the form of many sensations, which may counterbalance one another (Rejali 2007, 446–450). As the experience of pain is subjective, it is difficult to quantify or control. The experience of psychological torture is even more difficult to predict. This incoherence between the logic of rational information gathering and the subjective nature of pain is at the heart of interrogational torture. The subjective experience of pain suggests that the infliction of torture is not entirely consistent with an exercise of biopower, as it cannot be properly ordered or structured.

Biopolitics is also insufficient to explain the practices of torture at Guantánamo Bay because the prisoners are not being killed. In fact, the preservation of the lives of the prisoners despite their torture is at the core of the tension between biopower and sovereign power in the treatment of the prisoners at Guantánamo Bay. Foucault writes that the sovereign must make a distinction between who must live and who must die as a necessary component of the practice of sovereign power in biopolitical regimes (2003, 254–255). By this logic, in order to protect the lives of the domestic population, the source of risk must be killed. In the contemporary torture regime at Guantánamo Bay, however, sovereign power is exercised on "undesirables" in such a way that the object is not their deaths but their production as a particularly risky subject. Torture prevents its victims from having the kind of lives that biopolitics promotes in its positive form of furthering the health and longevity of the population. In the practice of torture, "the violence can unfold as something irresistible, even unlimitable, except that the death of the vulnerable one . . . always does constitute a limit" (Cavarero 2009, 31). Biopower, in this sense, has not led to the intentional deaths of the prisoners but, rather, has imposed a limit on the extreme use of sovereign power—the power to kill. Bodies are tortured, but they are not allowed to die. Death operates as a limit on the torturer as well as on the agency of the prisoner. The prisoner cannot be killed because he must be made to speak. This limit suggests a different interpretation of the role of sovereign power and biopower than the interpretation of those who suggest that sovereign power produces a subject who can be killed. While Guantánamo Bay may usefully be thought of as a zone of distinction, the fact that death still constitutes a murder or suicide suggests a need to rethink how power operates in relation to the livability of certain lives.

It could be argued that a strategic rationale exists for the decision to simultaneously torture prisoners for information, but not to let them die: to allow their deaths would mean that the prisoners could no longer supply the information needed to save lives. The point of analyzing the practice of torture by the United States in this context is not to argue that there is no strategic or instrumental logic being deployed. Rather, my purpose here is to examine the assumptions that underpin such strategic logics to show how they are embedded in particular discourses that are in tension with one another. The instrumental logic of torture given by its defenders is both constituted by, and in tension with, sovereign and biopolitical logics.

Further complicating a reading of torture in Guantánamo Bay as an exercise of sovereignty is that it is carried out behind closed doors, with officials denying that torture is being carried out. Modern torture is an invisible spectacle in which the emphasis is not on the visual spectacle for an audience, but on an exchange of pain and information. The emphasis on the subject of torture "breaking" and the release of certain kinds of information about the Guantánamo Bay prisoners (such as photographs showing prisoners in orange jumpsuits, shackled, wearing goggles, and kneeling on the ground) suggests that part of the process is also the performance of submission to the sovereign. The oxymoronic phrase "invisible spectacle" suggests that torture as a performance of sovereign power is still being carried out, but because of the need to operate within the terms of biopolitics, this spectacle is muted, only carried out with a great deal of anxiety.

TORTURE AS AN ANXIOUS PRACTICE OF SOVEREIGN POWER

As the prisoners at Guantánamo Bay have been declared enemy combatants who have no standing in international law, what then prevents the

United States from killing them outright, as they might have done if they encountered these "terrorists" in a battle? Despite the insistence on the prisoners' lack of legal status, the prisoners' lives are officially protected. They may be tortured, but they must be kept alive. Foucault defines the paradigms of sovereign power as the power to kill or let live, and it is exercised directly on the body of the criminal in the form of pain and death (Foucault 1979, 48). Torture, in this reading, marks the body directly and performatively establishes the power of the sovereign by its ability to mark bodies in this way. Judging by its willingness to use violence, but its unwillingness to take lives or let the prisoners take their own lives, the United States appears troubled by the exercise of sovereign power.

In ancient Greece, torture could be used to release the truth from a slave's body but not a citizen's. Slaves (and women and barbarians) were bodies, pure materiality, while citizens had reason (Dubois 1991, 52). But the distinction between slave and free is unstable, not "given by nature." Judicial torture served to maintain the distinction, as only the bodies of women and slaves were thought to be able to release truth through bodily pain. Torture served as a way of marking these social hierarchies. While the context and meaning of torture have changed, the use of torture to produce and sustain hierarchies of political subjectivities remains. Torture serves a similar function in the context of Guantánamo and the "war on terror": it produces its own rationale by using pain to unmake the subjectivity of the prisoner while making present the power of the sovereign. Violence is this instance is not done to a preexisting subject, but produces the subject that can be tortured.

By the infliction of pain, torture produces hierarchical relations through its demonstration of the torturers' strength in an act of sovereign power. Elaine Scarry's *The Body in Pain* describes how torture can destroy the victim's subjectivity. Undergoing intense pain and unceasing questioning, the victim is reduced to the space of the "natural body" incapable of speech, of entering the symbolic realm of language. Scarry's thesis is that torture reduces the body to a world of pain. The extreme pain of torture is inexpressible in language, and thus the subject's world is unmade because the pain has no referent in the outside world. The victim's lack of language destroys his or her subjectivity. Scarry writes:

> It is intense pain that destroys a person's self and world, a destruction experienced spatially as either the contraction of the universe down to the immediate vicinity of the body or as the body swelling to fill the entire universe. Intense pain is also language-destroying; as the content of one's world disintegrates, so that content of one's language disintegrates; as the self disintegrates, so that

which would express and project the self is robbed of its sources and its subject. (1985, 35)

Scarry presents a model of torture in which there are two distinct subjects: a torturer and a prisoner. The torturer becomes invulnerable, effectively disembodied, and comes to be identified with voice and world, while the prisoner experiences only pain and the body (1985, 36). The torturer speaks with the voice of the sovereign, and the victim, deprived of subjectivity, is made to speak as the sovereign wishes, making present the existence of the sovereign. The sovereign is made present in the body of the tortured, not by the death of the prisoner, but by the unmaking of the world of the prisoner.

Scarry's analysis of torture shows the extent of sovereign power in the twenty-first century. While her work has been criticized for its separation of language and body (Butler 1997a; Bkare-Yusuf 1997; Rivera-Fuentes and Birke 2001), it powerfully demonstrates precisely how language and bodies are mutually entailed. In torture, the victim is made to "speak the name of the sovereign," in Paul Kahn's telling phrase (2008, 42). Torture serves as the means not only of producing "truth" but also of making present the sovereign.

The tortured body is broken, but it must be kept alive so that it can provide information or labor. It must be able to speak or work. The imprisoned victim of torture is meant to provide information, his body made to speak, to subvert his own will to silence. As bodies reduced to pain, tortured prisoners are not liberal speaking subjects, able to consent or to make claims against the state. While torture is a bare display of sovereign power, it destroys the type of subject that would constitute that sovereignty. By disabling the prisoner's ability to speak, the United States prevents the speech act that underpins the consent of the ruled that characterizes liberalism; rather, the prisoners are forced to speak with the voice of the sovereign. Neither can the subjects of torture be "remade" as Scarry's exemplars are, because they are not being prepared for reintegration into society. The bare display of sovereign power destroys the very subjects of sovereign power. Scarry frames her discussion in terms of "world-making" and "world-destroying." World-making and world-destroying can have multiple intended audiences, however. While the torture may be world-destroying for the tortured, it can be world-making for its intended audience in the United States and abroad in terms of its substantiation of US sovereign power.

The torture of prisoners at Guantánamo Bay is an expression of sovereign power that is met with much anxiety in the United States. This anxiety is manifested in two modes of distancing the sovereign from torture: a geographical distancing and a political distancing. The special status, or lack of status, that the prisoners at Guantánamo Bay hold, as the United States has declared, suggests that the United States could claim the sovereign right to kill as well as torture, as the prisoners are enemies outside the protections of any social contract. Yet the prisoners are maintained and sustained in camps. The prisoners must be held by the sovereign—witness the outcry from politicians over various proposals in 2009 to release Guantánamo Bay detainees in the states represented by these politicians. Likewise, there is great anxiety over the proposal for housing Guantánamo Bay prisoners in maximum-security prisons in the United States, despite the presence of other persons convicted of terrorism within these very facilities.[5] The prisoners, and their torture, must be kept at a distance from the sovereign. Anxiety over the status of prisoners who were captured in Afghanistan as suspected Al Qaeda members who pose a threat to the United States has led to the quarantine of these prisoners within US control but outside US sovereign territory. Since 2002, the US government has used Camp Delta at the Guantánamo Bay naval base to house prisoners captured in Afghanistan and elsewhere, citizens of countries such as the United Kingdom, Saudi Arabia, Yemen, Pakistan, Afghanistan, and Syria. Guantánamo Bay is not the only such site; others include Bagram Airfield in Afghanistan, numerous prisons in Iraq including Abu Ghraib, plus an unknown number of Central Intelligence Agency black sites in a secret internment network that comprises facilities in Thailand, Afghanistan, Morocco, Poland, and Romania (Priest 2005; Danner 2009). The political battle that raged when President Obama tried to have Khalid Shaikh Mohammad tried in a civilian court in New York City, an attempt that was ultimately withdrawn, pivoted around security fears over the danger that the presence of one highly restrained prisoner might cause. Underlying these fears is the fear of more attention to the US torture regime and the fear of key evidence against Mohammad being excluded as it was gained under torture, which could lead to his release.

Torture is also distanced from the sovereign by the use of euphemism and official denial. Referred to as "enhanced interrogations," torture is not accepted outright. President Bush has famously stated, "we do not torture," while administration spokespeople and supporters vehemently assert the necessity of conducting these "enhanced interrogations." The Obama administration, while denouncing torture and promising to close Guantánamo, has yet to do so, ostensibly pending acceptable alternative arrangements for the prisoners.

While torture violates liberal values prohibiting the illegitimate use of violence by states against citizens, it also appears necessary or at least useful in performing the presence of the sovereign. One key example of torture in reproducing sovereign power through the obliteration of subjectivity is the repeated waterboardings of several "high-value" prisoners. Khalid Sheikh Mohammed was waterboarded 183 times and Abu Zubaydah was waterboarded at least 83 times, according to declassified Bush administration documents (Bradbury 2005b). The sheer number of waterboardings casts doubt on the official rationale of information gathering, as the likelihood that each successive waterboarding will make the subject more likely to share information he is holding back seems small, yet the rationale for the use of waterboarding remains that it will compel the prisoner to produce information. If the subject occasionally provides some information after waterboarding, the question then becomes at what point he has given all the information he has to give and how much of that information was false. This repeated performance of violence suggests an ongoing attempt at stabilizing sovereign power through the destruction of subjectivity. The medicalization of the torture techniques also shows unease with the practice of torture.

Torture as practiced in this context is dependent upon certain medical regimes of truth about the human body. Torture advocates cite the many safeguards in place to secure the life and health of the subjects of torture, and medical professionals object to the violation of patient's rights as well as to the inherent harm of torture. Modern practices of torture, unlike the ones Foucault describes as examples of sovereign power in *Discipline and Punish*, are designed to avoid leaving permanent marks on the body. The body of the torture victim is an intermediary rather than the object of the torture. Instead of the bloody spectacles of flogging, amputation, limb stretching, and beating associated with torture in the classical era, contemporary torture practices are aimed at bloodlessness and invisibility.[6] The torture techniques used by the US military and its proxies include waterboarding, sleep deprivation, exposure to heat and cold, electric shock, sensory deprivation, intimidation by dogs, insects, and humiliation by sexual abuse (Bradbury 2005a). These tactics have been labeled "stealth technologies" because they are difficult to document (Rejali 2003). The experiences of prisoners released from Guantánamo Bay and other detention sites suggest that different techniques were tried out in order to judge their efficacy at causing pain without seriously threatening the life of the subject (Danner 2009). Famously, the "Bybee memo" argued that to be considered torture, the pain inflicted had to be "equivalent in intensity to the pain accompanying serious physical injury, such as organ failure, impairment of bodily function, or even death" (Yoo 2002). Such discourses indicate that, for torture to be acceptable, a biopolitical rationale must underwrite the practice of sovereign power.

The torture program has created, and made use of, a body of knowledge about the human body and what it can endure without dying. The complicity and assistance of medical personnel are essential to the practice of torture. The discourse of the biological body, in its physical limitations, not only is essential to the practice of torture but is produced from the knowledge gained through torture. Medical professionals are on hand to ensure that such torture tactics are not taken so far as to permanently damage the bodies of the victims (Miles 2006, 50–67). In fact, part of the reasoning as to why these "enhanced interrogation techniques" do not constitute torture is that medical personnel are present to ensure the safety of the prisoners. Memos from the Justice Department to the CIA's Office of General Counsel, for example, provide numerous assurances that no detainee will be subjected to treatment that is "counterindicated" by psychological or physiological evaluations. The Justice Department claims, for example, that "OMS [the CIA's Office of Medical Services] closely monitors the detainee's condition to ensure that he does not, in fact, experience severe pain or suffering or sustain any significant or lasting harm" (Bradbury 2005b). This is not to say that prisoners subjected to torture techniques in truth do not experience "severe pain or suffering." Rather, this demonstrates the extent to which medical knowledge is integral to the practices of torture in not only producing effects on the prisoners but also attempting to limit harmful effects so that the prisoners are kept alive. The purpose of medical supervision is made clear in the statement of a CIA official speaking of Abu Zubaydah: "He received the finest medical attention on the planet. We got him in very good health so we could start to torture him" (Suskind 2006, 100).

Despite the protestations of the Justice Department, the attempt to conduct these "enhanced interrogations" in a perfectly controlled manner is based on the idea that health, life, and death are, in fact, controllable. At least 19 prisoners have died of their treatment at the hands of US soldiers and interrogators, though the deaths of many more may have been covered up (Miles 2006, 71). More than one hundred prisoners have died in US custody in Afghanistan and Iraq in the first three years of the "war on terror," a number that is surely higher today, although the government has not released more recent information (Nanji 2005). The claims that the techniques used by US forces do not cause severe or lasting harm have also been shown to be false (Physicians for Human Rights 2005). The dream of perfectly controllable violence, in which medical and legal safeguards prevent any lasting illness or harm despite increasing levels of deprivation, suffering, and violence, is a fantasy of sovereign power—the perfect gaze of the panopticon (Foucault 2007, 66). Bodies cannot be entirely controlled by sovereign power. In this space for accidents, the body resists sovereign attempts to manage it completely. The materiality of the body provides another space for resistance: the hunger strike.

HUNGER STRIKES AND THE BODY IN PAIN

Widespread hunger strikes at Guantánamo Bay began over allegations of mistreatment of the Koran and became a mode of resistance to the indefinite detention and ill-treatment more broadly (Worthington 2007, 271–276). In the spring and summer of 2013, more than two-thirds of the remaining prisoners were on hunger strike, with dozens being force-fed. Even in an environment in which sovereign power is exercised to a remarkable degree over the lives and bodies of prisoners, the refusal to consume food and water constitutes an act of resistance by the hunger strikers. In the face of a power whose goal is to keep prisoners alive but indefinitely imprisoned, the hunger strikers attack their own bodies by refusing to live indefinitely in such conditions. Under conditions in which their worlds and subjectivities are being so destroyed, hunger strikes are the only way of enacting self-government. By harming their own bodies, they attempt to exercise power over meaning. In trying to martyr themselves, they deny the presence of the sovereign and assert their own sovereignty over their bodies. Karin Fierke has recently incisively theorized the prison hunger strike as a "warden's dilemma" in which the hunger striker causes harm to his or her own body in a contest over the identity of the hunger striker as martyr or suicidal criminal (2013). Though Guantánamo Bay is not one of Fierke's cases, her performative account of political self-sacrifice as an attempt to change the "game" being played is an important contribution to thinking about the bodies and constitution of political subjects. The hunger strikes at Guantánamo Bay can certainly be read as an attempt to change the meaning of the prison camp from a site of punishment, or detention of shadowy subjects without a clear status, to a site of wrongful abuses against political subjects whose rights are being denied, but they also shed further light on how we think about the embodied subject of resistance. Hunger strike blurs the lines between active and passive resistance. Allen Feldman argues that hunger striking presents such a conundrum for the state precisely because it "fus[es] the subject and object of violent enactment into a single body" (1991, 62): the body is both the object of violence and the means through which violence takes place. It is also the site where the active and passive become blurred: the body of the patient is figured as passive, while that of the doctor or the medical personnel is actively intervening in the body. The hunger strikers' attempts to enact subjectivity comes at the cost of the very materiality of their bodies and challenges traditional IR's presumption of subjects as inherently self-preserving.

To demonstrate how the hunger strike exposes the inadequacies of IR's conceptions of the body, I return to Scarry's theorization of pain's unmaking of the subject to show its inadequacies in theorizing the potential of bodies to enact certain forms of politics. Scarry argues that the extreme pain of torture is inexpressible in language, and the subject's world is unmade because the pain has no referent in the outside world, it does not represent any "thing." Because of this lack of referentiality, the victim's lack of language destroys his or her subjectivity. The unrepresentability of pain means that the victim is unable to enter into the symbolic realm. This reading of the body in pain is limited because it does not posit any agency for the body. Veena Das's rethinking of the body in pain in reference to the tortured body is a fruitful opening into this problem and can help us to think about the kind of political claim that the hunger striker makes in this situation. While Fierke (2013) argues that the visual spectacle of the body in pain communicates resistance without language to an audience, Das (2007) argues that pain is not so much a matter of its unrepresentability in language, as much as it is a call for recognition. The key distinction is that the body in pain as a call for recognition is not necessarily expressing a message to a preexisting audience; rather, it can be read as a performative act of interpolating a community or audience. The expression of pain is a call for recognition in the body of the other. The experience of pain cries out for the response of the possibility that pain could be reversed, that it could reside in your body instead of mine in a kind of remembrance or imagining (Das 2007). Language may fail in expressing and communicating pain, but such a failure is always present in language, as language must be removed from "the thing" so it can fit into an existing signifier and therefore be mediated in language (Epstein 2010). A failure of the pain to be recognized as pain, as possibly reversible, is a failure of someone to be recognized as precisely human.

What this reading of Das suggests is that pain demonstrates that separateness or individuation between subjects and bodies is an accomplishment. This relationship between torture victim and torturer, whether that torturer is one or several people, or is connected to an entire state apparatus, can be thought of as exposing, and contributing to, a particular relationality in the acknowledgment of the realities of pain and the mutual constitution of ourselves as embodied subjects in a particular context that includes other embodied subjects as well. Thus, rather than creating distance between the "superempowered" torturer and the radically disempowered prisoners, pain can connect both embodied subjects through an imaginary of pain. As Asad reminds us, "What a subject experiences as painful, and how, are not simply mediated culturally and physically, *they are themselves modes of living in a relationship*" (2003, 84). Pain is a way of possibly entering into a relationship—but what relationship depends upon the response to pain, and how it is allowed to be expressed. Torture and other forms of violence are an exploitation of the primary vulnerabilities of bodies. Das and Asad give us a way of thinking about how we can differently establish relations and rethink connections—through attention to the material body in its social and political relations. The subject of torture in this way is not an autonomous subject trapped in his or her own body—or transcending it in the imperviousness of the torturer—but is bound in relations of recognition.

Thinking about bodies in terms of bodily relationships moves us away from thinking of justice in a Kantian, abstract sense toward a way in which we are not divorced from the social and political conditions we are acting in. The torture victim—whose torture and pain are hidden, denied, and justified at the same time—turned hunger striker contradicts the liberal presumption of the subject in International Relations and enacts a bodily politics of relationality and recognition. In seeking recognition as a political subject through his own painful demise, Binyam Mohamad and the other hunger strikers at Guantánamo Bay lay bare the contradictions and limitations in the way in which the subject is theorized in IR, especially in regard to matters of the biopolitical security state.

Binyam Mohamad's statement, "I do not plan to stop until I die or we are respected," is *not* a classical liberal appeal to the state on behalf of human rights so much as it is a call for *recognition* of the prisoners as political subjects by an international community. Indeed, had it been an example of the former, it could be judged an immediate failure: the official response to Guantánamo protestors has been to force-feed the hunger strikers. Mohamad's actual statement, however, suggests the limits of the liberal political subject and the biopolitics of security more broadly in his rejection of the preservation of his own body at the expense of recognition, a concept of relationality that would establish his political subjectivity.

By hunger striking, prisoners have been able to live their pain in a different relation to the liberal state and to the international community (or rather, *an* international community). The hunger strikers are living their pain agentically, in a way that they are not victimized by, and that, crucially, requires a material body that not only can experience pain, but also can weaken and die. The body of the hunger striker is an excessive body that makes pain manifest. The brutal domination of prisoners in Guantánamo Bay is based on "stealth" techniques of torture, calculated not to leave marks on the body and also calculated not to lead to the death of the person being tortured. In contrast, the body of the hunger striker will weaken and die; it will manifest the signs of violence. It will show the effects of sovereign power, even if the sovereign power being exercised here is of the prisoner over his own body. The body of the hunger striker is transformed into a weapon—in this way, officials are not precisely wrong in characterizing this act as a form of war or, at least, politics. This is a form of agency, however, that is not strictly based on decision by the conscious will of the subject, but rather depends upon the unpredictability of the material body in its need for supplementation through sources external to itself. Hunger strikers may be able to prolong their suffering, but they cannot precisely control their body's reaction to denial of the necessary supplementation that all bodies require to live. Bodies have an internal life all their own that we can never be free of. Hunger striking is a form of politics that, besides abandoning self-preservation as the essential prerequisite of politics, reveals the liberal ideal of freedom from external control to be a kind of myth or a flawed presumption because it assumes that we can leave our bodies behind. Hunger striking explicitly seeks *not* to leave one's body behind, but to make its functioning central to politics.

Mohammed's invocation of a "we"—a plural subject—in his statement "I do not intend to stop until I die or we are respected" suggests a call not only for recognition of political personhood for himself as a human individual, but also for the very possibility of a collective subject. The collective subject is disqualified in liberalism, at least in the public sphere (in contrast to the private sphere, in which the family is the preeminent unit). Of course, by "we" Mohamed could be referring to an aggregation of individuals who were and are being held in Guantánamo Bay, but that is not necessarily what this statement *does*. What this statement *does*, in conjunction with weakening and damage to the body of the hunger striker, is performatively invoke a collective subject deserving of recognition by an international community through the lived bodily vulnerability of Mohamed and the other hunger strikers. This claim for recognition is also not a claim for the recognition of what Mohamed or the other hunger strikers and prisoners already are, but also is a part of becoming something else in making that claim in relation to a collective subject and an international community (see Butler 2004a, 44). The body in pain here is a call for recognition that performatively constitutes its audience. This is part of the generative or productive capacities of bodies. Rosemary Shinko describes comparable instances of creativity in bodies that have altered the political terrain through drawing together of new forms of relations, a capacity of bodies that is missing from biopolitical analyses of bodies in pain that only focus on power as constraining or molding bodies, as well as from Scarry's account of the world-destroying capacities of extreme pain (Shinko 2010). The hunger strikes of the prisoners at Guantánamo Bay has inspired activism on their behalf, most compellingly that of Yasiin Bey, which I will return to in the next section.

If we understand pain as a lived relationship with others, how one lives one's pain depends on that relationship and whether that pain is acknowledged as pain. Pain in this sense is not a private or passive experience. Pain is also not only a negative, something to be avoided, as it is in liberalism. Pain can be lived agentically and with and through other people, in ways that cannot be understood through our frameworks for thinking about the subject as located only within a singular human body, or in a framework of Cartesian dualism, but it can form the basis for responsibility and responsiveness. The hunger strikes show that bodies can also be thought of as productive or agentic, and inscribed by power as the body of the Guantánamo Bay prisoners is through the violence of torture and regimes of race, gender, and sexuality that constitute the "terrorist" but that these same bodies can be thought of as productive or agentic in their resistance to their constitution not only as subjects being forced to live, but as individuated as well. Such a way of living in one's body challenges the biopolitical terms in which bodies are being made to live by revealing the political and material supplementation required for "natural" bodies to live. As a counter to such a response by the prisoners to the conditions under which they are being made to live, US officials have resorted to force-feeding the hunger strikers to continue their exercise of sovereign power through biopolitical strategies of "making live."

FORCE-FEEDING AND THE TRANSFORMATION OF POLITICAL STATUS

To the American people and the rest of the world, hunger strikes and the force-feeding of hunger strikers are part of the battle over the meaning of the violence committed against prisoners' bodies. United States officials defend the use of force-feeding, which medical ethicists claim is a violation of human rights, by insisting not only that the hunger strike is a tactic of war but also that they are force-feeding prisoners for the prisoners' own well-being. These seemingly contradictory logics of health and war are, in fact, part of the same logic of sovereign power. Only representatives of the United States are allowed to inflict pain and violence on the bodies of detainees—the detainees themselves are forbidden the same right. The exercise of biopower on the bodies of the hunger strikers is a perverse form of biopower's ability to "make live," as it is exercised directly on the bodies of the negative subjects of biopower, the dangerous bodies of "terrorists." Force-feeding has the effect of making the "terrorists" legible and forces a type of normative status onto them, as infantilized "dependents." This effort is aimed more at an American audience, as well as a broader global audience, in terms of assuring people of the safety and efficacy of such techniques of biopower.

The hunger striker is neither a juridical subject of sovereignty nor the liberal, rational subject of biopower, but a dangerous subject who is attempting to reconstruct a political subjectivity. Given that "terrorists" are not considered to act rationally, torture is somewhat paradoxical under the biopolitical rationale of seeking information through the infliction of pain and discomfort. To inflict pain upon a "terrorist" is to expect that person to act rationally to preserve his body from pain and injury and thus provide the information the interrogators seek. By courting death through hunger strikes, the prisoners at Guantánamo Bay refuse this attempt to normalize them. They resist the sovereign power's rights over life and death, as well as biopower's determination to ensure life (Foucault 2003, 247–248). The liberal subject as a rational, willing subject must single-mindedly strive for his self-interest. This also cannot meaningfully describe the hunger-striking prisoner, who suffers pain and harms his own body, eventually leading to his death if he is not force-fed.

The force-feeding of hunger strikers not only robs the prisoners of one possibility of enacting sovereignty over their own bodies but also has the effect of forcing normative status on them, not as moral subjects but as dependents of the state. They are made into legible subjects who, it might be said, never had it so good. The military reports that the detainees are fed very well and are gaining weight. Chief Petty Officer Colleen M. Schonhoff, who is in charge of preparing food for the detainees, stated, "I like to believe they're eating a lot better here than they were wherever they were before they got here. We take pretty good care of them" (Williams 2002). Senator Lindsay Graham has stated that the Guantánamo Bay detainees receive better treatment than the Nazis did because the Supreme Court ruled that the prisoners were entitled to habeas corpus (Raju 2008). Senator Jim Bunning, Republican of Kentucky, was impressed to learn that the detainees "even have air-conditioning and semiprivate showers" (Kirkpatrick 2005). Michael D. Crapo, Republican senator from Idaho, reported that the military personnel at the camp "get more abuse from the detainees than they give to the detainees" (Kirkpatrick 2005). Democratic senators Richard Durbin of Illinois and Ron Wyden of Oregon have also given assurances regarding the treatment of the prisoners after a visit to Guantánamo Bay. By affirming the camp's relative comfort, despite the complaints of prisoners, these accounts reinscribe the prisoners as a quasi-population in need of management, even though they neither are domestic subjects, nor are they intended to be a permanent population.

The use of force-feeding to keep hunger-striking detainees alive indicates a transformation of the political status of the prisoners from enemy combatants, to terrorists, to a quasi-population. Force-feeding makes the prisoners into objects of medical knowledge, a prerequisite for making them into objects that can be managed as dependents of the sovereign state. They are transformed from illegible terrorists into threats that are being managed competently. The force-feeding is conducted by medical professionals who are screened before they are deployed to Guantánamo to make certain they do not have moral objections to force-feeding (Miles 2006, 110). Around February 2006, the military began using restraint chairs to hold the prisoners while they were being force-fed. These chairs resemble dentist's chairs with restraints for the arms, legs, head, and torso. The military says they are necessary for the safety of the prisoners as well as to prevent them from throwing up after the feeding. In June 2013, 41 prisoners were being force-fed, a number so high that the US military had to send a backup team of medical personnel to assist with the assessment of the prisoners and their force-feeding (Williams 2013). Journalists have reported on the use of unnecessarily large nasal tubes that cause extreme pain and bleeding when forcibly inserted (Fox 2005). Overfeeding, which causes cramps, nausea, and diarrhea, is also frequently accompanied by prolonged restraint in these chairs, ostensibly to ensure absorption of the nutrients and to prevent self-induced vomiting.

Outside the terms of any social contract, the "terrorists" are transformed into subjects of a minimal exchange in which information is traded for the sustainment of life. This exchange is far from the liberal ideals of equal and autonomous subjects contracting with one another. By force-feeding the hunger-striking prisoners, the United States makes its sovereign power present over the bodies and lives of prisoners. In a fully biopolitical regime, not permitting the deaths of prisoners is central to the logic of sovereign power. Force-feeding is justified in biopolitical terms of preserving the lives of the prisoners and produces the prisoners as a quasi-population to be managed by doctors and administrators. A Pentagon spokesperson has responded to charges of ill-treatment in force-feeding by saying that

Defense Department officials "believe that preservation of life through lawful, clinically appropriate means is a responsible and prudent measure for the safety and well-being of detainees" (White 2006). In a facetious dismissal of accusations of abuse, one report asserted that hunger strikers were said to be given a choice of colors for their feeding tubes and lozenges to soothe their sore throats (Zagorin 2006). Hunger-striking prisoners are force-fed if they have refused 63 consecutive meals or have not eaten for 21 days, or if they drop below 85 percent of their healthy body weight. A doctor's approval is also needed, in the latter case (Reid 2009). Dr. William Winkenwerder, assistant secretary of defense for health affairs, insisted, "There is a moral question. Do you allow a person to commit suicide? Or do you take steps to protect their health and preserve their life? The objective in any circumstance is to protect and sustain a person's life" (Golden 2006). Officials have defended the force-feeding of prisoners by claiming that "it is our responsibility to make sure that the detainees are kept in good health" (Golden 2006). To suggestions that the policy of force-feeding violates the ban on "outrages upon personal dignity, in particular humiliating and degrading treatment" of Common Article 3 of the Geneva Conventions, officials have responded by invoking the language of Common Article 3, which states, "the wounded and sick shall be collected and cared for," to justify the force-feeding of prisoners (Mitchell 2009). While medical ethics and Defense Department guidelines allow for force-feeding only for cases in which immediate treatment is necessary to prevent death or serious harm (Department of Defense 2006), the fact that the prisoners are healthy enough to need restraint suggests that force-feeding was being done well before the lives of prisoners were in danger.

Military officials also claim that hunger strikers are operating under a strategic logic, as agents of Al Qaeda continuing their battle against the United States, even while in prison. A *Time* magazine articles reports: "Harris [Defense Department spokesperson] argues the camp will be needed for the foreseeable future, and that refusing to eat is not a cry for help, but a ploy drawn from the al-Qaeda playbook calculated to attract media attention and force the U.S. government to back down." Harris is also quoted as saying, "The will to resist of these prisoners is high. They are waging their war, their jihad against America, and we just have to stop them" (Zagorin 2006). The same article equates the hunger strikes with suicide attempts, arguing that both similarly seek to bring negative attention to Guantánamo so it will be shut down. Another spokesperson for Guantánamo Bay, Robert Durand, said, "The hunger strike technique is consistent with al-Qaeda practice and reflects detainee attempts to elicit media attention to bring international pressure on the United States to release them back to the battlefield" (Melia 2007). Durand also denied that the hunger strikers have made any specific demands or requests. Officials have declared the hunger strikes to be "acts of war." The framing of hunger strikes as part of the "al-Qaeda playbook" indicates the instability of the prisoners' new status as a quasi-population. This line of argument keeps the logic of both biopower and sovereign power in play. Against arguments that force-feeding is an abuse of sovereign power, the idea of hunger strikers as enemies and terrorists can be invoked. Against arguments of violating the human rights of prisoners, the biopolitical logic of preserving the lives of prisoners under the care of the United States may be invoked. Thus, the force-fed hunger strikers occupy an unstable position as not-fully-terrorist enemies, but not fully members of a population to be managed either.

While doctors have been involved in the force-feeding of prisoners at Guantánamo Bay from the beginning, ostensibly to ensure the safety of the prisoners, they have also led the charge against the practice of force-feeding hunger-striking prisoners under the banner of human rights. More than 250 medical professionals have signed an open letter to the *Lancet*, a British medical journal, demanding an end to force-feeding as a violation of the medical ethics of the American Medical Association and the World Medical Association. According to the codes of ethics of both organizations, force-feeding is considered an "assault on human dignity" so long as the prisoners or patients are capable of making an informed decision (Nicholl 2006). This view is premised on understanding hunger strikes not as a form of suicide but as a form of political protest—as essentially the political speech of a rational subject. Medical ethicists have also condemned the force-feedings by specifying the duties that doctors have to patients who decide to undergo hunger strikes: above respecting the sanctity of life and the health of the detainees, physicians are obliged to respect the autonomy of patients who freely choose to go on hunger strikes and who understand the consequences of their actions (Physicians for Human Rights 2005; Nicholl 2006). The labeling of force-feeding as torture per se, aside from the brutal measures used in its execution, is premised upon the Enlightenment view of the subject as an autonomous will that controls the body. It is also premised on a liberal subject that is *homo economicus*, with preexisting preferences and interests that the government cannot prevent him from pursuing. Medical ethicists insist that the refusal of food in this context is a matter not of pathology, psychological or otherwise, but of free choice. Medical ethicists consider force-feeding of competent persons, which intervenes in this control over the body, to constitute torture through an abridgement of the rights of hunger strikers.

In the discourse of medical ethics, hunger strikers are positioned as patients (as opposed to enemy combatants continuing their battle in prison) for whom certain rules govern relationships with doctors. The main object is the prisoner/patient and his subjectivity as a rational bearer of rights. Force-feeding, medical ethicists insist, is permissible only when it is first of all necessary for the health of a patient who is unable or refusing to eat and, second, when the refusing patient has been deemed mentally impaired and unable to understand the consequences of not eating and drinking. Force-feeding becomes a matter of psychiatry, in which doctors must determine if the patient is sufficiently rational to freely make the choice to refuse food. This medical discourse is inseparable from a liberal discourse of individuals as rights-bearing subjects, so long as they are deemed rational.

However, the discourse of force-feeding articulated by the military doctors and spokespersons suggests not an autonomous, rational subject with rights but rather a deranged subject who needs to be protected from himself. By force-feeding the hunger-striking prisoners at Guantánamo Bay, military personnel are not so much violating liberal principles of a subject's rational control over his or her own body but producing the detainees as irrational and "insane," in need of care and management. Judith Butler argues that the indefinite detention of the prisoners at Guantánamo Bay is comparable to the indefinite detention of patients in mental institutions (2004a, 72). Some hunger strikers are held in Guantánamo Bay's psych ward as suicidal and are under constant surveillance (Melia 2007). If the indefinite detention of mental patients is a suitable model for the indefinite detention of prisoners, then there is a corresponding analogy to the mental status of both kinds of patients. An advertisement from the company that makes the restraint chairs includes the slogan "It's like a padded cell on wheels" (Golden 2006). Force-feeding through nasal tubes is widely used with comatose patients or those suffering from psychiatric diseases. In these situations, it is not seen to be problematic, because such persons are deemed incapable of making rational decisions on their own behalf.

Force-fed prisoners are less Agamben's category of "exposed bare life" than what John Protevi names, after Foucault, "trapped bare life" (Protevi 2009, 125). Citing writer Lindsey Beyerstein, Protevi describes forcefeeding of women when they had previously declared themselves to be opposed to such procedures as "tube rape": a violation of their bodily integrity (Protevi 2009, 127). Theorizing force-feeding as a form of sexual assault usefully highlights two facets of this form of political violence: it is not pain per se that defines the violence of force-feeding, though force-feeding has been described as unbearably painful by those who have undergone it. In liberal political orders, it is not the pain associated with force-feeding that is the violation, but the violation of bodily integrity (Scarry 1990; Miller 2007). Judith Butler has noted the similarities between the indefinite detention of prisoners in Guantánamo Bay and the involuntary hospitalization of mentally ill patients without criminal charge who are deemed to be a threat to themselves or others (Butler 2004a). As Butler argues, such analogies only make sense if we presume that activities such as the "terrorism" that prisoners are suspected of are evidence of mental illness, or that detainees are outside any notion of rationality. Force-feeding has a similar performative effect: to position hunger strikers as not fully competent political actors. Here, they would have a similar status to that of comatose patients, anorexics, or British suffragettes. The gendering of the object of force-feeding goes beyond its association with women; rather, force-feeding is a *gendering* form of violence in that it performatively makes the person being force-fed into an incompetent person who must be cared for. The category of "trapped bare life" is a feminized category, as the prototypical examples involve women's reproductive bodies. John Protevi points out that the most famous cases involving controversies over force-feeding in the United States have been of white women of reproductive age, including Karen Quinlan (whom Agamben cites as an example of pure *zoē* because the law vacillates on whether or not she was dead), Nancy Cruzan, and Terri Schiavo, a woman who had been kept alive in a persistent vegetative state for 15 years, whose previous statements that she would not like to be kept alive in such a condition were bitterly litigated in various courts and in public opinion. Of one prisoner, naval surgeon Louis Louk said, "He's refused to eat 148 consecutive meals. In my opinion, he's a spoiled brat, like a small child who stomps his feet when he doesn't get his way" (Stafford Smith 2007, 189).

If the mental status of the hunger strikers is unfathomable and outside the bounds of accepted, civilized thought, then the detention and force-feeding can be justified. As figures of madness and dependency, the hunger-striking prisoners at Guantánamo Bay can be more comfortably detained indefinitely. Produced as both irrational and dependent, the prisoners do not need to be acknowledged as deserving the minimal human rights of trials to determine their guilt or innocence. However, it is not the preexisting mental status of the prisoners that leads to their indefinite incarceration and force-feeding; rather, it is the practices of detention and force-feeding that produce the prisoners as subjects of irrationality and unfathomability. This is consistent with the production of "terrorist" subjectivity, but with an added dimension of social responsibility. When we consider the military discourse of hunger striking as a tactic of war, the fact of hunger striking is not what is produced as unfathomable or unknowable; it is the minds of the prisoners themselves as agents of Al Qaeda that are produced as irrational and uncivilized. Once the prisoners and the hunger strikers in particular are produced as irrational subjects, then the state is authorized to intervene to "make live." The hunger strikers are figured not as dangerous but infantile, in need of the benevolence of the United States in order to remain alive. The production of hunger-striking prisoners into dependent figures of unfathomable moral and mental status not only has implications for the treatment of the prisoners but also, perhaps more crucially, has the effect of making the United States more comfortable with its exercise of sovereign power against its own liberal norms.

The dual techniques of sovereign power and biopower can be used to understand the transformation of the political status of American citizens. Aside from managing the prisoners, the force-feeding of hunger strikers serves to assure Americans that the technologies of biopower are safe—that they need not be concerned with interrogational torture nor suspect that prisoners' rights are being violated by force-feeding. Months and years after September 11, 2001, instead of decrying the decadence and complacency of American society that helped allow the attacks to occur, the discourse shifted to recapturing a sense of urgency and unity of purpose in addressing the threat of terrorism. Two years after September 11, President Bush stated in a speech that "the enemy is wounded, but still resourceful and actively recruiting, and still dangerous. We cannot afford a moment of complacency. Yet, as you know, we've taken extraordinary measures these past two years to protect America" (Bush 2003). Some of these extraordinary measures include authorizing torture. The "war on terror," as officials frequently reminded Americans, is a long, if never-ending war. The threat of terrorism is to be considered ever present, and everyday life is to be rearranged around the prevention of terrorist attacks. As one official said, "It is just a fact of life and we have to deal with it" (Baker 2002). Producing the prisoners as not only vaguely dangerous but also dependents in need of care makes Americans feel assured that the threat of terrorism is not only being managed but being managed in a humane way.

The act of force-feeding transforms the moral status of the hunger-striking prisoners from "terrorists" and "enemy combatants"—figures outside any social contract—to humans susceptible to management, of minimal interrelations. While force-feeding suggests that there is something incurably pathological about the "terrorists," it does not necessarily indicate their exclusion from any body politic (cf. Howell 2007). In sustaining the lives of hunger strikers by these means, the prisoners are included in the body politic in a way that produces them as figures of dependency. The threat of terrorism is thus managed by taking away freedom of speech in exchange for the speech of information. While medical ethicists attempt to assert that the prisoners are liberal subjects of rights, the continued force-feeding of hunger-striking prisoners makes the prisoners a symbol of diffuse danger on the border of political community. At the same time, it assures Americans that they are safe from the threat of terrorism because the terrorists are being managed competently. From this argument, we can read the Obama administration's delay in closing the prison at Guantánamo as based on not only operational difficulties but also difficulties in assuring the American people, as well as Obama's political opposition, that the former Guantánamo Bay prisoners would pose no threat if housed domestically. Force-feeding gives rise to a new understanding of Senator John McCain's 2005 statement against torture in response to an admonishment about the nature of the terrorists: torture "is not about who *they* are. It's about who *we* are" (Herbert 2005).

Just how this "we" is constituted is also affected by the productive capacities of bodies. If we understand pain and other bodily states to be lived in relation to others, we can focus on the ways in which such emotions, states, or affects are circulated and what kinds of alliances or assemblages of bodies they bring about (Ahmed 2004a). In the summer of 2013, actor, musician, and activist Yasiin Bey (formerly known as Mos Def) volunteered to undertake the same force-feeding procedure that hunger-striking prisoners at Guantánamo Bay are subjected to. With the help of Reprieve, a British human rights organization, Bey was shackled wearing an orange jumpsuit, while a feeding tube was forced through his nasal passages. The video shows Bey struggling against the nasogastric tube, crying out, protesting, yelling for it to stop, and ultimately the force-feeding is not carried out. After the attempted force-feeding ends, Bey struggles to describe what it feels like, describing it as "unbearable." It ends as it begins, with Bey stating "peace" and "good morning" (Reprieve 2013). Bey is a black man, a Muslim, an artist, a political activist, and a celebrity. In my reading, by donning the uniform and undertaking the force-feeding procedure, and by narrating such an ordeal with a simple statement of "peace" and positive recognition of the audience ("good morning"), Bey's performance asks the audience to imagine that this could also be them, just as it could be him. He (temporarily) made himself abject, treated brutally and inhumanely. As a black man and a Muslim, such a performance runs the risk of reproducing the equation of masculine, racialized bodies as abject bodies that deserve the harsh treatment they are so often subject to under racist criminal justice systems, and therefore producing contempt or indifference in racist audiences (see, for example, Dauphinée 2007). Yet, as an American, and as a musician and actor with a fair amount of celebrity, Bey is also someone whom (at least some) people are used to watching and paying attention to. Bey's is a "body that matters," or at least occupies multiple spaces in relation to social power and privilege.[7] What is perhaps too quickly dismissed as a publicity stunt can be read as a performance in the Butlerian sense of a speaking, feeling, resolutely human subject who, through his words and actions and the emotions they set into circulation, asks to be aligned with those who are both like him in some ways—Muslim, racialized, male— and unlike him in some ways—non-American citizens, non-famous. Bey's embodied performances as a black man donning an orange prison jumpsuit also works to performatively tie the treatment of prisoners at Guantánamo Bay to the US prison industrial complex and its mass incarceration of racialized men; at the time of the latest Guantánamo Bay hunger strikes, mass hunger strikes in the California Prison system took to place to protest, among other issues, the use of long-term solitary confinement. His act showed the potential of bodies to transform the relations of power under which they are constituted in biopolitical regimes, contributing to new alliances and political possibilities.

CONCLUSION

The practices of torture and force-feeding tell us little about the people tortured but much about the troubled exercise of sovereign power in a liberal, biopolitical society. Torture and the force-feeding of hunger-striking prisoners do not fully strip prisoners of their subjectivity, but remake their subjectivity as well as that of their captors. By constituting the prisoners of Guantánamo Bay as figures of indefinite captivity and dependency rather than as killable enemies or untenable risks, the United States exercises its sovereign power in a way that assures its American audience of the safety and desirability of biopolitical techniques, thus reforming the political status of American subjects as well as the "terrorist" subjects who must be held but kept at bay, tortured yet kept alive.

The broader issue here is of the undecidability of the subject position of the prisoners held at Guantánamo Bay. Their uncertain status means that their subject positions must be produced: through practices of torture and force-feeding on the bodies of these prisoners, they are transformed first into "terrorists" and then to irrational dependents. The violence is productive in the sense that it transforms these bodies into particular kinds of subjects and remakes the relations between the United States and the prisoners. With the ongoing pressure to close Guantánamo Bay and resettle those who have been imprisoned for a decade or more, and perhaps more important, with the intensification of the use of airstrikes on drones or otherwise to target suspected militants, the prisoners at Guantánamo Bay are increasingly being seen as something close to a subject of rights, at least in comparison to the targets of the precision warfare, which I discuss in Chapter 5.

The story of violence in Guantánamo Bay unsettles realist and liberal assumptions of the subject, which are both based upon sovereign power. The practice of hunger striking challenges the self-preserving subject as the basis for politics. Hunger striking in this case also suggests that the liberal presumption of the subject as an individual is inadequate. The experience of the body undergoing torture further challenges the liberal presumption of a speaking and willing subject, for torture erodes the subjectivity of the victim, including his or her ability to speak with his or her own will. Furthermore, reading the practices of violence in Guantánamo Bay has begun to introduce an alternative theorization of the body in International Relations by showing how bodies are both produced by discourse and by violence (in terms of the subjects of both "terrorist" and "dependent") as well as bodies that are productive (as the bodies of hunger strikers). These are not "natural" bodies that preexist politics, but bodies that are formed in and through violence and representations of that violence. Both of these points indicate a model or theorization of bodies as not existing as independent organisms; they require supplementation, either in terms of their social and political designations (as "terrorist," "dependent," or even as "individual"), or in their material needs, in order to exist. With the sovereign subjects of conventional IR theory destabilized, in the next chapter I turn my attention to the presumption of bodies as self-contained, naturally bordered by the skin, and argue that these bodies are only imperfectly produced in and through politics. To do so, I theorize suicide bombing as an embodied practice with political implications surpassing the intentions of the subject perpetrating this form of violence.

CHAPTER 3

Explosive Bodies

*Suicide Bombing as an Embodied Practice
and the Politics of Abjection*

At the moment of the bombing, the bodies of suicide bombers are obliterated, as are the bodies of those nearest to the bomber.[1] These bodies, once constituted as whole and autonomous vessels of subjects, become, in Adriana Cavarero's phrase, "heaps of meat" (2009, 98). This phrase is revealing of a consequence of suicide bombing: the separation of self and body so that only bodies are left behind, rendered inhuman by violence. This act and efforts at dealing with the aftermath of the bombing provide a window into the production of bodies, subjects, and borders. Bodies are shown as only ever partially and impurely differentiated from one another and the political conditions of their existence, dependent upon social and material supplementation. Biopolitical regimes of security, which attempt to minimize risk to the natural functioning of bodies, are disrupted by the practice of suicide bombing, not only through the injuring and killing of bodies, but also through the work that suicide bombing does to make apparent that the naturalized biopolitical body is indeed a specific historical formation. Practices of suicide bombing show bodies as contaminating, as not bordered by the skin, but deterritorialized, only appearing stable and fixed in essence and identity by practices of security.

The previous chapter complicated the story of sovereign practices of security by showing how they are infused with biopolitical rationality in the practice of torture and management of tortured bodies. This chapter argues that suicide bombing is a practice that explicitly disavows the biopolitical imperative of life and makes a mockery of its configuration of bodies.

Torture, as used in the "war on terror", ostensibly works to produce speech intended to preserve the lives of a threatened population, sacrificing the well-being of one life for many others, even as the tortured prisoner cannot be killed. In comparison to the invulnerability of the torturers, suicide bombing is a mode of violence in which the perpetrator makes him- or herself what we may consider *infinitely* vulnerable by accepting certain death in order to inflict not only death and injury upon a few, but vulnerability upon many more. Moreover, the immediate aim of suicide bombing as a form of violence is not the prevention of injury and death to a population, as in the contemporary torture regime, but quite the opposite: the destruction of life in a violent, public manner. While the previous chapter denaturalized the liberal body of security in terms of its capacity for speech and its existence as rational or irrational, this chapter denaturalizes bodies in terms of their boundedness and their passivity to political forces.

Suicide bombing troubles the broad narratives that International Relations tells about the practice of political violence. First, it upsets the assumption of the subject driven by self-preservation and the cultivation of the "good life"—motivations that define realist and liberal narratives of political community. This relationship of the distribution of life and death in political violence is associated with wars of the state, fought on behalf of sovereign power. Purposefully taking one's own life is seen as fanatical, while risking one's life on behalf of a cause is seen as a noble sacrifice. In this way, the suicide bomber is similar to the hunger striker, as neither conforms to the model of the self-interested, self-preserving subject. While self-sacrifice in military or altruistic endeavors is hardly unknown, what sets this mode of violence apart in the literature is the centrality or even necessity of the death of the bomber in carrying out a mission. International Relations theorists argue that the use of suicide bombers may be strategically rational from the perspective of a particular campaign. Crenshaw (2007), Bloom (2005), Hoffman (2003), Pape (2005), and O'Rourke (2008) all discuss the rationalities of terrorism in terms of the pre-conditions, grievances, and organizational strategies that explain why a group engages in terrorism and suicide terrorism in particular. However, this mode of violence is hardly rational from the perspective of self-preservation and the avoidance of pain and injury to the bomber.

Second, IR theorists have attempted to explain suicide bombing by probing the meaning that this form of violence has for particular communities, whether through the concept of martyrdom in Islamic societies or sacrifice on behalf of the nation. The subjectivity of the terrorist, specifically the suicide bomber, is thought of in terms of radical otherness or radical sameness—s/he is either a savage "wild man" whose motives are incomprehensible to the rational actor, or s/he is a rational actor, or part of a rational organization, and is merely choosing one military strategy among many for its effectiveness.[2] While this mode of violence is linked in popular discourses to radical varieties of Islam, locating the origins of this form of violence to particular religious or cultural contexts is of limited value because suicide bombing is a tactic employed by organizations espousing a variety of faiths, as well as secular organizations.

In this chapter, I set aside these questions of motivations or "causes" of suicide terrorism. Rather than attempting to figure out the "mind" of the suicide bomber in terms of his or her motivations, my analysis centers on the bodies of the bombers and the victims. I ask what the body of the suicide bomber *does* and what assumptions about bodies and political violence it unsettles. I also ask what kind of politics is expressed, or produced, by suicide bombing and the practices of recovery and burial that follow as embodied practices. I theorize agency not only as the actions taken by a self-directed subject, but as the effects of such actions, which may or may not be taken by a coherent, individual subject. This introduces an element of contingency—the effects of actions may not be consistent with the intentions of the actor and may transform the subject itself. In this sense, bodies may be considered agentic, whether or not such practices are intended or not (see also Bially Mattern 2011, 74–75).

I argue that suicide bombing is not only a destructive act of killing oneself in order to kill others, but also can be understood as a productive act as well. It does this by obliterating the borders of the body, borders that are produced by social and political forces. The bodies produced in this moment as corpses, lifeless flesh, are a source of horror and disgust. They are what feminist psychoanalyst Julia Kristeva calls "abject." By gathering the bodily remains of suicide bombers and victims, the practices of the Israeli organization ZAKA also participates in an economy of bodily sacrifice to reconstitute both bodies and community, acts that can be compared to the lack of reconstruction of the remains of the 9/11 bombers. Suicide bombing thus becomes a site that reveals how the state is produced through the production of bodies. Abjection, as an account of the lived experience of the body, provides an understanding of the power projected and revealed in the practice of suicide bombing. Thus the sacrifice in this context is not a religious ritual per se, but refers to the formation of the self through the exclusion of the bodily aspects of the abject, and of the disruption of the self by the abject that haunts the self, making it permanently vulnerable. Suicide bombing expresses how both the contours of the state and the gender order are tied to the production of bodies. In doing so, the abject bodies of suicide bombers serve as an example of how bodies are both produced by political practices as discrete, bordered entities signified as members of particular communities and genders, and how bodies are productive of politics, in that they can have political effects beyond the intentions of willing subjects.

I begin by theorizing sovereignty as a practice that produces an orderly, internal space and an outside space of danger and disorder; this practice of sovereignty is bound up in what is considered to be a "metaphor" of the *body politic* but what is in fact the mutual constitution of bodies and states. I then argue that these sovereign practices of state-making are also gendered practices of body-making. Having argued about the constitutive relationship between sovereignty and abjection, I turn to the suicide bomber as a figure of abjection that challenges the sovereignty of both states and bodies. Female suicide bombers, whose bodies are already viewed as abject, bear a troubling relationship to the state in this interpretation. When we look at efforts to reinstate sovereignty by reconstructing the bodies of suicide bombers and their victims (as shown by the example of the work of ZAKA in Israel), the haunting abject renders such practices of sovereignty incomplete.

SOVEREIGNTY, ABJECTION, AND BODIES

The practice of suicide bombing breaks down borders. It shatters the boundaries between the interior and the exterior of human bodies, between separated human bodies in using a body to kill others, and (in certain contexts) between state borders. This practice is emblematic of waning state sovereignty and poses a threat to state sovereignty itself. Here, I theorize sovereignty not as an attribute of a political actor, but as a practice of power both generated by and generative of subjects (Brown 2010, 52). Moreover, sovereignty is the practice of demarcating a separate space of law and disorder. This space of law or disorder in the modern world order is the space of the sovereign state. Sovereignty is the practice by which the inside and outside are distinguished, borders are drawn, and territory is demarcated. Sovereignty as a practice "should be understood as the discursive/cultural *means* by which a 'natural' state is produced and established as 'prediscursive'" (Weber 1998, 92). That is, sovereignty produces the ordered territory of the state as naturally distinguished from the chaotic outside. The spatial aspect of sovereignty is represented as boundedness. Sovereignty requires a space that is well defined and ordered, that has come into existence though interactions with the land. Lest it be forgotten, Lefebvre reminds us that sovereign spaces are produced by violence. "Sovereignty implies 'space' and what is more it implies space against which violence, whether latent or overt, is directed—a space established and constituted by violence. Every state is born of violence, and state power endures only by virtue of violence directed toward space" (1992, 280).

Sovereignty, then, is a performance that differentiates wild, ungovernable land from peace and order; it is only the sign of sovereignty that distinguishes a chaotic outside from an orderly inside. This hierarchy in space is familiar to International Relations theorists as the demarcation between the law and order of the inside and the danger, disorder, and unlaw outside sovereignty's bounds (Walker 1993; Campbell 2000 [1992]). Sovereignty expresses unity and agency, the ability to self-govern and to act autonomously. The ability to act autonomously outside the territory of the sovereign is dependent upon the subordination of powers internally that could fragment the *body politic*. In this framework, security discourses have produced violence as an intrusion upon the nation-state from an "other" located outside state boundaries, rather than stemming from the instability of bodies themselves. The division between the inside and outside, between domestic peace and external anarchy and danger, is produced by abjection.

Abjection describes the formation of subjects through the creation of individuated bodies and spaces. By expelling the abject, the self creates the boundary between the abject and itself—the expulsion of the abject is a necessary step in the formation of the self. In the process of self-formation, "I expel *myself*, I spit *myself* out, I abject *myself* within the same motion through which 'I' claim to establish *myself*," (Kristeva 1982, 3). The abject represents a part of the self that must be rejected in order to *become* a self. It is thus threatening to the self, and is regarded with disgust. The abject, though expelled, is thus an essential part of the self, lingering or haunting the unconscious, rendering it permanently vulnerable to disruptions. This act is never complete; it is always a process requiring maintenance, for, as Iris Marion Young writes, "any border ambiguity may become for the subject a threat to its own borders" (1990, 145).

The abject is founded on an attempted rejection of corporeality, stemming from the separation of the self from oneness with the maternal body. The abject is commonly associated with waste products and bodily fluids that leave the body through openings or wounds (Kristeva 1982, 52). However, abjection does not refer to corpses or bodily fluids per se, but rather, that which does not obey borders and challenges the existence of such borders. Abjection works symbolically to expose the psychic, social, and political work necessary to preserve the illusion of whole bodies with unbroken surfaces, bodies that are made to appear whole on the basis of expelling the abject. The abject is what must be expelled to maintain the "self's clean and proper body" (Kristeva 1982, 75). As Elizabeth Grosz writes, "the abject demonstrates the impossibility of clear-cut borders, lines of demarcation, division between the clean and the unclean, the proper and the improper, order and disorder" (1990, 89). The abject threatens the borders between inside and outside that must be maintained for the subject to remain a self-contained individual.

Butler reworks Kristeva's concept of abjection to understand subject formation while avoiding its essentialist reliance upon a female, maternal body. Norms are internalized, not by a preexisting subject encountering a norm and possibly internalizing it, but rather, the subject *becomes* a subject through the internalization of norms. One becomes a subject through literally becoming *embodied*. The subject is then marked by the absent presence of the "other." This other remains outside the subject, yet is still fundamentally a part of it. It is a corporeal other, as the subject in his or her striving to become a separate, individuated subject requires the rejection of a maternal body. This rejection is a form of melancholy or loss that *incorporates* the body (Butler 1990, 68). The embodied subject only becomes a subject through this bodily loss that continues to haunt it (Butler 1997b, 92). Butler's account of the production of a seemingly coherent identity necessarily entailing a loss is a useful way to understand the limits of the socially produced body. The materialization of bodies is never complete; it is a process that requires reiteration to maintain the effect of stabilization. The materialization of bodies is always insufficient, and bodies are always already *becoming* bodies. A body that seems complete and stable has already suffered a loss that is concealed, but nonetheless is a constitutive feature of the embodied subject. This loss that haunts the subject is referred to as the "constitutive other."

Theorizing sovereignty as a practice that maintains the abject at a distance allows us to see the connections between suicide bombing, borders of the state and nation, and the role of gender discourses in constituting both. The presence of the abject reminds us of the precariousness of bodies and subjectivity, and their indebtedness to one another in ways that collapse the distinction between self and body, nature and culture, order and disorder. Practices of security are not only about the threat beyond borders, but also about managing bodies within borders. Sovereignty is dependent upon bodies that are mortal (Dillon 1996). If we were not faced with the ever present threat of death, we would have no need of a Hobbesian sovereign to provide security. The body is an object that violence is done to, a container or location for violence. In order to provide security in terms of protecting the natural lives of bodies inside the state, the state needs bodies to be stable and legible (Scott 1998). The state can only protect or secure a stable form. Bodies that are not self-contained and individuated are much more difficult to contain (Manning 2007, 139–140). These stable bodies are produced through disciplinary techniques which form subjects into docile bodies that are also natural bodies that can be apprehended through scientific discourses (Foucault 1979, 155). Disciplinary techniques are how liberal societies pacify bodies within their own midst. Furthermore, subjects can only be integrated into the state so long as they are individualized (Foucault 1994, 334). Security is thus about securing bodies inside the state, as well as those outside.

The space that sovereignty produces is often analogized as a body. The analogy of the state as human body has a long history (Campbell 2000 [1992], 75–77; Fishel n.d.). Most famously represented by the figure of Hobbes's Leviathan, with the land and people as a body and the sovereign as the head, the state as *body politic* is a representation that produces both state and human body as containers. The Leviathan, as "artificial man," provides us with a compelling formulation of the articulation between state and bodies linked by the threat of violence. Sovereign power, in the artificial man of the Leviathan, is constituted precisely to protect the "natural man." The use of the term *body politic*, as well as bodily metaphors for the state, is not without political consequences for understanding the means of both the state and the body. How this body is represented has productive effects; as Judith Butler writes, "there is no reference to a pure body which is not at the same time a further formation of that body" (1993, 10). Cynthia Weber (1998) has influentially theorized the productive effects of performances of sovereignty in reference to Butler's work; here, I extend her arguments by connecting the performative production of bodies to the production of states.

The use of the phrase *body politic* to refer to a political community is usually described as a metaphor or a literary devise, but it is also more. Various feminists have argued that constitution of the state and constitution of the body are mutually entailed. Analyzing scientific discourse of the immune system in the 1980s, Donna Haraway argues that at this particular historical juncture, the body was constituted in terms of national security discourses of invasion, defense, and invulnerability (Haraway 1991c, 211). In early modern state-formation, scientific discourses argued that women's and men's bodies are not on a continuum of difference (as bodies had previously been understood) but are opposites. Women could thus be defined in terms of weakness, emotion, and impulse, in contrast to the masculine virtues of reason and force that governed the state apparatus (Laqueur 1990; Peterson 1992b; Towns 2010, 69–75). The body, as the site of impulses, must be kept in its proper (subordinate) place in the hierarchy, beneath reason, just as the state must maintain proper hierarchies to remain healthy (Cavarero 2002, 102–103). The constitution of women's bodies as "other" compared to men's is central to the constitution of the modern state, as it allowed for the demarcation of public/private spheres of activity and the categorical exclusion of women from public life on account of their association with the body and its deficiencies, compared to the affiliation of men with the mind and rationality—subjects supposedly free from the volatility of bodies. The representation of the political community as a human, able-bodied male also reifies the opposition between culture and nature, as it presents the "culture" of the state as a perfection of nature, as the "artificial man" simulates and supersedes the "natural man" (Grosz 1995, 106; Brown 1988, 108–110).

Sovereignty produces the state as a unified, singular entity: the *body politic* has one body and speaks with a single voice (Gatens 1996, 23). The *body politic* is represented as a generic, individual body, but of course there is no such thing. Rather, among other markers of difference, bodies are always sexed. Feminists have argued that this *body politic* is not only constituted by the exclusion of women, but also relies on masculine representations of bodies. The analogization of the state to a body, characterized by sharply delineated borders between inside and outside and between different units (other states, other bodies), is a representation of bodies (and thus states) as masculine and fully grown, without the inevitable decline of the life cycle (Cavarero 2002, 114)—the eternal body of the sovereign, rather than his fleshy, decaying body. The unitary of the state—one sovereign speaking on behalf of the state, and the social contract constituted by the voices of men (Pateman 1988; Gatens 1996)—is an erasure of sexual difference, using the masculine to represent the human.

The production of the state as a self-contained and bounded body reproduces sovereignty as a masculine practice. The representation of the state as a kind of container is sometimes considered a natural or inevitable metaphor. Lakoff (1987) asserts that because we live in bodies that are containers, we experience everything as inside a container or outside it. Because of our embodied experience, the "container" model of the state has an essential basis in our bodily life. However, the actual experience of embodiment for all people is not of self-contained bodies demarcated from the world by the boundaries of the skin, and experiencing one's body as a container is more common to men than to women (Battersby 1999). The modern, self-contained, bounded body that is seen as the normative body is culturally associated with white, heterosexual, able-bodied men rather than women, racial "others," sexual minorities, or disabled persons.

Women's bodies have not so much been constructed as absence, or lack, but as leaking or fluid, through a mode of seepage or liquidity (Grosz 1994, 203; Shildrick, 1997). As such, women's bodies have been figured as *abject* in their instability and their refusal to obey borders. These non-normative bodies are seen as particularly vulnerable and, as such, not suitable for full status as a sovereign subject.[3] Sovereign practices reproduce subjects and states in terms of masculine solidity and containment, which are destabilized by the practices of suicide bombing that violate the boundaries that sovereignty erects.

THE ABJECT BODY OF THE SUICIDE BOMBER

The body of the suicide bomber may be considered "abject," that is, a "constitutive outside," or what is sacrificed in order to bring about the appearance of unity and completeness of the self. Sacrifice, in the sense of abjection, acknowledges the necessary failure of the loss to bring about unity, as the expulsion of abject lingers and haunts the self, whether the individual or the state. Theorizing the body of the suicide bomber as abject allows us to grasp the implications of this form of violence in ways that are occluded by conventional treatments of this subject.[4] Namely, the suicide bomber as abject expresses a symbolic power that exceeds strategic calculations, as well as the work necessary to maintain the appearance of subject/body coherence, that is, of a singular, complete subject residing in a whole, solid body. The "leakiness" of the body of the suicide bomber represents the de-territorialization of the state.

By obliterating the borders between the interior and the exterior of the body, and between individual bodies, the suicide bomber not only harms bodies, but also destroys the sovereign processes that bind bodies into bounded individuals in the first place. At the same time, the suicide bomber poses a threat to the sovereign power of the state by bringing violence into the heart of its territory and making a lie out of the sovereign's role to protect its citizens. The presence of the abject reminds us of the precariousness of bodies and subjectivity, and their indebtedness to one another in ways that collapse the distinction between self and body, nature and culture, life and death. Because of the role of sovereignty in transforming wild, uncontrollable land and bodies into ostensibly ordered and demarcated unities, the suicide bomber (and attendant anxiety over suicide bombing) reveals the mutually constituting relationship between states and bodies, a relationship rife with gendered implications. The symbolic threat posed by the suicide bomber to the order of "clean and proper" bodies and states is suggested by the abject as the sacrificed, but haunting, specter of corporeality and femininity.

Suicide bombing is not only an act that collapses the inside and outside of the body's surfaces, but does so in order to cause the same damage to other bodies. More so than other forms of violence, suicide bombing is a particularly intimate form of killing that brings the bodies of victims and perpetrators together in death, injuring and killing in such a way that collapses the inside and outside of bodies, resulting in a gory spectacle. This evokes not only the corporeality that haunts the subject, but also points to the fluid boundaries between bodies. In deploying a means of violence that shatters the body's (illusory) wholeness, literally reducing it to corpses and fluid bits, the violence of the suicide bomber transforms the self into the abject while transforming his or her victims into symbols of the abject as well. Gayatri Spivak writes of suicide bombing, "Suicidal resistance is a message inscribed on the body when no other means will get through. It is both execution and mourning, for both self and other. For you die with me for the same cause, no matter which side you are on" (2004, 95). The suicide bomber not only pulverizes the boundaries of the self-contained body, but also breaches the boundaries that separate bodies from one another, and that separate political identities from one another. It is an act not only of destruction, but of *contamination*. Its message is not only that absolute security of the body's integrity is impossible, but also that the integrity of the social and political order that sovereignty attempts is impossible. The dissolution of the self by exploding the body erases boundaries between self and other as the body of the bomber in its flesh and blood merges with the anonymous others whom it targets. Suicide bombing erases differences between bodies produced by state discourses of self and other. It produces bodies not as same or other, clearly demarcated, but as *abject*, refusing boundaries, only a mass of flesh. It is the violent eruption of the abject, of a feminine symbolic, that has been disqualified in the sovereign state which values the impermeability of its borders and the absolute safety of its citizens above all else.

The body of the suicide bomber defies the modernist conception of the body whose wholeness and integrity is so taken for granted that it can be transcended, whether in a Cartesian thinking subject or a liberal deliberating subject. The figure of the suicide bomber suggests a non-normative bodily morphology that calls into question the perceived naturalness of the modern subject. Suicide bombing reverses the modernist conception of the body in which the inside is mysterious, hidden, and the outside, the skin, is what is presented to the world. The skin is a container for the inside and for the subject, which is located therein. The suicide bomber is a form of "leaky body" that is not stable, individual, or bound at the skin. It is a de-territorialized body, not ordered by sovereignty, and only appearing stable and fixed in essence and identity by practices of security.

While the broad category of "terrorist" may be associated with a certain kind of formlessness that is linked to abjection, the suicide bomber as a subtype of the "terrorist" is even more strongly linked to the abject. As discussed in Chapter 2, the figure of the "terrorist" is associated with a discourse of formlessness, a discourse that reveals the "abject" status of the terrorist. The terrorist, especially the suicide bomber, does not respect public boundaries, whether state borders, laws, or moral prohibitions on killing and suicide. His or her violent acts are, by definition, not tied to the legitimacy of the state and are considered to be unchained to morality as well in their targeting of random civilians. Terrorist organizations are loosely connected cells, operating underground and across state borders. Their operations are thought of as "shadowy" and "amorphous." The body of the suicide bomber, as one kind of "terrorist," brings another dimension to this formlessness, as the bomber's own body is made to explode, to exceed its own boundaries in order to destroy and wreak havoc. By randomly destroying the integrity of the bodies of citizens, the suicide bomber exposes the failure of states to provide security in terms of protecting its citizens from harm from external sources. In short, the suicide bomber reveals the instability of two boundaries simultaneously: the boundaries between states/national communities and between individual bodies.

The suicide bomber also becomes an abject figure by blurring the boundaries between nature and culture, biology and technology. The suicide bomber as such exists at the point of concealment of a bomb on, in, or about the body of the bomber. The body of the suicide bomber is not a "natural" body, but rather an amalgam of flesh and metal, biology and technology. The bomb carried by the suicide bomber is a form of technology concealed in a "natural" body. The "natural" body and the clothing worn by the bomber conceal the bomb. Clothing, as a cultural layer worn on the body that signifies a particular identity—of gender, of status, of religion or culture—is meant to conceal the "true" identity of the bomber. The suicide bomber must break the "law" to carry out his or her mission. He or she must "pass" in order to elude security measures and hide their intentions as well as their bombs. Bombers have dressed as Orthodox Jews, and women have pretended to be pregnant, for example, in order to escape close scrutiny and to better conceal bombs. The bombs become part of the bodies of the bomber, not only at the moment of detonation, but in an act of incorporation into the bomber's bodily presentation, a presentation necessary for the mission to be carried out. The statement in a video recording from Reem Al Rayashi captures the blurring of the boundaries between body and technology: "I have always dreamed of transforming myself into deadly shrapnel against the Zionists . . . and my joy will be complete when the parts of my body will fly in all directions" (quoted in Cavarero 2009, 97). In this way, the bomb plays a different role from that of a gun, a knife, or a grenade, which extends and enhances the destructive capabilities of the body. The body itself is the weapon, not only the wielder of technology (Oliver 2007, 32).

The explosion of the bomb is the moment of bringing to light that which is hidden—not only in the true intentions of the bomber, but what is hidden in bodies as well. In the gory scene of a bombing, the insides of bodies, once hidden by skin, are on full display. In its use of the body of the bomber as a projectile, the suicide bomber becomes a monstrous figure of ambiguity between nature and culture, and in its unreason, between animal and human. Very recently, suicide bombers have taken the concept of the "human bomb" a step further, and have placed bombs inside human bodies, both corpses and live bombers (Cavarero 2009, 96; Gardner 2009). From the amalgamation with the metal and other bomb components, to the moment of detonation, the suicide bomber is a body in transformation, a becoming-body rather than a permanent fixture. As such, the suicide bomber evokes the bodily horror of the inevitable bodily disintegration and death, even for those who are not threatened by this form of violence. The threat of suicide bombers as monstrous bodies, apart from the obvious ability to harm, lies in its capacity to contaminate, to spread disorder and the disintegration of identity.

Some might argue that to theorize the body of the suicide bomber as an abject, monstrous body is to denigrate this form of political violence as especially heinous compared to other forms of warfare that have similar, or worse, dangers for civilians (see Asad 2007). Such an argument, however, would require us to accept the logic of abjection: that what is abjected is bad, filthy, and unnatural. We couldn't see abjection as a possible strategy, or, more to the point, as something that not only makes social and political boundaries visible but also something that moves to erase these boundaries. Accepting the logic of abjection means that the presence of the abject is seen as *only* something that is repulsive, not as something that challenges the boundaries of the clean and proper itself.

Thinking of what the body of the suicide bomber *does* rather than what the bomber or his or her sponsoring organization intends leads us to think about bodies themselves as a type of agent, particularly as bodies-in-becoming in ways that challenge our conception of the body as self-contained and self-governing. In their ability to disturb boundaries between bodies, between inside and outside, nature and culture, bodies are a source of symbolic contamination that reveals the work necessary in upholding boundaries in the first place—boundaries that sovereign practices are driven to maintain control over.

ABJECTION, BORDERS, AND THE STATE

In the destruction of bodies in a way that seems meant to bring about the greatest possible damage, bodies are separated from political subjectivity, and thus are made abject. The mangled corpses that are left behind after a suicide bomber are no longer "clean and proper" bodies (Kristeva 1982, 72). The abject threatens not only the sovereign borders of the body, but the sovereign borders of the social and symbolic order as well. The borders of the symbolic order are maintained by ritual purification, an expulsion of the abject. In cases of suicide bombing, this ritual purification is undertaken in relation to the treatment of the bodies of the suicide bomber and his or her victims. The public nature of a suicide bombing makes the abject bodies of the bomber and his or her victims into a spectacle that exposes not only the instability of bodily integrity but the instability of the political order as well. As a public spectacle, it evokes the sacrificial logic of sovereign power, in which sacrifice is necessary to constitute the political order (see Foucault 1979). The recovery and burial of the bodies is a ritual that imbues the bodies with subjectivity through another form of sacrifice. The presence of the abject signals disorder and pollution, not just in the bodies involved, but in the social order as well; dead bodies are a management problem for states (see also Auchter 2014, 25–32). To return society to a state of perceived order, rituals must be undertaken to cleanse society of the pollution. As such, the recovery of bodies does more than attempt to re-establish subject/body coherence; it attempts to restore the appearance of integrity of the state as well. The work of ZAKA in Israel (and recently, around the world) is a particularly striking example of the effort deployed to maintain the semblance of subject/body/state coherence.[5]

This work in reconstituting bodies is part of a state practice to reinstate bodies into grids of intelligibility in which "us" and "them" are clearly demarcated. From an abject undifferentiated "heap of meat," bodies are produced as individual and self-contained, as well as signified with an identity. Bodies are thus produced as "whole" or "stable" forms that can be managed, rather than the leaky, de-territorialized bodies produced by suicide bombing.

Re-subjectification of Bodies

In Israel, a society known as ZAKA (an acronym for Identifiers of Victims of Disaster in Hebrew) is made up of volunteers who not only treat survivors, but also remove, identify, and bury body parts after bombings and other sudden deaths. ZAKA is the only organization that is authorized by the state to handle the recovery and identification of body parts, a duty that is normally undertaken by state institutions. ZAKA members are trained by the Israeli police and Magen David Adom (the Israeli Red Cross) in paramedic skills, proper management of forensic evidence, and Jewish law regarding the treatment of the deceased. Officially formed in 1995, ZAKA grew out of an informal network of Haredi (ultra-Orthrodox) volunteers who would gather at scenes of mass casualties (usually bomb attacks) to ensure that the bodies, regardless of the religion of the deceased, were being treated in accordance with Jewish law.

ZAKA effectively undertakes a purification ritual of making clean and proper what was disordered and defiled. ZAKA volunteers are motivated by a desire that the bodies of the victims be treated with respect. Showing respect means, first, that the bodies are covered up, restoring the hiddenness of the inside of bodies, which the bombers brought into the open. According to one volunteer, "if [the body] is visible, and everyone can see it, this is a lack of respect, shameful, and is why the first thing we do is to cover the body" (Stadler 2009, 146). Second, ZAKA strives to ensure that all body parts are recovered so that they can be buried according to Jewish law. They will spend hours ensuring that no blood or bits of flesh are left behind. ZAKA takes responsibility for locating, reassembling, and transferring victims' bodies to the Israeli Institute of Forensic Science, where they are identified using a variety of methods, including dental records and DNA analysis. In interviews, ZAKA volunteers frequently mention concerns that dogs, birds, or ants will consume human flesh, or that blood will be washed away by hoses (DiManno 2003; Ginsburg 2003). By treating bodies in accordance with Jewish religious law, ZAKA re-signifies that bodies are human and *Jewish*, not "heaps of meat."

The bodies of the suicide bombers are also treated with respect, despite whatever misgivings the volunteers may have. Body parts of suicide bombers that can be identified are given to the army to give back to the families of the bombers, if possible. As one ZAKA volunteer explained, "It is written in the Torah that each one should be buried properly in a Jewish cemetery . . . but it is not important if it is Jew or a Gentile, more specifically, it is written that all men have been created in God's image, even if he is the suicide bomber . . . by the very fact that he is a human being, all his organs should be gathered and buried, and this is exactly what ZAKA does" (Stadler 2006, 846).

The severed flesh left in the wake of a suicide bombing renders such bodies unidentifiable under the regimes of religion, nationality, gender, or race. Stripped of their production as certain types of political subjects, the parts of bodies that cannot be identified with any particular subjectivity are buried according to Jewish traditions. Given the nature of suicide attacks, many times it is difficult, if not impossible, to distinguish between the bodies of the perpetrator and the bodies of the victims. Frequently, the bodies of both the bomber and some of the victims are so mutilated as to be indistinguishable, despite the training of ZAKA members in the latest forensic technologies. In such cases, unidentified pieces are buried in a common grave according to Jewish tradition. One volunteer explains, "Although they are dead, we still honor every part of the body, every piece of flesh has to be brought to burial. Flesh we can't identify we bury together. Pieces of flesh are put in bags and the bags are buried in a special grave in the local cemetery" (BBC 2002). After death, the bodies of victim and perpetrator alike are reinscribed with political and religious meaning through the careful treatment of each body fragment as Jewish.[6] While the act of suicide bombing is an act of sovereign power that mutilates and destroys bodies, the practice of collecting all body fragments and fluids is an example of power regulating the body, turning objects only identifiable from a medical or anatomical viewpoint into remnants of a human subject. These actions are an attempt to (re)produce the body fragments as belonging to properly human subjects with a national and religious identity, an act that can never be completed, as these bodies cannot be made whole again, nor can they be entirely separated from that of the suicide bomber. While the bodies cannot materially be made whole (and of course cannot be brought back to life), they are made symbolically whole again, made into human subjects by identification and burial practices.

ZAKA volunteers explain their work in terms of a religious imperative that bodies should be treated like the Torah, that the damaged corpse must be reconstituted, put whole again. A volunteer explained this through the corporeal nature of the Torah: "The scroll of the Torah is something physical, corporeal. . . . A piece of leather or parchment that is used to write the sacred words of the Torah is not sacred until we begin writing the sacred words. . .. If a book of Torah is, God forbid, burned, a Jew will definitely hurry to save it with all his soul" (Stadler 2009, 143). This connection between the sacredness of the Torah and the human body is also seen in ZAKA's practice of recovering damaged or destroyed Torahs as part of their recovery mission, such as from synagogues damaged in Hurricane Katrina. For members of ZAKA, remaking a body into a subject, specifically, a Jewish subject, is an imperative of their own understanding of themselves as Jewish subjects. The practices of ZAKA not only entail the symbolic reconstitution of individual bodies, but are implicated in the reconstitution of national bodies as well.

ZAKA's politics in signifying the bodies of Jews is tied to the practices of burial in Israeli society more broadly. Of particular relevance for comparison is the treatment of deceased IDF (Israeli Defense Force) soldiers. Narratives of religion and nation played out over the handling of bodies of soldiers. While the bodies of victims of suicide bombing are collected to ensure the treatment of all flesh as human and divine, the bodies of soldiers are given even more care to ensure their representation of the nation and as generalizable "sons" belonging to all of Israel, not only as Jews or as members of particular families (Weiss 2002). The bodies of soldiers, like the bodies of victims of terrorism, are imbued with symbolic meaning. This is not, in itself, particularly surprising, as the memorialization of soldiers killed in war as a sacrifice to the nation is a common state practice. What is interesting, however, is the relationship between the practices of handling the bodies of IDF soldiers and the bodies of victims of suicide attacks. The bodies of soldiers are treated separately and differently from those of the general population. There is a "skin bank" available for the bodies of soldiers that may need it (from the bodies of non-soldiers) for reconstruction purposes, but no tissue from soldiers may be contributed to this supply. Samples of tissue or fluids may not be taken from soldiers for testing, as they are in other deaths (to be returned to the graves of the deceased later). Their bodies are also "perfected" in that they are treated specially to look whole and without injury (Weiss 2002, 59–60). Soldiers' bodies, as specific representatives of the state, must be as close to perfect as possible. This "perfect" or "whole" body is, of course, an unobtainable ideal—dead and mangled bodies cannot be brought back to life, nor can "actual" bodies ever manifest true perfection. The practice of attempting to reassemble, to make "perfect," is a means of attempting to cleanse the contamination of the corpse, the impure abject that can never be gotten rid of, either in the perfectly constituted body or the perfectly constituted state. The abject as remainder, that which cannot be made perfect, is a reminder of the inescapable contamination at the founding of the state and the seemingly self-contained body.

The reassembly of shattered bodies is a performative way of reassembling the cohesion of the world—not only of the subject, but of the community and sovereign state as well. As Kristeva writes, "the body must bear no trace of its debt to nature: it must be clean and proper in order to be fully symbolic" (1982, 102). The body fragments collected and identified by ZAKA are a synecdoche for the community and the nation, and the reassembly of them is an effort to remake the sovereignty of the state. The building of fences and border walls around state boundaries fulfills a similar function. Just as efforts to reconstruct bodies are destined to be incomplete, so too are the state's efforts to performatively establish its sovereignty by building walls around its territory. Wendy Brown recently argued that building walls such as the US–Mexico border fence and the Israeli "security fence"/apartheid wall is a sign not of resurgent state sovereignty, but rather of the loss of certain sovereign functions and the desire for performances of sovereignty. Walls fulfill a kind of psychic need for containment, rather than an actual purpose of deterring outsiders (Brown 2010). Efforts at reconstructing the bodies of the victims of suicide bombing or other political violence do even more to show the precariousness and ultimate illusory nature of sovereign unity, whether in states or in bodies.

The practice of memorializing suicide bombers as honored martyrs is common in the Palestinian context as well as others, such as the LTTE (Liberation Tigers of Tamil Eelam) in Sri Lanka, although the specific practice of handling remains by ZAKA appears to be unique. In contrast to the way in which remains are handled by ZAKA and the Israeli Forensic Institute, the remains of the September 11th hijackers seem to be treated in such a way as to ensure that they remain unpurified and unsubjectified, still "heaps of meat." This is in contrast to the extensive DNA testing that has been done on recovered remains from the World Trade Center towers; nevertheless, though thousands of samples of human remains were recovered, there are still over a thousand missing people from the World Trade Center site who have never been identified via their remains, and whose death has been certified only by legal documents (Edkins 2011, 129). Families of the victims of the World Trade Center's collapse on September 11, 2001, have expressed concern that the bodies of the hijackers would be mixed in with the bodies of their loved ones. Kurt Horning, whose son Matthew was killed in the WTC on September 11, 2001, and who cofounded the group WTC Families for Proper Burial, remarked, "It would be sadly ironic if they ended up being properly buried or sent to a Muslim country when many of the remains of the victims remain buried in a garbage dump" (Winter 2009). Horning's group supports the evacuation of the landfill on Staten Island where debris from the World Trade Center was buried, believing it may contain identifiable remains. The medical examiner's office has made efforts to distinguish and separate the tiny fragments of tissue and bone belonging to the hijackers from the body fragments that cannot or have not yet been identified. However, the task of completely sorting out the hijackers from the victims is deemed impossible because of how small, damaged, and scattered the body fragments are. The remains of the hijackers that have been identified are separated and sequestered in evidence lockers in undisclosed locations in New York and Virginia. To date, the remains of 13 of the 19 hijackers have been identified by DNA, although the FBI has refused to say which have been identified (Winter 2009). No official determination has been made about what to do with the remains, which have not been requested by any of the hijacker's families or governments (Conant 2009).

Robert Shaler, who was the head of New York's Department of Forensic Biology at the time of the attacks, reported of the families of the victims, "they did not want the terrorists mixed in with their loved ones. These people were criminals and they did not deserve to be with the innocent victims. No one knows what will happen, but I don't think they should be buried on American soil" (Winter 2009). The mention of "American soil" points to the bond between bodies, subjects, and states and suggests that burying bodies that have been identified as the suicide bombers in the United States is a disruptive, polluting act. The practices of identifying and burying the remains have resulted in the "purification" of the remains of the victims, but lack ZAKA's efforts at treating all remains as human. These un-reconstituted bodies remain "heaps of meat," lying in limbo as something other than human. While these abjected bodies remain unsignified, a great deal of effort has gone into interpreting and narrativizing other bodies: the bodies of female suicide bombers.

Gendering the Bomber

Scholars and the media alike are fascinated with female suicide bombers, who disrupt the image of women as maternal life-givers rather than life-takers. Women's participation in suicide missions has been of particular interest to feminists and gender theorists in International Relations because it appears to upset traditional gender roles in which women are victims, rather than perpetrators, of political violence (see Bloom 2005; Sjoberg and Gentry, 2007; Oliver 2007, 2008; O'Rourke 2008). Women who are suicide bombers challenge the myth of women as "beautiful souls" (Elshtain 1995 [1987]): innocents who need to be shielded from the harsh realities of the world by masculine protectors.[7] In what follows, I detour from this framing to focus on the politics of the sexed embodiment of the suicide bomber. I argue that what is interesting about the phenomenon of women as suicide bombers is not that women necessarily have different motivations for suicide terrorism, but that the symbolic politics differ when the suicide terrorist is embodied as a woman. As women are constituted by a different relationship to corporeality than men in Western culture, the suicide attack perpetrated by a woman represents a somewhat different politics that is not reducible to questions of agency or exploitation. In short, rather than the motivations of women who carry out suicide bombing, this section focuses on the performative effects of the disintegration and reformulation of female bodies.

The association of the suicide bomber with abjection is amplified in the presence of a female suicide bomber. The women's body, already associated with the abject, is made into a corpse, the "utmost of abjection" (Kristeva 1982, 4), as it makes others into corpses as well. The female suicide bomber does more than breach the boundaries between the inside and the outside of the body; she simultaneously disrupts and reinforces constructions of gender and women's embodiment by situating the polluting, contaminating bodies of women in a public setting. Female suicide bombers challenge the exclusion of women's bodies from the public sphere and from war-fighting in particular; yet by using their bodies as weapons, the construction of women's bodies as alluring but threatening is reproduced.

While bodily fluids in general are seen as abject and contaminating, men's and women's bodily fluids are not seen as contaminating in the same way or to the same extent. In Kristeva's writings, the abjection toward the signs of sexual difference—specifically, menstrual blood—is distinguished from the abjection typified by bodily waste, the corpse. While excrement evokes a threat stemming from outside the self, "menstrual blood... stands for the danger issuing from within the identity (social and sexual); it threatens the relationship between the sexes within a social aggregate, and through internalization, the identity of each sex in the face of sexual difference" (Kristeva 1982, 71). The threat of abjection that menstrual blood poses may perhaps best be thought of as related to the emphasis on women's reproductive capacities as the locus of sexual difference. For Kristeva, menstrual blood invokes the maternal body as the ultimate threat to individual autonomy. This emphasis is not, as Grosz reminds us, natural or inevitable, as many zones of the body could be taken to represent the essential difference between the sexes (1994, 196). Menstrual blood, as the mark of reproductive maturity, comes to signify not only sexual difference but also the female body as constituted by seepage and leakiness more broadly. By their association with signs of the abject, women's bodies have been discursively produced as bodies of fear and contempt. Their bodies are associated with monstrosity, in their potentiality for pregnancy and its rapid morphological changes, and in the troubling of the body as closed, autonomous, and secure in its boundaries—a normative image of what the body should be that is consistent with representations of the male body (Shildrick 2002). The presence of women in the public sphere, let alone seemingly violating gendered roles of women's passivity and victimhood, not only upsets the supposed unity of the body (which women are never fully identified with) but also exposes women's bodies in their most "monstrous" form, the terrifying formlessness that haunts the self. The figure of the female suicide bomber reproduces the production of women's bodies as abject, but provides a challenge to the exclusion of women from the public sphere and from committing acts of political violence.

Because of their association with abjection—a sense of fluidity and instability that is both captivating and repulsive—women's bodies themselves are threatening to the orderly space of sovereignty. Kelly Oliver argues that women's association with abjection makes them particularly effective as suicide bombers:

> Within popular discourse, women's bodies, menstrual blood, and female sexuality can be used as tactic of war because of the potency of their association with the danger of nature, of Mother Nature, if you will. Akin to a natural toxin or intoxicant, women's sex makes a powerful weapon because, within our cultural imaginary, it is by nature dangerous. (2007, 31)

Female suicide bombers are thus like Hollywood's *femme fatales*, using cultural narratives of their sexuality to hide destructive intentions, such as going unveiled to avoid suspicion. Women's bodies, already constituted as abject, are used as weapons to further blur the lines between individual bodies, and between the borders of state and community. The deployment of women's bodies as suicide bombers could be viewed as a parody of women's bodies as abject. In rejecting Kristeva's interpretation of abjection as rooted in a pre-political concept of the maternal body, Butler argues that abjection and maternal bodies are, in brief, cultural rather than natural phenomena (1990). Butler's concept of performativity describes the construction of gendered norms and gendered subjects through reiterated performance, thus leaving open the possibility of subversion and resistance through parodies, that is, performances that blatantly show that what should be natural is indeed constructed by exaggeration and caricature. Because women's bodies are not naturally fluid, leaky, or abject, any more then men's are, performances that heighten or intensify performances of abjection could work to undermine such naturalized discourses of women's embodiment. Yet, a parody is not enough to challenge representations of women's bodies or the sovereign *body politic*. Whatever emancipatory potential there may be for women or for rethinking the *body politic* in the practice of suicide bombing, especially by women, must be investigated in the space between action and the signification of that action.

As discussed earlier, the body of the suicide bomber is, in the moments after detonation, a "heap of meat," a body whose constitution in the symbolic order has been disrupted by the collapsing of the borders between inside and outside. Representing a radical separation between subjectivity and body, the suicide bomber and his or her victim(s) must be re-signified as part of an ongoing process of representations that constitutes not only a religious or national subject, but sexed and gendered subjects as well. Sometimes this signification happens in advance of the bombing, and is undertaken by the bombers themselves. In their testimonies, the women describe their actions in terms of seizing the reigns of political militancy. As female suicide bomber[8] Ayat al-Akhras said on her video testimony, "I've chosen to say with my body what Arab leaders have failed to say." Akhras continued: "I say to Arab leaders, stop sleeping. Stop failing to fulfill your duty. Shame on the Arab armies who are sitting and watching the girls of Palestine fighting while they are asleep" (Hasso 2005, 29). By killing and dying for their nation, these women challenged the gendered protector/protected dichotomy in which men fight wars to shield and protect women, who are in turn expected to be grateful and unquestioning of men's efforts (see Elshtain 1995 [1987]; Sjoberg 2006). However, at the same time, the framing of their suicide mission as a wake-up call to male leaders reproduces gendered roles of politics and war: both are the proper realm of men. Thus while her actions transgress gender roles, al-Akhras's statement serves to interpret her actions as feminine, and even as compelling traditional gender roles in her words cajoling Palestinian male leadership. Her performance, both in words and deed, are actions that disrupt Israeli sovereignty while instantiating a Palestinian sovereignty that reproduces the familiar relationship between women's bodies and the state. Other representations of the female suicide bombers serve to constitute them as wives and mothers in a heterosexual symbolic system.

The female suicide bomber is frequently represented as a bride. The female suicide bombers of the Syrian Socialist National Party (SSNP) were glorified as "Brides of the South," (O'Rourke 2008, 695) and Palestinian female suicide bombers have been referred to as "Bride[s] of Palestine" (Naamen 2007) or as "Bride[s] of Heaven" (Sjoberg and Gentry 2007, 124). Female suicide bombers are also represented as mothers, submissive and self-sacrificing on behalf of the nation. In such cases, the bomber is seen as metaphorically procreating through her actions: as one commentator on the first Palestinian female suicide bomber, Wafa Idris, proclaimed, "She bore in her belly the fetus of a rare heroism, and gave birth by blowing herself up!" (quoted in Cunningham 2009, 568). In both of these, the violence of women is made sense of by placing it in gendered and heteronormative narratives. The body of the female suicide bomber is subjectified according to gender and heterosexual norms as wife and mother.

The female suicide bomber marked as "pregnant" is figured as not only a mother-to-be, marked by her gendered embodiment, but a particularly monstrous embodiment—a body that is not quite one, not quite two. The pregnant body is deformed from within, not from an external threat. The pregnant female body also problematizes the boundaries between self and other, becoming an improper, abject body (Shildrick 2002, 31). As such, the pregnant woman is a source of fascination, but also fear and dread. The female suicide bomber as "pregnant" is an ambiguous figure, representing the heterogeneous space preexisting the division between self and other, but also, through the act of giving birth, of expulsion of the other from the self (the mother's body being expelled, abjected).

The constitution of female suicide bombers as maternal subjects by public declarations after their deaths is made clear by the following statement published about Wafa Idris: "what is more beautiful than the transformation of a person from a chunk of flesh and blood to illuminated purity and a spirit that cuts across generations?" (quoted in Cunningham 2009, 568). The discourse of the female suicide bomber after her death takes a body that is abject, stripped of subjectivity, and remakes it into a maternal, reproductive figure, akin to the "mother of the nation," which characterizes the role of women in nationalist discourses (Yuval-Davis 1997, 23). Her body is thus (re)produced as a sexed body under the regime of heteronormativity, "purifying" it from any contamination of gender roles. The gendering of the bodies of female suicide bombers, as well as the construction of the bodies of the victims of suicide bombers as Jewish in Israel, demonstrates the work that takes place both before and after the bomb to inscribe bodies with political subjectivity, as members of a community that must be reconstructed. This work suggests that the project of constituting bodies is ongoing as a performance of gender and a performance of sovereignty.

The language of weddings and reproduction to describe female suicide bombers transposes the role of women in nationalist discourses. While women are usually represented as the soil of the nation (that is, raped by invaders) or as reproducers of sons to fight for the nation (Massad 1995; Yuval-Davis 1997), female suicide bombers are represented as performing a similar role through their violence: birthing a nation by both dying and killing. Violence that might be taken as an act of resistance to sovereign boundary-making, as well as a kind of sovereign act in itself, is inscribed within a gendered order that codes women's political agency in terms of maternity. Such a reconstruction of female suicide bombers has ambiguous effects: women's political agency is recognized, yet only through gendered and heterosexual narratives. While such narratives are a way of "keeping women in their place" as wives and mothers, the public and political nature of this violence and the way it disrupts national borders, boundaries of the body, and gender roles suggest a more tenuous and uneasy relationship between the state's sovereign power and its ability to produce stable borders and bounded bodies. Female suicide bombers are figures of anxiety because their bodies, already abject in the sovereign order, violate the borders of bodies and states, but their bodies show sovereignty as precarious and inadequate to instill order on wild spaces.

CONCLUSION

Suicide bombing calls our attention to the political work that is necessary to constitute the illusion of individuated and self-contained bodies. By violently erasing the boundaries between the interior and the exterior of the body, the suicide bomber calls into question the model of the body as a self-contained vessel for the subject. The threat that the suicide bomber poses is not only the sovereign threat of taking lives, but of contamination, of the abject disrupting what has been constituted as the natural functioning of bodies and the circulation of populations. The body of the suicide bomber may be considered to be productive, or agentic, in that it has political effects beyond those intended by the willing subject choosing a suicide mission. The suicide bomber and the practices of (re)constituting the body of the bomber suggest that bodies are politically constituted, as well as *constituting* in the symbolic politics of abjection. At the same time, this rethinking of the body necessitates a rethinking of the terms of the state and sovereignty that are implied by the metaphor of the *body politic*. Efforts at reassembling and reconstructing the bodies of victims and perpetrators of this practice also show the self-contained body that is the body of IR to be an effect of material and discursive practices.

Suicide bombing and the recovery/identification of bodies as embodied practices reveal the construction of the state as *body politic* to be something more than "mere" metaphor or model; the boundaries of state sovereignty are produced though sacrificial politics of abjection not only in a metaphorical sense, but rather, through the production of abject bodies. By reading suicide bombing as an embodied practice, we are perhaps more inclined to view both states and bodies as "bodies without organs": bodies that are not unitary, confined to particular spaces, or possessing fixed structures (Deleuze and Guattari, 1980 [2004]; Rasmussen and Brown 2005, 479). The practice of suicide bombing challenges us to think of bounded bodies and bounded states as political performances that are only precariously reinforced by practices of sovereignty.

Having previously shown how practices of international security pose a challenge to the self-preserving, speaking subject presumed by realist and liberal IR as well as, in this chapter, how such practices also undermine the self-contained and individual subject, as well as the passivity of bodies, I turn now to attempts to protect bodies from suicide bombing and other violent practices that have been called "terrorism." Airport security assemblages are also implicated in practices that produce bodies as abject in the name of protecting natural bodies. While this chapter has theorized suicide bombing as a practice that reveals how bodies in International Relations are both produced by, and productive of, politics, the following chapter builds on this theme to consider a site in which bodies are both de-materialized into information, yet remain deeply material in the lived experiences of bodies in security practices.

CHAPTER 4

Crossing Borders, Securing Bodies

Airport Security Assemblages and Bodies of Information

In order to protect populations from suicide bombers and other forms of violence that target random people, as discussed in the previous chapter, states use a variety of technologies to locate bodies that may pose a threat in the form of terrorism, or to manage populations in immigration or asylum regimes. In this framework, security is knowledge—specifically, knowledge about bodies. The contemporary drive of security is not motivated so much by the search for concealed weapons or other contraband, but more by a desire to see beneath the possibly deceptive practices of dress, language, or identity presentation, to see the truth of the body and thus the future of security. Bodies are presumed fixed and unchanging as objects of the scientific gaze; in these security regimes, bodies are not only produced as *knowable* but also as *readable* by experts and machines (Van Der Ploegh 1999).

This chapter shifts from the embodied practice of suicide bombing to contemporary practices aimed at preventing such acts of violence, and from bodies whose individuation and separation from each other is an effect, to bodies whose materiality and immateriality are also subject to practices of violence and security. The security discourse includes the use of full-body X-ray or backscatter scanners, installed primarily in airports in North America and Europe, as an effort at rendering the bodies of the population legible to the state in order to locate and eliminate security risks. Contingency and risk are at the heart of the governing rationales of terrorism and the security politics of eliminating uncertainty; "what most characterizes global terror, we are persistently told, is the certainty of its radical uncertainty" (Dillon 2007, 9). While the "war on terror" has been analyzed in terms of biopolitical strategies of risk management (Rasmussen 2004; Dillon 2007a, 2007b; Kessler and Werner 2008; Amoore and de Goede 2008; Muller 2010; Lobo-Guerrero 2011), the prospect of another attack like those of September 11th or the 7/7 London bombing is deemed too catastrophic for its risk to be minimized or insured against by profiling techniques. The supposed incalculability and uninsurability of such events has led to states using precautionary and "zero risk" techniques in which people are presumptively assumed to be dangerous and must prove that they are harmless (Aradau and Van Munster 2007). Rather than normalization, such security procedures function as a "banopticon," as they seek proactive control and risk management rather than normalization (Bigo 2002, 82; Bigo 2007). The use of scanners is a primary example of such governing rationalities that attempt to build absolute knowledge so that risk may be eliminated. These scanners are part of a broader security assemblage that needs to secure and stabilize bodies by means of producing knowledge about them. The first part of this chapter is about how the body is understood as a particular artifact of discourse in the practices of airport security assemblages. The airport security assemblage can be read as a security strategy to detect a certain "biologized" internal enemy against whom society must defend itself (Foucault 2003), and as a technology for reading the population in order to better manage and control it (Scott 1998). What is new about the full-body scanners, or, more appropriately, the airport/border security assemblages that incorporate these scanners, is that bodies are viewed not only as organisms, as in the traditional dissections of modern medical practice, but as information. Bodily deviancy as a threat to security is dealt with not only through anatomization but through informationalization. The use of the scanners to detect anomalies in human bodies represents a moment of the simultaneous materialization and dematerialization of bodies. That is, identity and subjectivity are stripped away from bodies; persons are objectified *as* their fleshy, material bodies. At the same time, such bodies are *dematerialized*, transformed into digital images that are ultimately computer code: signs readable by technology and trained personnel. In this process, deviant bodies that do not fit with the boundedness of the state are excluded or are produced as suspicious or anomalous.

At the same time, the materiality of bodies is not completely obscured or made irrelevant. The second part of this chapter shifts focus from bodies to embodiment, that is, from bodies as signs in discourse to the experience of life as a body that people in culture can articulate (Hayles 1993, 148). I focus on the gap between the supposed "neutrality" of the body scanners and the security assemblage and the experiences of many who have protested the procedures as an invasion of privacy or a sexualized violation of their bodies and on the experience of trans- and genderqueer people as moments of contestation over the "truth" and materiality of the body. The informationalization of bodies in order to reveal deviancy and danger reveals the investment of "security" in rendering bodies legible— the experience of trans- people as presenting "anomalous" bodies in this assemblage exposes the dynamics of security as not revealing the truth of suspicious or dangerous bodies, but in producing deviant and "safe" bodies. These bodies are produced as deviant in the airport security assemblage not just because they do not conform to gender expectations, but because they do not conform to the state's desire to regulate bodies as fixed and unchanging, a desire that is undermined by the trans- disruption of the state's assumption of bodies and genders as fixed and immutable.

AIRPORT SECURITY ASSEMBLAGES AND BODIES OF INFORMATION

While the main focus of this chapter is the controversial body scanners, such technologies cannot be adequately theorized in isolation. Rather, they must be seen as part of a broader milieu, or assemblage. The body scanners are a component of a broader security assemblage of borders and especially airports that includes multiple bodies and technological artifacts and blurs the line between local and global in the provision of security.[1] Bodies here are not only human bodies. Mark Salter reminds us that the airport is part of an architecture of control that makes subjects into docile bodies (2007, 51–52). Bodies are produced by this security assemblage in relation to other bodies and artifacts. I consider this security assemblage to be a "practice of violence," related to the other practices of violence discussed in this book, because it is a form of managing violence, intervening on a field in which transportation networks and large crowds are sites where violence may occur both to the bodies of humans and to the flow and functioning of international capital. It is also implicated in practices of normative violence as it (re)produces certain bodies and certain lives as "real" and normal and others as aberrations. This assemblage includes the technological artifacts of scanners, the architecture of airports into "sterile" and "non-sterile" zones, the bodies of travelers, and the personnel trained to conduct searches and translate information about bodies into decisions about the riskiness of a body. In this security regime, everybody is perceived as at least potentially destructive (Epstein 2007, 155). Airport security procedures are boundary-producing practices, insofar as they not only enact the sovereignty of states over their territory (even if airports are not located at the geographic borders of states), but also produce boundaries between acceptable bodies and deviant bodies.

The territorial boundary between states is increasingly viewed as insufficient for thinking about the political effects of various forms of borders (Walker 1993; Rumford 2006; Walters 2006; Vaughan-Williams 2009). The airport serves as a de-territorialization of the border; it is a liminal space, a space of transition from one state to the next (Salter 2005). As such, it is a particularly significant place to investigate bodies as sites of politics, given the significance of the maintenance of bodies to securing the borders, as discussed in the previous chapter. In the context of the "war on terror" in which security threats are not associated with any particular territory or state but rather with mobile actors who seem to blend in to avoid detection, threats to security are not imagined as invading armies, but mobile individuals, actors, and processes (Adey 2004). Rather than the threat of nuclear war, which promoted a national security apparatus focused on the military, the post–Cold War era has resulted in a shift in security focus to non-state and transnational threats, including the drug trade, terrorism, and illegal immigration. Policing the borders has become a major security concern, and the line between law enforcement and intelligence/military operations is blurred (Andreas 2003). Airport security assemblage also cannot be understood apart from the broader movement toward increased state surveillance in Europe and North America, and especially toward the use of biometric technologies for both identification and verification of that identity (Pugliese 2010). Passports emerged as a way of regulating movement and of determining who is a citizen and who is a foreigner (Torpey 2000). The state borders (and the Schengen border in Europe) are increasingly managed biometrically. While border management serves to sort out "insiders" and "outsiders," desirable and non-desirable travelers, national identification schemes and attempts to both increase and centralize the data collected (including the "Real ID" program in the United States, which sets standards and coordinates local data) increase the surveillance capacities of states and enable their abilities to identify who does and who does not belong inside the state. In other words, the border, understood as a technology of social exclusion, does not end at the border as state surveillance capacities increase (Lyon 2005).

The United States deploys what it terms a "multilayered" strategy for border security. The "Secure Flight" program is about identifying individuals based on their name, birthdate, gender, and address, requiring people to give this information exactly as it appears on government-issued documents when they book flights. Thus, "Secure Flight" serves as a type of virtual border, tracking visitors before they reach the physical border. "Secure Flight" matches this information with the FBI's Terrorism Screening Center's "no fly" list, which uses data mining and profiling techniques to "pre-screen" individuals and create this list based on a statistical calculation of riskiness.[2] The focus here is not yet on the physical body of the traveler him- or herself, but on data that the state can search for signs regarding risk or trustworthiness. The addition of gender and date of birth to the information collected by the United States is intended to reduce the number of false positives of people selected for additional airport screenings and further visa scrutiny because their names are similar to those on the Terrorism Watch List (Currah and Mulqueen 2011).

The US VISIT (United States Visitor and Immigration Status Indicator Technology) program is a collection of over 20 existing databases, making use of biometric information, such as fingerprints and retina scans on visitors, non-citizen workers, and immigrants as part of its IDENT database. All non-citizens entering and leaving the United States are entered into this database. In the wake of the 9/11 attacks, the United States expanded the NSEER (National Security Entry-Exit Registration) program to require a special registration, photographing, and fingerprinting of men over the age of 16 in the United States who are nationals of 25 countries.[3] The people targeted for this special biometric registration are primarily Arab and Muslim men, with the exception of North Korea. Travelers of certain nationalities (Iran, Iraq, Libya, Sudan, and Syria) are automatically registered, along with other individuals who meet certain criteria and are identified as a security concern (Epstein 2007, 158). Europe uses similar methods, employing Eurodac, a series of cross-national databases to check visa status histories, as well as fingerprint data of persons who enter the EU illegally, including asylum seekers (Van Der Ploeg 1999). The United States is also piloting several programs such as "Global Entry" and "Pre-Check" or "Nexus" (at the US-Canada border), in which frequent travelers (known as "trusted travelers") can move more quickly through security checks by providing biometric data such as fingerprints and iris scans.

The quest for biometric data to enhance the state's efforts to screen out risky or undesirable people is rooted in the sense that the "securitization of identity" (Rose 1999, 240), in terms of everyday life requiring the verification of one's identity, is insufficient for keeping out undesirable people. Risk and danger are not found in a willing subject, but in a suspect body. Identity verification systems could not, for example, flag and collect data on the "shoe bomber" Richard Reid, traveling under his own British passport, despite his two days of interrogation before he boarded a plane. Technologies aimed at securing bodies themselves are seen to provide a more promising avenue to eliminate risk. Biometrics are rooted in a biopolitics of examining, diagnosing, and classifying individual bodies in order to maximize the health of the population, transforming bodies into objects to be measured, mapped, and manipulated (Pugliese 2010). Persons may misrepresent their identities or their intentions, documents can be faked, but, in this security imagination, "bodies don't lie" (Aas 2006). From photographs on passports to fingerprints and iris scanners, one's body must be presented at borders, where parts of the body are made to stand in for an entire identity (Salter 2004; Adey 2009, 277). Greater knowledge about bodies themselves seems to be the only way to ensure the state's ability to secure its borders and protect the bodies of its population from harm. As such, airport security assemblages are increasingly relying upon making human bodies into signs that can be read for the "truth" of deviance or trustworthiness.

Within the airport security assemblage, the traveler is subjected to passive examinations of his or her body for signs of risk. "Passive" here denotes that travelers are not subject to any additional procedures requiring their cooperation; rather, crowds are scanned as people go about their business. In the United States, the SPOT (Screening Passengers by Observation Techniques) program trains airport security agents in the interpretation of facial "micro-expressions" that presumably reveal emotions involuntarily, and can be used to predict intentions and locate suspicious persons (Adey 2009, 280–282) A number of new technologies are in place or are being developed to detect "terrorists" based on the premise that the bodies of terrorists emit signs that can be read to reveal their true intentions. First called "Protect Hostile Intent," later renamed "The Future Attribute Screening Technology," or FAST, a new system is being tested by the US Department of Homeland Security to identify signs of danger in bodies. This system uses video cameras, lasers, and infrared sensors to scour crowds for unusual behavior. This system can monitor eye movements, heart rate, skin temperature, and breathing in an effort to detect potential terrorists. It also monitors people's faces for "micro-expressions" or unintentional facial tics that could indicate deception. Radar beams can track the gait of people moving through crowds in order to detect whether a person is carrying a heavy object. Such technologies are based on the assumption that not just the weapons the body carries can be detected—as in the use of bomb-sniffing dogs—but the dangerous body itself can be detected. This system is meant to detect deception, as it "works like a polygraph" by looking for anomalies in body temperature, pulse, and breathing. Unlike a polygraph, however, the FAST machine works when people walk by a set of cameras, rather than when they are hooked up to a machine, answering questions (Frank 2008). Such readings would supposedly provide information about which persons were agitated. The project manager claims, despite criticism that agitation or anxiety could be signs of many other conditions and circumstances besides hostile intent, that the system makes use of research that can purportedly distinguish between planning to cause harm and merely being annoyed or anxious. These technologies create and utilize knowledge of bodily affects to make global mobility secure by determining one's intentions (Adey 2009). The use of such "passive" surveillance techniques to read bodies for internal signs is considered to have the advantage of not stopping or slowing the circulation of people.

The most controversial components of the airport security assemblage are what are known as body scanners (sometimes "full body scanners" or "security scanners"). These scanners, previously deployed in Europe, were not supported in the United States until the December 2009 failed attack of the "underwear bomber." Schiphol Airport in the Netherlands employed the first body scanners in 2007 and the United States has now installed around a thousand in US airports. Body scanners are also used, or are set to be installed, in airports in Canada, South Korea, Australia, Nigeria, Russia, and Japan. They are also being deployed in courthouses, train stations, and subways. These scanners supplement the use of metal detectors and luggage scanners. There are two main types: backscatter and millimeter wave (the latter is the most commonly used in the United States). Both emit high-speed particles that penetrate clothes but not skin in order to produce an image of the human body that can be reviewed for signs of anomalies that may indicate explosives or other contraband that would not be picked up by a metal detector. The millimeter wave machines produce 3-D images. These images are transmitted to a computer terminal that is located away from the screening area, out of view of the travelers. Travelers cannot see what images are produced, nor are they aware of who is viewing them or to what ultimate ends such images may be used. The security personnel viewing the images signals to the screening personal whether or not to subject the traveler to additional checks, such as an "enhanced pat-down" or a strip search. Passengers who refuse the body scanners are subject to additional checks, including pat-downs. The distinction between "border policing" and "domestic law enforcement" is meaningless in this context, as these scanners are not only used for passengers traveling internationally, but for any passenger, including those flying domestically. Such risk management technologies do more than "detect" potential suicide bombers like December 2009's "underwear bomber." These tactics produce the body as an object that can be mapped for evidence of the mind that controls it.

Technologies such as the FAST and body scanners do not search for a bomb or other contraband, but search for clues of a dangerous or, more precisely, "destructive" body. These detection systems render the body as a set of signs to be read. Such technologies reduce the human body to an organism that consists of biological functions such as pulse, breath, gait, and temperature: activities of bodies, rather than people. What was invisible is made visible through X-rays, video cameras, and other machines that penetrate the body beyond the surface to read its signs in body temperature, breathing, and pulse. These technologies embody a discourse in which the technological gaze can penetrate the body and make it transparent. "Seeing" the human organism in greater depth is meant to translate into "seeing" the subject as dangerous or not. Determining the level of risk of a subject is a matter of reading further and further into his or her body. The surveillance of suspicious bodies constitutes bodies in a modernist discourse that effects a radical separation of subjectivity and body. Those who market and sell these technological systems advertise them as objective and able to eliminate systemic forms of discrimination since these technologies are "a new way of using surveillance that looks at activities, instead of looking for people" (Nitkin 2007). Technologies are more reliable and are not prone to human prejudices: "To them, everyone is the same color" (quoted in Magnet and Rodgers 2012, 101). As such, biometric technologies obscure the racial and colonial politics of such technologies, which are rooted in colonial attempts at identifying native populations and have developed from the interplay of political and sociocultural influences such as cranial phrenology, which contains an implicit assumption of whiteness as the peak of hierarchical racial categories (Cole 2001; Pugliese 2010, 76). Programs like SPOT, in which trained agents seek to recognize facial micro-expressions on the assumption that such expression are unintentional, and that they are consistent among all people (they are not variable or influenced by difference in cultural background), build upon what Pugliese calls "infrastructural whiteness" in that the presumed neutrality of such technologies is built upon a sustained history of producing racial subjects by comparison to a white norm that is measured through bodily attributes (2010, 56–79).

It is not only these technologies, but the knowledgeable practices of which these surveillance tools are a part, that constitute the unruly and destructive bodies. These technologies are not just about seeing further and more accurately into what the body conceals, but rather, such technologies are bound up in power relations that constitute the knowing subject who interprets the signs from the scanners and X-rays into a judgment about the riskiness of a particular, individualized body. Here, there is a shift between the contemporary airport as a site where travelers are forced to confess their identities and intentions, becoming suspicious subjects who must submit to the questioning of the sovereign (Salter 2007, 58–59), and the airport as a site in which the body is made into an object that can confess itself through a "digital dissection," in Hall and Amoore's phrase (2009).

The comparison of the scanning technology to medical practices of dissection is revealing for its foregrounding of the relationship between bodies, knowledge, and death. The anatomical dissection, in Catherine Waldby words, "marks the point at which medical science itself develops out of a productive encounter with death" (2000, 142). The corpse, in the Cartesian view of medical science, is a body that is no longer animated by a subject. It is an object, broken apart from subjectivity. The corpse as an object is an object of knowledge, in which a knower, an essentially disembodied subject, can peer into the body. This gaze has an epistemological foundation that conceives of the body not as a surface, but as a three-dimensional space (Foucault 1994 [1973], 165). Medical science, the science of prolonging life, relies upon the corpse to enable such knowledge, as life prevents certain forms of viewing into the body. Life, in its vitality and complexity, hides the truth of the body. In order to be "secured," the body must be stripped of the contingencies and unpredictability of embodied subjects.

Foucault describes practices of dissection as being the moment at which man both becomes a voluntarist subject, that is, a transcendent knower, and an object of knowledge, a species-body, an organism. It was through the dissection of corpses that "Western man could constitute himself in his own eyes as an object of science, he grasped himself within his language, and gave himself a discursive existence, only in the opening created by his own elimination" (Foucault 1994 [1973], 197–198). Man is not only the creator of techno-knowledge, but he is constituted by it. Airport security assemblages (re)produce Cartesian conception of bodies, in which bodies are machines that are animated by an external and essentially disembodied subject. These symptoms observed by people operating surveillance technologies are only temporary signs, because it is only death that reveals, in Foucault's words, the "luminous presence of the visible" (1994 [1973], 165). The transparent body is the corpse; life shields the truth by limiting the signs that can be perceived. At the moment of the screening, everyone becomes a corpse; that is, everybody is a body that is open and can be read.

In attempting to reveal the "truth" of bodies, bodies are constituted as abject. This is a central irony of the contemporary practice of security: in order to secure the living body, the body as organism, security has to produce abject bodies. Here, the biopolitical division between what must live and what must, in a sense, die, comes together. In order to protect the lively body of the traveler, his or her body must be dissected, made into a corpse. Security is, in this sense, no different from biomedical practices more broadly, as anatomization and visualization projects that enable the biopolitical imperative to foster life, to prevent and cure disease are built upon the "sacrifice" of dead bodies, from early dissections of murderers and prostitutes to the Visible Human Project (Waldby 2000) and the contemporary use of cadavers and their tissues in medical schools. These risk management technologies, which attempt to eliminate the wounding of bodies and the wounding of the *body politic*, thus paradoxically partake in a politics of inscribing bodies as always already polluted and profane, as already a corpse. Just as biomedical knowledge cannot fully grasp and contain the living body, but must rely on the corpse, so must security only secure the body as a kind of "living dead" organism. The "corpse" is a body that is "just" a body; it is not invested with a subject who can lie or hide the truth: it must tell the truth. The biopolitical security logic of securing life builds upon a close relationship with death, but is dependent upon that which it can secure—not bodies as fleshy embodied subjects, but bodies as information or code (Dillon and Reid 2001, 2009).

Bodies of Information

The bodies that are scanned for signs of danger or deviancy are not only produced as objects or corpses but are "dematerialized": the biometric discourse conceptualizes bodies as informational flows and patterns (revealing the porous and malleable borders of the body).[4] The body is digitized, encoded, and made into an image, or representation of the body. In this instantiation, the biopolitics of security and governing terror are aimed at the informational body not as DNA, but as images that can be read for signs of risk and danger by either humans or machines. The difference between systems such as FAST (previously Hostile Intent), which scan crowds, and the much more controversial "body-scanners" is the production of an image of an individual body that is reviewed by a person. While both produce the body of security as a disembodied body of information, the transformation of this information into an image viewed by a person lies at the heart of the controversy behind these scanners. At first, the images produced by some machines resembled X-rays, similar to those in use at clinics and hospitals. After protests, software was developed to interpret the digital images of bodies, so that they resembled chalk outlines, or "generic humans," with boxes denoting any anomalies, or "potential threat areas." "ProVision ATD" software, available for the millimeter wave scanners but not for backscatter machines, is meant to "eliminate privacy concerns," in the words of its manufacturer, by providing an "image-free solution." The software scans the data "without human intervention" and determines whether any threats are present (L3 Communications 2012). In the words of one headline, travelers are "chalky aliens" to the operators (Hawkins 2010). This technology can focus on parts of the body, rather than the unity of the body, in order to screen out sexual organs: it shows "an a-sexed or 'castrated' body without sexual organs: the ultimate, naked image of *homo sacer* as a non-erotic 'body' that only consists of dismembered 'organs'" (Diken and Laustsen 2006, 449). In the scanners, bodies are not just signs to be read, but the relevant bodies themselves are digital representations of bodies that are examined for signs of suspicious anomaly by authorized personnel or by a computer program. The ability for bodies to be transformed into information is, however, dependent upon a TSA agent pressing a pink or blue button, signifying whether the person about to be scanned presents as a man or woman (Bohling 2012, 2014). This suggests that the body must be read for signs of its sex by a person in order to be screened "accurately" by a machine.

Other software in use transforms the digitized images of bodies not to outlines of "generic humans," but strictly to signals of safe or suspicious, okay or not okay, by the use of green or red lights. This process is described by Bellanova and Fuster as a "disappearance" of the body (2013), but it is more accurately described as a dematerialization of the body. Bodies are dematerialized in their transformation into an informational pattern. Beyond the objectification—and *abjectification*—of bodies as transparent objects of dissection, bodies here are produced as code to be read by a competent viewer. In this way, the process of scanning resembles and reproduces many prior projects that locate social deviance in bodies that can be read with the proper tools and authoritative viewers. The practice of photographing criminals, for example, was begun as a means to identify and classify them. The body was conceived of as the "visual template of the soul" (Lalvani 1996, 92). As in the dissection, the body cannot be grasped in its fleshy liveliness but only through its disassembly and transformation. The code produced by both the "hardware" of the scanning machines and the "software" that "reads" the images is dematerialized—not located in space and time, but fully and transferrable and rewriteable.

The scanners produce an image of the human body that is seen by a TSA agent (or equivalent in another country). The agent views the images in a room away from the screening procedures, and thus cannot be seen by the traveler (nor can the images be seen by the travelers, ostensibly in order to protect travelers' privacy. However, the screening personnel are, of course, agents of the state. And so, the images produce not only a "looker," a knowing gazer in the subject who views the images and judges them "safe" and "normal" or "abnormal" and subject to additional screening procedures, but a state that can perform what has been called a "virtual strip search" (see also Amoore and Hall 2009, 321). If this strip search were carried out by other means, such as the forced searches of vaginas and rectums, which are central features of imprisonment, the state's violence most likely would be broadly condemned. The violence of the virtual strip search of the body scanners lies not only in the objectification of bodies as abject "corpses" but in the production of the body as information. Information not only can be read, but also can be stored, retrieved, copied, transferred, and rewritten— circulated and accumulated and transmitted in all the ways characteristic of information economies (Waldby 2000, 7).[5] Like the body of the torture victim, permeable to violence and to being inscribed by power, the body of information is permeable in that it is no longer, in Cartesian terms, *res extensa*, that is, a material body that takes up space. Rather, it is a body that is not bound to any particular space. There is thus a certain pornographic aspect to these bodies of information in the lack of control that individuals have over these images. The images are commodities as they enter into exchange relations. The cost of participating in networks of global travel— a necessity for globalized circulations of goods and services—is allowing these images to be produced.[6]

Airport security assemblages are built upon the assumption that security can be based upon "seeing" into our bodies and making them into information that can be read. The ability of bodies to exhibit signs that can be read as trustworthy indicators of a subject's riskiness or desirability is challenged by the lived experiences of trans- and genderqueer people: people whose gender identity and/or presentation do not match their travel documents or what is expected of them based on their bodily morphology.

MATERIALIZATION OF BODIES

The airport security assemblage is site of the state's investment in gathering information and classifying bodies as part of a project of state building. David Campbell's book *Writing Security* (2000 [1992]) influentially argued that security is a discursive practice through which states demarcate certain forms of life as normal, healthy, civilized, and worthy, and others as abnormal, sick, and barbaric. Contemporary security practices surrounding the body scanners are an example of this practice by producing deviant, suspicious bodies through their simultaneous objectification and dematerialization of bodies. Such bodies are the biologized internal enemies against whom society must defend itself (Foucault 2003). The biometric practices of state surveillance, including body scanners, take the body as the ultimate sign of truth. Margrit Shildrik reminds us that these categories of safe bodies and unruly, "monstrous" bodies are unstable: "'monstrous bodies' after all, are disruptive; they refuse to stay in place and displace the distinctions that show the border of the human subject" (Shildrick 2002, 4). Security is not so much about identifying deviant bodies, but about producing deviant bodies that serve to define safe, healthy, and moral bodies. In the transformation of bodies to digital images at the border, "deviant" or "unruly" bodies are made to confess. This has the effect of "outing" trans- and genderqueer[7] people and constituting them as potential threats in the non-alignment of bodily morphology and gender presentation and/or the use of prosthetics to create "unnatural" bodies. The airport security assemblage becomes a site revealing the state's investment in securing gender and the conditions under which certain bodies can lead livable lives.

The "virtual strip search" of the body scanners is not experienced as "virtual" but rather affects the experience of lived embodiment. The bodily experience of the airport security assemblages undermines the distinction between a "really existing body" and a "virtual body," or a body of pure information. The experience of trans- and genderqueer bodies shows more than how certain bodies are produced as unruly or deviant; these "deviant" bodies show the instability of bodies as signs of the "truth" of either sex or gender and refocus our attention on how regimes of truth produce certain lives as intelligible and others as unreal. The airport security assemblage is thus both a site for the production of abject "bodies of information" and a site that reveals what is at stake in certain understandings of the materiality or "realness" of bodies.

Airport security assemblages produce a narrative about bodies in which biological sex is immutable and determined by the body, and is either one of two categories (M or F); while gender might be socially constructed, it is produced in a predictable relation to sex such that one's sexed embodiment "matches" one's gender identity and gender presentation. A "misalignment" between gender presentation and sexed embodiment that may be revealed by a body scanner therefore represents a security threat to trans- individuals, as would a gender presentation that does not match the sex listed on a person's government ID, required by "Secure Flight." The National Transgender Advocacy Coalition (NTAC) has reported that one in five transgender travelers have felt harassed by TSA agents, and has documented stories of transgender people who were detained for several hours because their bodies did not conform with the agents' expectations in either body scan images or pat-downs. Transpeople have been subject to detention, strip searches, humiliating questions, and reviews by bomb squads because their bodies do not match the expectations of security personnel (Keisling, Kendall, and Davis 2010; Bohling 2014; Sjoberg 2014, 85–90; Coyote 2010, Costello 2012).

The airport security assemblage orders bodies according to a normative sex/gender regime that casts trans-, genderqueer, and gender non-conforming people as threats and unruly bodies. The point here is not only that a relatively small number of people are discriminated against in airport security assemblages, although this is certainly true, and it is undoubtedly true regarding other non-normative bodies as well, such as the racialized bodies or the bodies of people with disabilities. What is also at stake is how materiality and language are understood in terms of securing bodies. In a regime in which the materiality of one's body is supposed to be the ultimate sign of riskiness, or truthworthiness, the experience of trans- and genderqueer people challenge the terms in which "materiality" is understood.

Butler's performative theory of gender argues that one cannot meaningfully distinguish between gender as a product of human ideas and culture, and sex, which is presumed to exist naturally as a brute fact outside human influence. In other words, Butler argues that sex is not to nature what gender is to culture; rather, gender "designate[s] that very apparatus of productions whereby the sexes themselves are established" (Butler 1999 [1990], 11). Sex differences are not only reproduced through discourses of gender, but both sex and gender are produced and regulated by what Butler refers to as the "heterosexual matrix." It is not only gender norm, but also the heterosexual matrix that produces the illusion of the naturalness of sex and gender. Norms of heterosexuality stabilize both sex and gender through a "grid of intelligibility." "Intelligible genders are those which in some sense institute and maintain relations of coherence and continuity among sex, gender, sexual practice, and desire" (Butler 1990, 17). Heteronormativity is premised on the belief that males are supposed to act masculine and desire females, and females are supposed to act feminine and desire men. If sex, gender, sexual practice, and desire do not line up in the way in which the heterosexual matrix demands, the subject will be unintelligible, not fully human. Any "break" between biological sex, gender performance, and desire is foreclosed as non-normative and "unreal" (Butler 1990, 17). Butler theorizes materiality not as a question of epistemological "reality," but as a matter of the livability of certain lives: whether the norms governing gender, race, sexuality, nationality, and other categories allow one to be recognized as a human subject. If lives deviate from recognizable, viable subjectivity, their lives will be unreal; they will not be bodies that "matter." The experience of trans- and genderqueer people, as those embodied in a way that does not cohere with the norms of the heterosexual matrix, provides insight into how norms of gender are embedded into the airport security assemblage.

Gender norms are not fixed or universal, nor do they exist in a vacuum. Gender norms are also linked to the production of racial distinctions, for example; Somerville argues that black people in the United States have been medically and culturally understood to have racialized physical characteristics that directly connect to their perceived abnormality in terms of gender and sexuality (2000). Stoler has also shown that gender and sexuality were sites in which European racial superiority was produced and maintained through the eroticization of racialized bodies and the surveillance of white bodies (Stoler 2002, 185–197). African-American women with "natural" or "Afro" style hair have had their hair patted down, despite not having set off any alarms or any other signs of "suspiciousness" in US airport security screening procedures (most famously in the case of Solange Knowles in 2011) (Sharkey 2011). As such, competently practicing gender in airport security practices also means conforming to ideas about proper gender appearance, which are grounded in ideals of whiteness, class privilege, and heterosexuality (see also Beauchamp 2009).[8]

Even before the installation of body scanners, the airport has been a place of insecurity for trans- and genderqueer people due to fears of being "outed" because their gender presentation does not "pass" in the eyes of officials or does not matching their official documents. The existence of body scanners has made this process especially fraught. First, in the United States, "Secure Flight" requires that a person booking a flight originating or departing within the United States submit a gender marker (M or F), which must match his or her state-issued documents. This information is also used to identify the individual at the airport. While plans are being developed and proposed to store biometric information on passports in various jurisdictions, in the United States, a gender marker (M or F)[9] is the only form of bodily information on passports (other than photographs, which may be up to 10 years old). This information is supposed to be compared with other databases in order to decrease the number of "false positives" of people being identified as someone on the "no-fly" list. In addition, the United States passed the REAL ID law in 2005 that enabled comparing identification data across agencies and jurisdictions in an effort to weed out invalid IDs or those obtained under false pretenses, which has led to considerable problems for trans- people whose official identification documents might be in more than one gender (Spade

2008). The inclusion of M or F as information about a passenger assumes that this is a permanent feature of the body. It furthermore assumes that there is a straightforward, commonsense relationship between the sex one is assigned at birth, one's gender identity, one's gender presentation (how one is perceived by others), and the gender classification on identity documents (Currah and Mulqueen 2011). Gender markers are also used by security agents to check the identity of the passenger being inspected. Flying thus requires a "match" between one's gender presentation (the gender that a person is recognized by others as) and the sex on one's official documents, which is by no means an easy or uncomplicated process. To understand why requires an understanding of how different state agencies determine "sex."

Sex is usually thought of as a binary and natural feature of bodies. If we are talking about sex as a biological characteristic, we might locate it in one's genetic makeup, or chromosomal sex, one's external morphological sex (visible genitals), one's internal morphological sex (testes, uterus, ovaries), one's secondary sex characteristics (breasts, Adam's apple), or one's hormonal sex (androgyne sensitivity). Usually a visual inspection of an infant's genitalia at birth is used to assign that child to a sex, but somewhere around one percent of children are born with atypical genitalia (Beemyn and Rankin 2011, 18). Such children are known as "intersex," or as patients diagnosed with a disorder of sex development. Surgery and other types of ongoing medical interventions are often performed on such infants to make their bodies conform to gender and heterosexual expectations, regardless of harm done to future reproductive or sexual capacities of the child (Fausto-Sterling 2000, 45–77; Wilchins 2004, 71–83; Karkazis 2008). It is ideas about gender and sexuality that determine, for example, the difference between a phallus that is large enough to be considered a penis, and one that is deemed too small and that must be altered into a clitoris. The M or F assigned to such children is not a reflection of the "truth" of sex based on genitals, but is the result of bodies being altered to fit sociocultural ideas about what "natural" bodies look like. The category of "intersex" exists because such bodies violate cultural rules about gender (Karkazis 2008, 5). The medical interventions taken to make bodies conform to ultimately arbitrary ideas about what proper genitals should look and function like poses a challenge to the "naturalness" of sex. In such cases, "[m]alleability is... violently imposed. And naturalness is artificially induced" (Butler 2004b, 66).

If sex assigned at birth is laden with the imposition of gendered ideas about bodies, so too are other means of identifying sex on official documents, such as driver's licenses, passports, Social Security cards, or other identification that is needed to access benefits, medical records, insurance, and so forth. Different jurisdictions have different requirements for changing one's legal gender identifier, while some countries refuse to allow legal changes to be made. Frequently, one must have a diagnosis of gender identity disorder and have undertaken permanent or semi-permanent bodily alternations through surgery and hormones. Such rules make the majority of trans- and genderqueer people ineligible to change their gender marker.[10] Canada's regulations prohibit travelers whose gender does not appear to match their official documents from flying. In order to officially change one's "sex" designation in Canada, one has to have proof that sex-reassignment surgery has taken place or will take place within a year. In the United States, states have the ability to amend or issue new birth certificates, although Idaho, Tennessee, and Ohio refuse to do so (and Texas will not without a court order) (Spade 2008). The US State Department has allowed gender marker changes to be made on passports, if a statement by a physician is given that the individual has undergone treatment for transitioning to the new gender.[11] The UK's Gender Recognition Act allows people to apply to a panel for the purposes of attaining a Gender Recognition Certificate entitling them to be identified with the gender on that certificate "for all purposes." Individuals seeking this certificate are required to obtain a diagnosis of persistent gender dysphoria and must convince a panel that it is their intention to live in the new gender for the rest of their lives (medical treatment, but not necessarily surgery, is required) (GIRES 2012).

Such requirements mean that trans- and genderqueer people who wish to be officially recognized as a member of a gender they were not assigned at birth must appeal to different state agencies, and such recognition is contingent upon pathologization and, frequently, undertaking permanent bodily alteration. In short, the state forces trans- people to align their sex with their gender. Because different jurisdictions have different requirements for changing the gender marker on one's birth certificate, driver's license, and other identity documents, the result is that trans- people who wish to officially change their gender markers have different requirements based on where they live, and where they were born (in the case of birth certificates). One telling example is the disparity between the laws of New York City and New York State. If one was born in New York City, changing the gender marker on one's birth certificate requires the surgical intervention of penectomy or hysterectomy and mastectomy (removal of the penis or removal of the uterus and breasts); if one was born in New York State, there is still a surgical requirement, only for a phalloplasty or vaginoplasty (the construction of a phallus or vagina) (Spade 2008, 736;

Salamon 2010, 189). Only a few jurisdictions have self-identification, that is, persons declaring they wish to be considered members of the opposite gender without proving some kind of medical intervention to a state agency.[12] Whereas one might "pass" for a particular gender in everyday life, the gender marker on identity documents, including those required for travel, depend upon the demands of the agency issuing the documents, which are often different or contradictory. The "M" or "F" on these documents is not a reflection of the truth of bodies, but is performatively the truth of sex, which is not necessarily the truth of the individuals in question. Such documents reveal that sex as a category belongs to the state, in its various administrative capacities (Salamon 2010, 183). While most cis-people associate transgender and transsexual people with sex reassignment surgeries and other medical interventions, the vast majority of people who identify as trans- or genderqueer do not undertake such measures (Beemyn and Rankin 2011, 124). According to one recent study carried out in the United States, 80 percent of trans-women and 98 percent of trans-men have not undergone genital surgery (Grant, Mottet, and Tanis 2010; Spade 2011, 145). Most trans- and genderqueer people are thus constituted as unruly bodies, bodies that have not been normalized according to the gendered imperatives of various agencies and jurisdictions of the state.

Airport security assemblages are a site at which adherence to gender norms designates one as "safe," and gender non-conformity can lead to the perception of one as a threat. The suspicion of trans- people in the airport security assemblage is partly linked to a fear that "cross-dressing" may be a tactic employed by terrorists to evade security. For example, a Department of Homeland Security memo warned, "Terrorists will employ novel methods to artfully conceal suicide devices. Male bombers may dress as females in order to discourage scrutiny" (DHS 2003). Certainly, men have worn "veils" as a tactic in various conflicts, most notably, in the Algerian War.[13] The danger of "men" dressed as "women" to the security assemblage is not just in "discouraging scrutiny" because women are assumed to be less dangerous, or because their bodies may not be inspected as closely for fear of complaints. It is also considered a threat based upon the state's (in)ability to identify certain subjects with certain bodies, as the airport security assemblage does in its "Secure Flight" program before the body scanning procedures, in which a person is required to submit a gender identification that matches state-issued documents. The "crossdresser" as potential "terrorist" also plays into trans-phobic discourses of trans- people as deceivers who conceal their "real" gender (see Bettcher 2007).

A "misalignment" between gender presentation and sexed embodiment that may be revealed by a body scanner therefore represents a security threat to trans- individuals, as would a gender presentation that does not match the sex listed on a person's government ID, required by "Secure Flight." Everyone might be the same color, according to the body scanners, but not everyone is the same sex and/or gender. The employees operating the body scanners are trained to seek out "anomalies" in bodies, which may "out" a trans- person. The body scanners that are outfitted with "ProVision ATD" (for Automated Threat Detection) scan bodies and produce images of "gender neutral" bodies (basically outlines) with anomalies marked in colored boxes. However, before a person is scanned, an employee must press a pink or blue button on the screen, indicating the gender of the traveler. The scanners thus rely upon the social recognition of a person's gender presentation as evidence of their sex, in order to better produce images of "gender neutral bodies." These images of "gender neutral bodies" have been described as "chalky aliens," reinforcing the idea that a body that is not marked by gender is an inhuman body (Amoore and Hall 2009). The United States has assured travelers that the Automated Threat Detection software is used to blur out images of genitals, and Canada has begun to use this technology as of 2013.

Security practices meant to identify the bodies of terrorists produce a discourse of embodiment that locates threat in queer bodies and reproduces the association of sexual and gender deviance with security threats (Campbell 2000 [1992], 157–160). This should not be understood as an example of a flawed process of "securitization" in which an object or category that was not previously associated with matters of security becomes discursively drawn into the realm of security by a matter of accident or oversight. Such a view would presume a subject doing the securitization, a speaking subject that exists prior to the practices involved in securitizing.[14] Trans- people are not securitized; rather, the emphasis that security practices place on the production and regulation of "natural" bodies reinforces what Butler refers to as a "heterosexual matrix." Through the airport security assemblage, the "naturalness" of bodies is revealed as not only a norm, but a norm that carries the weight of state control and invocations of security behind it.

How a body takes on or becomes a gender is a matter of how the body is lived, and can pose a challenge to bodily norms. The "gendering" of a body, as a performative practice, also poses a challenge to the "informationalization" of bodies, the attempt to make bodies (or rather, embodied subjects) disappear into the realm of language, the sign, or binary code. This is a fundamental aspect of what it means to be an embodied subject: the inscription of the body by powerful norms is never complete: "bodies never quite comply with the norms by which their materialization is compelled" (Butler 1993, 2). In her discussion of posthuman embodiment, N. Katherine Hayles reminds us, "Embodiment is akin to articulation in that it is inherently performative, subject to individual enactments, and therefore always to some extent improvisational. Whereas the body can disappear into information with scarcely a murmur of protest, embodiment cannot, for it is tied to the circumstances of the occasion and the person" (1993, 156). The bodies of trans- and genderqueer people demonstrate this point aptly: *bodies* can be made into information, digitized and referenced by technological assemblages as safe or unsafe, but our lived embodiment is much more complex and exceeds the norms that constitute our bodies. This in no way denies that people do not encounter the world with bodies that possess certain capacities and functions that differ. However, the lived body as a category is open to the ways in which people experience a "felt sense" of their bodies, desire, and sexual feeling in ways that do not necessarily correspond to sex, gender binaries, or heterosexual norms. For Young, the concept of the "lived body" recognizes that subjectivity is conditioned by the social world in ways that people have not chosen, but these unchosen facts are lived in their own way (Young 2002, 418).

Butler's articulation of the formation of the embodied explains the process of materialization as a "doing," a kind of practice, and thus changeable—but not entirely agentic. Trans- and genderqueer bodies are unsafe in and to the airport security assemblage because they have not been made secure, or docile, by the state or its various entities and agencies. While one of the goals of biometrics and their use in airport security assemblages is to use the body as a sign that a subject is the same over time (as compared to distinguishing one subject from another), the instability of gender as a marker of identity is central to the embodied experience of trans- and genderqueer people. Marked by a sense of fluidity, trans- and genderqueer can mean that the body is not understood as static, as an accomplished fact, but as a mode of becoming (Butler 2004b, 29). Because the lived experience of trans- people is of a body at odds with cultural expectations (including, in the case of some trans- people, that one is in the "wrong body") trans- people's lived bodies suggest that bodies can exceed what is "known" about bodies and can escape the attempts to secure them (see also Salamon 2010, 91–92). In a discussion about the formation of racialized bodies of surveillance in post–9/11 security regimes, Jasbir Puar writes, "what is being preempted is not the danger of the known subject but the danger of not-knowing" (2007, 185). A similar statement can be made about the danger that certain gender identities and presentations pose in airport security assemblages. In attempts at making bodies readable according to certain knowledgeable regimes, "knowing" the body is effectively an attempt to stabilize a certain gender regime of the sex one is assigned at birth. In such a regime, the bodies of trans- and genderqueer people are effectively erased as not conforming to certain bodily truths, and their lives become unthinkable, unlivable places to occupy. Airport security assemblages are thus a site at which the normative violence of sex and gender becomes visible, but can also be resisted.

Resistance

Airport security assemblages, especially the component of body scanners, are being resisted in various ways. While the TSA in the United States is probably correct that most people have acquiesced to the new procedures, there have been several strands of criticism and opposition to the post–9/11 security protocols. The question of resistance usually presumes an action taken by a willing subject to overcome a broader, often impersonal force; such a view of the subject is untenable if one understands subject formation to entail being formed, that is, being *subject to* norms that one did not choose and, indeed, norms such as gender binaries and heteronormativity that one might wish to change. This section addresses three categories of resistance to airport security assemblages, which I refer to as "don't touch my junk," "strategic visibility," and "fleshmobs."

If we are to think through the question of normative violence, that is, which bodies are intelligible according to norms, and how bodies live existing norms, Butler's example of drag as parody is an instructive contrast to a vision of resistance that would reaffirm a sovereign subject as the sole determinant of his body. Butler uses the practice of drag to (which, it should be noted, is not the same as being trans- or genderqueer) highlight the ways in which structures of gender can be parodied and possibly subverted. While her arguments on drag are often misunderstood by critics, these arguments point us toward thinking of the possibilities of undermining the heterosexual matrix and, specifically to the airport security assemblage, the regime of visual embodiment/disembodiment.

Butler argues that some practices within queer cultures, including drag, "often thematize 'the natural' in parodic contexts that bring into relief the performative construction of an original and true sex" (Butler 1990, viii). Not all "drag" performances are subversive; drag can be used to reinforce the supposedly natural corollary between sex, gender, and desire as well. However, what a subversive practice like drag can do is challenge the norm that certain gender performances, certain desires, and certain bodies are the natural order of things. Sandy Stone draws upon Butler's work to articulate the *genre* of the "transsexual" (not necessarily the individual "transsexual" person) as "a set of embodied texts whose potential for the *productive* disruption of structures sexuality and spectra of desire has yet to be explored" (1997, 352). Trans- people and genderqueer people's "performance" of gender is no more "false" or different from any other performance of gender, expect that the heterosexual matrix which insists upon a binary distinction between genders and a strict correspondence between sexed embodiment, gender, and desire makes certain performances of gender normative, and others "unthinkable" or "unlivable." The heterosexual matrix has the effect of making the correspondence between M and F sexed bodies, masculine and feminine genders, and heterosexual desire appear natural. Drag can question the means by which reality is made and asks us to consider the way in which being called real or being called unreal can be not only a means of social control but also a form of dehumanizing violence (Butler 2004b, 217). The attempts by the airport security assemblage to isolate bodies from such identity and history rely on a sense of the body as foundational—an essence of the person that cannot lie. In the context of the airport security assemblage, which is so intent upon revealing the "truth" of bodies in the name of security, having a non-normatively gendered body itself can be a performance that challenges the naturalness of sex and of bodies as stable referents more generally, regardless of the intentions of the trans- or genderqueer subject. The violence done to trans- and genderqueer bodies in the airport security assemblage is predicated upon a prior violence of the heterosexual matrix, which prescribes certain gendered performances for certain embodied subjects and renders non-gender-conforming people unintelligible to the state in this security assemblage. In what follows, I discuss three responses to the airport security assemblages in terms of whether they not only protest the security protocols, but whether they do so in a way that challenges the production of naturalized bodies as the sign of security.

The first protest strategy I'll call, in reference to the meme of early 2011, "don't touch my junk." This strategy is a protest based upon a comparison of the production of an image of the body (or a pat-down) with sexual assault, an affront to the body's integrity. For example, women have complained that they are being singled out for extra security screening by agents who are more interested in a voyeuristic look at their bodies than in conducting random checks. On these complaints, one journalist reported this statement by a woman: "'I feel like I was totally exposed,' said Ellen

Terrell, who is a wife and mother. 'They wanted a nice good look'" (Female Passengers Say They're Targeted by TSA 2012). That the journalist chose to mention that Terrell is a wife and mother seems to be an effort to note that Terrell's body is supposed to be "off-limits," protected from sexual advances and intrusions by the institutions of marriage and motherhood. The article also mentions that the TSA agent who sent her through the machine a total of three times also commented on the passenger's "cute figure." The "looker," the female TSA agent, is figured as a lesbian, sexually deviant and inappropriately using her status as an agent of the state to harass this respectable, "safe" woman who, because of her commitment to heteronormative institutions, should be off-limits and who cannot be a participant in sexually deviant practices. Here, we see a protest of the sexualization and objectification of a woman's body in the airport security apparatus take the form of a reassertion of the terms of bodily respectability—a body that is supposed to be "off-limits" to "lookers."

Because of the eroticism implicit in being an object of the gaze, anger is felt when bodies are turned into objects that we don't usually objectify, such as children and the elderly.[15] Famously, the words of John Tynor became a rallying cry against the full-body scanners. After refusing to go through the scanners, Tynor said to the TSA agent about to do a pat-down, "If you touch my junk I will have you arrested." A video clip of this encounter "went viral" and the phrase "don't touch my junk" became something of a rallying cry against airport security procedures, seen as unnecessary for most of the population and only installed to avoid profiling passengers by race or other outward signs of danger or otherness. As Charles Krauthammer restated this sentiment, "Don't touch my junk, you airport security goon—my package belongs to no one but me, and do you really think I'm a Nigerian nut job preparing for my 72-virgin orgy by blowing my johnson to kingdom come?" (2010). "Don't touch my junk" is a statement that protests the airport security regime under the privilege of white masculinity. The reference to "junk" is to masculine genitalia, and the threat to have the TSA agent arrested is a challenge to the power dynamics of the security assemblage, which posits TSA agents as privileged knowers and neutral observers of the body. The cry of "don't touch my junk" is a charge that the act of a pat-down (or perhaps the unauthorized viewing of the body involved in the full-body scanner, which Tynor refused) is an act of sexual assault, done by a perverted individual working on behalf of the state. Such protests and the resonance of "don't touch my junk" as a rallying cry against these invasive procedures also speak to the invisibility of racialized men's experience of police surveillance and harassment, such as "stop and frisk" policies that disproportionately target black and other minority men, but which are not met with widespread outcry or media attention. Protests on behalf of white men, married mothers, children, and the elderly forced to endure the "enhanced pat-downs" or full-body scanners reproduce the "normalcy" of certain bodies, in that they are not eligible for the sexualized objectification that these practices involve. As Jordanova puts it, "Unveiling men makes no sense, possibly because neither mystery nor modesty are male preserves but are attributes of the other" (1989, 110). Such protests reproduce the body (or rather, some bodies) as sovereign and inviolable, and a sovereign subject who can protect it and hide it from unwanted intruders. This logic reinforces the logic of the security state and the airport security assemblages themselves as protecting a territory by determining who can enter and who cannot.

While the "don't touch my junk" style protests that construct the body as a sovereign site of rights and privacy against the sexual predations of others are about decreasing the visibility of bodies, the "strategic visibility" (in the words of Beauchamp 2009) strategy is about increasing the visibility of the trans- body *as* trans-. "Strategic visibility" is not a protest against airport security assemblages; rather, it is an attempt to mold oneself to the requirements of the assemblage in order to pass through the security protocols more efficiently, thus minimizing the chance of being marked as a potential threat by an official. The National Transgender Advocacy Coalition (NTAC) has suggested that transsexual and transgender people disclose their status to security personnel, carrying with them papers with notes from surgeons and official name-change documents, if applicable. Such a strategy for "openness" may make travel easier for trans- people to travel without being subjected to additional screenings, but it comes with other risks. Under the advice of the NTAC, trans- and genderqueer people would also need to preemptively "out" themselves, which may carry implications for their personal lives and security, especially in smaller airports that service smaller areas in which travelers and security screeners may not be strangers to one another. Furthermore, this strategy relies upon obtaining official documentation and/or medical intervention, which, as discussed earlier, can be a very fraught process that most trans- and genderqueer people are not able to, or choose not to undertake. Choosing to be strategically visible as trans-, rather than "going stealth," as the NTAC advises, may be a less risky tactic for some trans- bodies, but it also comes at the cost of identifying oneself as trans- rather than as a member of the gender one identifies with or presents as. Thus, such a move reproduces assigned sex or "natural sex" as the truth of the body in asking trans- people to disclose that their gender presentation is anomalous or atypical in relation to their bodily morphology. Seeking "strategic visibility" as a means of avoiding extra screenings and delays at airports also entails aligning oneself as a "good" or "safe" trans- person, proving that one has nothing to hide, and erasing any similarity with the deceptive terrorist or immigrant. Such a move, as Beauchamp argues, requires the scapegoating of other bodies and shifts the focus in trans- politics from protecting trans-bodies from the violence of the state to helping the nation protect itself from the threatening terrorist (a move that relies upon privileges of race and economic class) (Beauchamp 2009, 364).

If "don't touch my junk" is about making bodies less visible, and "strategic visibility" is, precisely, about increasing visibility in order to streamline the airport security process, a type of protest known as "flesh-mobs" (after the performance art style of "flashmobs") is about making bodies hypervisible. In Germany, critics of the security procedures have subjected themselves to screenings while naked, or nearly naked. These "fleshmobs" critique the excess of vision that characterizes the scanners' "virtual strip search" (Magnet and Rodgers 2012) by making other travelers and airport personnel, rather than only authorized government personnel, into observers of bodies. Some of these protesters have done even more to make their bodies "legible" according to the terms of the security assemblage: one German protester wrote "prosthetic" on her arm, and "piercing" with an arrow pointed at her breast (Zetter 2010). John Brennan, a man from Portland, Oregon, was acquitted on charges of indecent exposure for stripping in protest of TSA screening procedures. Brennan's statement points to the reversal of the power dynamics in such an act: "The irony that they want to see me naked, but I don't get to take off my clothes off.. . . You have all these machines that pretend to do it" (KATU 2012).

Unlike "don't touch my junk" protests, which are about preserving the body as sovereign, especially for those viewed as unlikely to constitute terrorist threats (such as children, the elderly, "wives and mothers," and white men), "fleshmob" protests are not about defending a liberal sphere of autonomy against government intrusion so much as challenging the logics of bodily visibility. By stripping down, fleshmobs render body-scanning procedures a meaningless gesture in terms of producing information, and only valuable as a means of humiliation and domination. In his court testimony, Brennan described his act of stripping naked as intended to reveal to the TSA the effect its policies have on passengers, especially of the body-scanning procedures: "I want to show them it's a two-way street. . . I don't like a naked picture of me being available" (Duara 2012). Clearly, the "two-way street" Brennan is referring to does not mean that TSA personnel are made naked and subject to the gaze of passengers; rather, the "two-way street" is about control over viewing the body. Stripping naked at security screenings is a refusal to have one's body made into an image viewed and interpreted only by unseen, authorized viewers (and possibly leaked into wider circulation) and turns the tables by making the naked body visible to everyone in the vicinity. The airport security assemblages are made to appear meaningless by the redistribution of economies of observers and observed: bystanders are not only bodies waiting to be scanned themselves, but are viewers of the bodies of the fleshmobs as well. Such observers are necessary for the protest: this protest of excessive visibility only works if there is an audience to view bodies that are both "safe" in that they could not be concealing contraband, and are "pornographic" in the nakedness of their bodies. The protest hinges on the juxtaposition of the scandal of too much visibility of naked bodies in public spaces with the visibility of naked bodies as a security measure. The naked protesters, or "fleshmobs," court arrest that would reveal the hypocrisy of the state producing images of naked bodies for their own purposes, while disallowing nakedness in general. In these protests, the naked body of the security assemblage that was a "safe" body because it has nothing to hide becomes a dangerous body as it subverts the logic implicit in the security assemblages of the state as authorized viewer of the body. By becoming a "dangerous body," the "naked body" parodies the logic of the airport security apparatus. In making their bodies hypervisible, "fleshmob" protesters destabilize the state's prerogative to surveil bodies and the production of bodies as state-owned information.

CONCLUSION

The airport security assemblage highlights in stark terms the body of contemporary security practices as a body that is simultaneously made into "pure body," stripped of subjectivity and transformed into a sign of riskiness or non-riskiness. Such practices reveal how the desire to "make live" involves a close encounter with death, as the very bodies that are intended to be fostered and protected are transformed into digital corpses, as bodies that must die as subjects in order to live. The ontological and political dilemmas of such a system of security are made apparent in analyzing the lived experience of individuals whose gender performance, state-approved gender marker, and sexed embodiment do not conform to the expectations of the norm of the heterosexual matrix. The body as signifier for truth collapses under a Butlerian reading of such gender performances. Such disunities reveal the instability of the category of sex and also draw attention to the ways in which "the body" as a reference of security is also unstable. Attempts to secure "the body" are ultimately incomplete: not only do the experiences of trans- and genderqueer people subvert the assumptions of the airport security assemblage, but other forms of resistance, most notably those of "fleshmobs," are capable of challenging the state as the ultimate viewer and producer of knowledge about bodies. The lived body, the body that acts in and experiences the world, poses a challenge to regimes that would effectively dematerialize the body by making it either into a sign to be read, or, as the next chapter discusses, making it into a reader of signs.

CHAPTER 5

Body Counts

The Politics of Embodiment in Precision Warfare

RPAs [remote-piloted aircraft] are now part of our DNA.
— Major Bryan Callahan (Pitzke 2010)

Sitting in the "cockpit" of a windowless container filled with computer monitors and keyboards somewhere in the New Mexico desert, Brandon Bryant[1] received the order to fire a missile from the drone he was helping a pilot to operate on a house in Afghanistan. In the 16-second delay between the launch of the laser-targeted missile and the impact of that missile, a child walked around the corner, into view on the monitor. Bryant then saw the explosion and the building collapse, but no sign of the child. He related the next moments to a journalist:

"Did we just kill a kid?" he asked the man sitting next to him. "Yeah, I guess that was a kid," the pilot replied. "Was that a kid?" they wrote into a chat window on the monitor. Then, someone they didn't know answered, someone sitting in a military command center somewhere in the world who had observed their attack. "No. That was a dog," the person wrote. They reviewed the scene on video. A dog on two legs? (Abé 2012)

I recount this story not only because of the horror evoked by the casual violence and erasure of human suffering and death. This story also illustrates the specificity and detail of the visual imagery provided by drones, as well as the distribution of decision-making and action across a human/

technological system that constitutes the embodiment of precision warfare. In this practice of war, war is not disembodied, but relationally and asymmetrically embodied in the figure of the posthuman, a figure that enables not only the destruction of bodies, but the production of those bodies as ungrievable, as bodies that never existed in the first place. In Bryant's story, "[t]he child, if there had been a child, was an infrared ghost" (Power 2013).

Precision warfare is characterized by the use of precision-guided munitions, whether on manned aircraft or, increasingly, on drones, more formally known as unmanned aerial vehicles (UAVs) or remotely piloted aircraft (RPAs), used to target buildings, objects, or individuals. While the term "precision warfare" refers to a mode of violence, precision wars are waged as a form of global governance (Dillon and Reid 2001). Precision warfare, especially with the use of drones, is often perceived as a "disembodied" form of war because of the distance between the body of pilot or drone operator and the bodies that are killed or injured; however, viewed from a posthuman perspective informed by feminist theory, we see the violent practices of precision bombing as performatively constituting the figures of the precision bomber or drone operator, the targeted "militant," and the unknown or unseeable "civilians." These bodies are not prior to the practices of precision bombing, but exist in relation to one other and to technology in the practice of precision warfare.

PRECISION WARFARE AS BIOPOLITICAL WARFARE

The goal of precision warfare is absolute discrimination between combatants and civilians, a feat that depends upon absolute knowledge of the difference. It is also about protecting the lives of those fighting the wars. Precision warfare is predicated upon faith in technological solutions to the problem of discrimination: how to learn who is a civilian and who is a combatant, and how to spare civilians while killing the right people in the "vital massacres": what Foucault describes as necessary deaths for the purpose of fostering other lives (1978, 137). In precision warfare, this is not a political question but a question of timely information processing. Precision warfare is a very attractive form of security practice in liberal states for three related reasons. First, by using these technologies, civilian deaths are transformed from "massacres" to "accidents," or even are defined away altogether, and warfare can be presented as much more humane. Second, precision warfare takes place in a discourse of risk-management and is therefore is driven by a biopolitical rationale of state power. Third, there is (virtually) no reciprocal risk of death or injury to the pilots or drone operators; in the imagination of precision warfare, the pilots and drone operators are invulnerable.

In discourses of precision warfare, the deaths of civilians occupy a substantial, if not crucial, role. The sparing of civilian lives is given as a key rationale (second only to protecting the lives of servicemen and women) for the development and use of precision weapons. Wars are to be fought "humanely": for humanitarian purposes and waged with humane weapons and techniques (Coker 2001). Certainly the shift from the area bombing of World War II and Vietnam to the precision bombing of the Gulf War, Kosovo, Afghanistan, and Iraq may parallel the shift from punishment to more "humane," biopolitical forms of warfare, in which preservation of (certain) lives is necessary for the strategic and political success of the war. This allows for the greater use of military force on behalf of "humanitarian" projects because force can be deployed with less harm to "innocents," and citizens can be assured that due effort and care are being taken to spare the lives of civilians. Thus, military planners will use precision-guided bombs or drones in an attempt to destroy targets within cities or residential areas, targets that may have been off-limits in the past. Precision-guided munitions (PGMs) have increased as a percentage of total bombs dropped from 7 percent in the first Gulf War in 1991 to around 60 percent in the initial incursion into Afghanistan in 2001–2002. When civilians are killed, their deaths are not caused by the intentional killing of sovereign power, but are naturalized as unavoidable accidents, an inevitable if regrettable outcome (Owens 2003; Zehfuss 2011). The use of force on behalf of universal values such as human rights and the prevention of genocide can thus be justified.

Second, the technologies of precision warfare are governed by the logic of risk management and minimization that is well suited to the biopolitical governance of liberal societies.[2] Precision bombing, like its less accurate predecessor, strategic bombing, is an exercise of sovereign power by deciding who will die and who shall be left alone to live. The vision of precision bombing, of perfect accuracy in targeting, conveys a desire for absolute sovereign power—a desire manifest in the use of PGMs and drones to target specific individuals, with perfect knowledge and accuracy—and blurs the line between bombing and execution. The exercise of this sovereign power is made possible by various biopolitical networks of surveillance and precision targeting. Precision warfare is especially suited for a biopolitical approach because the very nature of precision bombing is of calculated risk, both in terms of the probability of hitting a target accurately and in the risk to civilians. The CEP, or circular error probability, is how "precision" is measured in laser or GPS-guided munitions. The CEP measures the average distance from a target that the bomb will hit in terms of 50 percent of hits within a certain radius. Such probabilities have been increasingly steadily.[3] Yet, the CEP is but the margin of error that is built into the system of targeting in precision warfare, which also includes the difference in where the target is and where the bomb is aimed at, as well as the vast realm of potential intelligence errors (Zehfuss 2011, 549). Challenging this vision of the perfectability of war, Beier argues, "there is an indeterminacy inherent in the use of precision-guided munitions (PGMs), even when the weapons themselves perform as intended" (2006, 267). Precision warfare also makes calculations about the risks to civilians, as targeting decisions are dependent upon an assessment of possible civilian casualties weighed against the importance of the destruction of the target. Such calculations often incorporate legal analyses as to the permissibility of attacks under the Geneva Conventions and other applicable laws.[4] Doctrines of risk-management entail bureaucratic and technocratic forms of governance that are dependent upon the production of a vast amount of information about the governed.

In the last decade or so, UAVs have been used not only for surveillance, but have been armed with missiles to fire on targets. Currently, the United States, the United Kingdom, and Israel are the only countries to use drones as weapons, though several others are attempting to buy or develop this technology. Israel has used drones to carry out targeted assassinations since at least 2000. The UAVs have been used to kill by the US and UK militaries in Afghanistan and Iraq, and by the United States in Libya, while the CIA controls drone missions in Pakistan, Somalia, and Yemen from its headquarters in Langley, Virginia, and a network of secret bases (Abé 2012). The number of people killed by precision bombs, either on drones or other aircraft, is hotly contested, especially concerning the number of civilians killed. The Bureau of Investigative Journalism has estimated the number of those killed by drone strikes in Pakistan as 2,537 to 3,646 in 381 strikes (2014), while US officials have denied that more than a few civilians have been killed, claiming that the rest are legitimate targets. The practices of contemporary precision warfare involve both the ability to target individuals and objects, causing much less unintended destruction than prior aerial bombardment practices; at the same time, difficulty in accounting for those that it does kill is a hallmark of precision warfare.

The third key advantage to the techniques of precision warfare to liberal states is the virtual invulnerability of the bombers. The precision bomber, like the torturer, accepts virtually no risk, especially when the precision bomber is a drone. The risk is entirely displaced to the target and surrounding population. In precision warfare, war is no longer, as Scarry writes, "a reciprocal activity for non-reciprocal outcomes" (1985, 85). In seeking to eliminate the risk of bodily injury to the armed forces involved, the non-reciprocal injuring that takes place in precision warfare makes this form of violence akin to torture. If the goal of precision warfare is to minimize or eliminate the risk of bodily harm by making the bodies of one side invulnerable, while maximizing the vulnerability of the target population, war doesn't need to be a sacrifice.[5] Violence and pain are seen as unnecessary and as purely negative, with no positive connotations, in liberal societies (Asad 2003), and they are at odds with the biopolitical imperative to foster life. As such, technological solutions to the problems of waging war without incurring deaths or bodily injuries are very attractive, especially for those who are in favor of the increased use of force for humanitarian purposes (see, for example, Beauchamp and Savulesu 2013).

The condition of embodiment, that is, the inescapability of living *as* a body, means that one is subject to violence and injury. An avoidance or escape from this vulnerability, especially in an activity such as war in which injury is precisely the point, is an effort to transform one's own body not only to enhance its capabilities, but also to overcome its weaknesses. While in war, one's body is an advantage in that it is a tool of violence as well as an object that can be injured; in liberalism, the body and its desires, vulnerabilities, and passionate attachments are to be disavowed. Bodies are at best instruments and are more often encumbrances. As discussed in Chapter 1, feminists have argued that in liberal political theory and in the practices of liberal states, an inability to overcome one's bodily passions and vulnerabilities is a disqualifier for political life. Precision warfare reproduces this attempt to separate the subject from his or her body, in order to create a more effective agent for the spread of liberal values, and a more perfect liberal subject in reducing the burdens and impediments of the body.[6] This disembodied way of fighting war means that the pilots will not become maimed or killed, showing the costs of war or symbolically demonstrating the weakness of the states or ideals on whose behalf they fight.

As "disembodied," the precision bomber or drone operator is seen as a "de-gendered" or "post-gendered" subject, in which it does not seem to matter whether the pilot or operator is a male or female. The drone operator is also "unmanned" because he is frequently stationed not in the war zone, but in the feminized space of the "home front" and is kept out of danger (Blanchard 2011). The "disembodiment" of the pilot or operator also means that he is not confined to the particularities and limited vision of his body; the satellite systems and the drone's video cameras mean that the bomber's eye view is the God's eye view of objectivity. Its vision is cartographic, viewing the world from above in order to carefully manage the land and the population (Scott 1998).

In Chapter 3, I argued that the explosive body of the suicide bomber and the various practices of handling the bodily remains of victims and perpetrators demonstrate the constitution of bodies as self-governing and self-contained with clear boundaries, which is a normative ideal requiring political work to sustain, rather than an ontological fact. Moving now from an intimate form of violence, in which the death of one person is required in order to kill others, to a form of violence in which the killers are shielded from the risk of death or injury, we might expect to see in this contemporary mode of violence a sharper image of bodies as natural entities, independent and isolated from one another. However, what becomes apparent is that the bodies of precision warfare—bombers/drone operators, targets, and the unknown dead—are not isolated; they exist together. To borrow Sara Ahmed's words, in the bodily encounters of precision warfare, "bodies are both de-formed and re-formed, they take form through and against other bodily forms" (2000, 39). The posthuman embodiment of the precision pilot makes possible the political conditions of life and death for a range of bodies touched by precision warfare.

Precision warfare is a practice that is performative of a biopolitical, statist moral order which allows for killing some people intentionally and allows for the deaths of some as "accidents" at the hands of bombers and planners, who are seemingly omnipotent. If noted at all, the deaths of those not specifically targeted are "accidental," and they remain unseen, their deaths ungrievable and uncounted as a means of official policy, their deaths the "boundaries of bodily life where abjected or delegitimized bodies fail to 'count' as bodies" (Butler 1993, 15). These people are the abject bodies that reveal the workings of power and the current political order. Rather than an effect of the distance between bomber and victim, the killability of the victims can be read as a result of the transformation of human bodies in precision warfare. Rather than allowing for the deaths of some bodies in order to spare the lives of others, this chapter describes the multiple bodies produced by material/discursive practices that theorize bodies as produced in relation to one another, as well as technologies and discursive practices. In this theorization, we see the violent practices of precision bombing as performatively constituting bodies marked by race and "killability," as well as omniscience and god-like sovereign power. These figures do not exist prior to the practices of precision bombing, but exist in relation to one other as the result of the intra-action between discursive practices and the materiality of posthuman bodies. The remainder of this chapter proceeds in two parts. In the first section, I argue that precision warfare is predicated upon the production of the human body as a computer or an information processor capable of being seamlessly integrated into a human/technology killing assemblage (that bodies nonetheless resist). In the second section, I argue that these bodies are productive of other bodies: the bodies of "terrorists," "enemy combatants," and others deemed killable by the precision warfare assemblage. These later bodies only exist in virtue of the posthuman bodies of precision warfare: they too are constituted as part of a posthuman bodily assemblage of bodies, technology, and violence.

POSTHUMAN EMBODIMENT

The production of the body of the precision bomber begins at the military, which has been, and is, a profound site of the formation of the masculine body. The militarized masculine body has been formed through rigorous training and discipline. The military has also formed masculine bodies by serving as an ideal to which males aspire (Goldstein 2001, 251–331; Hooper 2001, 82; Weiss 2002, 46). One iteration of the militarized masculine body is the body of technology, a body defined by its skilled melding with technology (Carver 2008). While this body is associated with the advanced technologies of contemporary warfare, the soldier as a site of technological transformation of the body is not a new phenomenon: eighteenth-century military training constructed bodies as interchangeable machines and objects of discipline (Foucault 1979, 153). This form of training served as the basis for liberal techniques of producing docile subjects. The intermeshing of bodies and machines in warfare has been brought to new heights in the development of advanced technologies to enable precision bombing. The human/machine integration into the machinery of war has perhaps reached its current zenith in the piloting of planes and operating of drones designed to drop GPS- and laser-guided bombs. Foucault's theory on the relationship between bodies, machines, and power has its limitations for theorizing this particular human/machine integration, in that his work implies the separate existence of bodies and machines prior to their fastening through disciplinary practices. Such a theorization preserves the existence of a natural human body that is modified by technology, not constituted by it.

Since biopower takes the subject as a species, just how this species-life is conceived and produced is crucial for understanding the nature of violence and the bodies it harms and re-forms. Donna Haraway's figure of the cyborg in feminist theory is juxtaposed to that of a goddess, a mythical figure of essentialized feminine power of embodiment and nature. Haraway's cyborg is a model of culture/nature integration that does not presume the irreducibility of either "culture" or "nature" in terms of embodiment, but rather, focuses on how "culture" and "nature" are mutually entangled. In the figure of the cyborg, "nature and culture are reworked; the one can no longer be the resource for appropriation or incorporation by the other" (Haraway 1991a, 151). Haraway's figure of the cyborg compels us to be attentive to how boundaries are formed that separate the "human" from the "machine," and the "person" from the "bomb." The cyborg, born of the drive toward military technological domination and the globalizing capitalist economy, is a figure that describes a posthuman conception of our embodied subjectivity. "The machine is not an it to be animated, worshiped and dominated. The machine is us, our processes, an aspect of our embodiment" (Haraway 1991a, 180). If we are the "machine," we are no longer the naturalized bodies of biopolitics whose organic functioning the government must not interfere with, but a complexly embodied subject whose boundaries are drawn in and through technologies and other bodies as part of broad projects of military domination and global capitalism. In N. Katherine Hayles's reading of the posthuman moment,

> ... there are no essential differences or absolute demarcations between bodily existence and computer simulation, cybernetic mechanisms and biological organism, robot teleology and human goals. ... [T]he posthuman subject is an amalgam, a collection of heterogeneous components, a material informational entity whose boundaries undergo continuous construction and reconstruction. (1999, 3)

This reading of the subject as a bodily process of the formation and re-formation of boundaries and the inclusion and exclusion of different elements is rooted in a feminist project of theorizing the historical specificities of embodiment in a way that privileges neither "nature" nor "culture" but is attentive to the ways that bodily difference is produced in specific formations.

The use of technological artifacts to wage war is hardly a new phenomenon. What distinguishes precision warfare is the transformation of the human into a source of code. Whereas the body scanners discussed in the previous chapter digitized the body into a text that could be read for signs of bodily deviance or devious intent, precision warfare produces bodies as information processors, active agents in networks, who make decisions about life and death in warfare. In precision warfare, the embodied subject of violence is figured as a mind, and that mind is an information processor. This posthuman view of embodiment is situated and produced by the biopolitical imperatives of warfare by liberal states. The production of the body as information processor has deep roots in the military and the development of computing and artificial intelligence.

Hayles argues that computing and, more specifically, the contemporary sciences of artificial life (AL) and artificial intelligence (AI) have refigured the human into the posthuman (1999). The project of artificial intelligence has its origins in Norbert Weiner's efforts to develop a machine capable of calculating the movements of aircraft in flight as well as the complexities introduced by a human pilot—and to be able to learn and evolve from this information (Hayles 1999, 85–86; Dillon and Reid 2009, 63). Hayles locates the development of artificial intelligence and computing more broadly, with ties to the postwar military industrial complex and the current needs of the militaries of wealthy, technologically advanced societies. The US military was heavily influential in the development of the computing industry, providing funding and guidance in the research and development stages in the postwar period (Edwards 1996). Artificial intelligence research has a close relationship with the US military, developing in concert with the military's own needs for technological solutions to war-fighting dilemmas (DeLanda 1997). AI research, which forms the basis of modern information and computing technologies, exists to enable militaries to fight wars more efficiently. Importantly, AI and AL (whose goal is the reproduction not only of human intelligence, but of essentially life processes) are quintessentially forms of embodiment, in that they conceptualize the capabilities of human bodies (especially their brains) as information processors that can be augmented, supplemented, and artificially recreated.

Artificial intelligence constructs the human in terms of a machine. The body is not imagined as an operator of machinery, but as a machine itself. This is a necessary formulation for the goal of AI and, especially, AL, as the need to replicate and improve upon the capabilities of human bodies requires not the creation of machines that are like human bodies (an unstable form/signifier), but a reformulation of what the human body and/or mind is, in order to suit the needs of AI/AL. In the framework of AI, the body is transformed into code, that is, into informational patterns (Hayles 1999, 61; Dillon and Reid 2009). AI challenges the boundaries of the biopolitical body, imaging bodies not as individuals or as species-life, but as flows of information. Precision warfare not only produces bodies in terms of information flows, but also is constitutively dependent upon these posthuman bodies.

The precision bomber or drone operator is integrated into a human/technological assemblage known in the military as a "kill chain." The kill chain consists of target identification, dispatching forces or weapons to the target, the decision and order to attack the target, and finally the destruction of the target. The kill chain involves a number of cognitive processes, described by John Boyd as OODA, for observe, orient, decide, and act. In the observe stage, information is absorbed. Orientation is the interpretation of this information, in which meaning is created and a range of responses is provided. A decision is then made, and action is taken (Bousquet 2009). In precision warfare, these cognitive functions are dispersed throughout a network of humans and technological artifacts. The human pilots or drone operators are one point in this "kill chain," analyzing information and deciding, along with the chain of command and the current rules of engagement, what actions to take, including the deployment of missiles. Reaper and Predator drones are based just outside conflict zones in bases in Afghanistan or Iraq, or in one of 60 bases in Africa, the Middle East, and Central Asia, in which launch and recovery crews control the drones though direct contact via an antenna on the aircraft; remote crews in Nevada and elsewhere take control half an hour after take-off, and relinquish control half an hour before landing, The pilot and sensor operator are located in small buildings about the size of trailers, surrounded by multiple screens and keyboards. The screens with information provided by the drones are also monitored by troops on the ground, military commanders in Afghanistan or Iraq, or intelligence analysts thousands of miles away (Blackhurst 2012), all of whom may also be in communication with the drone operators, giving feedback or orders. In cases where sites or individuals are monitored for many hours or days, legal advisors also review the visual images and communications from this network to provide guidance about the legal implications of a strike (Gregory 2011, 199).

Rather than being replaced by technology, the bodies of pilots are becoming integrated into a system as a fragment of what Foucault refers to as "mobile space" (1979, 164). The bodies of pilots are not, as in the case of the flying Aces of World War I, defined by strength or bravery. In fact, many of the drone pilots are not military personnel but civilians, including intelligence agents and private contractors (Mayer 2009). The technology of the airplane, surveillance, and weapons system, rather than "taking the human out of the loop," extends the body, or rather acts as a phenomenon that comes into being with its biological and technological capabilities. For example, a handful of Special Forces troops and CIA agents were able to kill more enemy fighters in the Shah-i-Kot Valley in Afghanistan than the rest of the 2,000 US troops in the area by using binoculars and laser pointers to triangulate the source of weapons fire, and then calling in air strikes (Mahnken 2008, 198). In terms of the progress of artificial intelligence and UAVs, the US Defense Department has set a goal for humans to be "on-the-loop" versus "in-the-loop," meaning that humans will monitor and override if necessary, rather than controlling certain aspects directly (Sharkey 2010, 378). Rather than the loss of the human in war, we are seeing the human in war transformed into a posthuman system of technological capabilities, spurred by a desire for seamless integration of human bodies into implements of war. The military's terminology has changed to reflect this understanding of precision warfare. While drones used to be called "UAVs," for "unmanned aerial vehicles," they are now referred to as "RPAs," or remotely piloted aircraft. "They are not unmanned at all," Air Force Colonel Hernando Ortega explained, "They're manned to the hilt" (Zucchino 2012).

The transformation of humans into information processors in technological systems is exemplified by the experience of drone operators. Drone operators report a proprioceptive sense of the drones as a part of themselves. That is, they experience the drones as merging with their bodies, sometimes imagining that they are the drones themselves (Power 2013). For example, Matt Martin writes part of his memoir of being a drone pilot in the first-person voice of the drone: "I carried a pair of Hellfire Missiles beneath my wings but my task was not to engage the enemy directly. . . . Sometimes I felt like God hurling thunderbolts from afar" (Martin and Sasser 2010, 3). Writing of the human/technological assemblage that constitutes the drones as an "I" indicates a sense of self, or subjectivity, expanded from the body bounded by the skin to a posthuman body made up of biological, technological, and social elements. Drones, or other technological "prosthetics," are not simply "tools" that are added onto bodies, imagined as separate or outside bodies; they are a transformation of the body, and of the human that is indicative of a posthuman framework. Other forms of artificial life in warfare evidence a similar phenomenon, such as robots used to scout for roadside bombs and other explosives, which soldiers sometimes treat as members of the unit (Singer 2009, 32).

While precision warfare is driven by a desire to wage war without risking the bodies of soldiers, the bodily knowledge and experience of military personnel play a role in the design of the war-fighting assemblages, such as the "cockpits" of drones, which are designed to emulate the experience of piloting a manned aircraft. The use of a pilot's embodied skills exemplifies the production of the human body as part of the "mind," a necessary part of a human's cognition. In 2006, Raytheon announced improvements to the control system to make it resemble an airplane cockpit in order to improve the pilot's "situational awareness," in fact, designing the operator stations in order to fit the body of the drone operator more seamlessly into the drone assemblage. This move was undertaken to reduce potential accidents, which until that point were largely attributable to pilot error (Raytheon 2006). In the summer of 2008, Raytheon replaced a keyboard on the console for pilots of UAVs with a video-game type console based on a discovery that "thumbs are the most energy-efficient and accurate way to control an aircraft" (Associated Press 2008). The new consoles also greatly enhance the view of the "pilots" with digital images for a nearly 180-degree view. In the future, Raytheon hopes to make the console and the chair vibrate to reflect the sensation of turbulence and landing. While attempting to fix some of the "pilot error" with new technologies, the aim is not to replace the human, but rather to enhance preexisting human capabilities, relying on making the controllers feel more as if they are in the cockpit of a plane. For example, drone operators were trained to feel as though they were in the Predator itself (Martin and Sasser 2010, 23).

The careful attention paid to the embodied skills of drone pilots suggests a post-Cartesian understanding of the role of the body in cognition. Contemporary neuroscience and cognitive science theorize the "mind" as a category that is not opposed to the body, but is always situated in a body and dependent upon that body (Varela, Thompson, and Rosch 1991; Gallagher 2005; Gibbs 2006). Intellectual awareness, that is, cognition, interacts with unconscious dimensions of bodily affect and contributes content to the workings of the mind. As neuroscientist Damasio writes, "The brain and the body are indissociably integrated by mutually targeted biochemical and neural circuits. . . body and brain form an indissociable organism" (1994, 87–88). Bodily affect may precede cognition, or cognition may precede affect, but these both interact in complex ways (Bially Mattern 2011, 66). Furthermore, just as the brain and body interact, the body also interacts with its environment. The body is, in Hayles's terms, "enculturated" (1999, 199) through practices—such as the training and experience of flying planes in the Air Force, or in Foucault's descriptions of Prussian military drills. Cognition is thus dependent upon a body that is formed through its environment and its history and training. This view is post-Cartesian, in that it considers the body to be more than a life-support system for the mind, but it also takes the materiality of the body as another kind of information source to be integrated into the human/machine assemblage.

"Prosthesis" is a technological term that is useful for understanding the ways in which technology performatively enables the posthuman subjectivity of the precision bomber. A prosthetic is a mechanical contrivance adapted to reproduce the form, and as far as possible, the function, of a lost or absent member. Elizabeth Grosz asks the question of whether a prosthetic is meant to correct a deficiency or a lack in the body, or whether the purpose is to supplement the body, giving it capabilities that exceed what is considered the norm (2005, 147). If there is no such thing as a "natural body" outside the knowledge practices that constitute bodies, how then can we draw the line between what is "natural" to the body and what is a human contrivance? Even if we could imagine a body in a "state of nature" outside sociality, that body is not self-sufficient, capable of existing without interacting with its environment. In fact, bodies do not so much interact with their environments, as if there were clear boundaries between the interior and exterior of bodies. Rather, bodies are always bodies-in-formation, adapting and recombining with other bodies (human and non-human). This is what I take Judith Butler to mean when she describes bodies as ontologically "precarious": bodies not only depend on their relations with others for their very existence, both in terms of defining the boundaries between bodies and in terms of the care necessary to sustain life, but bodies will necessarily cease to be, and are thus at risk of death at any time (Butler 2009, 30). Bodies are precarious precisely because they cannot exist independently of their environment. The precariousness of bodies suggests, on one level, that the use of technology to increase human capabilities is not a matter of adding on a layer of technology to an already existing, pre-defined biological platform. Rather, the integration of biology and technology in the figure of the "cyborg" suggests not an addition or subjection of the human, but a reconfiguration of subjectivity into the posthuman. In short, cybernetics was developed as a way to build better killing machines that ended up redefining and reorganizing the boundaries of the human body. Bodies are no longer considered a stable referent as agents of security; rather, figured as information or code, they can inhabit different relations and adapt in new combinations.

One ongoing feature of debates over precision warfare is to what extent humans are still "in the loop" in the weapons systems. The chaotic environments of war can make the use of automated weapons attractive, as the complexity of warfare can overwhelm a human's perception, reaction, and decision-making abilities. Automated weapons are imaged to eliminate mistakes and thus increase the ability to use force in a more frictionless way. This holds true whether drones or other robots are used for information-gathering purposes or killing, or both. As one CIA psychologist said, "The problem of every intelligence operation is how do you remove the human element" (Gray 1997, 198). Human intelligence is being replaced by satellite data, considered less fallible than humans in many ways. Critics, however, are concerned with the effects of total automation on moral responsibility in war. In this critique, "the human" is conceived as a known quantity, existing in a zero-sum relationship with material, technological forces. In reference to drones and other forms of artificial intelligence used in warfare, Peter W. Singer, author of *Wired for War*, has proclaimed, "Humankind is starting to lose its 5,000 year monopoly of fighting war" (Shachtman 2009). The more technological, the less "human" war is becoming, which has implications not only for the politics of the use of force, but for the very culture of war itself (Coker 2001; Masters 2005; Singer 2009). This concern regarding the relationship between humans and technology is especially prevalent in the issue of drones. Human subjects are considered to be the only kind of subjects able to make moral decisions, and fears of wars fought by autonomous machines drive much of the criticism of precision warfare (Singer 2009, 123–134). Humans are considered a type of "fail-safe" that ultimately maintains accountability and democratic control over the use of such weapons. This concern is a concern over the loss of the individual thinking and deliberating subject. In short, it is a concern about whether precision warfare is undermining the moral subject of liberalism. This subject is an autonomous subject whose reasoning is not unduly influenced by outside pressures. However, these critiques miss the nuance in the process of embodiment and technology provided by a posthuman reading of precision warfare. In light of such a reading, we are perhaps better off examining how precision warfare produces different kinds of relations that were not previously possibly or imaginable. In undertaking such a project, I begin with a reading of the visual politics of precision warfare.

Embodiment and the Bomb's Eye View

The visual capacities of posthuman bodies play a large role in structuring the relationship between the viewer and the viewed, the bomber and the bombed. The technological advances exemplified by laser- and satellite-guided bombs and the use of UAVs for surveillance, and now bombing, is driven by a desire for ever more powerful visualizing capabilities. Understood in posthuman terms, precision warfare is not about obtaining more accurate images of buildings, vehicles, or people. Rather, it is about producing or inventing these things and bodies and recasting relations among bodies. Here, I situate the politics of the embodied vision of precision warfare in feminist critiques of the technologies of vision and then turn to the objects and bodies that are produced by practices of embodiment.

The equation of the eye with the mind, Haraway has pointed out, has a long history. The seeing eye is the privileged means of representing the object of knowledge, creating in this performative process a knowing subject and a body as the object of that knowledge. Here, we see a reply of the dual move of biomedical knowledge that Foucault described in *Birth of a Clinic*, as in the body scanners of the airport security assemblages. The practice of opening up bodies and gazing at their insides produces a disembodied, knowing subject and an object of knowledge ripe for intervention and manipulation. It is not just biotechnology and instruments of security that wield this power, but instruments of war and destruction as well (a distinction that is blurred in biopolitical regimes). Feminists such as Haraway challenge the objectivity of this form of visual knowledge, denying the notion that vision is somehow unmediated and apolitical, even when performed by "one's own eyes," unassisted by technology. Rather, visual capabilities are a crucial aspect of political subjectivity, and vision is always embodied. The metaphors of vision associated with satellite imagery and the perspective of pilots and bombs appear to be tied to a disembodied subject, a view from nowhere and everywhere at the same time. The pretense of separating vision from embodiment is associated with masculine forms of knowledge. "Vision in this technological feast becomes unregulated gluttony; all perspective gives way to infinitely mobile vision, which no longer seems just mythically about the god-trick of seeing everything from nowhere, but to have put the myth into ordinary practice" (Haraway 1991b, 189). This "myth" is the Cartesian mind/body separation that divorces vision and knowledge from bodies, and this myth is put into practice in the apparatus of precision bombing, in which the view from above becomes the absolute truth, the view from nowhere.

The "god-trick" of the view from nowhere has played an essential role in modern state-building and colonial practices as a way to manage unfamiliar territories by mapping them and producing usable knowledge. Envisioning the territory from above is useful primarily to state elites interested in administering the land and remaking it so that is it more easily managed and ensuring the success of possible military action (Scott 1998, 55–57). The vision of the airplane, satellite, and drone is a vantage point of absolute power; it is similar to the disembodied vision of the medical gaze into the body, producing bodies and territories as intelligible and knowable from the outside, and ultimately, making these objects manipulable. The world is divided into an above and a below, in which instant destruction is the purview of those from above (see also Chow 2006, 35).

The technologies of precision bombing personify this "god-trick" in various ways. First, precision bombing is dependent upon "sight" beyond unenhanced human capabilities in order to be classified as "precision" at all. The two main types of precision-guided munitions are laser-guided and GPS-guided. In the former, a laser is used to point to a target, and the missile follows the path of the laser to "see" its way to the target. In the latter, satellites send information to correct the path of bombs, which are also equipped with backup systems in case this technology fails. GPS-guided bombs are generally more "accurate" because they function regardless of weather conditions. The ever increasing clarity of GPS systems, including the ability to target small and smaller CEPs, point to a greater drive toward accuracy and a minimization of risk of error, such that even "mistakes" fall within acceptable contingency parameters. Thus, the god-trick of "sight" from everywhere is relegated to GPS systems and drones, which are used to collect information, to substitute for eyes when it is too dangerous or difficult to obtain knowledge another way. Weary of the fascination with the drone, James Poss, a retired general who helped oversee the development of the Predator, remarks, "It's about the datalink, stupid" (Bowdon 2013). Surveillance video from drones has become crucial to the military campaigns in Iraq, Afghanistan, Pakistan, and recently has been approved for domestic use in the United States. Of drone-supplied video, Army Brigadeer General Kevin Mangum said, "It's like crack, and everyone wants more" (Shachtman 2010). The ability of drones to monitor large spaces is limited (the view from Predator cameras is often likened to looking through a soda straw); however, in 2011, the Air Force deployed an aircraft called "Gorgon Stare," made up of nine video cameras on a UAV, which can monitor movements around an entire town. The "Gorgon Stare" can send up to 65 images to different users, including drone crews and soldiers on the ground (Nakashima and Whitlock 2011). The US military currently has too much information from surveillance drones, which may be useful in future operations but is not needed immediately. To solve this problem, the military is working with DARPA (the US agency for advanced military research) to build "machine-machine" tools that can automate the cameras and help process data (Ackerman 2012b). With the data provided by the Gordon Stare, computers can track suspected terrorists or insurgents for months and analyze patterns of behavior, which can be compared to other forms of intelligence, such as cell phone or e-mail intercepts (Bowdon 2013).

Precision bombing reproduces the illusion of a disembodied subject with not only a privileged view of the world, but the power to destroy all that it sees. The Pentagon has stationed Reaper drones in the Horn of Africa, where militants in Somalia or Yemen, as well as pirates, may be targeted in the future (Entous 2010). Drones, although unarmed ones, have also been used to patrol the US–Canada and US–Mexico border (Davey 2008), and the military and Homeland Security are preparing "spy blimps" and drone helicopters that can transmit vast amounts of data (up to 80 years of footage plus audio in a single day) for use both domestically and abroad

(Shachtman 2011; Ackerman 2012a). The use of drones to conduct surveillance and possibly deliver lethal force is a tool not only of sovereign power, but also of the productive power of visual technologies as active components of posthuman bodies to produce particular subjects.

The posthuman production of the soldier is simultaneously redrawing and reconstituting the gendered culture/nature and mind/body dichotomies. While the soldier has been constituted as a dominant figure of masculinity, the cyborg subjectivity could be considered a means of de-gendering the soldier, as bodily difference between males and females are made less relevant in an environment that promotes technology as a solution to fallible human bodies. The posthuman bodies of precision bombers, relying on God's eye, or panoptical, views are produced as masterful, yet benign, subjects, using superior technology to spare civilians from riskier forms of aerial bombardment. The drones have also been described in benign terms by soldiers on mission on the ground in Afghanistan as unseen guardians and protectors of soldiers; drones have been used as a lookout so that weary soldiers could sleep (Zucchino 2010). The representations of drones as "guardian angels" is the partial enactment of the state's dream of total surveillance in the interests of management; portrayed as benign and helpful, instead of as killing machines, the use of drones as surveillance technologies is produced even as "motherly" in a benign metaphor of parental love, as a mother watches over her children sleeping. Whereas at one point, the use of technology in warfare was considered to be un-manly, dishonorable, and diminishing the warrior spirit that marked the superiority of a nation's men (Wilcox 2009, 221–225), technology is now inscribed as masculine. Technology, as "culture" or "mind," is not only the righteous warrior, but the protector of the feminine: here, not only the "beautiful souls" (Elshtain 1995 [1987]) of the women and children back at home, but the body of the soldier (Masters 2005). The soldier whose convoy is watched overhead by drones, or who is presumably spared from a dangerous mission by the use of precision airstrikes, is a body to be protected, rather than an embodiment of masculine bravery and strength, in comparison to the abilities of these technologies. Precision warfare represents the Enlightenment dream of transcending the body, with wars being waged on video screens. It is the technology that is the instrument of violence, not the bodies of soldiers. The soldiers of precision warfare can thus maintain the identity of the "just warriors" who are law-abiding and chivalrous in their attempts to spare civilians and serve as "guardian angels" for ground troops. As posthuman, the pilot or drone operator is also post-sex; his or her sexed embodiment is irrelevant to performing the tasks at hand, and to his or her integration into the technological system. Posthuman embodiment is shifting gendered categories by protecting soldiers (shifting them into a feminized category) through a masculine conception of bodies as technological tools.

Post-traumatic Stress Disorder and Posthuman Embodiment

The posthuman embodiment of precision bombers and especially drone operators is the result of a vision of warfare in which the bodies of one side are completely invulnerable; while a drone could (theoretically) be shot down, this would only prove a temporary disruption in the cybernetic human/technology assemblage. However, the production of human bodies as information processors is incomplete; that is, the human bodies are in excess of their integration into the precision "kill chain" or information-gathering and decision-making process. The materiality of bodies proves resistant to the desire of precision warfare to fully integrate them into the network of information processing and to fully protect them from vulnerability to war.

Drone operators have an embodied experience of warfare that is not subsumed by their role in information processing; they often have an affective, emotional experience to what they do, precisely because they can see the results. Drone operators stay in air-conditioned trailers in Nevada, while they watch their targets, sometimes for days in a row, getting to know their everyday lives; after a strike is authorized and missiles deployed, drone operators will survey the scene to confirm the target's death. The operators will witness these deaths, plus the unintended deaths and the deaths of soldiers in convoys they are supposed to protect (Martin 2011; Abé 2012). Colonel Albert Aimar, commander of the US 163rd Reconnaissance Wing, explains that, in a fighter jet, "when you come in at 500–600 mph, drop a 500-pound bomb and then fly away, you don't see what happens." However, when a Predator fires a missile, "you watch it all the way to impact, and I mean it's very vivid, it's right there and personal. So it does stay in people's minds for a long time" (Lindlaw 2008). Another drone operator vehemently denies the "video-game" metaphor for drone warfare, insisting the experience was quite different:

> You are 18 inches away from 32-inch, high-definition combat, where you are in contact [by headset with] the guys on the ground. . . .. You are there. You are there. You fly with them, you support them and a person you are tasked with supporting gets engaged, hurt, possibly killed, it's a deeply, deeply emotional event. It's not detached. It's not a video game. And it's certainly not 8,000 miles away. (Schogol 2012)

Matthew Power has called this a "voyeuristic intimacy" (Power 2013), but this is a one-sided intimacy: while drone operators and the network of commanders and analysts who view the images that the drones provide gain more and more visual access to the combat zones of Afghanistan and Iraq and the "ungoverned" or "unstable" spaces of Pakistan, Yemen, Somalia, Mali, Libya, Algeria, and other locales, the objects of such surveillance and violence have no such capabilities.

A further cause of high levels of burnout and post-traumatic stress disorder (PTSD) stems from the dual nature of life for drone operators. Drone pilots and sensor operators often work for 10–12 hours or more at a shift, and then go home, back to their everyday lives (Blackhurst 2012; Dao 2013). As one drone operator reported, "the weirdest thing for me—with my background [as a RAF jet pilot]—is the concept of getting up in the morning, driving my kids to school and killing people" (Blackhurst 2012). The affective states learned from being in a war zone do not necessarily translate well to the civilian world, in which people may experience affective states learned in war zones in different social environments. A recent study has found that drone pilots experience similar levels of health problems, such as depression, anxiety, and PTSD, as pilots of manned aircraft deployed to Iraq and Afghanistan, although information about the experiences of CIA pilots is not available (Dao 2013). When human bodies are combined into drone assemblages, they are not just information processors but are experiencing, feeling beings.

Post-traumatic stress disorder, or PTSD, a controversial diagnosis (see Howell 2011), refers to a condition with three sets of affective symptoms: hyperarousal, a constant expectation of danger; intrusion, the lingering imprint of trauma on one's body and mind; and constriction, or the numbing of feelings. The hyperarousal is a conditioned response to combat, which suggests that even though drone operators may be safe from the reciprocal violence that (once) defined warfare (Scarry 1985, 85), their bodies are still affected by combat. PTSD is the clinical term for the experience of a bodily reaction that may be well suited to dealing with a traumatic situation, such as combat, when it is experienced in an inappropriate setting (away from the battlefield). The experience of being in a war zone is a particular mix of physiological and social interactions that creates certain bodily sensations. The tension, excitement, and fear that one feels in moments of great stress are a complex result of emotions, cognition, and bodily responses, such as adrenaline, that is both a lived experience and a bodily practice. While drone operators spend up to 12-hour shifts at war, afterward they drive home and have to cope with the normal stresses of life such as parenting (Lindlaw 2008; Zucchino 2010; D. Chow 2013). One drone operator repeatedly refers to his experience of fighting a war while living at home with his family as making him "schizophrenic" (Martin and Sasser 2010). Air Force Colonel Hernando Ortega said, "This is a different kind of war, but it's still war. And they do internally feel it" (Zucchino 2012).

Despite the dreams of precision warfare and seamless human/technology information processing, the embodied experience of drone operators illustrates the ways in which human embodiment has lively, productive characteristics. The existence of the bodily response of PTSD in drone operators is evidence of the ways that bodies are still material and can "punch back" in ways that humans and their technologies cannot predict (Alaimo and Hekman 2008, 7). Human embodiment means that subjects are still material, and are still located in time and space, interacting with their environments. Hayles writes, "Formed by technology at the same time that it creates technology, embodiment mediates between technology and discourse by creating new experiential frameworks that serve as boundary markers for the creation of corresponding discursive systems" (1999, 205). While human subjects both create and are formed by technological systems, the subject as embodied means that there is material resistance from the immaterial norms of information flows. Bodies aren't as flexible or subject to molding to fit the operational needs of strategic doctrine as the dreams of precision warfare would have them.[7] While bodies are "leaky" and overflow the strict boundaries required of modern, liberal subjects (see Chapters 3 and 4), bodily experience is dependent not only on the openness of bodies to their environment, but also on maintaining some sort of boundary. To experience bodily sensations, to experience life *as* a body, there must be some kind of boundary or membrane (Colebrook 2011). The materiality of embodiment is dependent upon a material structure that must deviate from the norms placed upon it (Hayles 1999, 199; Butler 2004a, 217).

Posthuman bodies, in their leakiness between human and technology, resist the biopolitical tendency to naturalize life. While precision warfare seems to represent the ultimate in the liberal dream of warfare—disembodied, autonomous, and invulnerable—a posthuman reading suggests this understanding is flawed. Precision warfare is predicated upon the development of a subject that blurs the boundaries between human and machine. If the liberal state exercises its task of the protection of the naturalized lives of its population and its own sovereign existence through precision warfare, some of its foundational assumptions of the subject are undermined. The "prosthetic" nature of the precision bomber means that his or her body is not autonomous or individual, but rather is dependent on the supplementation of technology in his or her transformation into a (flawed) posthuman information processor. Such bodies are not only constituted by precision warfare, but constitute other bodies in their turn. In the next section, I turn to the bodies and relations that are produced by the posthuman embodiment of precision bombers.

PRECISION WARFARE AND "BODIES THAT DON'T MATTER"

Paul Virilio has argued that contemporary information networks have changed how military organizations conceptualize the enemy. After World War II, state boundaries were no longer sufficient to distinguish citizens and aliens, inside and outside (Virilio 2008 [1983], 114). New technologies are needed to identify enemies, as well as new imaginings about who these enemies are. The technologies of precision warfare are ultimately about producing certain bodies as legible, and legible as enemies. Bodies must first be made intelligible as objects of knowledge in order that certain forms of intervention can be made—in the practice of precision warfare, "intervention" means that certain bodies can be killed or not. The visual practices needed to project force internationally while upholding liberal values have resulted not only in the transformation of the objects of this gaze, but in the subjects that produce this gaze as well. In this, the embodiment of the precision bomber is shown to be productive of the bodies of "militants" and "civilians," or perhaps more accurately, "targeted bodies" and "unintended dead." These bodies are produced in mutual entanglement with the bodies of the precision bomber; the different categories of dead and injured bodies do not preexist their production in relation to posthuman bodies; they are made into objects of violent intervention through the practices of precision warfare, becoming part of the posthuman assemblages of contemporary war and technology.

Targeted Bodies

It has been argued that the norm of discrimination between civilians and combatants is strengthening and that technological developments in precision bombing have made it easier to distinguish between civilians and combatants (Thomas 2006). Precision bombing allows for greater penetration of this tactic; once entire cities were considered to be "civilian" and therefore morally suspect as bombing targets, now specific buildings within residential areas can be targeted. For example, in World War II, flying during the day with good weather conditions, it still sometimes took thousands of bombs for a few to reach their intended targets, which sometimes were defined in terms of hundreds of square acres (McFarland 1995, 160–195). In the Gulf War of 1991, bombs could famously take out single buildings, leaving others on a city block free of damage. The technology of precision warfare has now made it possible (theoretically) for the state to distinguish particular individuals in space, rather than neighborhoods or buildings; precision warfare has now allowed the state to demarcate, and kill, individual bodies. Precision bombing has made not only specific populations the targets of bombs, as in the aerial bombardment of World War II, but also has individualized the targets.

Targeted assassinations, which are perhaps better described as summary executions instead of the euphemism of "extrajudicial killings," form a significant component of recent counterinsurgency and counterterrorism wars. This kind of violence differs from the lethal force used by soldiers in battles, in that the targeted is identified in advance. Rather than soldiers being allowed to kill any combatants, in these summary executions the state has authorized the killing of specific, named individuals (Plaw 2008, 4), and more recently, anyone observed by a UAV as being involved in terrorist or insurgency activity or having a "pattern of life" suggesting involvement with militants. The targets of these summary executions are (mostly) the same as those deemed to be "enemy combatants" who are not given the rights of prisoners of war. The category of "enemy combatant" enabled the Bush administration to detain hundreds captured in Afghanistan in camps at Bagram and Guantánamo Bay, on the basis that persons affiliated with Al Qaeda or the Taliban were not representatives of a functioning state (Bybee 2002; Yoo 2002).

Quite apart from the concealed nature of much late twentieth-century warfare, especially in bodies of the dead (see, for example, Gusterson 2004, 62–81), the body of the suspected militant or terrorist is subject to the very public punishment of sovereign power. Summary executions can be usefully read as an extension of risk management in biopolitical warfare. On January 13, 2006, a UAV attempted to kill Ayman al-Zawahiri (a top Al Qaeda figure) and aides in Northern Pakistan (his wife and three of his children were killed in a similar attempt in 2001). In April 2003, the United States also tried to kill Saddam Hussein and some of his sons at a restaurant using precision targeting. Saddam and the others weren't there, and 14 civilians were killed. Targeted killing is legal in Israel, and has been used against several leaders of Hamas. UAVs are used by the United States to carry out targeted killings in Afghanistan and by the CIA in Pakistan, Somalia, and Yemen. Killings of high-profile Al Qaeda leaders, when successful, are frequently widely reported as triumphs in the "war on terror".

Although Osama bin Laden was not killed by a drone attack, drones provided the surveillance necessary to carry out the raid that led to bin Laden's death in 2011. Despite Defense Secretary Rumsfeld's declaration that "we don't do body counts on other people," reports about progress of the counterinsurgency in Iraq, for example, frequently reported the number of those claimed to be "enemies" who were killed (Graham 2005). While the number of civilians killed by drones is widely disputed, the targets killed are counted and triumphantly reported in the press when they are known or suspected Al Qaeda leaders.

The military advantage in using precision munitions and drones to carry out attacks on known and suspected militants is obvious: assassinations can be carried out without risking the lives of members of the CIA or military special forces. This tactic is justified by references to terrorists hiding in remote parts of the world that are inaccessible to US troops or any sovereign government. US Attorney General Eric Holder defended the use of drone attacks after the killing of Anwar al-Awlaki in 2012 as a necessary measure in which "due process takes into account the realities of combat" (Finn and Horwitz 2012). Furthermore, while it is illegal for an agent of the United States to carry out an assassination, the use of missiles and drones to carry out summary executions has not generally been defined as "assassination." Rather, it is framed as an extension of battlefield combat, especially in the ongoing global "war on terror". The US Congress endorsed Bush's post–9/11 policy authorizing the CIA to kill members and affiliates of Al Qaeda, using a rationale of "anticipatory self-defense," similar to Israel's rationale for similar killings (Mayer 2009). The Obama administration has continued this policy and dramatically increased the use of drones to kill in Afghanistan and Pakistan. Furthermore, the scope of the sovereign power that the drones enable not only is unlimited geographically, but also is not restricted based on the citizenship of those who may be designated targets. The Obama administration authorized and carried out the killing of Anwar al-Awlaki, a Muslim cleric and a US citizen, in September 2011, as well as his son two weeks later. Marking him for death is the performative act of the sovereign, making an exception of al-Awlaki, outside US and international law, a death that would have been much more difficult for the United States without the ability to kill him by drone attack.

The use of targeted killings by missile or drone is generally framed as an alternative to the deployment of US troops to kill or detain the suspect. While eliminating the risk to the potential captors, targeted assassinations also eliminate the option of taking suspects into custody, in which they might be questioned, held as a prisoner of war, or charged with a crime in order to stand trial. They occupy a different status than the prisoners held at Guantánamo Bay, who are subject to torture, indefinite detention, and force-feeding to keep them alive, but subjugated. The targets represent not an enemy who must be coerced into surrendering, or a fugitive who must be brought to justice, but the subject of extermination. This is the relationship that Foucault designates as racism, which is a way to mark the "break between what must live and what must die" (Foucault 2003, 254) and also the necessity of the death of some to secure the lives of others. The health of one population (the posthuman warriors and those they ostensibly protect) is made possible by the death of another population (the suspected "terrorists"). However, the terrorists are not figured as a population per se, but rather as a set of individuals who are marked as those who have or would disregard the sovereign's law, and who must be publicly, bodily, punished as a means of re-establishing the presence of the sovereign (Foucault 1979).

The use of drones continues the extension of the space of the battlefield, as well as the time of war, indefinitely. By the inculcation of posthuman subjectivities invested with sovereign power over life and death, precision warfare is a means of constituting the global reach of the panopticon: "the oldest dream of the oldest sovereign" (Foucault 2007, 66). Sovereign power over the individualized bodies of terrorists is exercised simultaneously with the biopolitical rationality of risk management that characterizes the "accidental" deaths of civilians who are killed as a result of the high-tech targeting of terrorists. Successfully waging the indefinite "war on terror" seems to depend more and more on the use of precision warfare, especially drones. Leon Panetta, the CIA director, has said that the drones are "the only game in town" in terms of effectively waging war in Afghanistan and Pakistan (Mayer 2009). Drones are used in cases in which other forms of sovereign power are unavailable, primarily in the Federally Administered Tribal Area (FATA) of Pakistan, and in Afghanistan, Somalia, and Yemen, where the government is unable or unwilling to capture or kill terrorist/enemy fighters itself, and the geography makes occupation more difficult. The Obama administration uses a process of "nominations" that are discussed by various agencies and then approved by President Obama (Becker and Shane 2012). This process of nomination has become institutionalized in what is known as a "disposition matrix" in which different factors, such as how dangerous the person is deemed to be, or whether they are inside the United States or in an allied country that can arrest the person. The shadow of the Orientalist trope of frontier or ungovernable spaces looms large in this "disposition matrix" that determines who is eligible for targeted killings. Furthermore, the Obama administration has expanded the Bush-era doctrine of "anticipatory self-defense" to argue that it has the right to use lethal force if "an informed, high-level official of the US government has determined that the targeted individual poses an imminent threat of violent attack against the US" (Department of Justice (US) n.d., 6). Importantly, "imminent" is not precisely defined, but the language of the White Paper excludes the necessity for a person to be actively plotting against the United States or its interests, and also defends using risk to US personnel in an attempted capture of the subject as a factor in determining whether an airstrike is legally permissible. This White Paper cites the right of self-defense of the United States, and says that approval for the use of military force in the US war against Al Qaeda is not geographically limited (Department of Justice (US) n.d., 3). In this White Paper, the United States asserts the legitimacy of using lethal force against any person defined as an enemy, based on unknown or secret criteria, potentially anywhere in the world. This logic of risk minimization to the United States and its soldiers through virtually limitless use of lethal force on individuals seems to realize Asad's admonition that "the absolute right to defend oneself by force becomes, in the context of industrial capitalism, the freedom to use violence globally" (2007, 62).

This power of individualizing targets has broadened as well, with drones being used to target and kill not only individuals who are deemed to be leaders among the "enemy combatants," but lower level "foot soldiers" as well. A rule of thumb used to be that the CIA had to have enough intelligence on a subject to know his name in order for a suspect to be targeted. This is no longer necessary, as acting as if you pose a threat is now enough to be targeted for a drone killing (Muir 2010). Lower-level militants are now being targeted, especially in Pakistan. One report suggests that, while the media has emphasized high-level Al Qaeda and Taliban leaders such as Ayman al-Zawahiri, more than 12 times as many mid- or low-level fighters have been killed by drones as named targets (Entous 2010). The Obama administration has also broadened the list of "approved targets" to include about 50 Afghani drug lords accused of helping to finance the Taliban (Mayer 2009).

With the Obama administration's unfulfilled promise to close Guantánamo Bay and the dramatic rise in the number of targeted killings since Obama took office, suspected Al Qaeda, Taliban, and affiliated fighters are no longer the visible symbols of torture and indefinite detention who are the subjects of legal and humanitarian advocacy. They are not individualized bodies that have been transformed from "enemy combatants" into dependents and, increasingly, subjects of rights. As targets in precision warfare, their deaths do not constitute murder, and they are also celebrated as a triumph of the state's ability to demarcate individuals in space and use lethal force against them. In the practices of precision warfare, bodies of "terrorists" are bodies of information as well. They show up as heat signatures on the drone pilot's infrared screens (Martin and Sasser 2010, 52). They are not neutrally represented by an image on the screen any more than the body of a traveler is represented by the "Automated Threat Detection" image of "generic outlines." Bodies that are killed by drones are made killable by drones; that is, they exist as bodies to be killed only by virtue of their representation on the screens of UAV assemblages. Where once a person located in "ungoverned" or "ungovernable" places was literally "off the grid" in terms of state intervention, drones and other surveillance technologies of precision warfare produce potentially every human in the world as watchable, and killable. While drone operators (unlike the pilots of bomber planes) can often see clear images of the bodies they target, the people who are targeted by drones, on the other hand, often cannot see or hear the drones at all. Predator drones, for example, hover three miles above the ground over Afghanistan (Muir 2010). This gaze is the gaze of the panopticon, a one-sided gaze that has as its ideal perfect knowledge and control, in which the source of the gaze cannot be seen (Foucault 1979, 200–201). This role of the gaze suggests that it is not the abstraction or distance from the targets per se that is a necessary condition for killing; rather, it is the masculine posthuman embodiment that enables such killing.

"Patterns of Life"

In February 2011, the *Washington Post* reported that the CIA has shifted its targeting procedure to focus on militants who meet a criteria kept secret, but which is referred to as a "pattern of life" that includes certain "signatures" such as traveling in or out of an Al Qaeda compound (Miller 2011). "Signature" strikes target people in Pakistan, Yemen, and Somalia based on their activities, even if they are not persons known to officials (Becker and Shane, 2012). "Pattern of life" analysis was also used as evidence in the decision to decimate an Afghan village using 25 one-ton bombs (Ackerman 2011). Obama administration officials have defended their targeting practices, which assume that males traveling in areas of Al Qaeda activity or who are found with Al Qaeda operatives, are involved in terrorist activity and are thus eligible to be targeted by drone strikes (Becker and Shane 2012). Once targets have been identified, "pattern of life" analysis is also used to predict their movements so that non-target casualties can be minimized (Lewis 2013). Here, there is a striking similarity between the bodies of precision bombers and the bodies of their targets in that "life" and the bodies in which such life is embedded are not seen as material objects so much as informational patterns (Hayles 1999, 104). The US National Security Agency (NSA) has recently been revealed to use tracking "pods" drones to collect data from wireless routers, computers, smart phones, and other electronics, which are used to facilitate airstrikes (Scahill and Greenwald 2014). Metadata are used to identify the individual SIM[8] card; metadata refer not to the content of mobile calls, but to the activity on the SIM card: who contacts whom. The metadata are analyzed to identify specific SIM cards, which may or may not be held by the person intended. Nor is this metadata analysis always accurate as to who is involved in militant organizations, as it lacks human, or "on-the-ground," intelligence. Precision warfare, which transforms the human body into a computer or information processor, can only relate to other bodies through this paradigm of information: like the bodies produced by full body scanners in airport security assemblages, bodies of the targets of violence in precision warfare exist in dematerialized form, as images and information.

The critique of the "pattern of life" criteria is not so much that some of the people identified by this technology may be "misidentified" and not actually be Al Qaeda or Taliban militants, though this is certainly a concern, or whether "patterns of life" analysis ends up sparing more civilian lives by predicting the movements of targets and enabling strikes when targets are not near civilians. On one level, we might critique this kind of criteria as straying from the traditional "just war" as well as international law from determining who is a combatant and thus a legitimate target, as this criterion is notably looser than the standard of providing "material support" for hostilities. From the perspective of posthuman embodiment, the use of "pattern of life" analysis reveals the inadequacies of thinking about contemporary warfare from the "just war" perspective in the first place. Here, the use of drones to target certain bodies is based on a kind of biopolitical discourse—the term "life" also connects the regime of precision warfare with biology and ecology—a discourse suggesting a kind of transformation from the subject position of terrorist, to a more vague designation of "undesirability." The apparent unacceptability of certain "patterns of life" and the need to remake the world and destroy those who are not complicit represent continuity with colonial struggles to manage "ungovernable" lands and reform native populations. The visual and computational abilities that accrue to posthuman precision bombers enable the killing of others to be understood as accidents, outside political accountability, in the realm of the naturalized disaster, more akin to a tornado or an epidemic. The designation of killability stems from a process in which those marked for death are identified and individuated by images and code as a "pattern of life" rather than as corporeal entities: from a "virtual life" made known only through images and algorithms to a targeting decision leading to very real deaths (Pugliese 2013; Gregory 2014). This form of surveillance marks a shift from mapping and targeting based on terrain, cities, and military installations to a mapping of bodies: bodies that are materialized as information patterns. Marking people for death—for elimination—based on "pattern of life" suggests that precision warfare is being used not only on behalf of the sovereign power's ability to punish and kill globally, but of the ability and desire to kill based on a particular way of being in the world, that, while not articulated in racial terms, uses language associated with both biology and information processing to designate individuals marked for death. The production of knowledge as a precursor to targeting here has a more complicated relation to the visual: "seeing" the target is not the criterion used to enable destruction; seeing is only part of the process that involves the production and collection of diverse forms of data (including "metadata") that are used to target based on nodes in communications networks, which here stand for life itself (see *inter alia* R. Chow 2006).

Unknowable Bodies

While the "terrorists" are targeted for death, a large number of the people actually killed in precision warfare are those whom we might consider "civilians" if such a term, associated with just war theory and international law, were still relevant and meaningful. The "spectacle" of punishment in bombing is the destruction of buildings and non-human targets; the death of people, whether soldiers or civilians with some important exceptions, is hidden from view. Whereas the just war tradition sees death in war as glorious sacrifice on behalf of the nation (Elshtain 1995 [1987]), deaths of those other than the enemy are mistakes or accidents in precision warfare, if they are seen to exist at all. Like "terrorists," "enemy combatants," "militants," and others marked for death, those other than targets who are killed exist as *killable* through the production of posthuman precision bombers. Here, the concept of "civilian," while still used to protest the killing of unintended victims, is not longer a useful category of analysis when killing is less about the distinction between "us" and "them," friends and enemies, than the elimination of certain forms of life (see Dillon 2007b). Such bodies enter into the posthuman assemblage of precision warfare as an actively produced ignorance: in the discourse of precision warfare, "civilians" only exist insofar as assurances of looking out for their welfare are used as a justification for certain practices of violence; few dead "civilians" are said to actually exist.[9]

Those to whom violence is done to "accidentally" are constituted as "bodies that don't matter." In the conflicts in Afghanistan and Iraq, government officials have refused to keep count of civilian deaths, referring to the difficulties in ascertaining an accurate count. One UK official said, "It should be recognized that there is no reliable way of estimating the number of civilian casualties caused during major combat operations" (BBC 2005). The deaths of civilians are not in view of either the bombers or the viewers thousands of miles away, who witness the war through a media restricted from showing the caskets of dead soldiers returning to the United States (Milbank 2003; Stolberg 2004). The Pentagon has also disavowed the possibility of ascertaining how many civilians have been killed, despite the existence of many techniques for counting civilian dead (Norris 1991, 228). The limits of the discourse of precision can be seen in the contrast between the capability to bomb buildings accurately, but not count civilian deaths accurately. The discourse of the unknowability of body counts distinguishes precision warfare from prior modes of warfare. By means of contrast, in the Vietnam War, progress was often measured by "body counts" of the number of enemies (or suspected enemies killed). Accordingly, very precise records were kept of the number of deaths.

In terms of contemporary precision warfare, especially in the debates about the use of drones by the US and Coalition forces, the number of civilians killed have varied widely. The CIA's covert operations in Pakistan have led to the most disagreement about the numbers of civilians versus militants killed, at least in part because the drone campaign has been considered an official secret, so most of the information comes from local press reports and interviews with witnesses. In 2009, Kilcullen and Exum cited local Pakistani sources to claim that 50 civilians have been killed for every militant, including over 700 civilians killed (Kilcullen and Exum 2009). Byman estimated that drones reportedly kill 10 civilians for every militant death (Byman 2009). On the other hand, US officials have claimed that very small numbers of civilians have been killed. Bergman and Tiedemann reported in 2010 that US government officials have claimed that just over 20 civilians have been killed in the prior two years, while more than 400 fighters have been killed by drones (Bergen and Tiedemann 2010). Obama administration officials have also claimed that the number of civilians killed have been in the "single digits" and that both local populations and militants have an incentive to claim that those killed are innocent of any wrongdoing (Becker and Shane 2012). One assessment of four databases based on local media reports concluded that actual civilian deaths are between about 4 percent and 24 percent of the total number of those killed by drone strikes in Pakistan (Plaw 2013, 142).

In the above debates over the number of civilians versus militants killed by drones, or by precision warfare more generally, the difficulty of distinguishing between civilians and combatants is presented as an epistemological problem of insufficient vision in surveillance, or insufficient intelligence. In other words, distinguishing between civilians and combatants, and only killing combatants, is possible with better information that is not necessarily available because locals may lie. The God's eye vision of precision warfare is not only the perspective of the pilots, but an epistemology that constructs absolute knowledge as finite and attainable.

One of the most striking features of the contemporary drone warfare is the US government's method of counting civilian casualties: deaths by drone strikes in Pakistan are counted as combatants if they are military-age males, and independent estimates of civilians killed that range in the hundreds are considered by the Obama administration to be influenced by propaganda (Becker and Shane 2012). As women are presumed to be non-combatants, the presence of women killed at the scene is read as a missed target and the death of non-combatants (Entous 2010). Here, we see an example of the violence of gender norms to erase certain lives. Butler writes, "To the extent that gender norms... establish what will and will not be intelligibly human, what will and will not be considered to be 'real,' they establish the ontological field in which bodies may be given legitimate expression" (Butler 1999 [1990], xxiii). In the designation of all military-age men as "combatants" and thus killable, and women as civilians and their deaths as mistakes, the gendered operation of the civilian/combatant distinction serves to render the question of an individual's conduct or threat meaningless. If, as Kinsella persuasively argues, the civilian/combatant distinction is constitutively gendered, with women serving as the quintessential civilians who cannot be a threat (2005, 2011), the decision to count all military-aged men killed as combatants compounds this logic by anchoring threat or danger in the body of man. The category of "civilian" as one not involved in planning or carrying out war or violence is effectively meaningless, and sexed embodiment has replaced it as a determination of whose deaths should be regretted (even if they aren't mourned). Another way to define away the concept of civilian is simply to not record their deaths, as in Brandon Bryant's story that opened this chapter.

In effect, there are no civilians in precision war, there are only individuals who, by a variety of processes, have been targeted for death rained by above. They are not a vague "enemy" group and they are not, by and large, openly carrying arms. They are individualized, even the ones who are identified not by guilt in a court of law like a criminal, not by gathering intelligence data, but by exhibiting a certain "pattern of life" that is at least partially determined by algorithms (Gregory 2014). The expanded definition of an imminent threat made explicit in the US Department of Justice White Paper, which suggests that clear evidence of an attack planned in the immediate future isn't necessary, also broadens the terms of legitimate military targets (especially when the US has not declared war). In short, the combination of technologically enabled targeting practices, legal justifications, and gender discourses creates a population that can be killed with virtual impunity: deaths are not only un-punished, they are nonexistent.

Epistemologies not only produce objects of knowledge, but also produce "unknowns." The lack of precise body counts, as well as the difficulty in distinguishing between civilians and combatants in precision warfare, should not be understood as a temporary shortcoming in a progression of ever-increasing knowledge, but as an actively produced ignorance.[10] Applied to "body counts," the difficulties in accurately calculating the number of civilian and combatant deaths are not a matter of unreliable systems of measurement and the methodological and political issues surrounding attempts to enumerate casualties, but rather the result of a discursive system that actively produces the "accidental" deaths of civilians as unknowable, as a matter of the unreliability of counting practices or enemy propaganda, in short, of the failure of the very state whose failure brought about the bombings in the first place.

Defenses of precision warfare are often about the rigor to which the laws of armed conflict and the principles of distinction and proportionality are applied. Harold Koh, the Legal Advisor to the State Department during the first Obama administration, was a notable defender of drone strikes: "In my experience, the principles of distinction and proportionality that the United States applies are not just recited at meetings. They are implemented rigorously throughout the planning and execution of lethal operations to ensure that such operations are conducted in accordance with all applicable law" (Koh 2010). John Rizzo, who served as chief counsel at the CIA for six years, has said that CIA drone strikes required approval by him and 10 other agency lawyers before they were authorized (Hastings 2012). In the United States, controversies over precision warfare and the use of UAVs to carry out targeted killings specifically, generally revolve around legal questions, such as whether or not it is legal to target US citizens, such as Anwar al-Awlaki. The legal structures, such as the Geneva Conventions or the question of whether the Obama administration procedures were properly followed,[11] and the emphasis placed on avoiding civilian casualties are one way of avoiding focusing on the dead bodies that such strikes cause

(Asad 2007; Gregory 2014). By debating the legal and moral rationales in terms of the existing discourses that privilege the intentions of military commanders, violence is made acceptable if it is done in a way that is procedurally correct.[12] The gaze is focused on questions of accountability in US political leadership, rather than the complex military apparatus and related political conditions that make certain bodies killable and even erasable in the first place.

The use of precision weaponry is justified by reducing the number of civilian deaths; yet, these very deaths cannot be counted under this regime and, moreover, the practices of precision warfare make civilians "killable" in the first place. "Mattering" in this sense is less about an objective empirical reality that reproduces the "god's eye view" of certain privileged epistemologies, but a question of normative violence; that is, the norms of bodily life that foreclose, often violently, the kinds of lives that are livable. As such, Butler's contribution toward theorizing the embodiment of norms of gender and sexuality is not only, or even primarily, an epistemological contribution. It is a political intervention aimed at the question of livable lives in a context in which so many lives have been deemed unreal, and, in the face of their violent demise, ungrievable (Butler 2004a). Implicit in Butler's formulation of normative violence is a critique of Agamben's concept of *homo sacer*, the original figure of sovereign power, the "bare life" outside political status who can be killed without it being considered a murder or sacrifice (Agamben 1998). Agamben writes that the concept of the body "is always already a biopolitical body and bare life, and nothing in it or the economy of its pleasure seems to allow us to find solid ground on which to oppose the demands of sovereign power" (1998, 187). Agamben's *homo sacer* is someone who was first recognized as a life, and then abandoned by power to become only biological life. Butler's work is an insistence that life cannot be "bare." The *homo sacer* is constituted by sovereign power and thus is not "outside power" as it exists by virtue of its exclusion. However, Butler's "unintelligible" or "ungrievable" life is far from a bare life; it is not abandoned by power, it is not an apolitical body or an animal life, which is what remains after one is stripped of political status. Such categories are impossible for Butler, as the production of such a category requires apparatuses of power; being "unintelligible" or *homo sacer* requires being mired in power relations, rather than abandoned by them. Butler insists that there is no "pure" or "raw" body prior to the intervention of power or outside power (Butler 1993; Bell 2010, 149). The function of normative violence is to prevent some lives from being recognized as lives in the first place.

The production of certain bodies as killable yet ungrievable, whose guilt or innocence is irrelevant, reveals not only the political work needed to strip their bodies of subjectivity, but also the interconnection between the bodies of civilians and the bodies of posthuman soldiers. The bodies of civilians are produced in relation to the production of posthuman soldiers. In order for the military personnel to commit violence from afar, the bodies of civilians are produced as biopolitical bodies who live or die as a matter of rational calculation and risk management. Subjected to the aleatory nature of precision weapons and complicated formulae factoring into targeting decisions, including the weather and how much a threat the intended target is, the civilians are not individualized as the targets of the bombs are. They exist only as members of a population, whose management entails not the injunction to "make live" but rather the minimization of threat, rather than a serious effort at its elimination.

While counting bodies is one step toward a critical analysis of precision warfare, the mere counting of bodies does not necessarily challenge the production of certain bodies as killable, especially as such numbers are compared (3,000 US soldiers killed in Iraq versus 3,000 killed on September 11th, Iraqi civilians killed by Coalition forces versus Iraqi civilians killed by Saddam Hussein). The recording of numbers of deaths, whether in the hundreds for drone warfare and other uses of precision weaponry, or as part of the broader casualties in land wars and occupations such as the US-led invasion of Iraq, are in a sense *incomprehensible*. The suffering of others, whether by atomic bomb, displacement by war, or other atrocity, is erased, becoming unthinkable, because of who the sufferers are made to be.[13] As one theorist noted, "common practices of reporting casualties have become so normalized that they at once obscure and reproduce the workings of geopolitical power that frame these numbers" (Hyndman 2007, 38). Just as the imaging capabilities of satellites and drones make it possible to view individual people targeted, while not necessarily bringing about greater sensitivity and reluctance to use force, the enumeration of deaths does not necessarily constitute a politics of re-humanizing or "subjectivizing" those who have been made into "mere bodies." Butler echoes this concern, arguing that the act of representing, or "seeing" the other is not enough to ensure the humanization of the subject. It is not the "human" that is represented, but rather, the "human" is the limit of the possibility of representation. What has been produced as "inhumane" or outside the bounds of humanity cannot be brought in by representation. For Butler, following Levinas, "The human cannot be captured through the representation, and we can see that some loss of the human takes place when it is 'captured' by the image" (2004a, 145). The representation of suffering beings does not necessarily bring them into the ethical moment, but rather, representation practices can be used to produce some humans, some bodies, as "other," as lives not worth mourning. The "human" exceeds representation because representation is what brings "beings" into being—a process that forces the question of the ethical from the deployment of sovereign, physical violence per se to questions of ethical representational, boundary-producing practices. The precision bomber as "posthuman" suggests that both bomber and the people on his or her screen are flows of information on a screen—existing as texts or codes. The production of certain subjects through their integration in informational frameworks constituted by the practices of precision warfare suggests that a greater emphasis on "seeing" the victims of warfare is not an adequate critique: it is the "coding" of such people that matters.

CONCLUSION

This chapter has probed the political implications of the mutually entangled bodies of posthuman precision bombers and the killable bodies of "militants" and unfortunate bystanders. By mutually entangled, I mean that the physical/political production of these bodies with certain capabilities and powers comes in terms of the formation of other bodies. There is no "terrorist" marked for death by a hovering drone without posthuman drone pilots, nor are there "accidental" unnamed, uncounted, and uncountable deaths of civilians (a concept that is also inadequate when the category of "marked for death" is so broad to include those who might otherwise be counted as civilians). These bodies exist only in relation to one another, the sovereign power of the posthuman bomber existing only by the performative force of its ability to view the movements of, and launch missiles at, people half a world away. Precision warfare thus simultaneously produces a subject that is (seemingly) invulnerable and subjects that can or must die, but at the same time erases responsibility for this very regime. Bomber pilots and drone operators are not the only "posthuman" bodies; the killable bodies of "terrorists" and civilians only come into being by virtue of the human/technological assemblages of precision warfare. They, too, are posthuman bodies: constituted in and through their relation to the killing machines of precision warfare.

In a regime in which the biopolitical imperative operates with such force, the bodies that the regimes of precision warfare work to secure are shown to be *unnatural* bodies, constituted in reference to historical political conditions and divergent material capabilities. "There is no unmediated photograph or passive camera obscura in scientific accounts of bodies and machines; there are only highly specific visual possibilities, each with a wonderfully detailed, active, partial way of organizing worlds" (Haraway

1991b, 190). Precision warfare, as producing and making use of bodies-as-computers with particular embodied visions, organizes and makes legible a world of individual targets and accidental deaths of civilians. It is these unnatural bodies that constitute the biopolitical practice of precision warfare as a tool of "humanitarian" global liberal governance. In the next chapter, I take this project's overall themes of the problems of embodiment in biopolitical security practices, including the naturalization of bodies, bodies as material and cultural/political and bodies as precarious, and bring them to bear on an emerging doctrine governing the practice of violence internationally: the "responsibility to protect."

CHAPTER 6

Vulnerable Bodies and the "Responsibility to Protect"

In this work, I have argued that contemporary practices of violence and security demonstrate the need to take the embodiment of the subject seriously in ways that neither conventional International Relations theory nor biopolitical approaches have thus far. Feminist approaches, on the other hand, argue that it is inadequate to separate something called "the body" from the broader social, political, and environmental milieu. Bodies have no independent existence as such, but require supplementation in a variety of ways, from the work needed to conceptualize bodies as the objects of torture or as legible to security apparatuses, to the material and discursive relations needed to make certain bodies killable in the regime of precision warfare. Sovereign power is one form of supplementation of the body insofar as sovereign power is necessary to live a life free of violence, deprivation, and an early death, in the Hobbesian state of nature. In a biopolitical reading, the bodies that comprise the populations are constituted, as I have argued, as bodies that not only must be managed, but also must be *known*; that is, they must be constituted as objects of knowledge in order to survive and thrive under responsible stewardship. The existence of bodies *qua* bodies is the result of political interventions, though bodies also possess productive or agentic capacities for altering political relations. The framework that this work has developed for thinking about bodies, subjects, and violence suggests that ethical accounts of political violence should take into account more than the injuring or killing of natural bodies; they should also be responsive to the ways in which social relations—including security practices—are implicated in (and reliant upon) producing different kinds of bodies and configurations of bodily relations.

In this chapter, I show how the theorization of bodies that I have developed in this project can be applied to critique an emerging framework for understanding and addressing contemporary security threats: the doctrine of "responsibility to protect," often abbreviated RtoP or R2P. In light of the previous chapters—which argued that bodies are both produced by, and are productive of, politics and are not contained in themselves or in their relations to others—we can now think about bodies in connection to RtoP in a way that challenges the terms of "responsibility" by thinking about not only harm done to existing bodies, but also the production of certain bodies as those that can be harmed. Specifically, I attempt to think through the paradigm of RtoP from Butler's theorization of vulnerable bodies, which is in accord with the dimensions of bodily life that this work has developed. I show that thinking through the ethical implications of RtoP from an ontology of vulnerability has broader implications for the way in which we think about ethics and responsibility.

Butler's thesis of bodily vulnerability and ontological precariousness is an argument that bodies do not exist in their own right, but rather exist only in virtue of certain conditions that make them intelligible as human. Humans are not only vulnerable to violence as natural bodies that can be harmed; they also are vulnerable precisely because they exist only in and through their constitution in a social and political world, in and through their relations with other bodies. Human bodies are vulnerable to each other precisely because there is no "we" or "I" outside the other. Butler writes, "if the ontology of the body serves as a point of departure for such a rethinking of responsibility, it is precisely because, in its surface and its depth, the body is a social phenomenon: it is exposed to others, vulnerable by definition" (2009, 33). This sentence highlights the connection between rethinking the subject as embodied and rethinking the terms of ethics and responsibility that attend to us as embodied subjects. Having shown in preceding chapters that bodies targeted, harmed, or protected by practices of violence and its management are unnatural (as they are produced by political relations as well as productive of relations), that bodies are both material and symbolic, and that they are formed in ongoing relations with one another, I put this formulation to work in a critique of the "responsibility to protect," a recent development in International Relations that redefines sovereignty.

RESPONSIBILITY TO PROTECT

In recent years, the doctrine of "responsibility to protect" (RtoP) has been promoted as a norm that encourages states to override the principle of state sovereignty in order to stop genocide and other "mass atrocities" (Bellamy

2009). Set up by the Canadian government, the International Commission on Intervention and State Sovereignty (ICISS) promoted the concept of "responsibility to protect" as way of resolving the debates in the 1990s over humanitarian intervention. Over 150 states agreed to RtoP, and it was formally adopted at the 2005 World Summit. In 2011, the United Nations invoked RtoP in a mission to protect civilians from mass atrocities in Côte d'Ivoire, as well as in Resolution 1973, which authorized NATO's military action in its mission in Libya.

The Rwandan genocide, the killing of over seven thousand men and boys at Srebrenica, and the ongoing rapes and killing of civilians in Darfur and the Democratic Republic of Congo (DRC) are all instances of the kinds of mass violence that the doctrine of RtoP was initiated to prevent; RtoP develops a framework to provide guidance to the international community on how to address such atrocities. The outcome document for the 2005 World Summit states, "Each individual state has the responsibility to protect its population from genocide, war crimes, ethnic cleansing and crimes against humanity" (United Nations General Assembly, para. 138). Military interaction is not intended to be the first step to address such atrocities; rather, other coercive measures are to be taken first, including diplomacy, sanctions, or the use of judicial instruments such as the International Criminal Court. RtoP formally includes not only the "responsibility to react" in terms of the international community's use of military or other forms of intervention, but also the "responsibility to prevent" (of both states and the international community in monitoring emerging situations) and the "responsibility to rebuild" (in the case of the use of force to stop or prevent mass atrocities, the international community must remain involved in efforts to rebuild and fix the damage caused). This norm essentially makes sovereignty conditional upon upholding certain standards of human rights.

If we are seeking, then, to determine who is sovereign, that is, who has the right to let live or kill without it counting as murder, we might locate this power in NATO or its most powerful member states. However, we might also see this, as its proponents do, as making human life sovereign, as the preeminent political value. RtoP is a development of a broader agenda in international politics to redefine security from the protection of the state to the protection of the individual. The concept of "human security" has, in the past few decades, become a frequently invoked term in the international community, especially in the United Nations, changing the referent of security from the state to the individual person, and specifically regarding the ways in which individual human life is insecure. While the human security approach strives to change the conceptual apparatus, it relies on the established logic of security, as human bodies are produced as objects to be protected from outside threats, just as states are in conventional international security discourse. As one of RtoP's architects and leading proponents, Ramesh Thakur, proclaims, "human security puts the individual at the center of debate, analysis and policy. He or she is paramount, and the state is a collective instrument to protect human life and enhance human welfare" (Thakur 2010, vii). The agenda of human security emerged in the post–Cold War shift from what was considered "traditional" security threats of interstate war to "nontraditional" security issues, such as civil war, genocide, terrorism, the use of indiscriminate weapons of landmines and cluster bombs, and even non-violent causes of bodily vulnerability, like the lack of food and clean water as well as health issues, including the HIV pandemic. Summing up these diverse developments, Kaldor writes, "security is about confronting extreme vulnerabilities—not only in wars but in natural and man-made disasters as well" (2007, 183).

The political problems that RtoP addresses stem from a theorization of the security problematic as constituted by the threat of sovereign power: the power to take life or let live. The problem that RtoP is meant to address is the abuse of this power to take life. RtoP is meant to prevent and address violence against individuals—either violence by the government itself, or violence that the government cannot or will not stop. As such, RtoP is a vision of security from the perspective of sovereign or juridical power. RtoP implicitly theorizes bodies and security in ways that are familiar in the mainstream of security studies: naturalized bodies that will live unless they are intervened upon by outside forces that would injure or kill them.

The responsibility to protect does more than reinforce sovereign power; it defines sovereignty as biopower through the term "responsibility," although from a Foucauldian perspective, sovereignty was already constituted in terms of responsibility (Fishel 2013, 213). RtoP enshrines the concept that rights-bearing individuals are the basis from which state sovereignty is derived. State sovereignty is redefined not as an absolute principle of non-interference from other states, but as a responsibility. Non-interference is made contingent upon government's protecting the rights of their citizens, defined as a lack of certain forms of violence. As stated by the co-chairs of the ICISS, "it is now commonly acknowledged that sovereignty implies a dual responsibility: externally, to respect the dignity and basic rights of all the people within the state. In international human rights covenants, in UN practice and in state practice itself, sovereignty is now understood as embracing this dual responsibility. Sovereignty as responsibility has become the minimum content of good international citizenship" (Evans and Sahnoun 2002, 102).

This is a shift from prior definitions of sovereignty. Sovereignty as it is traditionally theorized in International Relations bestows a formal equality on all states and enables them to use violence and make war legitimately. We are still within the terms of sovereign power, but RtoP is a way in which security is now also articulated in biopolitical terms. Evans and Sahnoun write, "at the heart of this conceptual approach is a shift in thinking about the essence of sovereignty, from control to responsibility" (2002, 101). The reformulation of sovereignty as responsibility casts sovereignty in biopolitical terms: no longer the power to take life over a specific territory, sovereignty is a beneficent form of patriarchal power, governing the population with its best interests in mind (Foucault 2007, 100, 129). RtoP takes seriously the concept of human security, itself a critique of how the "narrow perception of security leaves out the most elementary and legitimate concerns of ordinary people regarding security in their daily lives" (ICISS 2001, 15). Failing to protect citizens from hunger, disease, flooding, unemployment, and environmental hazards are given as examples of human security issues that RtoP is designed to address. Such phenomena take place not at the level of individuals, but at the level of population. By recasting sovereignty as responsibility, RtoP installs a biopolitical understanding of sovereignty as promoting the lives of citizens as a population of organisms—preventing mass violent deaths and ensuring the proper circulation of basic necessities. However, the responsibility to protect explicitly applies only to the four violations of genocide, war crimes, ethnic cleansing, and crimes against humanity—instances of "calamities" such as HIV/AIDS, climate change, or natural disasters are explicitly considered to undermine the consensus over the concept (UN General Assembly 2009, para. 10b). RtoP is meant to protect against certain forms of violence but not others: it protects against forms of widespread direct violence usually associated with wars or mass atrocities, but not broader forms of structural violence, deprivation, or precaritization.

In the discourse of "human security" the focus is on the dying, suffering bodies of people located someplace else, in the Third World, the Global South, the (former) colonies. These are de-politicized bodies, bodies to be kept alive, to be fed and healed. They are bodies that are the objects of Western intervention to save, as their states have failed to save them. Security, in the context of biopolitics requires a complex system of coordination and centralization, including various non-governmental, governmental, and inter-governmental aid agencies aimed at "developing humans" (Duffield and Waddell 2006, 4). Furthermore, RtoP is meant to be applied solely to "failed" states, or states in the South. The Commission report specifies that RtoP is not to be applied to "major powers" because interventions in these states are likely to cause larger conflicts (ICISS 2001, 37). As such, the biopolitical imperative of RtoP seems to be based on monitoring, control, and regulation of a non-Western population's life (Weber 2009, 587). "The proposition that human security prioritizes people rather than states is more accurately understood in terms of effective states prioritizing populations living within ineffective ones" (Duffield and Waddell 2006, 10).

The biopolitical, as that which takes control of life processes, collapses such a distinction between war and politics that sovereignty produces by reserving violence and war for itself. The biopolitical critique of security practices focuses our attention on the ways in which security not only forbids, but is also productive. While we might fruitfully locate RtoP in terms of the biopolitical nature of contemporary security practices, this critique is not sufficient to account for the proliferation of this new norm and its consequences for thinking about ethics and responsibility in terms of embodied subjects. A biopolitical critique of RtoP calls upon us to be attentive to the workings of power in producing certain kinds of subjects and, importantly, certain kinds of bodies who are vulnerable or invulnerable. Just as various technologies are involved in producing certain bodies as intelligible as targets in the case of precision warfare, or through violence as terrorists who can be tortured or irrational figures who can be force-fed, certain knowledgeable practices are implied in producing a certain people as the objects of intervention. This chapter is not intended to contribute to the literature in International Relations on the question of "humanitarian intervention" and why certain atrocities affecting certain people at certain times have been deemed eligible for intervention while others have not been.[1] The contribution of my work in theorizing bodies in International Relations is not only to call attention to how certain bodies are produced intelligibly as "lives worth saving" but also in highlighting the need to think relationally about bodies—the bodies of "targets" as well as civilians produced as killable by the creation of precision bombers as posthuman bodies, for example. The production of certain bodies as lives worth saving is bound up in the production of other bodies as not worth saving, or other bodies who deserve to die. Even less frequently discussed in the International Relations literature is what the production of certain bodies as vulnerable lives that need saving (and other bodies as lives already lost) implies about an "us"—the people who debate such issues in international forums and write about them in the academy under the auspices of the discipline of International Relations.

In thinking about the political and ethical question of creating and sustaining the conditions for "livable lives," there is a way in which we can read RtoP as precisely the kind of increased recognition of humanity, of "humanness" of subjects that allow us to recognize their lives precisely as lives worth living. One might argue that RtoP is acknowledgement of the precariousness of life, as it is an acknowledgement of responsibility for the preservation of lives in distant places, lives that are not necessarily tied to an "us" through family, culture, or nationality. Such a reading is possibly borne out by Judith Butler's recent writings on bodily precarity. Butler specifically addresses 9/11 as an injury to the United States as a subject, and reads subsequent wars as a way of trying to shore up the United States as an invulnerable subject by maximizing vulnerability for others. In opposition to such a model of increasing feelings of security by making others insecure, Butler advances bodily vulnerability as a generalizable condition to encourage a more thoughtful and less violent approach to the question of ethics and responsiveness in the face of violence. There is a way in which, given the emphasis on egalitarianism in recognition of mutual vulnerability, the doctrine of RtoP is a way of doing precisely what Butler, or a particular reading of Butler, would have us do. In contrast to the practices of torture and precision warfare, which seek to eliminate bodily vulnerability by maximizing vulnerability for others, RtoP appears to be about seeking greater bodily security for all. RtoP is about lessening the consequences that being born within certain political borders has on the precariousness of life, specifically death in genocide or other mass atrocities, and the expansion of the number of people whose lives "matter" politically. RtoP is only possible in a world in which the definition of people whose lives are worth saving is expanded beyond the state, or from the perspective of a Euro-American-centric world, to non-white, non-Christian peoples (Finnemore 2004). Butler even suggests that military interventions to stop genocide may be justified at one point. This is a plausible interpretation of Butler and the concept of bodily vulnerability insofar as it seeks a more egalitarian understanding of whose lives are worth living and whose lives are worth saving—an expansion of the possibilities of "livable lives."

However, a reading of Butler's concept of precariousness in terms of the theorization of bodies, subjects, and violence put forth in this project gives us pause before too quickly celebrating the responsibility to protect. We must be careful to distinguish an approach that takes seriously bodies as produced by, and productive of, International Relations, from a model of humans as rights-bearing subjects, which a celebration of RtoP as an expansion of the ability of the international community to protect human rights would entail. Butler's formulation of the question of ethics—drawing on her theory of the formation of embodied subjects—stresses that ethics is not only matter of inclusion and exclusion of individuals into particular communities as subjects with particular rights. Butler writes, "It is not a matter of simple entry to the excluded into an established ontology, but an insurrection at the level of ontology, a critical opening up of the questions, What is real? Whose lives are real? How might reality be remade?" (2004a, 33). In other words, the questioning of bodily ontology entailed in Butler's concept of bodily precarity is not about applying concepts of human rights or human security to greater numbers of people. Rather, such an approach would question the portrayal of RtoP as a process that increases recognition of certain subjects who are *already* constituted by a certain set of rights, including the right to be protected from sovereign violence. RtoP poses a sovereign subject, but locates it in the individual rather than the state. It is the individual that should not be impinged upon, that should not suffer violence—it is not the state that should be left alone. The individual as a subject whose rights to bodily integrity and inviolability are sacrosanct is precisely not a subject constituted by vulnerability; it is an autonomous body that this work has shown is untenable for theorizing contemporary practices of violence.

Butler's account of the production of the embodied subject and the kind of ethical response that is entailed in such an understanding of bodies compel us to consider the co-production of differentiated embodied subjects. Crucially, to understand the body as precarious is not to understand the body as at risk in the sense that its integrity and autonomy are threatened from outside forces. The relationship of RtoP to the sovereign state and the sovereign individual presumes coherent, preexisting subjects in way that denies primary vulnerability. Butler's concept of normative violence—the violence that attends to the formation of the subject—stands in contrast to this model of embodiment. Understanding the subject as constituted by violence, and vulnerability to violence as a generalizable phenomenon rather than a characteristic of certain groups, suggests a rethinking of the question of agency and responsibility. In a recent work in conversation with Athena Athanasiou, Butler discusses the tension between two readings of vulnerability: the first as an ontological matter of subject formation in which we are formed by our "passionate attachments" to lost objects (see also Butler 1997b) and our embodied relationality: that we are driven by passions and dependent upon environments and others that sustain us (2013, 3–4). The other sense of this vulnerability is enabled by the first but not reducible to it: in seeking to avoid a depoliticizing sense of this constitutive vulnerability to that which is outside the self, but through which we have no "self" to speak of, Butler clarifies the need to avoid allowing this framing of precarity to legitimize or excuse certain forms of human deprivation and exploitation, which are historically specific (2013, 5–7). Butler distinguishes between *precarity* as a general condition and *precariousness* as a condition that is the result of some lives not mattering, that is, lives that are being made unintelligible. While precariousness may be thought of as those who live as the "constitutive outside," those whose lives are rendered unintelligible as lives, *precarity* signifies the constrictive vulnerability that is the cost of becoming a subject; we are subjected to and by norms that we did not choose. In light of this distinction, we are called upon to see how historical processes depoliticize certain bodies, making them objects for rescue, intervention, and manipulation, which appear as "bodies in pain on the horizon!" in Muppidi's words (2012, 120), calling out for their lives to be sustained as "bare life," as the passive beneficiaries of aid. In order to do this, we must examine normative violence as a way of relating the process of subject formation to the issue of violence. Following this, I show how this enables a re-reading of issues implied by this relation to RtoP and the different subjects that RtoP produces: a subject to be saved, a subject that can do the saving, and an inhuman subject that can be killed in order to save others. I close with a consideration of how the question of normative violence suggests a reorientation of ethical thinking in International Relations.

NORMATIVE VIOLENCE

A critical examination of RtoP through the tools for understanding embodiment that this work has utilized would thus entail not only a critique of violence as injuring, as something to be avoided except as a last resort in defense of the lives of citizens; it would also require a critical examination of normative violence that is centrally concerned with the production of abject bodies. These abject bodies are the constitutive outside that haunts the seemingly coherent subject, for the very concept of "human life" requires a relationship with the category of the nonhuman (Butler 2004b, 13). The naming of the "human" implies the naming of that which is not human, the drawing of a boundary demarcating the constitutive outside, the inhuman (Butler 1993, 8). Violence is also implicated in the formation of subjects relative to the various modes of violence under consideration in this project—torture, suicide bombings, the precision warfare of bombs and drones, as well as many more. These are bound up in norms that make us who we are, so that we are never fully in control of subject positions or whether we are recognized as humans at all. Butler insists that while we are formed from violence, that is, made intelligible or partly intelligible and subject to certain kinds of social risks through the violence of norms, we do not have to perpetuate this violence (2009, 167). Having been formed through violence, we have access to modes of non-violence that can pertain not only in the injunction not to harm individuals in terms of the use of sovereign power to hurt or to kill, but the use of non-violence in terms of our own implication in the possibilities of embodied subjects leading livable lives.

The prisoners held at Guantánamo Bay exist in such conditions of "unlivability;" tortured, denied status under international law, and held indefinitely, with measures taken even to prevent their suicide or protest by hunger strikes. Such violence happens to subjects that have already been "derealized," or made into "bodies that don't matter," through their designation as "enemy combatants" and "detainees." Their torture, then, is not considered torture, as this is an injuring of a subject that has already been subject to the normative violence that posits these people as outside the bounds of the recognizably human. Normative violence is connected to violence as we usually think of it, in that if "violence is done against those who are unreal, then, from the perspective of violence, it fails to injure or negate those lives since those lives are already negated" (Butler 2004a, 33). By denying that the treatment of prisoners at Guantánamo Bay and elsewhere constitutes torture, but is rather "ill-treatment" or "abuse," the humanity of those who have suffered this violence is also denied, as torture names a practice against a human subject, against whom violence is always a violation. Violence against the targets and bystanders of precision warfare also fails to count against these "bodies that don't matter," as these bodies are constituted as ungrievable, killable bodies by the production of the bodies of precision bombers and drone operators as invulnerable through their production into legal and technological systems of protection and enhanced killing capacities.

If we consider bodies as produced by particular social and political circumstances, and even more important, as requiring supplementation in terms of certain conditions to make life livable, we are pushed to consider the conditions that not only create the possibility for mass atrocities, but also the conditions that make certain lives eligible for supplementary protection by an "international community." Butler insists that bodily precariousness is not about some lives being precarious while others are not. The condition of being an embodied subject entails supplementation, both materially in terms of bodily needs and a certain set of social conditions that sustain lives as livable. "The very idea of precariousness implies dependency on social networks and conditions, suggesting that there is no 'life itself' at issue here, but always and only conditions of life, life as something that requires conditions in order to become livable life and, indeed, in order to become grievable" (Butler 2009, 23). Because bodies are vulnerable and, indeed, mortal, there can be no such thing as a "right to life" itself: there are only conditions for sustaining life, and for creating the social and political conditions for livable lives.

In taking bodies seriously in their social and political production as intelligible "bodies that matter" or as abjected bodies, we see in RtoP a practice that (re)produces three types of embodied subjects. First, there are bodies of protection—that states must protect, or in the case that states cannot or will not protect, that other actors are called upon to protect. This schema also implies a subject that is the agent of protection, empowered to use force in order to eradicate violence—that is, a sovereign subject who designates who must live and who must therefore die. There is also the subject that may be killed so that others might live, the lives that can be sacrificed and who are the face of inhumanity. In considering the role of normative violence and RtoP, I start by considering the production of the bodies to be saved as those who are already lost.

The object of the intervention that RtoP produces are subjects whose lives are being lost, not only as individuals, but as members of populations. They are the victims of ongoing genocides, massacres, and other atrocities. RtoP sets the standard for intervention as "actual or anticipated" large-scale loss of life or ethnic cleansing, which may include killing, expulsion, rape, or "acts of terror" (Evans and Sahnoun 2002, 103). They are those whose states have failed to protect them, or who are actively targeting them in either a failure or an abuse of sovereign power. They are not subjects of agency, but are bodies that breathe, suffer, and die, who are "just bodies." They can then become civilians who are killed accidentally, because they are always already lost. These bodies are what Mbembe refers to as the "living dead" (2003, 40), those which are subject to massacre; such massacres are the deaths of those who, politically and socially speaking, are already dead.

Like Butler in her concept of bodily precariousness, Mbembe calls attention to the social and political conditions that differentially structure risk and vulnerability and, in particular, formulate massacres and atrocities of the sort that RtoP is meant to address. Such deaths are not a failure of sovereign power to recognize human rights. Rather, these deaths are due to certain practices of sovereign power that certain bodies are made killable, already socially dead. RtoP is meant to protect bodies that have, in Butler's terms, failed to materialize as "bodies that matter." They are the abject bodies that inhabit "unlivable" zones of social life (Butler 1993, 3). By recognizing certain bodies as in need of saving from forms of sovereign power, RtoP is complicit in a regime that recognizes certain people as *only* vulnerable bodies that need protecting from sovereign power, who are thus differentiated from those empowered to save them. They are only the naturalized bodies of biopolitics, the objects of intervention and various representational practices depicting them as bodies to be saved. Deprived of context, "what impels actions, what bring[s] about a 'moral imperative to act' is the vision of the injured, bleeding, dying body of the Other" (Muppidi 2012, 119, citing Rieff 2002, 33). A focus on saving these bodies is limited in its ethical imagination to the terms of "responsibility": it is a responsibility to save only those who have already been deprived of the social and political conditions of a "livable life," who have been marked out as targets for genocide and ethnic cleansing, whose lives are the abject that must be expelled.

From the perspective of bodies as ontologically precarious, focusing on the vulnerability of certain bodies in their constitution of always already vulnerable is not sufficient to "solve" the problem of vulnerability. It does not acknowledge the vulnerability of those killed or injured in an effort to save others, and also does not acknowledge the precariousness of those who are "protected," whose states are presumably doing a good enough job, the citizens of states who are presumed interveners. Such vulnerabilities exist, but RtoP is a framework that does not acknowledge this vulnerability and serves to manage the political distribution of this vulnerability. I turn next to the question of vulnerable bodies and, in particular, the implications for the denial of such vulnerability.

VULNERABLE BODIES

RtoP presumes that people are made vulnerable by sovereign violence and that by removing state sovereignty as a shield, people will be less vulnerable and more secure. As the previous section discussed, RtoP locates vulnerability in states that fail in their biopolitical responsibility to provide protection from mass death. As a next resort, RtoP posits an agentic subject above the state, the "international community" who can act, including through the use of violence, to eliminate violence and protect vulnerable people. On what terms does this actor assume this kind of power over life? Taking seriously the critique of exogenous, natural, and fully self-conscious actors that I have developed throughout this work, as well as the reformulation of bodies as produced in and through social relations and in relation to other bodies, means that we cannot consider this agent to preexist its establishment as a "protector of last resort." This sovereign subject, in its presumed agency, is a subject whose own vulnerability is erased and who is constituted as an invulnerable subject. Individual bodies that represent the "international community" may be killed in such interventions, but the subject of the "international community" is constituted as a sovereign subject that can never be killed. As such, it is a disembodied subject akin to the "king's two bodies": the sovereign has the power to inflict violence but is immune from suffering from it—even though the individual king may die, the sovereign subject is immortal (Kantorowicz 1957).

To take Butler's thesis of bodily precarity seriously is to challenge the designation of some populations as vulnerable and others as invulnerable; vulnerability is a generalizable condition that is constitutive of what it means to be an embodied human subject. In locating vulnerability to violence "elsewhere"—and presenting the question of "responsibility" as located in a more secure, "invulnerable" subject of the state or the international community—is to neglect how the subject that is presumed to provide security in the event of state failure is also, by definition, a vulnerable subject. This "invulnerable" subject is not literally impermeable to violence; rather, I use the term *invulnerable* in this sense to indicate a denial of the embodied subject's constitutive vulnerability not only to violence as we commonly understand it, but also to normative violence in the social and political formation of the subject. This invulnerable subject is a fully agentic subject whose violent formation is obscured.

Explicitly defining sovereignty as responsibility and including, in former UN High Commissioner for Human Rights Louise Arbor's words, a state "duty to care" for its citizens could be seen as a progressive move in feminist terms (Arbour 2008). As I briefly discussed in Chapter 1, feminists have argued that caring labor has been devalorized as feminized labor. "Care" represents an ethical tradition that some feminists have argued is associated with women and has been devalued in favor of the masculine "justice" tradition.[2] However, when located as an attribute of the state, the caring aspect of RtoP is less about recognition of universal human vulnerability (rather than the vulnerability of certain populations) and the valuing of caring labor as necessary for human flourishing than it is about positing certain agents of this care, and certain recipients. Butler's thesis of the embodied subject as vulnerable suggests a critique of the terms of agency that RtoP implies. The discourse of RtoP locates agency in two places: an international community and the people/states that are doing the harm that constitutes the failure to protect. Agency is posed as a matter of exogenous subjects acting on the world. By locating agency elsewhere, such a model reinforces the association of people in "Third World" or "developing nations" (especially women) with helplessness (see *inter alia* Mohanty 1984; Orford 1999). Feminist scholars have argued that logics of protection feminize those being protected (who are placed under the patriarchal power of their protectors) as weak and helpless children (Elshtain 1995 [1987]; Tickner 2001; Young 2003; Sjoberg 2006; Carver 2008; Wilcox 2009).

Philip Cunliffe has recently echoed this point, arguing that a perverse effect of creating a "duty to care" for the state actually undermines political accountability in the name of paternalism: "states have responsibilities *for* their people rather than *to* their peoples" (2010, 93). As Cunliffe points out, the recipients of RtoP seem to be politically passive; they provide a convenient constituency for elites. Cunliffe cites Marx's dictim, "they cannot represent themselves, they must be represented"; but perhaps Spivak's famous interpretation of this point in "Can the Subaltern Speak?" is even more relevant. Spivak analyzes this dictim in terms of Western discourses to produce knowledge about non-Western subjects without reproducing colonialist systems of knowledge and power (1985 [1988]). The responsibility to protect reinforces the status of some people as objects of pity or charity, but not as proper political subjects who can make claims and can be dealt with as equals (see also Butler 2013, 113). The "human" of human security and humanitarianism that underpins the revisioning of sovereignty in world politics are "humans" stripped of the social, political, economic, and environmental worlds in which they are embedded—not subjects of constitutive vulnerability, in Butler's terms, but as people whose lives have been made unlivable, whose "bare life" is to be sustained, and whose suffering is taken not as evidence of radical relationality but as evidence of how distinct and distant they are from an "us." RtoP also reinforces a heroic understanding of the "international community" as agents capable of rescuing such helpless people, as well as deciding upon whether such people are indeed helpless and in need of rescuing in the first place.

However, if we understand embodied subjects to be in an ongoing process of becoming in relation to other embodied subjects and the social and material environments, we must critique not only *where* agency is to be attributed but how that agency is to be understood. The subject who is in a position to decide or deliberate over whether a state is meeting its obligations under RtoP, or who is empowered to act to protect those lives being lost or threatened, is not isolated from the processes of normalization, or social and political production, as a certain kind of embodied subject. Furthermore, this subject, like other subjects, is formed in relation to others and norms in ways that can never be fully grasped. In analyzing RtoP, we must then not neglect to consider the norms that constitute certain subjects as agentic, as saviors and protectors. While such subjects may not be, strictly speaking, invulnerable in terms of imperviousness to violence, in this scheme their vulnerability in terms of their formation in and through social relations is denied. Such subjects are formed in a history that they did not choose, but are formed nonetheless. As Butler writes, "the very capacity to judge presupposes a prior relation between those who judge and those who are judged" (2005, 45). The formation of this subject of invulnerability includes the exclusion of the abject as the "constitutive outside" of the subject; for this subject—the "international community"—to appear as a coherent subject vulnerability must be shifted elsewhere—onto both vulnerable subjects who need saving, as well as to inhuman subjects who can be killed.

Butler establishes the constitutive vulnerability of our embodiment in her sentence that serves as this book's epigraph: "the body implies mortality, vulnerability, agency: the skin and the flesh expose us to the gaze of others, but also to touch, and to violence" (2004a, 26). In her essay "Besides Oneself: On the Limits of Sexual Autonomy," Butler continues this thought: "The body can be the agency and the instrument of all these as well, or the site where 'doing' and 'being done to' become equivocal" (2004b, 21). In this follow-up to her depiction of the physical and social vulnerabilities of the bodies, Butler acknowledges that these very same bodies are instruments of the violence, neglect, objectifications, and death, through our embodied gaze, through the use of our bodies to commit acts of violence. They are agents of various forms of violence as well, but also are fundamentally constituted by forms of political and social determination of our embodied selves that we cannot control. Our bodies as the site of "doing" and "being done to" make them the site in which power relations are complicated precisely because it is the site in which both occur simultaneously, blurring the lines between agency and passivity. Bodies as simultaneously active and passive, inscribed by exterior forces yet productive of agency as well, can be seen in the painful body of the hunger striker protesting his or her imprisonment in Chapter 2, or in the naked(ish) bodies of the "flesh mob" as both protesters and objects of the gaze. The body can be a witness, and in one's own marking and refiguring of the body, violence can contribute to the re-subjectification of bodies.

Taking seriously our bodies as constitutively vulnerable means that we must locate agency in the conditions that formed particular agents, but this does not mean that these agents are absolved of responsibility—we are never *completely* formed by conditions. We should ask ourselves, what performances of the "natural" are occurring that disguise and hide the constitutive vulnerability of those who are constituted as "responsible" subjects rather than subjects needing protection? As the "power to produce what it claims to represent," performativity suggests a double movement: it not only produces an effect of the natural and inevitable, but also conceals this construction as it appears to be natural. One's formation as a subject is ongoing, iterative, and citational—as it is never complete, the subject can be reformulated over time. Certainly, the histories that constitute certain subjects as wielders of various forms of violence are important here, whether the subjects of violence are those who perpetrate and threaten the mass atrocities that RtoP is meant to address, or the subjects of violence who would use force in order to stop such atrocities. Such histories do not mean that there is *no* question of responsibility or that people cannot be held accountable for their actions. Butler's vulnerability thesis suggests that locating responsibility in sovereign subjects is not the *only* way of thinking about responsibility, and that ethics requires more than the presumption of sovereign subjects.

After all, as Butler writes, "if the violent act is, among other things, a way of relocating the capacity to be violated (always) elsewhere, it produces the appearance that the subject who enacts violence is impermeable to violence" (2009, 178). By locating violence "somewhere else," in places that have always already failed to accede to the norm of sovereignty, RtoP, then, has the effect of (re)producing certain subjects as invulnerable. The violence that RtoP proposes and enables—in the sense of military force used to end or forestall genocide or ethnic cleansing—is productive in the sense that it produces both the subjects perpetrating this violence as invulnerable and the subjects that are the target, or possible victims, of such violence as always already vulnerable, or even already dead.

RtoP (re)produces this break between vulnerable and invulnerable subjects in part by distinguishing between zones of regular politics, in which states are fulfilling their biopolitical responsibilities, and certain "death-worlds," in which life is not promoted, but is taken in a failure or a perversion of the state's responsibilities to foster and regulate life. Created by a committee established by the United Nations through Canada's leadership, the norm of RtoP and its accession took place under conditions that have been demarcated as normal politics: the deliberation and consensus of rational subjects with particular sets of interests. RtoP then takes place as an aspect of politics far from the circumstances it is meant to address: the realm of unreason and the violence of war, especially wars that turn on citizens and civilians and subject them to mass killing. RtoP sets up a mechanism in which the reason of politics can intervene in the unreason and passion of such wars and can bring them back to normalcy, back to the political. It enacts a division between the stable worlds of sovereignty and impermeability to violence and the violent worlds in which bodies are always already vulnerable.

In making this break, RtoP simultaneously supports and challenges state sovereignty. First, it supports state sovereignty by emphasizing that it is first and foremost the state's responsibility to protect its citizens. In cases of civil war leading to massacres and other such atrocities, the state is to be supported in its efforts to stop the violence. RtoP only challenges state sovereignty by insisting that when states cannot or will not stop this violence, the international community then has a duty to bestow the protection that the state is not providing. Security, in the regime of RtoP, is defined as protection from violent death in the hands of, or with the complicity of, the state. As Stefanie Fishel points out, this framing elides other logics of extreme violence: "the shift from 'sovereignty as right' to 'sovereignty as responsibility' only evades the deeper questions that remain about the violence inherent in the state and the international system of states" (2013, 209).

The responsibility to protect instantiates a liberal vision of disqualifying violence from the domestic realm. The subject does not owe strict obedience to the sovereign, and the subject to be protected is the individual subject of rights. RtoP is an insistence that states do not have the right to use violence against their own citizens and must uphold their protection from violence both internally and externally: sovereignty as responsibility is duty to provide care and protection for citizens. Sovereignty is ostensibly being reformed to no longer include the equality of all states in their right to wage war against one another; rather, RtoP instantiates a norm of "good global citizenry" for states, in which to refuse to comply is unthinkably cruel or irrational (see also Piiparinen 2012). To an extent, this is a reformulation of an older norm in which "civilized" states could wage war against one another, but the colonies, or frontiers that are not properly constituted into states, are the zone of exception from which the law can be suspended, and violence outside the law can be perpetrated (Mbembe 2003, 24). Redefining sovereignty in the biopolitical terms of responsibility means that the violence of military intervention is defined in terms of the civilized order of "the international community" against the inhuman violence that spurs such interventions.

Redefining state sovereignty from a concept of absolute authority over a defined territory to a duty to protect individuals from widespread violence also implies a reshaping of the constitutive relationship between the human body and the state. The boundaries of the state have been imagined, and conceptualized, as akin to the skin of the human body as the boundaries between the inside and outside, and between different states and bodies. As I argued in Chapter 3, the human body as self-contained, with the skin marking a solid boundary between inside and outside and demarcating one subject from another, is not a natural or ontological fact but the result of various political, symbolic practices. In short, this is contingent upon articulation of what bodies are; it is not an essential truth of bodies. Likewise, the state as *body politic*, an entity modeled on this self-contained body, is an effect of various political discourses. RtoP reproduces this logic, denying the constitutive vulnerability of human bodies as well as the particular histories and articulations of this model of the state.

Having theorized bodies and states as mutually productive in terms of their solid borders and the strict demarcation between like units, the doctrine of responsibility to protect can be seen as an attempt to discipline states into enacting just such a model of governance. Of chief concern here is the concept of the failed state, or the state with "ungoverned" or "ungovernable" regions where the central government does not exercise effective control over the borders. Here, the primary examples given are Somalia for a failed state, and Pakistan and Yemen as states with ungoverned regions. Such states are the constitutive others, the "abject" that constitutes liberal states in the West as the norm, the "clean and proper" subjects whose bodies—both in terms of the bodies of their citizens and states as *bodies politic*—are inviolable. If some lives are deemed "unlivable" or "ungrievable" because of the failure of their bodies to live up to the norm, these are the states whose existence *as* states is unlivable because of a similar failure, who are then subject to violence that is considered legitimate.

If it is the figure of the human who is the sovereign subject, as RtoP would have it, then an injury to this subject can lead to sovereign practices of violence to locate injury elsewhere. If the subject then becomes a subject identified with this injury, it becomes a subject who legitimates its own violence to avenge its injury. Butler is especially concerned with the injury of 9/11 and the wars that were undertaken as a result, but her writings on the charge of anti-Semitism and critiques of Israeli state policy suggest that the myriad historical injuries suffered by Jewish people, and especially the Holocaust, can be taken as similar examples to the US wars in response to 9/11—as attempts to use violence to deny a constitutive vulnerability and instead shore up one's own sovereignty by inflicting violence on others. RtoP works somewhat differently from these two examples, in that it is not the injury suffered by a subject that is used to legitimate violence, but rather, the injury to *other* subjects that is used as a potential reason for the use of violence on their behalf. There is, undoubtedly, some measure of solidarity involved here. However, might we also see this relationship as a defense not only of particular sovereign subjects, but also of sovereign subjects and sovereignty itself? Attempts to eliminate vulnerability in shoring up sovereign power and sovereign subjects are only displacements and denials of the vulnerability that attends to all human subjects. By recasting sovereignty as responsibility, the sovereignty of the individual, the state, and the international community are all reproduced, albeit through biopolitical terms. Sovereign power is reaffirmed in such a way that it can be exercised not only against domestic subjects, but against subjects that are deemed to lack humanity.

SUBJECTS OF INHUMANITY

The production of humanity as subjects to be saved, who must be made to live by subjects who are always already alive and invulnerable, implies a constitutive other, an "inhuman" subject. This inhuman subject is primarily those who perpetrate the crimes of genocide or ethnic cleansing on behalf of the state or whom the state cannot or will not prevent from committing such crimes. In constituting the invulnerable subjects of "the international community" that speaks on behalf of humanity in terms of human rights and human security, these subjects of inhumanity are the abject, that which is excluded as the founding repudiation of such a subject. To have a humanity that is embodied, we must have an inhuman embodiment as well (Devji 2008, 26–27). The naming of the "human" entails the drawing of a boundary demarcating the constitutive outside, the inhuman (Butler 1993, 8). The subject of the "international community" is linked to an older discourse of civilization that speaks on behalf of the human, claiming that it represents humanity against an inhuman(e) other.

The condition of "inhumanity" in the contemporary world order cannot be separated from the sovereign foundation of the state in protecting the "natural life" of citizens. States involved in not only killing people, but also committing genocide—the killing of populations—are subject to military intervention. In the "war on terror," as in so many conflicts, the enemy is seen as synonymous with a particular callousness and inhumanity toward human life. The Taliban's lack of respect for human life and the abysmal conditions in Afghanistan leading to premature deaths under Taliban rule are both justifications given for US-led military operations in Afghanistan (Elshtain 2003, 60). Condemnation of the practice of suicide bombing is focused on the celebration of the deaths of "martyrs" who are willing to die in order to kill non-combatants. Similar conditions constitute the inhuman others of RtoP, as interventions are justified in terms of the lack of respect for life and subsequent mass killings. Killing or failing to prevent the deaths of populations, under the doctrine of RtoP, makes one a legitimate target of violence, as do "acts of terror," although violence is not intended as the first step to addressing such atrocities. As those who can be killed, the existence of such subjects of inhumanity blurs with the populations that RtoP attempts to save, the people who are already targets of extermination, who are already socially dead. Under such conditions, the vulnerable bodies of the population in need of protection can be killed as "collateral damage" in attempts to save them by using violence against their killers: both are already constituted as bodies that do not matter. The broader implications of this include the legitimation of violence against those who are deemed to have insufficient respect for life. Importantly, this "inhumanity" in not protecting life in RtoP only applies to the domestic population; one might ask why states that do not exhibit the kind of respect for the lives of populations in *other* states are not subject to the same sovereign violence.

This is, of course, not a defense of genocide or any other violent practices but an examination and critique of the terms in which RtoP constitutes certain forms of violence as ethical. We may have very good reasons to do so—to make decisions to use force to stop genocide—but this kind of decision does not exhaust our ethical responsibilities. The question of normative violence—the violence that attends to the formation of subjects—is another site of our ethical responsibilities. Butler's turn to Levinas can be seen in light of the concern with normative violence and her rejection of methodological individualism—that individuals are the basic unit of ontology and, thus, ethics. The question of how one responds to other humans fails precisely when the subject of the address is not recognized as human. Her engagement with Levinas is a way of struggling with the question of ethics not only as a question of how one treats existing individuals, but of a responsibility that attends to the subject that preexists the subject's very formation. It is a sense of violence that is prior to violence as we usually understand it.

Butler's use of the Levinasian face is a way of addressing the problem of normative violence, the violence that attends to the formation of subjects rather than injuring a subject that already exists. The Levinasian concept of the face posits discourse as arriving before we do, before we are formed as subjects. The face is the *bodily* aspect of the other, but like the subject, it is not a self-contained, clearly delineated body. Butler uses the terminology of exposure when discussing the vulnerability of the body—bodies as exposed to others, and bodies as exposed to the gaze, to touch, and to violence (2004a, 26). The face represents the normative violence that is always present as a possibility. Yet, the face is a responsibility that one cannot avoid, as its call is part of the discursive structure that produces the self. In the confrontation with the face, the subject-in-becoming is called to non-violence through a responsibility to this other. Butler extorts: "Let's face it. We're undone by one another. And if we're not, we're missing something" (2004a, 23). In these lines, Butler addresses the reader directly, even beyond the author-audience structure of academic writing. By this direct address, Butler does what grief, what the "face," stands for: her address interpolates the reader into a subject constituted with this responsibility, and constituted in the precariousness that is social and political life as well as bodily existence that is made possible through relations with others.

In theorizing our bodies as ontologically precarious, the question of ethics becomes not a condemnation or defense of subjects of inhumanity—the murderers, perpetrators of genocide, or terrorists—but of reflection about the processes in which subjects become human or not, and the terms of humanization, as this is ultimately the question about how certain bodies come to "count" and the terms on which livable lives are established. As a matter of ethics, this becomes a matter of how we recognize the vulnerability in ourselves and in other subjects. Vulnerability has to be recognized in order to restructure the field of ethics (Butler 2005, 43). In the process of recognition, neither side is precisely what one was before. This means that one cannot recognize another subject as vulnerable without rethinking one's own subjectivity relative to vulnerability. Recognition is the process "by which I become other than what I was and so cease to be able to return to what I was" (Butler 2005, 27).

We perform recognition of vulnerability by various practices, such as speech acts acknowledging vulnerability and various representational practices of vulnerability. Striving for recognition is not a claim to be recognized as we are—for before we are recognized, we are in sense outside subjectivity—but in making a claim, we are in a process of becoming something else (Butler 2004a, 44). Here we see more implications of the hunger strikes at Guantánamo Bay and the statement of Binyam Mohammad: "I do not intend to stop until I die or we are respected." This is speech act that is made by a body being made to perform weakness and vulnerability—a body that will weaken and die, whose precariousness is being made to be acknowledged. Butler writes, "To say that a life is precarious requires not only that a life be apprehended as a life, but also that precariousness be an aspect of what is apprehended in what is living" (2009, 13). Speech acts and other representation practices are necessary but perhaps not sufficient conditions for the humanization of subjects in their precariousness *as* humans. In order to think about the social and political conditions for "livable lives," I have turned to the question of representing the other, especially the vulnerable other, the other that is always already wounded, as a means of thinking about what form responsibility may take given an ontology of generalized precariousness, rather than an ontology of self-contained individuals.

The representation of injured or killed bodies, or those who have been excluded from the normative frameworks constituting "livable lives," is not sufficient to counter the production of these lives as "unlivable" or "ungrievable." As I argued in the previous chapter, the "human" is what is brought into being by representation, and therefore the category of the "human" exceeds representation. The unlivability of certain lives is not a matter of a lack of information, or a discursive failure to produce such knowledge; rather, as with the deaths of civilians, ignorance in this instance has been actively produced. Thus, the problem is not only that the media do not report on the human suffering of war—especially of the "other" side or that, until recently, photographs of coffins of soldiers killed in the US wars in Afghanistan and Iraq were forbidden from being photographed. The circulation of representations of broken bodies and the use of the wounded and killed as the consequences of war may be necessary and important for any number of political projects, not the least of which is bringing to light the costs of war, which are so often papered over.

However, there are some problematic aspects in focusing on wounded and dead bodies as a way of "humanizing" the victims of violence that apply to questions of ethics, violence, and representation more broadly. Such images may provoke horror and disgust: this may be useful if it is a first step to recognizing commonality and mutual vulnerability, but the horror and disgust that is the felt response to the presence of the abject does not necessarily lead down this path. It is possible, even likely, that the revulsion that accompanies images of broken bodies can lead to a desire to buttress one's own sense of stability through various forms of rejection. Such images may also provoke pity, which is a kind of ethical response, though it is also a response implicated in hierarchical relations. The visual record of abuse, such as the photographs depicting torture at Abu Ghraib, may extend the torment, as the recording of the torture was an integral part of the humiliation and shaming (see Dauphinée 2007, for example), and some people take a perverse pleasure in such images. As violence against others can have the effect of shoring up one's own feeling of *invulnerability* by the location of violence elsewhere—far away, or in a different time, or to someone not "like me"—such images can reinforce a sense of victims of violence as "always already" dead. This does not also mean that the absence of such images is ethically and politically unproblematic either. What is perhaps necessary but not sufficient is an inquiry into what Deleuze referred to in his concept of the visual as that which "distributes what is seen and who sees" (1988, 58). Precision warfare, as a form of violence that relies heavily on particular configurations of bodies, weapons, and visual technologies, is one site of the use of representation to produce bodies as human or inhuman; another site that functions in an overlapping way is the surveillance technologies used to detect "dangerous bodies," such as those of suicide bombers.

The representation of suffering beings does not necessarily bring them into the ethical moment, but rather, representation practices can be used to produce some humans, some bodies, as "other," as lives not worth mourning. Images of broken human bodies do not always generate pity and compassion: the widely distributed images of the bodies of the sons of Saddam Hussein were used to demonstrate American power. The controversy over whether or not photographs of Osama bin Laden's corpse should be distributed demonstrates a similar principle: concern over the "unseemliness" of trumpeting images of a man's death and the possibility that outrage over such triumphalism would bring about more violence. Representation always entails a "loss," a gap between the subject's desire and what can be expressed in words or other symbolic representations. It is not the "human" that is represented, but rather, the "human" is the limit of the possibility of representation. Bodies are "in excess" of speech such that (in Hansen's paraphrase of Butler) "speech can never fully convey the body, and the body is never constituted outside of speech" (2000, 302). What has been produced as "inhuman" or outside the bounds of humanity cannot be brought in by representation. The "human" exceeds representation because representation is what brings "beings" into being—a process that forces the question of the ethical from physical violence per se to questions of ethical representational, boundary-producing practices. In thinking about the problem of ethics from a perspective of mutually constituted bodies and normative violence, we are called to be responsible not only for the protection of those we can see (that we have been made aware of through representational practices and speech acts), but also for the ways in which various subjects are produced *as* human or inhuman.

HOW RESPONSIBILITY IS RESTRUCTURED

The core conclusion that the previous discussion suggests is that ethics and responsibility cannot *only* be considered a matter of responding to others as if "we" and "they" existed as socially and politically separate entities. By taking embodiment seriously as an effect of, and cause of, entangled engagements, responsibility is rethought as accountability for who and what "matters" in the world—and who and what does not matter—in sharp contrast to discourses of "responsibilization" that shift the site of ethics onto individuals, as in neoliberal discourses. We are mutually entangled with each other such that we cannot separate. Our bodies themselves do not precede social entanglements, and thus we cannot consider an ethics of violence differently from existing frameworks that separate bodily existence from power. Rather than ethics being conceptualized as the proper treatment of others, "ethics is therefore not about the right response to a radically exterior/ized other, but about responsibility and accountability for the lively relationalities of becoming of which we are a part" (Barad 2007, 393). Responsibility has to do less with seeking security than with resisting regimes of inequality by addressing what Athena Athenasiou describes as "the differential allocation of humanness; the perpetually shifting and variably positioned boundary between those who are rendered properly human and those who are not" (Butler 2013, 31).

The broader implications of theorizing bodies as precarious and bound to one another in their production as seemingly autonomous entities is that the question of ethical responsibility lies not only in protecting or rescuing those who have been constructed as grievable but also in the challenging of those discursive practices that constitute some people as grievable tragedies in death, others as justifiably killable. Because we are formed through the violence of norms, it is incumbent upon us to resist imposing the same violence on others (Butler 2009, 169). Butler posits a mode of protection, but it is clear that she does not mean, or does not only mean, the protection of an existing body from violence. Protection from violence is also a struggle with the social and political norms that structure the production of livable lives: to be responsible, to protect from violence in this instance is to work to lessen the violent effects of the norm, to trouble the power of bodily norms to mark certain lives as unlivable and unreal. Responsibility is about where the "cut" between self and other is made. We do not have recourse to the "god's eye view," to approach the question of ethics in terms of a disconnected appraisal of a situation in which "we" have no part. Our constitution in and through the world is not only a matter of our perspective being limited or partial. Our subjectivity is a material engagement in the world, creating it as it produces knowledge about it. Taking seriously the bodily precariousness means being attentive to the discourses that produce certain subjects as inhuman or as only bleeding, suffering bodies outside the full political context under which we and they are constituted.

Conclusion

This work has interrogated contemporary practices of violence through the critical lens of feminist theories of embodiment. However, this work was never intended to speak only to feminists; rather, the purpose in highlighting feminist work, and particularly that of Judith Butler, is to show how feminist work contributes to a revisioning of the terms of political violence more generally, through an analysis of the constitution of embodied subjects in and through violent practices. While Chapters 2 through 5 each focused on a particular set of violent practices and their management, each chapter also adds a thread toward the three main arguments of this book. First, contemporary practices of violence necessitate a different conception of the subject as *embodied*: understanding the dynamics of violence means that our conceptual frameworks cannot remain "disembodied." Second, taking the embodied subject seriously entails conceptualizing the subject as ontologically precarious, whose body is not given by nature but is formed through politics, and who is not naturally bounded or separated from others. Feminist theory in particular offers keen insights for thinking about our bodies as both *produced by* politics as well as *productive of* politics. Third, theorizing the embodied subject in this way requires violence to be considered as not only destructive, but also productive in its ability to remake subjects and our political worlds. In what follows, I underscore the specific threads of the main contributions of this book and discuss the potential for future work.

Chapter 1 showed how different strands of IR theory either implicitly or explicitly conceptualize the relationship between bodies, subjects, and violence, in which the body is an "absent presence" in terms of conventional theories and remains under-theorized in critical/feminist theories. I suggested that feminist theories of embodiment, particularly the work of Judith Butler, offer a way of theorizing the embodied subject in a way that is better suited for the challenges of thinking about contemporary practices of violence. I turned to establishing the inadequacies of existing frameworks empirically through discussions of contemporary violent practices, dismantling IR's assumption about bodies and subjects, and showing what a view of the embodied subject in feminist terms can contribute to how we theorize these practices. The hunger-striking prisoners discussed in Chapter 2, "Dying Is Not Permitted," differ from realism's assumptions of self-preservation and, more strikingly, liberal presumptions of the rational, speaking, consenting subject. The torture of prisoners is not a sovereign practice of punishing a subject under the law, but seeks to use the body's response to pain to override the will of the subject. The practice of torture reveals a biopolitical logic that uses violence against some bodies in order to promote the lives of others. Its contradictions in assuming a rational subject of pain-avoidance, but an irrational subject of force-feeding, demonstrate the need to rethink the foundational assumptions about the nature of violent practices from a biopolitical perspective, which sees violence as a performative act that produces subjects rather than harms pre-existing subjects.

Chapter 2 thus demonstrated how the practices of torture, hunger striking, and force-feeding undermine realist and liberal presumptions about the relationship between subjects and bodies, as well as the need to think about such practices of violence *biopolitically*. Chapter 3, "Explosive Bodies," continued the critique of IR's assumptions about bodies by showing that bodies are not naturally bounded containers for the subject. The boundedness and individuality of the subject are revealed in the practice of suicide bombing and various reactions to this form of political violence as an illusory effect of practices. Chapter 4, "Crossing Borders, Securing Bodies," continued this theme of the realness and materiality of certain bodies as they move across state borders and gender borders. Even the "body itself," as something that can be read by man or machine, as part of state security apparatuses, is an unstable signifier: the "body" as something that can be stripped of its meaning in broader cultural and political contexts is challenged by the experience of trans- and gender non-conforming people, whose lives demonstrate how thoroughly the notion of a material body is shaped by norms and state practices determining whose bodies and whose lives count as "real."

In Chapter 5, "Body Counts," the narrative of bodies in global politics develops another layer: bodies in their material existence as "bodies that matter" are produced in relation to other bodies; that is, the bodies of those killed by practices of precision warfare are only made possible by the "posthuman" embodiment of precision bombers and drone operators. The bodies of the purveyors of violence are "posthuman" in the sense that their boundaries do not end at the skin, but rather, they are integrated into a human/technological "kill chain" that seeks to transform the human body into a seamless component in an information-processing machine. The bodies produced by precision warfare are not strictly those of biological humans operating advanced technologies; nor are we capable of positing the "bare life" of those subjected to the all-seeing gaze and tremendous destructive capability of precision warfare and its cyborg denizens. Rather, we are called upon to see the ties between them in their asymmetrical co-production and of the normative violence implicit in such practices, which renders the lives of those killed as uncountable and unknowable.

The second main argument developed in this book is that bodies are not organisms that exist outside politics, as in conventional IR theories, but bodies are both produced by, and productive of, politics. Under contemporary biopolitical state security practices, bodies are produced by designating certain bodies as risks or threats, while other bodies are constituted as those to be protected. For example, the "terrorist" subject is produced and transformed through, among other practices, the violence of torture and force-feeding. Through the practice of torture, the tortured prisoner comes to be embodied in such a way that he is *only* a body; he is stripped of subjectivity and reduced to physical embodiment such that torture becomes rationalizable and calculable. Simultaneously, the torturer becomes "disembodied," as his or her body is not subject to violence or violation; it is no longer the self's vulnerable interface with the world. When prisoners attempt to resist by one of the only means of agency left to them, the refusal of food, they are force-fed, transforming them into dependent objects of biopower, rather than fully political subjects exercising autonomy over their own bodies.

In a different context from the torture and force-feeding of Guantánamo Bay, the terrorist subject is also produced by practices of surveillance and detection that purport to "read" the body for signs of ill intent. Such practices dematerialize bodies, virtually stripping them in order to make them transparent and readable; however, the experiences of trans- people show that such practices are deeply embedded in discourses of gender that presume and reinforce the alignment of bodily morphology to gender presentation and official documentation.

By these practices, the terrorist is constituted as a dangerous body that must be separated from the *body politic*. In instances of what could be read as a failure to maintain the boundaries between dangerous bodies and protected bodies, suicide bombing and the following recovery efforts reveal the political work necessary to constitute what Kristeva calls the self's "clean and proper body" (1984, 75). As I argued in Chapter 3, efforts to identify and reconstruct the bodies of victims by ZAKA members and the Israeli Forensic Institute transform victims' bodies into meaningful political subjects as Israeli Jews, while discourses of gender and heterosexuality produce bodies of female suicide bombers as gendered subjects sacrificing for the nation. Efforts at recovering and identifying the bodies do more than reflect the subjectivities of victim and perpetrator: they work to establish them. As suicide bombing results in a shattering of bodies, frequently rendering the victims indistinguishable from the perpetrators, the bodies must be reconstructed from their condition as "heaps of meat," bodies without subjectivity, in order to reconstruct the semblance of national wholeness and unity. The practices of ZAKA, the organization that collects the bodily remains, and the Israeli government provide a case study of how the body is politically produced through practices of International Relations, as well as how this constitution of bodies is directly tied to the formation and maintenance of the borders of the state and self.

Security practices that attempt to protect bodies from violent damage and death also produce bodies as abject—as de-subjectified "just bodies" that can be read by scanners for signs of risk and danger. While security apparatuses rely upon the body as a legible object in order to sort out safe and desirable bodies from deviant or unruly bodies, the experiences of trans- and gender non-conforming people demonstrate that sex and gender are properties of the state; bodies do not exist outside bodily norms of gender and sexuality. The existence of a material body that is legible to security practices is dependent upon the production of that body both as information and as intelligibly sexed; the failure of certain bodies to meet such standards results in their "unreality" as a traveler circulating across borders governed by the norms of liberal security governance. Bodies are not only killed, but are made to be "killable" by practices of International Relations. Some of the key political changes instituted by technologies of war not only increase the lethal capabilities of governments, but also result in profound changes in the nature of human embodiment. Such technologies—including both technological systems like drones and political/legal methodologies such as summary executions—produce certain bodies as killable targets and others whose deaths are seen as regrettable but inevitable.

If contemporary practices of international violence compel us to not only focus explicitly on the embodiment of subjects, but also theorize bodies as materialized through practices, we might be tempted to think of our bodies as objects that exist only as they are molded or given form but which are themselves passive, rather than politically active in any way. Not only does this ontology of bodies reproduce mind/body and culture/nature dualism by attributing agency solely to "mind" or "culture," but this view is countermanded by bodily practices in IR. The bodies that are produced by International Relations are also *productive* of IR; they play an agentic role in constituting practices of IR that cannot be reduced to the motivations of disembodied subjects.

The practice of suicide bombing provides a stark illustration of the manner in which bodies are themselves productive of world politics. I argued in Chapter 3 that, more than being a deliberately destructive act, suicide bombing as a mode of violence can be theorized as an act of contamination. By violently destroying the self in order to kill others, the suicide bomber disrupts the sovereign, self-enclosed, individualized body of the modern state. Interpenetrating and merging the bodies of self and other, the "nature" and "technology" of body and bomb, and the "inside" and "outside" of the body, the body of the suicide bomber performs a politics of contamination. Suicide bombing thus has political effects that are not reducible to conventional understandings of political violence as coercion. Thinking of suicide bombing as an embodied practice sheds light on the role of the body in international security; more than an object to be protected, bodies can be used to threaten security and to disrupt the stable borders of the state. The practices of recovering and reconstructing the bodies of victims and bombers in the wake of suicide bombings also illustrate how bodies can be productive of International Relations. Such practices do more than create the illusion that bodies are cohesive and self-contained. These bodily practices redraw boundaries between identities and produce bodies as synecdoche for the state and nation: reconstructing bodies as whole and discrete performatively rebuilds the state as a whole and discrete body as well.

The body of the hunger-striking prisoner in Guantánamo Bay is another example of the transformative power of bodies. In the tightly regulated environment of the prison camp, the prisoners may have decided to go on a hunger strike, but it is the weakening of their bodies that forces a transformation in the status of the prisoners from "enemy combatant," outside any law, to "dependent," an object of care made possible by the constitution of the "war on terror" as a biopolitical project. Yet another example is the posthuman body of the pilots in precision warfare, which renders the bodies of both militants and civilians "killable" in the sense that the material capacity exists to kill them. Perhaps more important, these bodies are rendered "killable" in a political and normative sense through their exclusion from political life as bodies that matter, or that can even be counted.

The posthuman bodies of precision bombers are productive of other bodies such that their embodiment allows some bodies to be subject to summary execution or anonymous death as collateral damage. The bodies of the same drone pilots also demonstrate the ability of bodies to exert agentic capacities against their production as instrumental information processors: despite the development of technological systems of surveillance and destruction aimed at keeping the bodies of soldiers out of harm's way, drone pilots experience signs of stress and even PTSD, embodied responses to the trauma of fighting in war.

Having illustrated that the bodies are produced by violent practices, yet also exhibit capacities, we can think more clearly about what theorizing the subject as embodied might mean in reference to violent practices in IR. This is the third main contribution of this work. In this work, I've focused on the human subject as the object of violence in order to move us from the individual and voluntarist conceptions of the subject prevalent in IR theory to a nuanced appreciation of the political nature of the *embodiment* of the subject. However, as the practices of suicide bombing and precision warfare illustrate, the embodiment of the subject is an effect of politics, and its instantiations need not end at skin. As a body-in-formation—that is, a body whose materialization is ongoing and subject to change, rather than fixed by biology or any other discourse—the embodied subject of International Relations is a posthuman body: an assemblage of organic and technological, natural and cultural materials and forces, whose existence as demarcated from others and from its discursive formation is only ever an illusory effect of political practices.

The consequences for thinking about embodied subjectivity as posthuman in terms of how we think about violence is eloquently theorized in Butler's work on precarity, which emphasizes violence and loss that exist as an ever-present reality of social life. Paying attention to the "constitutive outside" of bodies exposes the precariousness of all bodies: the abject other that is included by its exclusion. While Butler's theory of performativity can be understood as a theory of norms that are embodied, Butler's precarity thesis also speaks to the body as it is viewed in reference to norms, and of the exclusions of particular bodies. Among these exclusions are the bodies of women and queer people, and non-white and disabled bodies, an exclusion based on the norms that set male, heterosexual, white, and healthy/able-bodied as the standard, neutral, or universal body. Precarious populations are those that require protection by the state, but who are therefore also subject to the state's violence (Butler 2009, 26). They are the inflexible bodies and the *too* embodied that exceed the state's need for them as "clean and proper bodies" (Kristeva 1982) and whose bodies may becomes bodies that "don't matter," vulnerable to neglect and physical violence that does not register as such.

While the concept of the "posthuman" was only introduced in Chapter 5 of this work, the conception of the subject as existing only through supplementation with discursive and technological artifacts applies to both other "cases" under discussion in this work, and more broadly still. To be "posthuman" is not a function of a specific moment of technological or capitalist development. To posit the posthuman as a recent development suggests that there was a time when the human was never included in the category of nature, and existed in a state of purity outside its relation to technologies and the material world (Kirby 1997, 147; Waldby 2000, 48). Rather, to think of the embodied subject as "posthuman" is to theorize a subject in which the lines between the natural and cultural are not clear. This is precisely what is captured by the terms in which Butler articulates the precariousness of life: bodily vulnerability is not only a matter of finitude and the ever-present possibility of death, but the ontology of embodied life in which subjects exist only in relation to norms and desires they did not choose and the material conditions for sustaining life. The posthuman is a challenge to the body as object, as bounded organism and species, whose capabilities, limits, and boundaries are known in advance.

"Posthuman" bodies not only are sites for the inscription of cultural norms, they are sites of the active production of discourse as well. As sites of the convergence of "doing" and "being done to" (Butler 2004b, 21) bodies exist on what Hayles refers to as field of interaction between the material and cultural (1999, 199). Bodies are enacted through interaction with environment, but embodied subjectivity entails the capacity for subjects to enter into new formations and alliances. Our dependence on social relations and relations with the environment, even relations of violence, transform us. Such an ontology of bodies aims to move past nature/culture dualism as well as the sex/gender dichotomy to foreground the interplay between the materiality of bodies and their normative production in discourse.

Precision bombers and suicide bombers represent two poles of posthuman embodiment; in the former, the naturalized and individualized body is modified and extended in order to kill without risk to this body, and in the latter, the same body is put at infinite risk, deliberately obliterating the illusion of the "clean and proper" boundaries of bodies in order to kill. In both the seemingly unrelated cases of suicide bombing and precision warfare, body parts, bombs, and other weapons are not merely tools to extend the body's capability, but apparatuses that fundamentally reshape what it means to be a body. In neither of these cases can we think of subjects in liberal terms as autonomous; yet this is not the same as an anti-human perspective in which humans have no agency. In the contemporary biopolitical context, these posthuman bodies are not only harmed by sovereign practices of political violence, but some are formed as objects of intervention and made to live, while others are not only made to be killable, but are "ungrievable" lives whose deaths never really count as death. The embodied subject of IR, as both precarious and posthuman, suggests a rethinking of the way in which violence is theorized in IR.

Biopolitics denies the constitutive vulnerability of the embodied subject, focusing on dividing the population into seemingly stable categories, protecting and fostering the lives of some—whether in interventions aimed at regulating the lives of dependent populations, such as Guantánamo Bay inmates, efforts to screen for terrorists, building precision bombing apparatuses, and so forth. Biopolitical practices of security are aimed at maximizing vulnerability for some, and minimizing it for others. Violence expresses the instability in the founding of subjects as *embodied* subjects that is the result of the "constitutive outside," the abject that is not fully expelled and that lingers and drives the production of embodied that is never fully complete. Violence is present at the founding of subjects that appear to be stable and of bodies that appear to be natural. Theorizing bodies as produced through social and political relations challenges the myth of the sovereign man who rules over his otherwise inert body, as bodies are made and remade through discourse and through violence, and themselves exert a form of agency not reducible to the subject.

Sovereign relations of political power and violence act upon already existing bodies to punish and coerce; this form of relation is the primary focus of most IR theorizing about violence and security. However, biopolitical techniques have not so much replaced, but have been incorporated into techniques of sovereignty: this set of relations is evident in some of the practices of violence in Guantánamo Bay and the rationale for using torture to obtain information to save lives, and the insistence upon force-feeding hunger striking prisoners both as an act of war and an act of care. The emerging normative framework of "responsibility to protect," discussed in Chapter 6, legalizes biopolitical notions of responsibility within the sovereign framework of nation states, making sovereign contingent upon a minimal level of care for populations. Under the contemporary regime of RtoP, sovereignty *is* biopolitical. Biopolitical perspectives have drawn attention to the ways that practices of security meant to protect bodies from harm do not incidentally result in violence to other bodies; rather, violence is required (Foucault 2003). Biopolitical perspectives encourage us to view violence as productive; violence is not just something that is done to punish or coerce state and individuals; rather, such sovereign practices of violence are infused with the biopolitical imperative to foster life and promote the welfare of certain populations. As such, biopolitical perspectives have pushed us to be attentive to the ways in which what is seemingly stable is only an effect of practices. The bodies that sometimes appear to be both fixed and foundational to our subjectivity are in fact sites of the investment and transformation of relations of power.

Contemporary practices of violence reveal the body that conventional IR theory has taken for granted, a supposedly "clean and proper" body that is violated by violence, to be an appearance that is produced through exclusion and abjection in which certain bodies are disqualified from consideration as fully human. Security is, in this sense, a performance that attempts to create the illusion of the body's integrity and wholeness by producing a threatening "other" as lacking this proper body. Airport security assemblages are dependent upon the legibility of the body as a natural organism, but the seeming "naturalness" of this body, untainted by human artifice, is always in debt to practices of gender, which normatively constitute certain bodies as legitimate and safe, and others as inappropriate and risky. Violence is one way to produce the illusion of this properly differentiated subject, as the torture and force-feeding of the prisoners at Guantánamo Bay are a way of marking them as terrorists, and then as "dependents" who are not fully political subjects. Suicide bombing and the practices of handling and burying the human remains show the boundaries of the body and the assumption of self-governing individuality to be an illusory effect of politics rather than exogenously given. The suicide bomber troubles the naturalized body by collapsing the distinction between subject and object, nature and culture, inside and outside. The bodies protected through the practice of precision warfare are dependent upon the posthuman embodiment of precision warriors. Such bodies, along with the bodies of the suspected terrorists and the bystanders they kill, are not only "unnatural" bodies, bodies that require supplementation through their entanglement with technology. The bodies of precision bombers are also productive bodies, in the sense that their embodiment makes other bodies into killable bodies, in ways that were previously impossible, through the use of visual and weapons technologies. The production of "clean and proper bodies" moves from marking the borders of national communities through bodily reconstructions and efforts to ensure the safe circulation of travelers and migrants across spatial borders, to the creation of spaces of exception without reference to state borders in the prison camp at Guantánamo Bay (and similar camps worldwide) and in the posthuman bodies of precision warriors.

Foucault's concept of biopower centers on the individual and populations, maintaining the idea of the self-contained, integral body, with preexisting borders. Dillon and Reid (2009) extended Foucault's analysis to the ways that biopower intervenes to manipulate and foster life on the molecular level, and even in digitizing life. The interrelated modes of violence discussed in this work have shown that the borders of the body are always a political effect and are subject to transformation; whether in regard to their constituent parts or their formation as part of broader assemblages, as in the case of precision bombers. What is less explored in the literature on biopolitics and war are the dynamics of bodies "pushing back" and having agentic effects in the kinds of relations that biopolitics would make them into. The body's vulnerability is a feature of what Butler describes as its "socially ecstatic structure" (2009, 33)—that its very being is radically dependent upon others. This structure is a pre-condition for the practice of hunger striking to impel force-feeding and a transformation in the subject position of (some) prisoners at Guantánamo Bay and for the production of "killable" bodies by the technology-infused embodiment of precision bombers, as well as the stress and PTSD symptoms suffered by precision bombers despite designs to distance soldiers from the risks of the battlefield. Bodies may be produced as information or "code": infinitely flexible, legible, and movable, but bodies in their material instantiations are still relevant; embodiment entails reactivity and affects that are not necessarily predictable. Thinking about bodies as productive, that is, with capacities to transform other bodies and discursive formations, also suggests a shift in the ways we think about violence. If, as in the example of the abject body of the suicide bomber, bodies have political effects that exceed the intentions of self-conscious subjects, bodies are not only tools used by subjects to effect violence; bodies can have productive political effects as well in the ways they are organized and assembled with other bodies to create new kinds of political subjectivities.

In securing life, biopolitical security practices have attempted to separate political subjectivity from physical embodiment, understanding both the referents of security and the threats to this security as biological organisms or populations. One particular irony of these practices is that attempts to secure the life of subjects have resulted in the production of the bodies of the subjects as unanimated corpses, as "just bodies" stripped of subjectivity that can be read by professionals and machines for signs of their security risk. The promotion of life becomes dependent upon a virtual death; the production of the referent of security as not only an abject corpse, but a dematerialized image, or in the case of RtoP, the bodies of those always already dead. The promotion of life also becomes dependent upon a form of normative violence: the violence that designates certain bodies and lives as unlivable. IR theory has remained complicit in this movement by failing to take into account the politics and politicization of bodies, implicitly treating them as if they were the natural organisms that biopolitics would resign them to.

Power and violence are in the service of "making life live," in which the body becomes a site not only of investments of power, but also of resistance. Resistance does not take the form of a rejection or surpassing of power relations; rather, resistance is an integral part of power relations. As such, the body, which is both object and effect of violent practices, becomes the vital site of resistance and possible transformation of power relations. From the bodies of hunger strikers in Guantánamo Bay, to refugees sewing their lips shut in camps in Australia, to the self-immolation that sparked uprisings across the Middle East and North Africa, and the bodily occupation of space that is the hallmark of the Occupy Wall Street movement, the biopolitical operations of sovereign power demand an accounting for dynamics of bodily resistance to the domination and de-legitimization done in the name of life. Being attentive to the multiplicity of ways that the politics of life forms our horizon of possibilities necessitates greater attention to relations among bodies and embodied relations.

A central feature of Butler's concept of bodily precarity is that our bodies are formed in and through violence. Humans, as always already produced in relationality to others who are similarly produced, are vulnerable to each other in ways that surpass physical violence. Butler stresses that we do not encounter power and norms on their own, but through our encounters with others (2005, 30). We are mutually entangled with each other such that we cannot separate.

This social and relational ontology of the body suggests that we bear a kind of responsibility for the lived experiences and livability of certain lives—but not as fully conscious, rational subjects. Humans, as always already produced in relation to others who are similarly produced, are vulnerable to each other in ways that surpass physical violence. Our bodies themselves do not precede social entanglements, and thus we cannot consider an ethics of violence differently from existing frameworks that separate bodily existence from power. Whether one is subject to such harm and physical coercion is a social matter: whether one's life is survivable is dependent upon how the body is socially constituted. Ethical questions about violence and International Relations not only revolve around the use of force in regard to harming preexisting bodies, but also must take seriously the question of normative violence as well, in particular, how norms constitute certain bodies as "livable lives" or as abject "bodies that don't matter" that may be injured or killed. Bodily precariousness as ontology also provides a new language for thinking about violence and vulnerability in IR: we are not only accountable for violence done to pre-given bodies and subjectivities but also implicated in the production of certain bodies as killable and certain bodies as protected or as "livable." The recent promotion of the norm of "responsibility to protect" to revise the contemporary norm of sovereignty points to the biopolitical concern to foster and shepherd life as the basis for sovereign power; as such, RtoP poses a site in which the production of differentiated bodies through norms and practices can be seen.

While the field of security studies is fundamentally about overcoming, containing, or applying rational controls to vulnerability (or more precisely, the *distribution* of vulnerability), the violence of the self's very founding reveals vulnerability to be an inescapable aspect of our being. Bodies, under the sign of sovereignty, are vulnerable bodies seeking to eliminate this vulnerability through the political action of constituting the sovereign state and the sovereign man under the regime of rights. Bodily vulnerability thus functions as that which simultaneously *must* be overcome, but which can never be overcome. The concept of risk in International Relations illustrates a logic that attempts to overcome this constitutive vulnerability through technological superiority and expert knowledge. Theorizing bodies as ontologically as well as physically precarious necessitates a different view of violence in IR, in particular, that violence is an expression of the instability of bodies in their social existence and relations to one another.

Biopower, as the governance of populations, is a practice that seeks to deny the precarity of life through classifying individuals according to their differences, insulating groups from contact with other groups, and normalizing groups suffocating difference within groups. Biopower also legitimizes and sometimes institutionalizes these strategies to manage and eliminate difference through the creation of discrete, homogenized units by making such strategies appear natural (Ettlinger 2007). While Butler's recent work on bodily vulnerability is primarily framed in terms of state violence, rather than the differential material conditions for life that exist in the contemporary political economy (although see Butler and Athenasiou 2013),[1] her concepts of normative violence and bodily precarity are useful for thinking through how to theorize violence when taking into consideration an embodied subject. When normative frameworks establish in advance what kinds of lives will be livable, what lives are worth preserving and mourning, these views implicitly justify contemporary practices of violence. Butler suggests the possibility that a politics of bodily vulnerability could provide an alternative to the sovereign strategies of managing violence: denying vulnerability by appearing impermeable, and/or becoming violent oneself. Violence is an act that attempts to eradicate one's vulnerability and relocate it elsewhere; it produces the illusion that one is invulnerable.

Violence, then, is a manifestation of the instability and undecidability in the constitution and management of contemporary political subjects as *embodied* subjects. Rather than a reversion to a previous era, and a betrayal of liberal political values, violence expresses the instability in the founding of subjects that is the result of the "constitutive outside," which provides the energy for the disruption and renewal of the ever-precarious subject. In contrast to the liberal vision of eliminating violence from political life, Talal Asad (2003) reminds us that liberal, modern societies have never been free of physical pain and cruelty. It is not cruelty per se that is perceived as wrong, but excessive cruelty beyond what is needed to control and discipline subjects. Torture has been defined as the infliction of *unnecessary* cruelty and suffering (if it is deemed necessary, it is euphemized as "enhanced interrogation"), and certain technologies of war are considered to be unnecessarily cruel (such as chemical and biological weapons) as opposed to others (aerial bombing). Excessive cruelty and pain inflicted upon subjects are seen as a sign of backwardness and a lack of civilization. Though we have mechanisms to regulate and redirect the exercise of violence, in fact, we have simply made the expression of these energies more civilized in their violent precision—through complicated legal rationales and procedures for "enhanced interrogations" and through legally and technologically enabled bombings. We are shocked by expressions of political violence such as suicide bombings, which seem barbaric and irrational by comparison, but which may in fact be a similar indication of the abject, or the excess, that haunts the seemingly uncorrupted subject.

Violence is thus not only a destructive practice that is to be avoided, or only a rational course of policy, but rather, is also in some sense a creative force, as an "outside" that is not fully expelled, that lingers and drives the production of bodies and subjects. Such violence challenges the myth of the sovereign man. It is a commonplace in political theory that sovereignty exceeds legal codes. Sovereignty is performatively produced; that is, it is made to exist through practices, through the Schmittian decision on the exception, or Agamben's *homo sacer*, for two examples. Twentieth-century political thought from Kantorowicz (1957) to Foucault's performative theory of the sovereign has considered sovereignty something exceeding the law, bestowing the ability to inflict violence on others. The sovereign state is not only founded and maintained by violence or the fear of violence, but the sovereign man is produced by violent exclusions to maintain the appearance of wholeness and integrity. The appearance of sovereign men and sovereign states is thus predicated upon bodily vulnerability—for the sovereign to exist, bodies must be made vulnerable to the violence of the sovereign.

By re-politicizing bodies, feminist theory is a productive resource for thinking about our bodies as "given over from the start" to vulnerability and political forces. In myriad ways, feminists have exposed our bodies as both fundamental to subjectivity and political themselves, the implications of which have not been fully explored in the field of International Relations. Our bodies, as the basis for political subjectivity, are politically constituted—they are effects of political discourses of violence and vulnerability, security and power. Violence is a means of reconstituting subjection as the expression of the excess that haunts the subject as evidence of the incompleteness of bodies whose form and function in the political community must be renewed. Violence expresses the instability of bodies, as it is instrumental in the making and remaking of embodied subjects and their place in the political community. This is to say that the violence serves to make and remake subjectivities. We know that violence is bodily harm and injury, and that violence involves legal transgression. But it is more than this. As feminists and other critical theorists have argued, violence is also about social standing; it is used as a tool to reproduce hierarchies. Violence as expressive of excess and instability means that violence has political effects in constituting subjects, rather than merely harming only preexisting subjects or violating the rights of preexisting subjects; it forms and reforms our bodies and worlds.

Recent work in International Relations and in the study of political violence more generally has begun to take the embodiment of the subject seriously. One such example is work in the last decade foregrounding practices as objects of study or explanation of phenomena in international politics. Two prominent proponents of this approach, Emanuel Adler and Vincent Pouliot, define practices as "socially meaningful patterns of action which, in being performed more or less competently, simultaneously embody, act out and possibly reify background knowledge and discourse in and on the material world" (Adler and Pouliot 2011, 6). Such an approach is promising for thinking about the embodiment of discourses in their manifestation and production in everyday life, but thus far the "practice turn" in International Relations is not necessarily compatible with feminist and queer approaches to embodiment that stress how discourses can be subverted through practices, the formation of differences, and the multiplicity of ways to embody a certain practice (see Wilcox n.d.). It is also not clear from work thus far that bodies can in any way be productive, rather than absorbing and reflecting broader power structures.

Other examples of recent work rethinking bodies and embodiment include Sylvester's call for prioritizing the embodied experiences of war (Sylvester 2011, 2012, 2013) and Barkawi and Brighton's argument for the centrality of the wartime experience as distinct from security studies (2011), as well as broader sociologies of contemporary war and the body (McSorley 2012). Feminist theorists bring a distinct perspective to thinking about the embodiment of war, as this work has discussed; there is more work to be done, however, in thinking about the embodiment of what has come to be called affect: emotions or bodily states that are not entirely conscious to the subject. Feminists and queer theorists such as Sara Ahmed (2004a, 2004b), Jasbir Puar (2007), and Lauren Berlant (2011) have been at the forefront of thinking about affect as a relatively autonomous force that is *embodying* and productive of shifting demarcations along lines of race, gender, and sexuality. In International Relations, such work has the potential to bring together studies of subjectivity, emotion, and embodiment to think more holistically about what it means to live as a "becoming-body" in our contemporary world. Moving from the biopolitical emphasis on the production of bodies in discourse to the potentialities of bodies to affect and be affected is necessary in order to take seriously the potential of bodies not only to be written or inscribed by relations of power, but also to create or enact new relations themselves. In the contemporary age of risk and danger managed by the production of bodies into information or information processors, it is incumbent upon us to think through ways in which we live in and through bodies, and of the complex movements and formation of such bodies, which may serve as a site for creatively rethinking our future political horizons.

ACKNOWLEDGMENTS

Writing the acknowledgements for a book begun many years ago is powerful lesson in the breadth and depth of connections, exchanges, and relationships without which this project could not have materialized. *Bodies of Violence* began as my doctoral dissertation in the Department of Political Science at the University of Minnesota. I wish to thank my advisor, Bud Duvall, for supporting this project and my development as a scholar from the very beginning of graduate school, for his wisdom, patience, and encouragement, for giving me the space to grow, and for asking the right questions at the right time to move my work forward. I am also grateful to Bud for leading an outstanding group of intellectually and politically engaged scholars; only a tiny fraction of the many conversations from Bud's dissertation groups and seminars could make it into this work but they continue to shape my growth as a scholar. Many thanks also to Ron Krebs and Nancy Luxon for their many close readings, for challenging discussions, and for pushing me further in my work. Thanks also to Lisa Disch and Naomi Scheman for their guidance on this project.

I owe much to Jennifer Lobasz, Sheryl Lightfoot, Aaron Rapport, and Joyce Heckman for their unfailing support as friends, colleagues, and fellow-travelers throughout the long and sometimes difficult journey through graduate school and whatever lies beyond. With great thanks and affection also to Quinn Gorman, Julia Cohen, Priya Outar, Krzysztof Karski, Erin Seiberlich Karski, and Mary Thompson.

I'm also grateful for a vast network of colleagues, mentors, and friends who have read, commented on, discussed, and supported this project and its various iterations over the years including: Jessica Auchter, Alex Barder, Tarak Barkawi, Andreas Behnke, Janice Bially Mattern, Linda Bishai, David Blaney, Jesse Crane-Seeber, Kara Ellerby, Stefanie Fishel, Caron Gentry, Jen Heeg, Kimberly Hutchings, Lene Hansen, Patrick Thaddeus Jackson, Heather Johnson, Paul Kirby, Daniel Levine, Debbie Lisle, Renée Marlin-Bennett, Ellen Messner-Davidow, Alex Montgomery, Pashmina Murthy, David

Mutimer, Daniel Nexon, Mark Salter, Laura Shepherd, Rosemary Shinko, Laura Sjoberg, Vicki Squire, Maria Stern, Mustafa Tagma, Ann Tickner, Cindy Weber, Gillian Youngs, and many more that I have undoubtedly and unfortunately missed. An extra thank you to David Blaney for his mentorship in matters of scholarship, teaching, the discipline, and life in academia that began when I was his undergraduate advisee at Macalester College and continues to this day. Thanks again to Laura Sjoberg for her friendship and mentoring over the years and for many conversations about this work.

This book was honored in the best possible way (with an hour of critical engagement) at the 2013 ISA-NE Northeast Circle. Thanks to Samuel Barkin for nominating the work and to Anna Agathangelou, Ty Solomon, and Eric Blanchard for reading the entire manuscript and providing many helpful insights and critiques.

I spent 2011 to 2013 as a Charles and Amy Scharf postdoctoral research fellow in the Department of Political Science at Johns Hopkins University; there I found strong community of interlocutors, mentors, and friends including Renée Marlin-Bennett, Siba Grovogui, Sam Chambers, Jane Bennett, Lester Spence, Isaac Kamola, Serena Laws, Bentley Allen, Ben Meiches, Alex Livingston, Willy Blomme, David Pak Yue Leon, Stuart Gray, Moira Lynch, and members of the Feminist/Queer Theory reading group.

I came to the University of Cambridge as a Lecturer in Gender Studies in the fall of 2013, where I completed the final revisions on this text. I want to thank Jude Browne and Lesley Dixon from the University of Cambridge Centre for Gender Studies, as well as many colleagues from the Department of Geography and Department of Politics and International Studies for their kindness in welcoming me to Cambridge and their support for this project.

Thanks also to audiences at the University of Minnesota, Johns Hopkins University, American University, the University of Delaware, and the University of Belfast, as well as many ISA and ISA-NE conferences for the opportunity to present my work and the engaging conversations that followed.

I would also like to thank the reviewers at Oxford University Press for many helpful comments and suggestions that helped improve the text immensely. Thanks to series editors Ann Ticker and Laura Sjoberg for their unwavering support for this book and to Angela Chnapko and Peter Worger at Oxford University Press for their help making this book a reality.

My deepest thanks go to my family who have been a constant source of support for me and who have (mostly) patiently awaited this book's arrival: my mother, Nancy Wilcox Wiessner, sister Leslie Wilcox Rosedahl, brother Evan Wilcox, and a large extended family in Todd, Emily, Dan, Kevin, Megan, Val, Dick and the next generation: Owen, Grant, and Britta. They are my first and best lesson in what it means to be "undone by each other". This book is for them.

NOTES

INTRODUCTION
1. Additionally, see Chambers (2007), Chambers and Carver (2008) and Butler (1999[1990]) on the centrality of normative violence to Butler's work on questions of gender and sexuality as well as post-9/11 ethics and politics.

CHAPTER 1
1. For further debate on the metaphor of the "body politic" and the "organic" model of the state, see Krishna (1994); Weber (1998); Cavarero (2002); Bigo (2002, 67); Turner (2003); Neumann (2004); Rasmussen and Brown (2005); Luoma-Aho (2009); and especially Fishel (n.d.).
2. Some of the many works on the relationship of biopolitics, liberalism, and contemporary warfare include Jabri (2006b); Reid (2006); Dauphinée and Masters (2006); Dillon (2007a, 2007b); Dillon and Lobo-Guerrero (2008); Dillon and Reid (2009); Evans (2010, 2011).
3. See Chambers and Carver (2008, 51–72) for a nuanced comparison of Butler and Coole's positions vis-a-vis agency and the body.
4. Butler's description of subject formation refuses the opposition between a "social construction" that implies the possibility of change and a determinism that insists upon the stability of categories of social oppression (see, for example, Butler 1993, 94). In an early article, Butler describes the body as a situation (1989a); as such, she bypasses voluntarism/determinism dualism. For Butler, "becoming" a body does not mean that gender is imposed on subjects (see also Lloyd 2007, 39). If gender were something that was "culturally constructed," it would imply that there was a subject, an "I," before the imposition of gender. Butler reinterprets Beauvoir, not as a theorist of "gender" as a culturally constructed imposition upon a preexisting subject, but as a theorist of how one comes to embody a "historical idea," the norm of gender. Gender as an aspect of our bodily reality is not set—in fact, it requires constant work to uphold—but neither is it something an existing agent can change. Rather, it is a core component of the subject itself—"there need not be a 'doer behind the deed'... the 'doer' is variously constituted in and through the deed" (Butler 1990, 142). Theorizing our bodies as socially constituted means that power does not just act on our bodies, but forms our bodies and subjectivities in ways that we are not fully aware of or can control. See also Chambers and Carver (2008) for a much more detailed account of Butler's theory of the embodiment of the subject and its relationship to the political.

5. See also Shinko (2010) for an especially provocative use of McNay's theory of generative bodies for thinking about bodies and their capacities for resistance in International Relations.
6. Cf. Reid (2011).

CHAPTER 2

1. An earlier version of this chapter was published as "Dying Is Not Permitted: Sovereignty, Biopower, and Force-Feeding at Guantánamo Bay" in *Torture: Power, Democracy and the Human Body*, edited by Shampa Biswas and Zahi Zalloua (University of Washington Press, 2011). Permission to reprint copyrighted material is gratefully acknowledged. The chapter title is taken from Zagorin (2006).
2. This is not to say that prisoners have not died at Guantánamo Bay, or that they have not been intentionally killed. Three prisoners who had been reported to have committed suicide in June 2006 are suspected of being murdered, based on testimony from prisoners and former military personnel. See Horton (2010).
3. Following a wave of abortion clinic bombings in 1994, the FBI refused to investigate the crimes as terrorism. As such, there was no coordinated federal effort to stop the violence for more than a decade (Jenkins 1999).
4. Ahmed Khalfan Ghailani was acquitted in a civilian court in November 2010, of all but one of 280 charges against him related to the 1998 US embassy bombings after being held in various CIA "black sites" and Guantánamo Bay after his capture in 2004.
5. Convicted foreign terrorists in the Supermax prison include Zacarias Moussaoui, the so-called twentieth hijacker; Wadih el-Hage, of the 1998 embassy bombings; and Ramzi Yousef, leader of the 1993 World Trade Center bombings. See Johnson and Pincus (2009).
6. Detainees have also reported being beaten at Guantánamo as well as other detention camps. These forms of abuse were intended to be kept secret and, unlike tactics such as sensory deprivation, stress positions, and waterboarding, have not been justified as crucial for information gathering.
7. In 2014 Bey cancelled concert dates in the United States citing unspecified immigration/legal reasons that led to reporting that he had been "banned from the US" but this story was almost immediately found to be false and corrected (see Beaumont-Thomas and Gambino 2014).

CHAPTER 3

1. A modified version of this chapter was published as Lauren Wilcox, "Explosive Bodies and Bounded States: Abjection and the Embodied Practice of Suicide Bombing," *International Feminist Journal of Politics*, Volume 16 no 1, 2014, pp. 66–85. 2013. Reprinted by permission of the publisher, Taylor & Francis Ltd.
2. These portraits of the suicide bombers are often conflated. As Slavoj Žižek has pointed out, attributing the motivations of the suicide bomber to the access to dozens of virgins in the afterlife as a type of rational reason ends up portraying the suicide bomber as a ridiculously strange "other" (Žižek 2008, 83).
3. While the representations of women's bodies as leaky and penetrable and men's bodies as solid and impenetrable have much cultural currency, it should be noted that masculine embodiment, even for members of the military, can also involve "penetrability" (Belkin 2012) and can be seen as vulnerable and in need of protection by technology (Masters 2005). I would argue that such representations are necessary for men's violence and death as part of military forces to be seen as a necessary sacrifice for protecting those who "must live" in biopolitical terms.

Bodily vulnerability, in this sense, is ultimately in service of the reproduction of sovereignty.
4. On the suicide bomber as abject, see also Asad (2007).
5. ZAKA's work is not confined to Israel/Palestine, as in recent years they have used their expertise at forensic identification after the South Asian tsunami and Hurricane Katrina in 2005, the 2008 Mumbai bombings, and the 2010 earthquake in Haiti. Nor, of course, are suicide bombings in general or by women specifically limited to Israel/Palestine: it is the conjunction of suicide bombings plus the work of ZAKA that makes this a valuable "case" for thinking about bodies, borders, and orders.
6. Of course, not all victims are Jewish; approximately 25 percent of Israelis are Arab or members of another minority group. Furthermore, as the group was founded and is largely made up of Haredim, or "ultra-Orthodox" Jews, ZAKA's relation to the Israeli state is complicated. Haredim typically reject Zionism and the legitimacy of the state; however, ZAKA's humanitarian work and work on behalf of the victims of terrorism and other disasters has been acknowledged and accepted by the state, which coordinates efforts with ZAKA. In addition, the effort to signify bodies as Jewish in the context of the Israeli/Palestinian conflict has the effect of signifying bodies as belonging to a national as well as religious identity because of the promotion of Israel as a Jewish state.
7. The Chicago Project on Security and Terrorism's database lists 125 total attacks by women in the years 1981 to 2011, covering all applicable conflicts. While this can give us a rough idea of the relative frequency of women versus men as suicide bombers, the high number of attacks in which the gender is unknown in this database suggests that the numbers of women suicide bombers are almost certainly under-counted. Their data indicate 17 out of 198 attacks in Israel/Palestinian territories/Lebanon were perpetrated by women, and 29 out of 107 total attacks in Sri Lanka were perpetrated by women, as were 20 out of 60 attacks in Russia by Chechen separatists (CPOST 2011). These data also do not take into account bombings that were thwarted: while there may have been 17 successful suicide bombings by women in the Israeli/Palestinian conflict, up to 96 women have attempted to complete a suicide mission (Bloom 2011, 128). Bloom (2011, 141, 214) estimates that 40 percent of suicide bombers affiliated with the PKK in Turkey and around 43 percent of participants in suicide attacks by the LTTE in Sri Lanka were women, and around a third of the Al Qaeda–Iraq bombings were perpetrated by women.
8. I refer to "female" suicide bombers even while discussing the production of their bodies as sexed and gendered to acknowledge the performative effects of discourses of gender in constituting the sex of particular bodies, including the gendered representations of female suicide bombers, both before and after their deaths.

CHAPTER 4

1. See Abrahamsen and Williams (2009). In the United States, airport security is run by the Transportation Security Administration, a division of the Department of Homeland Security, but certain airport security functions may soon be privatized.
2. Canada has a similar program called "Passenger Protect" that operates a "no-fly" list, but does not use statistical indicators of riskiness.
3. These countries are: Iran, Iraq, Libya, Sudan, Syria, Afghanistan, Algeria, Bahrain, Eritrea, Lebanon, Morocco, North Korea, Oman, Qatar, Somalia, Tunisia, the

United Arab Emirates, Yemen, Pakistan, Saudi Arabia, Bangladesh, Egypt, Indonesia, Jordan, and Kuwait.
4. See also Ajana (2013).
5. Although the TSA in the United States claims that the images are not digitally stored, and thus cannot be retrieved or shared, multiple incidences of images being "leaked" have been reported (see for example Johnson 2010).
6. The images produced by backscatter and millimeter wave body scanners, with or without the "Provision ATD" software that creates the "neutral human" image with "anomalies" blocked out are widely available online and are also available at Bellanova and Fuster (2013). However, I was unable to secure the rights to reproduce these images in this book.
7. "Transgender" is often thought of as an umbrella term that describes people whose gender identity or gender presentation does not match the sex they were assigned a birth. It sometimes includes, and sometimes excludes, transsexuals who undergo surgery and other medical interventions to change their bodies in ways that present as a different sex from the one they were assigned at birth. "Genderqueer" includes people who reject the gender binary and may see themselves as gendered in ways other than how they were assigned at birth without wishing to fully embrace being identified with the "opposite" sex. I use both "trans-" and "genderqueer" as inclusive terms to refer to people whose gender identification or presentation may be at odds with social expectations based on their sex assigned at birth and/or designated on state-issued ID cards. The opposite of trans- is cis-, a prefix referring to people who do not experience their sexed embodiment to be at odds with their gender identities. See Stryker (2008); Beemyn and Rankin (2011); as well as Sjoberg and Shepherd (2012) and Sjoberg (2012) on the category of trans- in International Relations.
8. Stoler further notes the similarities between the goals of project "Hostile Intent" and the risk management strategies of colonial governance in the Dutch Indies to ascertain and monitor mental states that might prove disruptive (2008, 356). Butler's own thinking has recently been engaged with the relationship between race, sexuality, and being a "body that matters" (Bell 2010).
9. According to prevailing feminist usage, the M and F, which stand for male and female, designate sex, a biological category, rather than the social category of gender. However, the TSA refers to this as a "gender marker" and I've chosen to retain this terminology here because it indicates how "sex" is a function of "gender."
10. States have diverse requirements for changing the gender marker on one's passport; Australia recently has allowed intersexed persons and transgender persons who are in the midst of a transition to have a third gender "X" on their passports; India and Nepal also have "third gender" options for their passports.
11. In 2010, the US State Department eliminated the need for genital surgery for gender reclassification on passports, but still requires medical and/or psychiatrist intervention (Currah and Mulqueen 2011, 561).
12. Argentina recently became the first country to allow individuals to change their gender markers based on solely on self-identification.
13. The threat of cross-dressing is linked with fear of the *niqab* or *burka* that covers most of the body and face. Some arguments of those seeking to outlaw face-covering garments, worn primarily by Muslim women, are based on perceiving these garments as security threats because they cause the identity of the wearer to be concealed. France, Italy, and several municipalities in Belgium, for example, have made it illegal to cover the face in the public sphere, stressing,

along with the promotion of secularism, the anti-terrorist logic. Aside from singling out Islamic religious dress for such measures, a ban on certain forms of clothing as an anti-terrorism measure because they are easy for terrorist *men* to hide under (as in the case of Mohammed Ahmed Mohamed, suspected of links to al-Shabab, who eluded security agents following him by donning women's garments) (Quinn 2013) may be read as evidence that gender markers, whether on documents or in clothing choices, are actually very ineffective at consistently identifying individuals.
14. This critique of the Copenhagen school of "securitization" is made by Lene Hansen (2000).
15. The security protocols required for children and the elderly have recently been relaxed in some places in the United States because of extensive criticism (Ahlers 2012).

CHAPTER 5

1. Bryant has since become an outspoken critic of US drone policies.
2. See also Shaw (2002).
3. One of the first precision tools, the Norden Bombsight, within a 1,000-meter radius was said to be able drop a "bomb into a pickle barrel," but its accuracy was measured in percentage of bombs hitting the given target (McFarland 1995). The mean CEP in the Gulf War was 100 feet, while the mean CEP of bombs dropped in Iraq in 2003 was 25 feet, meaning that even if the bombs hit where they were intended to, massive amounts of damage nearby the target will like ensue. Combined with intelligence errors, targeting errors, and GPS errors, the risks of unintended deaths from precision missiles, whether launched from manned or unmanned aircraft, are frequently greater than the popular imagination of these weapons as virtually error-proof.
4. For at least several decades, lawyers and legal analyses have been integrated into targeting decisions: it is often reported by government officials in the United States that legal considerations for civilian casualties have prevented strikes from occurring. Whether the close integration of lawyers into the "kill chain" of decision-making serves as a moralistic rubber stamp for military operations or a significant restriction on the use of various forms of bombardment is a matter of debate (ah Jochnick and Normand 1994; Ignatieff 2001; Koh 2010; Chatterjee 2011; Mckelvey 2011; Hastings 2012).
5. See also Pin-Fat and Stern (2005), who argue that the military is an exceptional space created by sovereign power and that military personnel are *homines sacri* who cannot truly be sacrificed, and for whom the myth of heroic sacrifice is dependent upon gendered norms of protecting women and children.
6. Masters (2005) argues that the bodies of soldiers in high-tech warfare are feminized, in that they are treated as weak and vulnerable. Technology becomes the masculine subject, as it protects feminized bodies and fulfills masculine desires of absolute power and knowledge. While Masters powerfully shows the political implications of high-tech warfare for democratic politics, her work reifies a distinction between "fleshy bodies" and "technology" that is rejected by the posthuman approach.
7. For more on the prominence of "flexible bodies" in neoliberal societies, see E. Martin (1994).
8. SIM stands for "subscriber identity module." SIM cards are plastic integrated circuits that are used to identify and authenticate users on a mobile network.

9. Thanks to Tarak Barkawi for pointing out the tensions between the term "civilian" and the arguments of this chapter.
10. See Tuana (2004) and Scott (1998), 12–13, for other examples of actively produced ignorances.
11. For example, the *Washington Post* reporting on Human Rights Watch's report on the US drone attack on a Yemeni marriage procession in December 2013 focused on how the strike did not comply with the policies for civilian protection that Obama had previously outlined (Miller 2014).
12. See also Talal Asad's critique of the privileging of military commander's judgment in just war theory (2007, 21).
13. See Muppidi (2012) for a trenchant discussion of the colonial logics of counting bodies and the incomprehension of suffering.

CHAPTER 6
1. See, for example, Wheeler (2000); Crawford (2002); Finnemore (2004); Mamdani (2009).
2. Some key works in the "care" tradition include Gilligan (1983); Ruddick (1989); Tronto (1996); Robinson (1999); Held (2006).

CONCLUSION
1. Butler has been criticized for her focus on state violence at the expense of a more systematic critique of the distribution of various forms of violence and precariousness in the contemporary global political economy (Reid 2011; Watson 2012). In recent speeches addressing the Occupy movement, Butler has extended her concept of precarity to "precaritization" as the effect of policies associated with neoliberalism (Butler 2011; Butler and Athenasiou 2013).

BIBLIOGRAPHY

Aas, Katja Franko. 2006. "'The Body Does Not Lie': Identity, Risk and Trust in Technoculture." *Crime, Media, Culture* 2, no. 2: 143–158.

Abé, Nicola. 2012. "Dreams in Infrared: The Woes of An American Drone Operator." *Spiegel Online International*. December 14. http://www.spiegel.de/international/world/pain-continues-after-war-for-americandrone-pilot-a-872726.html.

Abrahamsen, Rita, and Michael C. Williams. 2009. "Security beyond the State: Global Security Assemblages in International Politics." *International Political Sociology* 3: 1–17.

Abdul-Ahad, Ghaith. 2009. "'I Took a Piece of Flesh with Me Home and I Called It My Son.'" *Guardian*. September 12. http://www.guardian.co.uk/world/2009/sep/11/afghanistan-airstrike-victims-stories/print.

Abu-Lughod, Lila. 2002. "Do Muslim Women Really Need Saving?: Anthropological Reflections on Cultural Relativism and Its Others." *American Anthropologist* 104, no. 3: 783–790.

Ackelsberg, Martha A., and Mary Lyndon Shanley. 1996. "Privacy, Publicity, and Power: A Feminist Rethinking of the Public-Private Distinction." In *Revisioning the Political: Feminist Reconstructions of Traditional Concepts in Western Political Theory*, eds. Nancy J. Hirschmann and Christine Di Stefano, 213–234. Boulder, CO: Westview Press.

Ackerman, Spencer. 2012a. "Homeland Security Wants to Spy on 4 Square Miles at Once." *Danger Room*. January 23. http://www.wired.com/dangerroom/2012/01/homeland-security-surveillance/.

Ackerman, Spencer. 2012b. "Air Force Chief: It'll Be 'Years' before We Catch Up on Drone Data." *Danger Room*. April 5. http://www.wired.com/dangerroom/2012/04/air-force-drone-data/.

Adey, Peter. 2004. "Secured and Sorted Mobilities: Examples from the Airport." *Surveillance and Society* 1, no. 4: 500–519.

Adey, Peter. 2009. "Facing Airport Security: Affect, Biopolitics and the Preemptive Securitisation of the Mobile Body." *Environment and Planning D: Society and Space* 27: 274–295.

Adler, Emmanuel and Vincent Pouliot. 2011. "International Practices: Introduction and Framework." In *International Practices*, eds. Emmanuel Adler and Vincent Pouliot, 1–35. Cambridge: Cambridge University Press.

Agamben, Giorgio. 1998. *Homo Sacer*. Translated by Daniel Heller-Roazen. Stanford, CA: Stanford University Press.

Agamben, Giorgio. 2005. *State of Exception*. Translated by Kevin Attell. Chicago: University of Chicago Press.

ah Jochnick, Chris, and Roger Normand. 1994. "The Legitimation of Violence: A Critical Analysis of the Gulf War." *Harvard International Law Journal* 35, no. 2: 388–416.

Ahlers, Mike M. 2012. "TSA Set to Test New Screening Protocols for Elderly." *CNN Travel*. March 14. http://articles.cnn.com/2012-03-14/travel/travel_tsa-elderly-screening_1_full-body-scanner-tsa-officers-passengers?_s=PM:TRAVEL.

Ahmed, Sara. 2000. *Strange Encounters: Embodied Others in Post-Coloniality*. New York: Routledge.

Ahmed, Sara. 2004a. "Affective Economies." *Social Text 79*, 22, no 2: 117–139.

Ahmed, Sara. 2004b. *The Cultural Politics of Emotion*. Edinburgh: Edinburgh University Press.

Ajana, Btihaj. 2013. *Governing Through Biometrics: The Biopolitics of Identity*. Basingstoke, Hampshire: Palgrave MacMillan.

Alaimo, Stacy, and Susan Hekman, ed. 2008. *Material Feminisms*. Bloomington: Indiana University Press.

Amoore, Louise, and Marieke de Goede. 2008. *Risk and the War on Terror*. New York and London: Routledge.

Amoore, Louise, and Alexandra Hall. 2009. "Taking People Apart: Digitised Dissection and the Body at the Border." *Environment and Planning D: Society and Space* 27: 444–464.

Andreas, Peter. 2003. "Redrawing the Line: Borders and Security in the Twenty-first Century." *International Security* 28, no 2: 78–111.

Aradau, Claudia, and Rens Van Munster. 2007. "Governing Terrorism Through Risk: Taking Precautions, (un)Knowing the Future." *European Journal of International Relations* 13, no. 1: 89–115.

Arbour, Louise. 2008. "Responsibility to Protect as a Duty of Care in International Law and Practice." *Review of International Studies* 24: 445–458.

Asad, Talal. 2003. *Formations of the Secular: Christianity, Islam, Modernity*. Stanford, CA: Stanford University Press.

Asad, Talal. 2007. *On Suicide Bombing*. New York: Columbia University Press.

Associated Press. 2008. "Military Drones, a la Video Games." July 20. http://www.boston.com/business/technology/articles/2008/07/20/military_drones_a_la_video_games/

Auchter, Jessica. 2014. *The Politics of Haunting and Memory in International Relations*. London and New York: Routledge.

Baker, Al. 2002. "For Emergency Official Touched by 9/11's Horrors, Fears of Complacency." *New York Times*. May 21 http://www.nytimes.com/2002/05/21/nyregion/traces-terror-security-for-emergency-officials-touched-9-11-s-horrors-fears.html.

Barad, Karen. 2007. *Meeting the Universe Halfway: Quantum Physics and the Entanglement of Matter and Meaning*. Durham, NC: Duke University Press.

Barkawi, Tarak. 2011. "From War to Security: Security Studies, the Wider Agenda and the Fate of the Study of War." *Millennium: Journal of International Studies* 39, no. 3: 701–716.

Barkawi, Tarak, and Shane Brighton. 2011. "Powers of War: Fighting, Knowledge, and Critique." *International Political Sociology* 5: 126–143.

Barnett, Michael, and Raymond Duvall. 2005. "Power in International Relations." *International Organization* 59: 39–75.

Battersby, Christine 1999. "Her Body/Her Boundaries." In *Feminist Theory and the Body*, eds. Margrit Shildrick and Janet Price, 341–358. London: Routledge.

BBC. 2005. "Counting the Civilian Cost in Iraq." June 6. http://news.bbc.co.uk/1/hi/world/middle_east/3672298.stm.

BBC. 2009. "CIA Agents Guilty of Italy Kidnap." November 9. http://news.bbc.co.uk/2/hi/8343123.stm.

Beauchamp, Toby. 2009. "Artful Concealment and Strategic Visibility: Transgender Bodies and U.S. State Surveillance after 9/11." *Surveillance and Society* 6, no. 4: 356–366.

Beauchamp, Zack, and Jilian Savulesu. 2013. "Robot Guardians: Teleoperated Combat Vehicles in Humanitarian Military Intervention." In *Killing by Remote Control: The Ethics of an Unmanned Military*, ed. Bradley Jay Strawser, 106–125. Oxford and New York: Oxford University Press.

Beaumont-Thomas, Ben and Lauren Gambino. 2014. "Yasiin Bey, aka Mos Def, cancels US tour amid 'legal' wrangles." *The Guardian*. May 22. http://www.theguardian.com/music/2014/may/22/yasiin-bey-mos-def-cancels-tour-denied-entry-us.

Beauvoir, Simone de. 1989 [1952]. *The Second Sex*. Translated by H. M. Parshley. New York: Vintage.

Becker, Jo, and Scott Shane. 2012. "Secret 'Kill List' Proves a Test of Obama's Principles and Will." *New York Times*. May 29. http://www.nytimes.com/2012/05/29/world/obamas-leadership-in-war-on-al-qaeda.html?pagewanted=all&_r=0.

Beemyn, Genny, and Susan Rankin. 2011. *The Lives of Transgender People*. New York: Columbia University Press.

Belkin, Aaron. 2012. *Bring Me Men: Military Masculinity and the Benign Façade of American Empire, 1898–2001*. New York: Columbia University Press.

Bell, Vicki. 2010. "New Scenes of Vulnerability, Agency and Plurality: An Interview with Judith Butler." *Theory, Culture & Society* 27, no. 1: 130–152.

Bellamy, Alex. 2006. "No Pain, No Gain? Torture and Ethics in the War on Terror." *International Affairs* 82, no. 1: 121–148.

Bellamy, Alex. 2009. *Responsibility to Protect: The Global Effort to End Mass Atrocities*. Cambridge: Polity Press.

Bellanova, Rocco, and Gloria Gonzalez Fuster. 2013. "Politics of Disappearance: Scanners and (Unobserved) Bodies as Mediators of Security Practice." *International Political Sociology* 7, no. 2: 188–209.

Bergen, Peter, and Katherine Tiedemann. 2010. "The Year of the Drone: An Analysis of U.S. Drone Strikes in Pakistan 2004–2010." *Foreign Policy*. April 26. www.foreignpolicy.com/articles/2010/04/26/the_year_of_the_drone.

Berlant, Lauren. 2011. *Cruel Optimism*. Durham: Duke University Press.

Bettcher, Talia Mae. 2007. "Evil Deceivers and Make-Believers: On Transphobic Violence and the Politics of Illusion." *Hypatia* 22, no. 3: 43–65.

Bially Mattern, Janice. 2011. "A Practice Theory of Emotion for International Relations." In *International Practices*, eds. Emmanual Adler and Vincent Pouliot, 63–86. Cambridge: Cambridge University Press.

Bigo, Didier. 2002. "Security and Immigration: Toward a Critique of the Governmentality of Unease." *Alternatives: Global, Local, Political* 27: 63–92.

Bigo, Didier. 2007. "Detention of Foreigners, States of Exception, and the Social Practices of Control of the Banopticon." In *Borderscapes: Hidden Geographies and Politics at Territory's Edge*, eds. Prem Kumar Rajarman and Carl Grundy-Warr, 3–34. Minneapolis: University of Minnesota Press.

Bkare-Yusuf, Bibi. 1997. "The Economy of Violence: Black Bodies and Unspeakable Terror." In *Feminist Theory and the Body*, eds. Janet Price and Margrit Shildrick, 232–311. London: Routledge.

Blackhurst, Rob. 2012. "The Air Force Men Who Fly Drones in Afghanistan by Remote Control." *Telegraph*. September 24. www.telegraph.co.uk/news/uknews/

defence/9552547/The-air-force-men-who-fly-drones-in-Afghanistan-by-remote-control.html.

Blakely, Ruth. 2007. "Why Torture?" *Review of International Studies* 33: 373–397.

Blanchard, Eric. 2011."The Technoscience Question in Feminist International Relations: Unmanning the U.S. War on Terror." In *Feminism and International Relations*, eds. J. Ann Tickner and Laura Sjoberg, 146–163. New York and London: Routledge.

Bloom, Mia. 2005. *Dying to Kill: The Allure of Suicide Terror*. New York: Columbia University Press.

Bloom, Mia. 2011. *Bombshell: Women and Terrorism*. Philadelphia: University of Pennsylvania Press.

Bohling, Alissa. 2012. "Transgender, Gender Non-Conforming People among First, Most Affected by War on Terror's Biometrics Craze." *Truth Out*. April 16. http://truth-out.org/news/item/8506-transgender-gender-non-conforming-people-among-first-most-affected-by-war-on-terrors-biometrics-craze.

Bohling, Alissa. 2014. "Exclusive: Transgender travelers singled out in TSA screenings, docs show." *Al Jazeera America*. May 26. http://america.aljazeera.com/articles/2014/5/26/groin-anomalies-andpatdownstravelingwhiletrans.html.

Bordo, Susan. 1990. "Feminism, Postmodernism, and Gender-Scepticism." In *Feminism/Postmodernism*, eds. Linda J. Nicholson, 133–156. New York and London: Routledge.

Bordo, Susan. 1993. *Unbearable Weight: Feminism, Western Culture and the Body*. Berkeley: University of California Press.

Bousquet, Antoine. 2009. *The Scientific Way of Warfare: Order and Chaos on the Battlefields of Modernity*. New York: Columbia University Press.

Bowdon, Mark. 2013. "The Killing Machines: How to Think about Drones." *The Atlantic*. August 14. http://www.theatlantic.com/magazine/archive/2013/09/the-killing-machines-how-to-think-about-drones/309434/.

Bradbury, Steven G. 2005a. "Re: Application of 18 U.S.C. §§ 2340–2340A to the Combined Use of Certain Techniques in the Interrogation of High Value al Qaeda Detainees." *US Department of Justice, Office of Legal Counsel*. May 10. http://luxmedia.vo.llnwd.net/o10/clients/aclu/olc_05102005_bradbury46pg.pdf.

Bradbury, Steven G. 2005b. "Re: Application of United States Obligations under Article 16 of the Convention Against Torture to Certain Techniques That May Be Used in the Interrogation of High Value al Qaeda Detainees." *US Department of Justice, Office of Legal Counsel*. May 30. http://luxmedia.vo.llnwd.net/o10/clients/aclu/olc_05302005_bradbury.pdf.

Brecher, Bob. 2007. *Torture and the Ticking Time Bomb*. Malden, MA: Blackwell.

Brown, Wendy. 1988. *Manhood and Politics: A Feminist Reading in Political Theory*. Totowa, NJ: Rowman and Littlefield.

Brown, Wendy. 1995. *States of Injury: Power and Freedom in Late Modernity*. Princeton, NJ: Princeton University Press.

Brown, Wendy. 2010. *Walled States, Waning Sovereignty*. Brooklyn, NY: Zone Books.

Buck, Lori, Nicole Gallant, and Kim Richard Nossal. 1998. "Sanctions as Gendered Instrument of Statecraft: The Case of Iraq." *Review of International Studies* 24, no. 1: 69–84.

Bush, George W. 2003. "Remarks by the President on Homeland Security." *Office of the Press Secretary*. September 10. http://georgewbush-whitehouse.archives.gov/news/releases/2003/09/20030910-6.html.

Butler, Judith. 1989a. "Gendering the Body: Beauvoir's Philosophical Contribution." In *Women, Knowledge, Reality*, eds. Ann Garry and Marilyn Pearsall, 253–262. Winchester, MA: Unwin Hyman.
Butler, Judith. 1989b. "Foucault and the Paradox of Bodily Inscription." *The Journal of Philosophy* 86, no. 11: 601–607.
Butler, Judith. 1993. *Bodies That Matter: On the Discursive Limits of 'Sex.'* New York and London: Routledge.
Butler, Judith. 1997a. *Excitable Speech: A Politics of the Performative*. New York: Routledge.
Butler, Judith. 1997b. *The Psychic Life of Power*. Stanford: Stanford University Press.
Butler, Judith. 1999 [1990]. *Gender Trouble: Feminism and the Subversion of Identity*. New York and London: Routledge.
Butler, Judith. 2004a. *Precarious Life: The Power of Mourning and Violence*. London and New York: Verso.
Butler, Judith. 2004b. *Undoing Gender*. New York and London: Routledge.
Butler, Judith. 2005. *Giving an Account of Oneself*. New York: Fordham University Press.
Butler, Judith. 2009. *Frames of War: When is Life Grievable?* London: Verso.
Butler, Judith. 2011. "Bodies in Alliance and the Politics of the Street." *European Institute for Progressive Social Policies*. http://eipcp.net/transversal/1011/butler/en.
Butler, Judith, and Athena Athenasiou. 2013. *Dispossession: The Politics in the Performative*. Cambridge: Polity Press.
Butler, Judith, Lynne Segal, and Peter Osborne. 1994. "Gender as Performance: An Interview with Judith Butler." *Radical Philosophy* 67: 32–39.
Buzan, Barry. 1991. *People, States and Fear: An Agenda for International Security Studies in the Post-Cold War Era*. London: Harvester Wheatsheaf.
Byman, Daniel. 2009. *Do Targeted Killings Work?* Brookings Institute. http://www.brookings.edu/opinions/2009/0714_targeted_killings_byman.aspx.
Campbell, David. 2000 [1992]. *Writing Security: United States Foreign Policy and the Politics of Identity*. Minneapolis: University of Minnesota Press.
Campbell, David, and Michael Dillon. 1993. "The End of Philosophy and the End of International Relations." In *The Political Subject of Violence*, eds. David Campbell and Michael Dillon, 1–47. Manchester: Manchester University Press.
Carver, Terrell. 1996. *Gender Is Not a Synonym for Women*. London and Boulder, CO: Lynne Rienner.
Carver, Terrell. 2008. "The Man in the Machine." In *Rethinking the Man Question: Sex, Gender and Violence in International Relations*, eds. Jane Parpart and Marysia Zalewski, 70–86. London and New York: Zed Books.
Cavarero, Adriana. 2002. *Stately Bodies: Literature, Philosophy, and the Question of Gender*. Ann Arbor: University of Michigan Press.
Cavarero, Adriana. 2009. *Horrorism: Naming Contemporary Violence*. Translated by William McCuaig. New York: Columbia University Press.
Chambers, Samuel A. 2007. "Normative Violence after 9/11: Rereading the Politics of *Gender Trouble*." *New Political Science* 29 no. 1: 43–60.
Chambers, Samuel A. and Terrell Carver. 2008. *Judith Butler and Political Theory: Troubling Politics*. New York: Routledge.
Chatterjee, Pratap. 2011. "How Lawyers Sign Off on Drone Attacks." *Guardian*. June 15. http://www.theguardian.com/commetisfree/cifamerica/2011/jun15/drone-attacks-obama-aministration/print.
Chicago Project on Security and Terrorism. 2011. "Suicide Attack Database." Available at http://cpost.uchicago.edu/search.php (accessed 10 September, 2012).

Chow, Denise. 2013. "Drone Wars: Pilots Reveal Debilitating Stress beyond Virtual Battlefield." *Live Science*. November 5. www.livescience.come/40949-military-drone-war-psychology.html.

Chow, Rey. 2006. *The Age of the World Target: Self-Referentiality in War, Theory, and Comparative Work*. Durham, NC, and London: Duke University Press.

Cohn, Carol. 1987. "Sex and Death in the Rational World of Defense Intellectuals." *Signs: Journal of Women in Culture and Society* 12, no. 4: 687–718.

Coker, Christopher. 2001. *Humane Warfare*. London: Routledge.

Cole, Simon. 2001. *Suspect Identities: A History of Fingerprinting and Criminal Identification*. Cambridge, MA: Harvard University Press.

Colebrook, Claire. 2011. "Time and Autopoiesis: The Organism Has No Future." In *Deleuze and the Body*, eds. Joe Hughes and Laura Guillaume, 9–28. Edinburgh: Edinburgh University Press.

Conant, Eve. 2009. "Remains of the Day." *Newsweek*. January 12, 43–45.

Coole, Diana. 2005. "Rethinking Agency: A Phenomenological Approach to Embodiment and Agentic Capacities." *Political Studies* 53 no. 1: 124–142.

Coole, Diana. 2007. "Experiencing Discourse: Gendered Styles and the Embodiment of Power" *British Journal of Politics and International Relations* 9, no. 3: 413–433.

Coole, Diana, and Samantha Frost. 2010. "Introducing the New Materialisms." In *New Materialisms: Ontology, Agency, Politics*, eds. Diana Coole and Samantha Frost, 1–46. Durham, NC: Duke University Press.

Costello, Cary Gabriel. 2012. "TSA Body Screening and the Trans Body" Transfusion. March 25. http://trans-fusion.blogspot.co.uk/2012/03/tsa-body-scanning-and-trans-body.html

Coyote, Ivan. 2010. "Flying While Butch." Daily Xtra. Dec 15. http://dailyxtra.com/vancouver/ideas/flying-butch

Crenshaw, Martha. 2007. "Explaining Suicide Terrorism: A Review Essay." *Security Studies* 16, no. 1: 133–162.

Cunliffe, Philip. 2010. "Dangerous Duties: Power, Paternalism and the 'Responsibility to Protect.'" *Review of International Studies* 36: 79–96.

Cunningham, Karla. 2009. "Female Survival Calculations in Politically Violent Settings: How Political Violence and Terrorism Are Viewed as Pathways to Life." *Studies in Conflict and Terrorism* 32, no. 7: 561–575.

Currah, Paisley, and Tara Mulqueen. 2011. "Securitizing Gender: Identity, Biometrics, and Transgender Bodies at the Airport." *Social Research* 78, no. 2: 557–582.

Damasio, Antonio. 1994. *Descartes' Error: Emotion, Reason, and the Human Brain*. New York: Penguin.

Danner, Mark. 2009. "US Torture: Voices from Black Sites." *New York Review of Books*. April 9. http://www.nybooks.com/articles/archives/2009/apr/09/us-torture-voices-from-the-black-sites/

Das, Veena. 2007. *Life and Words: Violence and the Descent into the Ordinary*. Berkeley and Los Angeles: University of California Press.

Dao, James. 2013. "Drone Pilots Are Found to Get Stress Disorders Much as Those in Combat Do." *New York Times*. February 23. http://www.nytimes.com/2013/02/23/us/drone-pilots-found-to-get-stress-disorders-much-as-those-in-combat-do.html?_r=0.

Dauphinée, Elizabeth. 2007. "The Politics of the Body in Pain: Reading the Ethics of Imagery." *Security Dialogue* 38, no. 2: 139–155.

Dauphinée, Elizabeth, and Cristina Masters, eds. 2006. *The Logics of Biopower and the War on Terror: Living, Dying, Surviving*. New York: Palgrave.

Davey, Monica. 2008. "Drone to Patrol Part of Border with Canada." *New York Times*. December 7. http://www.nytimes.com/2008/12/08/us/08drone.html.

De Goede, Marieke. 2008. "Beyond Risk: Premediation and the Post-9/11 Security Imagination." *Security Dialogue* 39, no. 2–3: 155–176.

DeLanda, Manuel. 1997. *War in the Age of Intelligent Machines*. London: Zone Books.

Deleuze, Gilles. 1988. *Foucault*. Translated by Sean Hand. Minneapolis: University of Minnesota Press.

Deleuze, Gilles, and Felix Guattari. 2004 [1980]. *A Thousand Plateaus*. Vol. 2 of *Capitalism and Schizophrenia*. Translated by Brian Massumi. London and New York: Continuum.

Department of Defense. 2006. "Medical Program Support for Detainee Operations, DoD instruction no. 2310.08E." June 6. http://www.dtic.mil/whs/directives/corres/pdf/231008p.pdf.

Department of Justice (US). "Lawfulness of a Lethal Operation Directed Against a U.S. Citizen Who Is a Senior Operational Leader of Al-Qa'ida or an Associated Force." msnbcmedia.msn.com/i/msnbc/sections/news/020413_DOJ_White_Paper.pdf (accessed July 5, 2013).

Dershowitz, Alan. 2002. "Want Torture? Get a Warrant." *San Francisco Chronicle*. January 22, A19.

Deudney, Daniel. 2007. *Bounding Power: Republican Security Theory from the Polis to the Global Village*. Princeton, NJ, and Oxford: Princeton University Press.

Devji, Faisal. 2008. *The Terrorist in Search of Humanity: Militant Islam and Global Politics*. New York: Columbia University Press.

Diken, Bulent, and Carsten Bagge Laustsen. 2006. "The Camp." *Geografiska Annaler: Series B Human Geography* 88, no. 4: 443–452.

Dillon, Michael. 1996. *The Politics of Security: Towards a Political Philosophy of Continental Thought*. London and New York: Routledge.

Dillon, Michael. 2004. "The Security of Governance." In *Global Governmentality: Governing Global Spaces*, eds. Wendy Larner and William Walters, 76–94. London: Routledge.

Dillon, Michael. 2007a. "Governing Through Contingency: The Security of Biopolitical Governance." *Political Geography* 26, no. 1: 41–47.

Dillon, Michael. 2007b. "Governing Terror: The State of Emergency of Biopolitical Emergence." *International Political Sociology* 1, no. 1: 7–28.

Dillon, Michael, and Luis Lobo-Guerrero. 2008. "Biopolitics of Security in the 21st Century: An Introduction." *Review of International Studies* 34: 265–292.

Dillon, Michael, and Julian Reid. 2001. "Global Liberal Governance: Biopolitics, Security and War." *Millennium: Journal of International Studies* 30, no. 1: 41–66.

Dillon, Michael, and Julien Reid. 2009. *The Liberal Way of War: Killing to Make Life Live*. London: Routledge.

DiManno, Rosie. 2003. "Cleaning Up the Carnage When Terror Strikes in Israel." *Toronto Star*. May 5, A2.

Dingley, James, and Marcello Mollica. 2007. "The Human Body as Terrorist Weapon: Hunger Strikes and Suicide Bombers." *Studies in Conflict and Terrorism* 30: 459–492.

DiStefano, Christine. 1991. *Configurations of Masculinity: A Feminist Perspective on Modern Political Thought*. Ithaca, NY, and London: Cornell University Press.

Downes, Alexander B. 2009. "Desperate Times, Desperate Measures: The Causes of Civilian Victimization in War." *International Security* 30, no. 4: 152–195.

Duara, Nigel. 2012. "Judge: Man Who Stripped Nude at Airport Not Guilty." *Associated Press*. July 18. http://www.google.com/hostednews/ap/article/

ALeqM5giTyifXFF_Xp1akq82rm65nqEVtQ?docId=a974540d1050421b9e24ce
b74092c886.
Dubois, Page. 1991. *Torture and Truth*. New York: Routledge.
Duffield, Mark, and Nicholas Waddell. 2006. "Securing Humans in a Dangerous World." *International Relations* 43: 1–23.
Edkins, Jenny. 2011. *Missing: Persons and Politics*. Ithaca, NY: Cornell University Press.
Edkins, Jenny, and Véronique Pin-Fat. 2004. "Introduction: Life, Power, Resistance." In *Sovereign Lives: Power in Global Politics*, eds. Jenny Edkins, Véronique Pin-Fat, and Michael J. Shapiro, 1–22. New York and London: Routledge.
Elshtain, Jean Bethke. 1995 [1987]. *Women and War*. Chicago: University of Chicago Press.
Elshtain, Jean Bethke. 2003. *Just War Against Terror: The Burden of American Power in a Violent World*. New York: Basic Books.
Enloe, Cynthia. 1983. *Does Khaki Become You? The Militarization of Women's Lives*. Boston: South End Press.
Enloe, Cynthia. 2000. *Maneuvers: The International Politics of Militarizing Women's Lives*. Berkeley: University of California Press.
Entous, Adam. 2010. "Special Report: How the White House Learned to Love the Drone." *Reuters*. May 19. http://www.reuters.com/article/idUSTRE64H5SL20100518.
Epstein, Charlotte. 2007. "Guilty Bodies, Productive Bodies, Destructive Bodies: Crossing the Biometric Border." *International Political Sociology* 1, no. 2: 149–164.
Epstein, Charlotte. 2010. "Who Speaks? Discourse, the Subject and the Study of Identity in International Politics." *European Journal of International Relations* 17, no. 2: 1–24.
Ettlinger, Nancy. 2007. "Precarity Unbound." *Alternatives* 32: 319–340.
Evans, Brad. 2010. "Foucault's Legacy: Security, War and Violence in the 21st Century." *Security Dialogue* 41, no. 4: 413–433.
Evans, Brad. 2011. "The Liberal War Thesis: Introducing the Ten Principles of Twenty-First-Century Biopolitical Warfare." *South Atlantic Quarterly* 110, no. 3: 747–756.
Evans, Gareth, and Mohamed Sahnoun. 2002. "Responsibility to Protect." *Foreign Affairs* 81, no. 6: 99–110.
Fausto-Sterling, Anne. 2000. *Sexing the Body: Gender Politics and the Construction of Sexuality*. New York: Basic Books.
Fearon, James, and Alex Wendt. 2002. "Rationalism v. Constructivism: A Skeptical View." In *The Handbook of International Relations*, eds. Walter Carlsnaes, Thomas Risse, and Beth A. Simmons, 52–72. London: Sage Publications.
"Female Passengers Say They're Targeted by TSA." 2012. *CBS Dallas*. February 3. http://dfw.cbslocal.com/2012/02/03/female-passengers-say-theyre-targeted-by-tsa/.
Ferguson, Kathy. 1993. *The Man Question: Visions of Subjectivity in Feminist Theory*. Berkeley: University of California Press.
Fierke, K. M. 2009. "Agents of Death: The Structural Logic of Suicide Terrorism and Martyrdom." *International Theory* 1, no. 1: 155–184.
Fierke, K. M. 2013. *Political Self-Sacrifice: Agency, Body and Emotion in International Relations*. Cambridge: Cambridge University Press, 2013.
Fineman, Martha Albertson. 2008. "The Vulnerable Subject: Anchoring Equality in the Human Condition." *Yale Journal of Law and Feminism* 20, no. 1: 1–23.
Finn, Peter, and Joby Warrick. 2009a. "Detainee's Harsh Treatment Foiled No Plots." *Washington Post*. March 29. http://www.washingtonpost.com/wp-dyn/content/article/2009/03/28/AR2009032802066.html.

Finn, Peter, and Joby Warrick. 2009b. "In 2002, Military Agency Warned Against 'Torture.'" *Washington Post*. April 25. http://www.washingtonpost.com/wp-dyn/content/article/2009/04/24/AR2009042403171.html.

Finn, Peter, and Sari Horwitz. 2012. "Holder: US Can Lawfully Target American Citizens." *Washington Post*. March 5. http://www.washingtonpost.com/world/national-security/holder-us-can-lawfully-target-american-citizens/2012/03/05/gIQANknFtR_story.html.

Finnemore, Martha, and Kathryn Sikkink.1998. "International Norm Dynamics and Political Change." *International Organization* 52, no. 4: 887–917.

Finnemore, Martha. 2004. *The Purpose of Intervention: Changing Beliefs about the Use of Force*. Ithaca: Cornell University Press.

Fishel, Stefanie. *Bodies and Worlds in International Relations: New Metaphors for Global Living*. Unpublished manuscript.

Fishel, Stefanie. 2013. "Theorizing Violence in the Responsibility to Protect." *Critical Studies on Security* 1, no. 2: 204–218.

Foot, Rosemary. 2006. "Torture: The Struggle over a Peremptory Norm in Counter-Terrorist Era." *International Relations* 20, no. 2: 131–151.

Foucault, Michel. 1972. *The Archeology of Knowledge*. Translated by A. Sheridan Smith. New York: Tavistock Publications.

Foucault, Michel. 1978. *The History of Sexuality*, Vol. 1. New York: Random House.

Foucault, Michel. 1979. *Discipline and Punish: The Birth of the Prison*. Edited by Alan Sheridan. New York: Vintage Books.

Foucault, Michel. 1980. *Power/Knowledge: Selected Interviews and Other Writings 1972–1977*. Edited by Colin Gordon and translated by Colin Gordon, Leo Marshall, John Mepham, and Kate Soper. New York: Pantheon Books.

Foucault, Michel. 1994 [1973]. *The Birth of the Clinic*. Translated by A. M. Sheridan Smith. New York: Vintage Books.

Foucault, Michel. 2000. "The Birth of Social Medicine." In *Essential Works III: Power*, by Michel Foucault, 134–156. New York: The New Press.

Foucault, Michel. 2003. *Society Must Be Defended*. Translated by David Macey. New York: Picador.

Foucault, Michel. 2007. *Security, Territory, Population: Lectures at the College de France, 1977–78*. Translated by Graham Burchell. Basingstroke, Hampshire: Palgrave Macmillan.

Fox, Ben. 2005. "Guantanamo Hunger Strikers Say Feeding Tubes Employed as Punishment." *Associated Press*. October 20. http://www.informationclearinghouse.info/article10689.htm.

Frank, Thomas. 2008. "Anxiety-Detecting Machines Could Spot Terrorists." *USA Today*. September 18. http://usatoday30.usatoday.com/news/nation/2008-09-18-bioscanner_N.htm?csp=Forbes.

Gambetta, Diego, ed. 2005. *Making Sense of Suicide Terrorism*. Oxford: Oxford University Press.

Gatens, Moira. 1996. *Imaginary Bodies: Ethics, Power and Corporeality*. New York: Routledge.

Gibbs, Raymond W. 2006. *Embodiment and Cognitive Science*. Cambridge: Cambridge University Press.

Gilligan, Carol. 1983. *In a Different Voice: Psychological Theory and Women's Development*. Cambridge, MA: Harvard University Press.

Ginsburg, Mitchell. 2003. "Enduring Horror." *Jerusalem Report*. September 22: 12.

GIRES. 2012. "United Kingdom Gender Recognition Act." *Gender Identity Research and Education Society*. http://www.gires.org.uk/GRA.php.

Glanz, James. 2004. "Torture Is Often a Temptation and Almost Never Works." *New York Times*. May 9. http://www.nytimes.com/2004/05/09/weekinreview/the-world-torture-is-often-a-temptation-and-almost-never-works.html.

Golden, Tim. 2006. "Tough U.S. Steps in Hunger Strike at Camp in Cuba." *New York Times*. February 9. http://www.nytimes.com/2006/02/09/politics/09gitmo.html?pagewanted=all.

Golden, Tim. 2007. "Guantanamo Detainees Stage Hunger Strike." *New York Times*. April 9. http://www.nytimes.com/2007/04/09/us/09hunger.html?ex=1179633600&en=5274585f8ae4039e&ei=5070.

Goldstein, Joshua S. 2001. *War and Gender: How Gender Shapes the War System and Vice Versa*. Cambridge: Cambridge University Press.

Graham, Bradly. 2005. "Enemy Body Counts Revived." *The* Washington Power, October 24. http://www.washingtonpost.com/wp-dyn/content/article/2005/10/23/AR2005102301273.html.

Grant, Jaime M, Lisa A. Mottet, and Justin Tanis. 2010. *National Transgender Discrimination Survey Report on Health and Health Care*. Washington, DC: National Gay and Lesbian Task Force and National Center for Transgender Equality.

Gray, Chris Hables. 1997. *Postmodern War: The New Politics of Conflict*. New York: Guilford Press.

Gregory, Derek. 2004. *The Colonial Present: Afghanistan, Palestine, Iraq*. Malden, MA: Blackwell Publishing.

Gregory, Derek. 2011. "From a View to Kill: Drones and Late Modern War." *Theory, Culture and Society* 28, no. 7–8: 188–215.

Gregory, Derek. 2014. "Drone Geographies." *Radical Philosophy* 183: 7–19.

Grossman, Dave. 1995. *On Killing: The Psychological Costs of Learning to Kill in War and Society*. Boston: Little, Brown and Co.

Grosz, Elizabeth. 1994. *Volatile Bodies: Toward A Corporeal Feminism*. Bloomington: Indiana University Press.

Grosz, Elizabeth. 1995. *Space, Time, and Perversion: Essays on the Politics of Bodies*. New York and London: Routledge.

Grosz, Elizabeth. 2005. *Time Travels: Feminism, Nature, Power*. Durham, NC, and London: Duke University Press.

Gusterson, Hugh. 2004. *People of the Bomb: Portraits of America's Nuclear Complex*. Minneapolis: University of Minnesota Press.

Hafez, Mohammed M. 2006. *Manufacturing Human Bombs: The Making of Palestinian Suicide Bombers*. Washington, DC: United States Institute of Peace Press.

Hannah, Matthew. 2006. "Torture and the Ticking Time Bomb: The War on Terrorism as a Geographical Imagination of Power/Knowledge." *Annals of the Association of American Geographers* 96, no. 3: 622–640.

Hansen, Lene. 2000. "The Little Mermaid's Silent Security Dilemma." *Millennium: Journal of International Studies* 29, no 2: 285–306.

Hansen, Lene. 2006. *Security as Practice: Discourse Analysis and the Bosnian War*. New York: Routledge.

Haraway, Donna. 1991a. "Situated Knowledges." In *Simians, Cyborgs and Women*, by Donna Haraway, 183–202. New York: Routledge.

Haraway, Donna. 1991b. "A Cyborg Manifesto: Science, Technology, and Socialist-Feminism in the Late Twentieth Century." In *Simians, Cyborgs and Women*, by Donna Haraway, 149–182. New York: Routledge.

Haraway, Donna. 1991c. "The Biopolitics of Postmodern Bodies." In *Simians, Cyborgs and Women*, by Donna Haraway, 203–230. New York: Routledge.

Hasso, Frances S. 2005. "Discursive and Political Deployments by/of the 2002 Palestinian Women Suicide Bombers/Martyrs." *Feminist Review* 81: 23–51.

Hastings, Michael. 2012. "The Rise of the Killer Drones: How America Goes to War in Secret." *Rolling Stone*. April 16. http://www.rollingstone.com/politics/news/the-rise-of-the-killer-drones-how-america-goes-to-war-in-secret-20120416.

Hawkins, Robert J. 2010. "You're Nothing But a Chalky Alien to TSA Scanners." San Diego Union Tribune. August 31. http://www.signonsandiego.com/news/2010/aug/31/youre-nothing-chalky-alien-tsa-scanners/.

Hayles, N. Katherine. 1993. "The Materiality of Informatics." *Configurations* 1, no. 1: 147–170.

Hayles, N. Katherine. 1999. *How We Became Posthuman: Virtual Bodies in Cybernetics, Literature, and Informatics*. Chicago: University of Chicago Press.

Held, Virginia. 2006. *Ethics of Care: Personal, Political, and Global*. New York: Oxford Unviersity Press.

Herbert, Bob. 2005. "Who We Are." *New York Times*. August 1. http://www.nytimes.com/2005/08/01/opinion/01herbert.html.

Hobbes, Thomas. 1996 [1651]. *Leviathan*. Edited by Richard Tuck. Cambridge: Cambridge University Press.

Hoffman, Bruce. 2003. "The Logic of Suicide Terrorism." *The Atlantic Monthly* 291, no. 5: 40–47.

Hooper, Charlotte. 2001. *Manly States: Masculinities, International Relations, and Gender Politics*. New York: Columbia University Press.

Horton, Scott. 2010. "The Guantanamo 'Suicides': A Camp Delta Sergeant Blows the Whistle." *Harper's*. January 18. http://www.harpers.org/archive/2010/01/hbc-90006368.

Howell, Allison. 2007. "Victims or Madmen? The Diagnostic Competition over "Terrorist" Detainees at Guantanamo Bay." *International Political Sociology* 1, no. 1: 29–47.

Howell, Allison. 2011. *Madness in International Relations: Psychology, Security, and the Global Governance of Mental Health*. London and New York: Routledge.

Hyndman, Jennifer. 2007. "Feminist Geopolitics Revisited: Body Counts in Iraq." *The Professional Geographer* 59, no. 1: 35–46.

Ignatieff, Michael. 2001. *Virtual War: Kosovo and Beyond*. New York: Picador.

International Commission on Intervention and State Sovereignty. 2001. *The Responsibility to Protect*. Ottawa: International Development Research Centre.

Jabri, Vivienne. 2006a. "Shock and Awe: Power and the Resistance of Art." *Millennium: Journal of International Studies* 34, no. 3: 819–839.

Jabri, Vivienne. 2006b. "War, Security and the Liberal State." *Security Dialogue* 37, no. 1: 47–64.

Jenkins, Philip. 1999. "Fighting Terrorism as if Women Mattered: Anti-Abortion Violence as Unconstructed Terrorism." In *Making Trouble: Cultural Constructions of Crime, Deviance, and Control*, eds. Jeff Ferrell and Neil Websdale, 319–346. Hawthorne, NY: Aldine De Gruyter.

Johnson, Carrie, and Walter Pincus. 2009. "Supermax Prisons in the US Already Hold Terrorists." *Washington Post*. May 22. http://www.washingtonpost.com/wp-dyn/content/article/2009/05/21/AR2009052102009.html.

Johnson, Joel. 2010. "One Hundred Naked Citizens: One Hundred Leaked Body Scans." *Gizmodo*. November 16. http://gizmodo.com/5690749/these-are-the-first-100-leaked-body-scans.

Joint Task Force–Guantanamo. 2003. "Camp Delta Standard Operating Procedures." 200328-March. http://www.dod.mil/pubs/foi/operation_and_plans/Detainee/CampDeltaSOP_dec07.pdf (accessed 2012 28-July).

Jordan, James. 2010. "9/11 Victims Identified with DNA Tests." *Sky News*. January 8. http://news.sky.com/skynews/Home/World-News/September-11-New-York-World-Trade-Centre-Attack-Victims-Identified-After-DNA-Tests/Article/2 01001215516767?f=rss.

Jordanova, Ludmilla. 1989. *Sexual Visions: Images of Gender in Science and Medicine Between the Eighteenth and Twentieth Centuries*. Madison: University of Wisconsin Press.

Kahn, Paul W. 2008. *Sacred Violence: Torture, Terror and Sovereignty*. Ann Arbor: University of Michigan Press.

Kaldor, Mary. 2007. *Human Security: Reflections on Globalization and Intervention*. London: Polity.

Kantorowicz, Ernst. 1957. *The King's Two Bodies: A Study in Medieval Political Theology*. Princeton, NJ: Princeton University Press.

Karkazis, Katrina. 2008. *Fixing Sex: Intersex, Medical Authority, and Lived Experience*. Durham, NC: Duke University Press.

KATU. 2012. "Judge: Naked Man at TSA Screening Protected by Free Speech." *KATU.com*. July 18. http://www.katu.com/news/local/Man-who-stripped-for-TSA-search-at-PDX-found-not-guilty-162935416.html.

Keisling, Mara, Kate Kendall, and Masen Davis. 2010. "Letter to John S. Pistole, TSA Administrator." December 17. http://transequality.org/PDFs/NCTE_NCLR_TLC_121710.pdf.

Kessler, Oliver, and Wouter Werner. 2008. "Extrajudicial Killing as Risk Management." *Security Dialogue* 39, no 2–3: 289–308.

Kirby, Vicki. 1997. *Telling Flesh: The Substance of the Corporeal*. New York and London: Routledge.

Kilcullen, David, and Andrew Exum. 2009. "Death from Above, Outrage from Below." *New York Times*. May 16. www.nytimes.com/2009/05/15/opinion/17exum.html?pagewanted=all&_r=0.

Kinsella, Helen. 2005. "Securing the Civilian: Sex and Gender in the Laws of War." In *Power and Global Governance*, eds. Michael Barnett and Raymond Duvall, 249–272. Cambridge: Cambridge University Press.

Kinsella, Helen. 2011. *The Image before the Weapons: A Critical History of the Distinction Between Combatant and Civilian*. Ithaca, NY: Cornell University Press.

Kirkpatrick, David D. 2005. "Senators Laud Treatment of Detainees in Guantanamo." *New York Times*. June 28. http://www.nytimes.com/2005/06/28/politics/28gitmo.html.

Koh, Harold Hongju. 2010. "The Obama Administration and International Law." *US Department of State*. March 25. http://www.state.gov/s/l/releases/remarks/139119.htm.

Koo, Katrina Lee. 2002. "Confronting a Disciplinary Blindness: Women, War and Rape in the International Politics of Security." *Australian Journal of Political Science* 37, no. 2: 525–536.

Krauthammer, Charles. 2010. "Don't Touch my Junk." *Washington Post*. November 19. http://www.washingtonpost.com/wp-dyn/content/article/2010/11/18/AR2010111804494.html.

Krishna, Sankaran. 1994. "Cartographic Anxiety: Mapping the Body Politics in India." *Alternatives* 19: 507–521.

Kristeva, Julia. 1982. *Powers of Horror: An Essay on Abjection*. Translated by Leon S. Roudiez. New York: Columbia University Press.

L3 Communications. 2012. "ProVision ATD Image-Free Technology." L3 Communications Security and Detection Systems. http://www.sds.l-3com.com/advancedimaging/provision-at.htm.

Lakoff, George. 1987. *Women, Fire, and Dangerous Things*. Chicago: University of Chicago Press.
Lalvani, Suren. 1996. *Photography, Vision, and the Production of Modern Bodies*. Albany: State University of New York Press.
Laqueur, Thomas. 1990. *Making Sex: Body and Gender from the Greeks to Freud*. Cambridge, MA: Harvard University Press.
Lefebvre, Henri. 1992. *The Production of Space*. Malden, MA, and London: Blackwell.
Leonnig, Carol. 2005. "More Join Guantanamo Hunger Strike." Washington Post, September 13 http://www.washingtonpost.com/wp-dyn/content/article/2005/09/12/AR2005091201690.html.
Lewis, Jeffrey. 2007. "Precision Terror: Suicide Bombing as Control Technology." *Terrorism and Political Violence* 19: 223–245.
Lindlaw, Scott. 2008. "Drone Operators Suffer War Stress." *Military Times*. August 7. www.militarytimes.com/news/2008/08/ap_remote_stress_080708/.
Lloyd, Moya. 2007. *Judith Butler: From Norms to Politics*. Cambridge, UK: Polity Press.
Lobo-Guerrero, Luis. 2011. *Insuring Security: Biopolitics, Security and Risk*. New York and London: Routledge.
Locher, Birgit, and Elisabeth Prügl. 2001. "Feminism and Constructivism: Worlds Apart or Sharing the Middle Ground?" *International Studies Quarterly* 45, no. 1: 111–129.
Luban, David. 2005. "Liberalism, Torture, and Ticking Bomb." *Virginia Law Review* 91: 1425–1461.
Luoma-aho, Mika. 2009. "Political Theology, Anthropomorphism, and Person-hood of the State: The Religion of IR." *International Political Sociology* 3, no 3: 293–309.
Lyon, David. 2005. "The Border Is Everywhere: ID Cards, Surveillance and the Other." In *Global Surveillance and Policing: Border, Security, Identity*, eds. Elia Zureik and Mark B. Salter, 66–82. Portland, OR: Willan Publishing.
MacKinnon, Catharine. 1989. *Toward a Feminist Theory of the State*. Cambridge, MA: Harvard University Press.
Magnet, Shoshana, and Tara Rodgers. 2012. "Stripping for the State: Whole Body Imaging Technologies and the Surveillance of Othered Bodies." *Feminist Media Studies* 12, no. 1: 101–118.
Mahnken, Thomas. 2008. *Technology and the American Way of War since 1945*. New York: Columbia University Press.
Mamdani, Mahmood. 2009. *Saviors and Survivors: Darfur, Politics and the War Against Terror*. New York: Pantheon Books.
Martin, Emily. 1994. *Flexible Bodies: The Role of Immunity in American Culture from the Days of Polio to the Age of AIDS*. Boston: Beacon Press.
Martin, Matt J., with Charles J. Sasser. 2010. *Predator: The Remote-Control Air War over Iraq and Afghanistan*. Minneapolis: Zenith Press.
Martin, Rachel. 2011. "Report: High Levels of 'Burnout' In U.S. Drone Pilots." *NPR*. December 19. http://www.npr.org/2011/12/19/143926857/report-high-levels-of-burnout-in-u-s-drone-pilots
Masters, Cristina. 2005. "Bodies of Technology: Cyborg Soldier and Militarized Masculinities." *International Feminist Journal of Politics* 7, no. 1: 112–132.
Mbembe, Achille. 2003. "Necropolitics." *Public Culture* 15, no. 1: 11–40.
McFarland, Stephen. 1995. *America's Pursuit of Precision Bombing, 1910–1945*. Washington, DC: Smithsonian Institution Press.
Mckelvey, Tara. 2011. "Inside the Killing Machine." *Newsweek*. February 15. http://www.newsweek.com/inside-killing-machine-68771.

McKeown, Ryder. 2009. "Norm Regress: US Revisionism and the Slow Death of the Torture Norm." *International Relations* 23, no. 1: 5–25.

McNay, Lois. 1992. *Foucault and Feminism: Power, Gender and the Self*. Cambridge: Polity Press.

McNay, Lois. 2000. *Gender and Agency: Reconfiguring the Subject in Feminist and Social Throught*. Cambridge: Polity Press.

Melia, Michael. 2007. "More Gitmo Detainees Join Hunger Strike." *Associated Press*. January 8. http://www.sfgate.com/cgi-bin/article.cgi?f=/n/a/2007/01/08/international/i152839S55.DTL.

Milbank, Dana. 2003. "Curtains Ordered for Media Coverage of Returning Coffins." *Washington Post*. October 21: A23.

Miles, Steven H. 2006. *Oath Betrayed: Torture, Medical Complicity, and the War on Terror*. New York: Random House.

Mill, John Stuart. 1989 [1859]. *On Liberty and Other Writings*. Ed. Stefan Collini. Cambridge: Cambridge University Press.

Miller, Greg. 2011. "Increased U.S. Drone Strikes in Pakistan Killing Few High-Value Militants." *Washington Post*. February 21. http://www.washingtonpost.com/wp-dyn/content/article/2011/02/20/AR2011022002975.html.

Miller, Greg. 2014. "Report: Deadly Drone Strike in Yemen Failed to Comply with Obama's Rules to Protect Civilians." *Washington Post*. February 20. www.washingtonpost.com/world/nationa-security/report-deadly-drone-strike-in-yemen-failed-to-comply-with-obamas-rules-to-protect-civilians/2014/02/19/46bc68f2-997d-11e3-b931-0204122c514b_story.html.

Miller, Ruth A. 2007. "On Freedom and Feeding Tubes." *Law and Literature* 19, no. 2: 161–186.

Milliken, Jennifer, and David Sylvan. 1996. "Soft Bodies, Hard Targets and Chic Theories: US Bombing Policy in Indochina." *Millennium: Journal of International Studies* 25, no 3: 321–359.

Mitchell, Luke. 2009. "Six Questions for Cynthia Smith on the Legality of Force-Feeding at Guantanamo." *Harper's*. June 4. http://harpers.org/archive/2009/06/hbc-90005110.

Moghadam, Assaf. 2009. "Motives for Martyrdon: Al-Qaida, Salafi Jihad, and the Spread of Suicide Attacks." *International Security* 33, no. 3: 46–78.

Moon, Katherine H. S. 1997. *Sex Among Allies: Military Prostitution in U.S.-Korea Relations*. New York: Columbia University Press.

Muir, David. 2010. "Inside the Drone War: On the Ground and in the Virtual Cockpit with America's New Lethal Spy." *ABC News*. January 12. http://abcnews.go.com/WN/inside-predator-drones-game-changing-technology-war-afghanistan/story?id=9543587.

Muller, Benjamin. 2010. *Security, Risk and the Biometric State: Governing Borders and Bodies*. New York: Routledge.

Muppidi, Himadeep. 2012. *The Colonial Signs of International Relations*. London: C. Hurst & Co.

Nakashima, Ellen, and Craig Whitlock. 2011. "With Air Force's Gorgon Drone 'We Can See Everything.'" *Washington Post*. January 2. www.washingtonpost/cp-dyn/content/article/2011/01/01/AR2011010102690.

Nanji, Ayaz. 2005. "Report: 108 Died in U.S. Custody." *CBS News*. March 15. http://www.cbsnews.com/stories/2005/03/16/terror/main680658.shtml?cmp=EM8706.

Nayak, Meghana. 2006. "Orientalism and 'Saving' US State Identity after 9/11." *International Feminist Journal of Politics* 8, no. 1: 42–61.

Neumann, Iver B. 2004. "Beware of Organicism: The Narrative Self of the State." *Review of International Studies* 30: 259–267.

Nicholl, David. 2006. "Guantanamo and Medical Ethics." The Jurist, June 13. http://jurist.org/forum/2006/06/guantanamo-and-medical-ethics.php.

Nicholl, David, et. al. 2006. "Forcefeeding and Restraint of Guantanamo Bay Hunger Strikers." *Lancet* 367, no. 9513: 811.

Nitkin, Karen. 2007. "Walking Like a Bomber." *Technology Review*. January 17. http://www.technologyreview.com/printer_friendly_article.aspx?id=18072.

Norris, Margot. 1991. "Military Censorship and the Body Count in the Persian Gulf War." *Cultural Critique* 19L: 223–245.

Okin, Susan Moller. 1989. *Justice, Gender, and the Family*. New York: Basic Books, 1989.

Oliver, Kelly. 2007. *Women as Weapons of War: Iraq, Sex and the Media*. New York: Columbia University Press.

Oliver, Kelly. 2008. "Women: The Secret Weapon of Modern Warfare?" *Hypatia* 23, no. 2: 1–16.

Orford, Anne. 1999. "Muscular Humanitarianism: Reading the Narratives of the New Interventionism." *European Journal of International Law*, 1999: 679–711.

O'Rourke, Lindsey. 2008. "What's Special about Female Suicide Terrorism?" *Security Studies* 18, no. 4: 681–718.

Owens, Patricia. 2003. "Accidents Don't Just Happen: The Liberal Politics of High Technology 'Humanitarian' War." *Millennium: Journal of International Studies*, 32 no. 3: 595–616.

Pape, Robert. 1996. *Bombing to Win: Air Power and Coercion in War*. Ithaca, NY: Cornell University Press.

Pape, Robert. 2005. *Dying to Win: The Strategic Logic of Suicide Terrorism*. New York: Random House.

Parpart, Jane L., and Marysia Zalewski. 2008. "Introduction." In *Rethinking the Man Question: Sex, Gender and Violence in International Relations*. London: Zed Press 1–22.

Pateman, Carole. 1988. *The Sexual Contract*. Stanford, CA: Stanford University Press.

Pateman, Carole. 1989. "Feminist Critiques of the Public/Private Dichotomy." In *The Disorder of Women: Democracy, Feminism, and Political Theory*, ed. Carole Pateman. Stanford, CA: Stanford University Press 118–140.

Peterson, V. Spike. 1992a. "Transgressing Boundaries: Theories of Knowledge, Gender and International Relations." *Millennium: Journal of International Studies* 21, no. 2: 183–206.

Peterson, V. S. 1992b. "Security and Sovereign States: What Is at Stake in Taking Feminism Seriously?" In *Gendered States: Feminist (Re)Visions of International Relations Theory*, ed. V. S. Peterson. Boulder, CO, and London: Lynne Rienner Publications 31–64.

Peterson, V. Spike, and Anne Sisson Runyan. 2010. *Global Gender Issues in the New Millennium*. Boulder, CO: Westview.

Physicians for Human Rights. 2005. "Forced Feeding of Gitmo Detainees Violates International Medical Codes of Ethics." September 16. http://physiciansforhumanrights.org/library/news-2005-09-16.html.

Piiparinen, Touko. 2012. "McDonaldisation of Sovereignty: A Foucauldian Analysis of Responsibility to Protect." *Global Society* 26, no. 4: 473–493.

Pin-Fat, Véronique, and Maria Stern. 2005. "The Scripting of Private Jessica Lynch: Biopolitics, Gender and the "Feminization" of the U.S. Military." *Alternatives: Global, Local, Political* 30: 25–53.

Pitzke, Marc. 2010. "Interview with a Drone Pilot." *Spiegel Online*. March 12. http://www.spiegel.de/international/world/0,1518,682420,00.html.

Plaw, Avery. 2008. *Targeting Terrorists: A License to Kill?* Burlington, VT: Ashgate.

Plaw, Avery. 2013. "Counting the Dead: The Proportionality of Predation in Pakistan." In *Killing by Remote Control*, ed. Bradley Jay Strawser, 126–153. Oxford: Oxford University Press.

Plumber, Thomas, and Eric Neumayer. 2006. "The Unequal Burden of War: The Effect of Armed Conflict on the Gender Gap in Life Expectancy." *International Organization* 60, no. 3: 723–754.

Power, Matthew. 2013."Confessions of a Drone Warrior." *GQ*. October 13. www.gq.com/news-politics/big-issues/201311/drone-uav-pilot-assassination.

Press, Darryl. 2011. "The Myth of Airpower in the Gulf War and the Future of Warfare." *International Security* 26, no. 2: 5–44.

Priest, Dana. 2005. "CIA Holds Terror Suspects in Secret Prisons." *Washington Post*. November 2. http://www.washingtonpost.com/wp-dyn/content/article/2005/11/01/AR2005110101644.html.

Protevi, John. 2009. *Political Affect: Connecting the Social and the Somatic*. Minneapolis: University of Minnesota Press.

Puar, Jasbir. 2007. *Terrorist Assemblages: Homonationalism in Queer Times*. Durham, NC: Duke University Press.

Pugliese, Joseph. 2010. *Biometrics: Bodies, Technologies, Biopolitics*. New York and London: Routledge.

Quinn, Ben. 2013. "Police Search for Missing Terror Suspect Who Escaped in Burqa." *The Guardian*. November 4. http://www.theguardian.com/uk-news/2013/nov/03/police-search-missing-terror-suspect.

Raju, Mana. 2008. "Graham: Detainees Get Better Treatment Than Nazis." *The Hill*. June 12. http://thehill.com/leading-the-news/graham-gitmo-detainees-get-better-treatment-than-nazis-2008-0612.html.

Rasmussen, Claire, and Michael Brown. 2005. "The Body Politic as Spatial Metaphor." *Citizenship Studies* 9, no. 5: 469–484.

Rasmussen, Mikkel Vedby. 2004. "'It Sounds Like a Riddle': Security Studies, the War on Terror and Risk." *Millennium: Journal of International Studies* 33, no. 2: 381–395.

Raytheon. 2006. "Advanced Multi-Unmanned Aerial System's Cockpit." *Defense Update*. http://defense-update.com/products/u/UCS.htm.

Reid, Julian. 2006. *The Biopolitics of the War on Terror: Life Struggles, Liberal Modernity and the Defence of Logistical Societies*. Manchester: Manchester University Press.

Reid, Julian. 2011. "The Vulnerable Subject of Liberal War." *South Atlantic Quarterly* 110, no. 3: 770–779.

Reid, Tim. 2009."One in Five Guantanamo Bay Detainees Is on Hunger Strike." *Times (London)*. January 15. http://www.thetimes.co.uk/tto/news/world/americas/article1999151.ece.

Rejali, Darius. 2003. "Modern Torture as Civic Marker: Solving a Global Anxiety with a New Political Technology." *Journal of Human Rights* 2, no. 2: 153–171.

Rejali, Darius. 2007. *Torture and Democracy*. Princeton, NJ, and Oxford: Princeton University Press.

Reprieve. 2013. "Yasiin Bey Force-Feeding Video Launches Campaign to Support Guantanamo Hunger-Strikers." July 8. http://www.reprieve.org.uk/press/2013_07_08_guantanamo_force_feeding_yasiin_bey/.

Richter-Montpetit, Melanie. 2007. "Empire, Desire and Violence: A Queer Transnational Feminist Reading of the Prison 'Abuse' in Abu Ghraib and the Question of 'Gender Equality.'" *International Feminist Journal of Politics* 9, no. 1: 38–59.

Rieff, David. 2002. *A Bed for the Night: Humanitarianism in Crisis*. New York: Simon and Schuster.

Reid, Julian. 2011. "The Vulnerable Subject of Liberal War." *South Atlantic Quarterly* 110, no. 3: 770–779.

Rivera-Fuentes, Consuela, and Lynda Birke. 2001. "Talking with/in Pain: Reflections on Bodies under Torture." *Women's International Studies Forum* 24, no. 6: 653–68.

Roberts, Michael. 2007. "Suicide Missions as Witnessing: Expansions, Contrasts." *Studies in Conflict and Terrorism* 30: 857–887.

Robinson, Fiona. 1999. *Globalizing Care: Ethics, Feminist Theory and International Relations*. Boulder, CO: Westview Press.

Rose, Nikolas. 1999. *Powers of Freedom: Reframing Political Thought*. Cambridge: Cambridge University Press.

Rousseau, Jean-Jacques. 1997 [1762]. *The Social Contract and Other Later Political Writings*. Edited and translated by V. Gourevitch. Cambridge: Cambridge University Press.

Rubin, Gayle. 1975. "The Traffic in Women: Notes on the 'Political Economy' of Sex." In *Toward an Anthropology of Women*, ed. Rayna Reiter, 157–209. New York: Monthly Review Press.

Ruddick, Sara. 1989. *Maternal Thinking: Toward a Politics of Peace*. New York: Ballantine Books, 1989.

Rumford, Chris. 2006. "Theorizing Borders." *European Journal of Social Theory* 9, no. 2: 155–169.

Salamon, Gayle. 2010. *Assuming a Body: Transgender and the Rhetorics of Materiality*. New York: Columbia University Press.

Salter, Mark. 2004. "Passports, Mobility and Security: How Smart Can the Border Be?" *International Studies Perspectives* 5: 71–91.

Salter, Mark B. 2005. "At the Threshold of Security: A Theory of International Borders." In *Global Surveillance and Policing: Borders, Security, Identity*, ed. Elia Zureik and Mark B. Salter, 36–50. Portland, OR: Willan Publishing.

Salter, Mark B. 2007. "Governmentalities of an Airport: Heterotopia and Confession." *International Political Sociology* 1: 49–66.

Scahill, Jeremy, and Glenn Greenwald. 2014. "The NSA's Secret Role in the U.S. Assassination Program." *First Look*. February 10. firstlook.org/theintercept/article/2013/02/10/the-nsas-secret-role/.

Scarry, Elaine. 1985. *The Body In Pain: The Making and Unmaking of the World*. New York: Oxford University Press.

Scarry, Elaine. 1990. "Consent and the Body: Injury, Departure, and Desire." *New Literary History* 21, no. 4: 867–896.

Schelling, Thomas. 1966. *Arms and Influence*. New Haven, CT, and London: Yale University Press.

Schogol, Jeff. 2012. "Demand Grows for UAV Pilots, Sensor Operators." *Air Force Times*. April 21. http://www.airforcetimes.com/article/20120421/NEWS/204210318/Demand-grows-UAV-pilots-sensor-operators.

Seelye, Katharine Q. 2002. "Some Guantanamo Detainees Will Be Freed, Rumsfeld Says." *New York Times*. October 23. http://www.nytimes.com/2002/10/23/

world/threats-responses-detainees-some-guantanamo-prisoners-will-be-freed-rumsfeld.html

Scott, James C. 1998. *Seeing Like a State: How Certain Schemes to Improve the Human Condition Have Failed*. New Haven, CT, and London: Yale University Press.

Scott, Joan W. 1991. "The Evidence of Experience." *Critical Inquiry* 17: 773–797.

Scott, Joan Wallach. 1986. "Gender: A Useful Category of Historical Analysis." *The American Historical Review* 91, no. 5: 1053–1075.

Shachtman, Noah. 2009. "Inside the Rise of the Warbots." *Danger Room*. February 4. www.wired.com/dangerroom/2009/02/peter-singers-w/.

Shachtman, Noah. 2010. "Army Preps 'Unblinking Eye' Airship for Afghanistan." *Danger Room*. June 17. http://www.wired.com/dangerroom/2010/06/army-preps-unblinking-eye-airship-for-afghanistan/.

Shachtman, Noah. 2011. "All-Seeing Blimp Could Be Afghanistan's Biggest Brain." *Danger Room*. January 18. http://www.wired.com/dangerroom/2011/01/all-seeing-blimp/.

Shane, Scott, and Charlie Savage. 2011. "Bin Laden Raid Revives Debate on Value of Torture." *New York Times*. May 3. http://www.nytimes.com/2011/05/04/us/politics/04torture.html?_r=1&scp=1&sq=torture%20bin%20laden&st=cse&gwh=116DF161F6C7E3F47CE746A4AEBF02DF.

Shane, Scott, and Mark Landler. 2011. "Obama Clears Way for Guantanamo Trials." *New York Times*. March 7. http://www.nytimes.com/2011/03/08/world/americas/08guantanamo.html?ref=guantanamobaynavalbasecuba&gwh=D728E42FED7C0A07C7938345FC1902DD.

Shildrick, Margrit. 1997. *Leaky Bodies and Boundaries: Feminism, Postmodernism and (Bio)ethics*. London and New York: Routledge.

Shildrick, Margrit. 2002. *Embodying the Monster: Encounters with the Vulnerable Self*. London: Sage.

Shue, Henry. 1978. "Torture." *Philosophy and Public Affairs* 7, no. 2: 124–143.

Sharkey, Joe. 2011. "With Hair Pat-Downs, Complaints of Racial Bias." *New York Times*. August 15. http://www.nytimes.com/2011/08/16/business/natural-hair-pat-downs-warrant-a-rethinking.html?_r=4&src=tp&.

Sharkey, Noel. 2010. "Saying 'No!' to Lethal Autonomous Targeting." *Journal of Military Ethics* 9, no. 4: 369–383.

Shaw, Martin. 2002. "Risk Transfer Militarism, Small Massacres and the Historical Legitimacy of War." *International Relations* 16, no. 3: 343–359.

Shepherd, Laura. 2006. "Veiled References: Constructions of Gender in the Bush Administration Discourse on the Attacks on Afghanistan Post 9/11." *International Feminist Journal of Politics* 8, no. 1: 19–41.

Shepherd, Laura. 2007. "'Victims, Perpetrators and Actors' Revisited: Exploring the Potential for a Feminist Reconceptualization of (International) Security and (Gender) Violence." *British Journal of Politics and International Relations* 9: 239–256.

Shepherd, Laura J. 2008. *Gender, Violence and Security: Discourse as Practice*. London and New York: Zed Publishers.

Shinko, Rosemary E. 2010. "Ethics after Liberalism: Why (Autonomous) Bodies Matter." *Millennium: Journal of International Studies* 38, no. 3: 723–745.

Shklar, Judith. 1984. *Ordinary Vices*. Cambridge, MA: Harvard University Press.

Shklar, Judith. 1998. "The Liberalism of Fear." In *Political Thought and Political Thinkers*, by Judith Shklar, ed. Stanley Hoffman, 3–20. Chicago: University of Chicago Press.

Singer, P. W. 2009. *Wired for War: The Roboties Revolution and Conflict in the Twenty-first Century*. New York: Penguin Press.
Sjoberg, Laura. 2006. "Gendered Realities of the Immunity Principle: Why Gender Analysis Needs Feminism." *International Studies Quarterly* 50: 899–910.
Sjoberg, Laura. 2012. "Toward Trans-Gendering International Relations?" *International Political Sociology* 6: 337–354.
Sjoberg, Laura. 2014. Gender, War, and Conflict. Cambridge: Polity Press.
Sjoberg, Laura, and Caron Gentry. 2007. *Mothers, Monsters, Whores: Women's Violence in Global Politics*. London: Zed Books.
Sjoberg, Laura, and Laura Shepherd. 2012. "Trans-Bodies in/of Wars: Cis-privilege and Contemporary Security Strategies." *Feminist Review* 101: 5–23.
Smith, Thomas. 2002. "The New Law of War: Legitimizing Hi-Tech and Infrastructural Violence." *International Studies Quarterly* 46: 367–376.
Somerville, Siobhan. 2000. *Queering the Color Line: Race and the Invention of Homosexuality in American Culture*. Durham, NC: Duke University Press.
Sontag, Susan. 1990 [1978]. *Illness as Metaphor and AIDS and Its Metaphors*. New York: Doubleday.
Spade, Dean. 2008. "Documenting Gender." *Hastings Law Journal* 59: 731–832.
Spade, Dean. 2011. *Normal Life: Administrative Violence, Critical Trans Politics and the Limits of Law*. Brooklyn, NY: South End Press.
Spivak, Gayatri Chakrovarty. 1988 [1985]. "Can the Subaltern Speak?" In *Marxism and the Interpretation of Culture*, eds. Cary Nelson and Lawrence Grossberg, 271–313. Champaign: University of Illinois Press.
Spivak, Gayatri Chakrovarty. 2004. "Terror: A Speech after 9-11." *boundary 2* 31, no 2: 81–111.
Stadler, Nurit. 2006. "Terror, Corpse Symbolism and Taboo Violation: The 'Haredi Disaster Victim Identification Team ("ZAKA") in Israel." *Journal of the Royal Anthropological Institute* 12, no. 4: 837–858.
Stadler, Nurit. 2009. *Yeshiva Fundamentalism: Piety, Gender and Resistance in the Ultra-Orthodox World*. New York: New York University Press.
Stern, Maria, and Marysia Zalewski. 2009. "Feminist Fatigue(s): Reflections on Feminism and Familiar Fables of Militarisation." *Review of International Studies* 35: 611–630.
Stoler, Ann Laura. 2002. *Race and the Education of Desire*. Durham, NC: Duke University Press.
Stoler, Ann Laura. 2008. "Epistemic Politics: Ontologies of Colonial Common Sense." *Philosophical Forum* 39, no. 3: 349–361.
Stolberg, Sheryl Gay. 2004. "Senate Backs Ban on Photogs of G.I. Coffins." *New York Times*. June 22.
Stone, Sandy. 1997 [1987]. "The Empire Strikes Back: A Posttransexual Manifesto." In *Writing on the Body: Female Embodiment and Feminist Theory*, eds. Katie Conboy, Nadia Medina, and Sarah Stanbury, 337–359. New York: Columbia University Press.
Stryker, Susan. 2008. *Transgender History*. Berkeley, CA: Seal Press.
Suskind, Ron. 2006. *The One-Percent Doctrine: Deep Inside America's Pursuit of its Enemies since 9/11*. New York: Simon and Schuster.
Sylvester, Christine. 1994. *Feminist Theory and International Relations in a Post-Modern Era*. Cambridge: Cambridge University Press.
Sylvester, Christine. 2002. *Feminist International Relations: An Unfinished Journey*. Cambridge: Cambridge University Press.

Sylvester, Christine. 2011. "Experiencing War: An Introduction." In *Experiencing War*, eds. Christine Sylvester, 1–7. Abingdon and New York: Routledge.

Sylvester, Christine. 2012. "War Experiences/War Practices/War Theory." *Millennium: Journal of International Studies* 40, no 3. 483–503.

Sylvester, Christine. 2013. *War as Experience: Contributions from International Relations and Feminist Analysis*. Abington and New York: Routledge.

Thakur, Ramesh. 2010. "Foreword." In *New Perspectives on Human Security*, eds. Malcolm McIntosh and Alan Hunter, vii. Sheffield: Greenleaf, vii-xiv.

Thomas, Evan. 2006. "'24' versus the Real World." *Newsweek*. September 20. http://www.newsweek.com/does-torture-really-work-109235.

Thomas, Ward. 2006. "Victory by Duress: Civilian Infrastructure in Air Campaigns." *Security Studies* 15, no. 1: 1–33.

Tickner, J. Ann. 1992. *Gender in International Relations: Feminist Perspectives on Achieving Global Security*. New York: Columbia University Press.

Tickner, J. Ann. 1997. "You Just Don't Understand: Troubled Engagements Between Feminist and IR Theorists." *International Studies Quarterly* 41, no. 4: 619–623.

Tickner, J. Ann. 2001. *Gendering World Politics: Issues and Approaches in the Post-Cold War Era*. New York: Columbia University Press.

Torpey, John. 2000. *The Invention of the Passport: Surveillance, Citizenship, and the State*. Cambridge: Cambridge University Press.

Towns, Ann. 2010. *Women and States: Norms and Hierarchies in International Society*. Cambridge: Cambridge University Press.

Tronto, Joan. 1993. *Moral Boundaries: A Political Argument for an Ethic of Care*. London: Routledge.

Tronto, Joan. 1996. "Care as a Political Concept." In *Revisioning the Political: Feminist Reconstructions of Traditional Concepts in Western Political Theory*, eds. Nancy J. Hirschmann and Christine Di Stefano, 139–156. Boulder, CO: Westview Press.

Tuana, Nancy. 2004. "Coming to Understand: Orgasm and the Epistemology of Ignorance." *Hypatia* 19, no. 1: 194–232.

Turner, Bryan S. 2003. "Social Fluids: Metaphors and Meanings of Society." *Body & Society* 9, no. 1: 1–10.

US Department of Homeland Security. 2003. "DHS Advisory to Security Personnel, No Change in Threat Level." *Department of Homeland Security*. http://www.dhs.gov/xnews/releases/press_release_0238.shtm.

Van Der Ploeg, Irma. 1999. "The Illegal Body: 'Eurodac' and the Politics of Biometric Identification." *Ethics and Information Technology* 1: 295–302.

Varela, Franciso J., Evan Thompson, and Eleanor Rosch. 1991. *The Embodied Mind: Cognitive Science and Human Experience*. Cambridge, MA: The MIT Press.

Vaughan-Williams, Nick. 2009. *Border Politics: The Limits of Sovereign Power*. Edinburgh: Edinburgh University Press.

Virilio, Paul. 2008 [1983]. *Pure War*. Los Angeles: Semiotext(e).

Waldby, Catherine. 1996. *AIDS and the Body Politic: Biomedicine and Sexual Difference*. Abingdon and New York: Routledge.

Waldby, Catherine. 2000. *The Visible Human Project: Informatic Bodies and Posthuman Medicine*. London and New York: Routledge.

Walker, R. B. J. 1993. *Inside/Outisde: International Relations as Political Theory*. Cambridge: Cambridge University Press.

Walt, Stephen. 1991. "The Renaissance of Security Studies." *International Studies Quarterly* 35, no. 2: 211–239.

Walters, William. 2006. "Border/Control." *European Journal of Social Theory* 9, no. 2: 187–203.
Washington, Wayne. 2002. "Rumsfeld Defends Detainee Conditions." Boston Globe, January 28, A1.
Weber, Cynthia. 1998. "Performative States". *Millennium: Journal of International Studies* 27, no 1: 77–95.
Weber, Cynthia. 2001. *International Relations: A Critical Introduction*. New York and London: Routledge.
Weber, Patricia. 2009. "Too Political or Not Political Enough? A Foucauldian Reading of the Responsibility to Protect." *The International Journal of Human Rights* 13, no. 4: 581–590.
Weiss, Meira. 2002. "The Body of the Nation: Terrorism and the Embodiment of Nationalism in Contemporary Israel." *Anthropological Quarterly* 75, no. 1: 37–62.
Weiss, Meira. 2002. *The Chosen Body: The Politics of Embodiment in Israeli Society*. Stanford, CA: Stanford University Press.
Wendt, Alexander. 2001. *Social Theory of International Politics*. Cambridge: Cambridge University Press.
Wheeler, Nicholas. 2000. *Saving Strangers: Humanitarian Intervention in International Society*. Oxford: Oxford University Press.
White, Josh. 2006. "Guantanamo Force-Feeding Tactics Are Called Torture." *Washington Post*. March 1. http://www.washingtonpost.com/wp-dyn/content/article/2006/02/28/AR2006022801344.html.
Whitworth, Sandra. 2008. "Militarized Masculinity and Post-Traumatic Stress Disorder." In *Rethinking the Man Question; Sex, Gender, and Violence in International Relations*, eds. Jane L. Parpart and Marysia Zalewski, 109–126. London and New York: Zed Books.
Wilchins, Riki. 2004. *Queer Theory, Gender Theory: An Instant Primer*. Cambridge, MA: Alyson Books.
Wilcox, Lauren. 2009. "Gendering the 'Cult of the Offensive.'" *Security Studies* 18, no. 2: 214–240.
Wilcox, Lauren. "Practicing Gender, Queering Theory." Unpublished manuscript.
Williams, Rudi. 2002. "Detainees Eat Well, Gain Weight on Camp Delta's Muslim Menu." *American Forces Press Service*. July 3. http://www.defenselink.mil/nedws/newsarticle.aspx?id=43686.
Winter, Stuart. 2009. "Remains of 9/11 Killers Found." January 11. http://www.express.co.uk/posts/view/79402/Exclusive-Remains-of-9-11-killers-found.
Worthington, Andy. 2007. *The Guantanamo Files: The Stories of 774 Detainees in America's Illegal Prison*. Ann Arbor, MI: Pluto Press.
Worthington, Andy. 2009. "A Truly Shocking Guantanamo Story." *Andy Worthington*. September 9. http://www.andyworthington.co.uk/2009/09/30/a-truly-shocking-guantanamo-story-judge-confirms-that-an-innocent-man-was-tortured-to-make-false-confessions/.
Yoo, John. 2002. "Memorandum to Alberto Gonzales." *US Department of Justice, Office of Legal Counsel*. August 2. http://www.usdoj.gov/olc/docs/memo-gonzales-aug1.pdf.
Yoo, John. 2005. "Memorandum to Willian Haynes II, January 9, 2002." In *The Torture Papers: The Road to Abu Ghraib*, eds. Karen Greenberg and Joshua Dratel, 38–79. Cambridge: Cambridge University Press.
Young, Iris Marion. 1989. "Polity and Group Difference: A Critique of the Ideal of Universal Citizenship." *Ethics* 99: 250–274.

Young, Iris Marion. 1990. *Justice and the Politics of Difference*. Princeton, NJ: Princeton University Press.
Young, Iris Marion. 2002. "Lived Body vs. Gender: Reflections on Social Structure and Subjectivity." *Ratio* 15, no. 4: 410–428.
Young, Iris Marion. 2003a. "The Logic of Masculinist Protection: Reflections on the Current Security State." *Signs: Journal of Women, Culture and Society* 29, no. 2: 15–35.
Young, Iris Marion. 2003b. "Feminist Reactions to the Contemporary Security Regime." *Hypatia* 18, no. 1: 223–231.
Youngs, Gillian. 2004. "Feminist International Relations: A Contradiction in Terms? Or: Why Women and Gender are Essential to the World 'We' Live in." *International Affairs* 80, no. 1: 75–87.
Yuval-Davis, Nira. 1997. *Gender and Nation*. London: Sage Publications.
Zagorin, Adam. 2006. "At Guantanamo, Dying Is Not Permitted." *Time*. June 30. http://www.time.com/time/nation/article/0,8599,1209530,00.htm.
Zehfuss, Maja. 2001. "Constructivism and Identity: A Dangerous Liaison." *European Journal of International Relations* 7, no. 3: 315–348.
Zehfuss, Maja. 2011. "Targeting: Precision and the Production of Ethics." *European Journal of International Relations* 17: 543–566.
Zetter, Kim. 2010. "German 'Fleshmob' Protests Airport Scanners." *Wired*. January 12. http://www.wired.com/threatlevel/2010/01/german-fleshmob/.
Ziarek, Ewa Plonowska. 2008. "Bare Life on Strike: Notes on the Biopolitics of Race and Gender." *South Atlantic Quarterly* 107, no. 1: 89–105.
Žižek, Slavoj. 2008. *Violence: Six Sideways Reflections*. New York: Picador.
Zucchino, David. 2010. "Drone Pilots Have a Front-Row Seat on War, from Half a World Away." *Los Angeles Times*. February 21. http://articles.latimes.com/2010/feb/21/world/la-fg-drone-crews21-2010feb21/4.
Zucchino, David. 2012. "Stress of Combat Reaches Drone Crews." *Los Angeles Times*. March 18. http://articles.latimes.com/2012/mar/18/nation/la-na-drone-stress-20120318.

INDEX

Note: Surnames starting with al- or el- are indexed under the subsequent part of the name (e.g., al-Zawahiri is in the Z's).

Aas, Katja Franko, 109
Abdul-Ahad, Ghaith, 1
Abdulmutallab, Umar Farouk, 57–58
Abé, Nicola, 131, 134, 148
Abject bodies: nature of, 13–14; normative violence as producer of, 174–177; of precision warfare, 136; in RtoP, 180; of suicide bomber, 82–83, 88–92, 103; women's bodies as, 88. *See also* Bodies that don't matter
Abjection: borders and the state and, 92–102; description of, 82, 84–85; of female suicide bombers, 97–98; resubjectification of bodies and, 93–97; sovereignty, bodies, and, 83–88
Abortion clinics, bombing of, 208 *n*3 (ch.3)
Abu Ghraib, 1, 62, 187
Abu-Lughod, Lila, 37
Ackelsberg, Martha A., 30
Ackerman, Spencer, 146, 147, 156
Actorhood, 35–36
Acts of war, hunger strikes as, 73
Adey, Peter, 107, 109, 110
Adler, Emmanuel, 203
Affect, embodiment of, 204
Afghanistan: CIA black sites in, 62; deaths in, 1, 159; drone surveillance of, 149; gendering of war in, 37; US-led military operations in, justifications for, 184
Agamben, Giorgio, 23, 25, 42, 50, 75, 162

Agency, 68, 178
Agentic capacities, 45–46, 51, 69, 166, 199
Ahmed, Sara, 77, 136, 204
AI (artificial intelligence), 139
Aimar, Albert, 148
Airport security assemblages, 104–130; bodies of information and, 113–115; Cartesian conception of bodies (re)production of, 112; conclusions on, 129–130; context for, 106–113; embodied subjects at, 28–29; management of violence by, 27; materialization of bodies, 115–129; overview, 14, 104–106; readings of, 105; resistance to materialization of bodies, 124–129
Al-Akhras, Ayat, 100
AL (artificial life), 139
Alaimo, Stacy, 45, 150
Algerian War, 121
Al Qaeda-Iraq, numbers of female suicide bombers in, 209 *n*7
Al Qaeda members and detainees, 56, 62, 152, 155
American Medical Association, on force-feeding, 73
Amoore, Louise, 105, 112, 115, 122
Ancient Greece, torture in, 60
Andreas, Peter, 107
Anomalous bodies, 106
Anticipatory self-defense, 153, 154–155
Anxiety, over US use of torture, 61–62

Aradau, Claudia, 105
Arbour, Louise, 178
Architecture of control, 106
Argentina, changing gender markers in, 210 n12
Arms and Influence (Schelling), 3–4
Artificial intelligence (AI), 139
Artificial life (AL), 139
Asad, Talal, 20, 67, 91, 135, 155, 162, 202, 209n4, 212
Associated Press, 142
Athenasiou, Athena, 189, 201
Auchter, Jessica, 92
Australia: body scanners in, 110; gender markers in, 210 n10
Automated weapons, 143–144
Autonomous subjects, of liberalism, 31
Al-Awlaki, Anwar, 153

Backscatter scanners, 110
Bagram Airfield, Afghanistan, 62
Baker, Al, 76
Banopticons, 105
Barad, Karen, 11, 46, 189
Bare life (*homo sacer*), 23, 25, 42, 50, 162, 179, 192
Barkawi, Tarak, 3, 4, 10, 204
Barnett, Michael, 36
Battersby, C., 87
BBC, 94, 159
Beauchamp, Toby, 118, 127, 128
Beauchamp, Zack, 135
Beauvoir, Simone de, 34, 35
Becker, Jo, 154, 156, 159, 160
Beemyn, Genny, 119, 121
Belkin, Aaron, 40, 42, 208n3
Bell, Vicki, 162
Bellamy, Alex, 5, 21, 167–168
Bellanova, Rocco, 114
Bergen, Peter, 159
Berlant, Lauren, 204
Bettcher, Talia Mae, 121
Bey, Yasiin (Mos Def), 69, 77–78, 208n7
Beyerstein, Lindsey, 74
Bially Mattern, Janice, 82, 142
Bigo, Didier, 105
Binaries, gendered, 38
Bin Laden, Osama, 58, 153, 188
Biometric technologies, 7, 107, 109, 111

Biopolitics: biopolitical security regimes, 80; biopolitical subjects, 27–28; conclusions on, 197–198, 199; as moral discourse, 56–57; precision warfare as biopolitical warfare, 132–137; security and IR and, 23–29
Biopower: conclusions on, 199, 201; contradictions in exercise of, 54; exercise of logic of, at Guantánamo Bay, 52–53, 56–57; Foucault on, 23–24, 27, 52; hunger strikes and, 70; locus of, 25; as moral framework, 26; practices of violence and, 17; sovereignty as, in RtoP, 169; subject of, 137; torture as sovereignty, discipline, and, 54–59
Birke, Lynda, 61
Birth of a Clinic (Foucault), 145
Bkare-Yusuf, Bibi, 61
Blackhurst, Rob, 140, 149
Black people, racialized physical characteristics of, 118
Black sites, 62
Blakely, Ruth, 5
Blanchard, Eric, 135
Bloom, Mia, 81, 97
Bodies: conclusions on, 192; enculturation of, 142; gendered representations of, 208 n3 (ch.3); individualization of, 25–26; influence of discursive practices on, 46–47; informalization of, 106; meaning of, 36; normalization of, feminist theory on, 7; production of, 199; reading of, for risks, 111; relational constitution of, 5; sex, violence and, 40–48; sex of, 6–7; simultaneous materialization and dematerialization of, 105; technological effacement of, 40; transformative powers of, 194–195. *See also* Airport security assemblages; Embodiment; Guantánamo Bay; International Relations; Precision warfare; Subjects; Suicide bombing; Supplementation; Violence; *following headings starting with "Bodies"*; *specific types of bodies (e.g., abject bodies, maternal bodies, violent bodies)*

Bodies, nature of: agentic capacities, 45; as autonomous individuals, 47; as containers, 87–88; dependency, 52; as focus of violence, 1–2; genderedness, 86–88; as generative of war and political violence, 3; incompleteness of, 85; instability of, 10, 46; natural vs. unnatural, in biopolitical practices of security, 26–27; as objects of knowledge, 166; as objects of security practices, 50–51, 85–86; ontological status of, 30, 47, 143; as performative, 8, 45; as socially constructed, 207n4; stable vs. leaky, 93; as truthful, 109; as useful, 52. *See also* Vulnerability
Bodies-as-information, in precision warfare, 29
Bodies-in-becoming (in formation), 91–92, 143, 195
Bodies in pain, hunger strikes and, 65–69
Bodies of information, 113–115, 116, 156, 193. *See also* Airport security assemblages
Bodies of protection, 176
Bodies of violence: airport security assemblages and, 104–130; bodies, subjects, and violence in IR, 17–48; conclusions on, 190–204; at Guantánamo Bay, 49–79; overview, 1–16; precision warfare and, 131–165; responsibility to protect and, 166–189; resubjectification of, 93–97; suicide bombing and, 80–103
Bodies, subjects, and violence in IR, 17–48; biopolitics, security, and IR, 23–29; conclusions on, 190–191; feminist theorizations of violence in IR, 29–48; overview, 11–12, 17; subjects of IR, 18–23; under-theorization of, 4
Bodies that don't matter (not worth saving): conclusions on, 195–196; inhuman subjects as, 185; patterns of life and, 156–158; prisoners of Guantánamo Bay as, 175; production of, 171; targeted bodies, 151–156, 175; unknowable bodies, 158–164. *See also* Abject bodies
Bodies without organs, 103
Bodily fluids, 98
Body cavities, searches of, 115
Body counts, unknowability of, 161. *See also* Deaths; Precision warfare
The Body in Pain (Scarry), 60–61
Body politic, 86, 87, 100, 102–103, 183, 192
Body scanners, 105, 106, 110–111, 113–115. *See also* Airport security assemblages
Bohling, Alissa, 114, 117
Bombers, gendering of, 97–102. *See also* Precision bombers
Bombs, corporality of, in suicide bombings, 91
Bomb's eye view, 144–148
Border fences (walls), 96
Borders and boundaries: abjection, the state, and, 92–102; biometric management of, 107; bodies' need for, 150; drone patrol of, 146; of embodied subjects, 138; between human and nonhuman, 174, 184; between states, 107; suicide bombing's effects on, 83–84, 89–92, 102–103, 194
Bordo, Susan, 37, 38
Boundaries. *See* Borders and boundaries
Bousquet, Antoine, 140
Bowdon, Mark, 146
Boyd, John, 140
Bradbury, Steven G., 57, 63, 64
Brecher, Bob, 52
Brennan, John, 128–129
Brides, female suicide bombers as, 100–101
Brighton, Shane, 3, 204
Brown, Michael, 103
Brown, Wendy, 31, 87, 96
Brute facts, bodies as, 3
Bryant, Brandon, 131, 132, 160
Buck, Lori, 33
Bunning, Jim, 70
Bureau of Investigative Journalism, on deaths from drone strikes, 134
Bush, George W., 50, 56, 62, 76, 153

INDEX [237]

Butler, Judith: on abjection, 85, 99; on bodies, productiveness of, 86; on bodies, vulnerability and precariousness of, 15–16, 47–49, 143, 167, 172–176, 178, 179–181, 185–186, 195–196, 200; critiques of, 46, 212n1 (concl.); on drag as parody, 124–125; on ethics, 172–173; Foucault, differences from, 46, 51–52; on gender and gender norms, 8, 11, 117, 160; on heterosexual matrix, 122; on indefinite detention of prisoners at Guantánamo Bay, 74, 75; on individualism, 185; on Israel and Jewish people, 183; on judging, 180; on materialization, 8, 123; on naturalness of sex, critique of, 51; on normative violence, 9, 173, 201–202; otherness, injurability and, 55; performativity, concept of, 8, 46, 99–100; on protection from violence, 189; on sex, imposition of, 119; on subject formation, 207 n4; on subjects, humanization of, 163; theorization of, as political intervention, 162; works cited, 10, 37, 43, 44, 57, 61, 68, 136, 150, 184, 199
Buzan, Barry, 4
Bybee memo, 63–64
Byman, Daniel, 159

Cadavers, 113
California Prison system, 78
Campbell, David, 18, 19, 22, 84, 86, 115, 122
Camp Delta, 62
Canada: body scanners in, 110; Passenger Protect program, 209 n2; travel regulations, gender and, 120
Caring labor, in feminist theory, 30–31, 178. 212n2
Carver, Terrell, 33, 39, 40, 137, 179, 207n1, 207n3, 207n4
Castrated bodies, 114
Cavarero, Adriana, 59, 80, 87, 91
Central Intelligence Agency (CIA): black sites, 62; drone missions and, 134, 152, 161; Office of Medical Services, 64; Pakistan, covert operations in, 159; suspect targeting, intelligence needed for, 155; targeting procedures, secret criteria for, 156
CEP (circular error probability), 133–134
Chambers, Samuel, 207n1, 207n3, 207n4.
Chicago Project on Security and Terrorism, 209n7
Children, killed by drones, 131
Chow, Denise, 149
Chow, Rey, 145, 158
Citizens, bodies of, 21
Civilian-combatant distinction, 160
Civilians: bodies of, and bodies of posthuman soldiers, 163; combatants, differentiation from, 151–152; deaths of, in precision warfare, 132–133, 158–162, 164; as unintended dead, 151; unknowability of deaths of, 161, 162
Clean and proper bodies: conclusions on, 193, 195, 196, 198; suicide bombing and, 85, 92–93, 96
Clothing, 90–91, 210–211n13
Cohn, Carol, 40–41
Coker, Christopher, 133, 144
Cole, Simon, 111
Colebrook, Claire, 150
Collateral damage, bodies as, 10, 185, 195
Colonialism, 145, 182
Combatants (militants), 151–152. See also Soldiers
Common Article 3, Geneva Conventions, 56, 72
Conant, Eve, 97
Congress (US), targeted killings, approval for, 153
Constitutive others, 85
Constitutive outside: bodies of suicide bombers as, 88; conclusions on, 195; in embodiment of subjects, 9; femininity as, 38, 41; formation of subject of invulnerability and, 180; naming of the human and, 174, 184; violence and, 202
Constructivism, 3, 35–36
Contamination, suicide bombing as, 89, 90, 91, 92, 102
Contingency, in suicide bombing, 82
Control, architecture of, 106

Coole, Diana, 11, 45
Corporeality, 45
Corpses, as objects, 112
Costello, Cary Cabriel, 117
Coyote, Ivan E., 117
Cranial phrenology, 111
Crapo, Michael D., 70–71
Crenshaw, Martha, 4, 81
Criminals, photographing of, 114
Cross-dressing, 121, 210n13
Crossing borders. *See* Airport security assemblages
Cruelty, 20, 202
Cruzan, Nancy, 75
Culture vs nature, 45
Cunliffe, Philip, 179
Currah, Paisley, 108, 119
Cybernetics, 143
Cyborgs, 40, 137–138

Damasio, Antonio, 142
Dangerous bodies, 109, 129, 188, 192. *See also* Terrorists
Danner, Mark, 56, 62, 63
Dao, James, 149
DARPA, camera automation by, 146
Das, Veena, 66, 67
Dauphinée, Elizabeth, 77, 187
Davey, Monica, 146
Davis, Masen, 117
Deaths: accidental, in precision warfare, 136; from drone strikes, 134, 153; Foucault on, 112; as limit to exercise of sovereign power, 52, 58–59; living dead, 176; numbers of, 163; of US prisoners from torture, 64. *See also* Hunger strikes
Death-worlds, 181
Defense Department, 72, 140–141
De Goede, Marleke, 105
DeLanda, Manuel, 139
Deleuze, Gilles, 103, 187
Dematerialization of bodies, 14, 113, 114, 157, 192
Dependent bodies, 52
Dershowitz, Alan, 52
Deudney, Daniel, 18–19
Deviant (unruly) bodies, 105, 106, 115–116, 121. *See also* Unnatural bodies
Devji, Faisal, 184

DHS (Homeland Security Department), 109, 121
Differentiation, and linking, in formation of woman as subject, 38
Digital corpses, 129
Digital dissection, 112
Diken, Bulent, 114
Dillon, Michael, 18, 23, 25, 85, 105, 113, 132, 139, 158, 199
DiManno, Rosie, 93
Dingley, James, 4
Discipline and disciplinary power, 27, 54–55, 86. *See also* Torture
Discipline and Punish (Foucault), 53, 63
Discourse analysis, 37–38
Discourses, performative, 8
Disembodiment, of precision bombers, 135–136
Disposition matrix, for targeted killings, 154
Dissections, 112
Distancing, in anxiety over torturing, 62
DiStefano, Christine, 31
Doing and being done to, 180, 196
Domestic violence, 32
"Don't touch my junk," 125–127
Downes, Alexander B., 6
Drag, as parody, 124–125
Drone helicopters, 146–147
Drone operators, 141–142, 147–148, 149
Drones (unmanned aerial vehicles, UAVs, remotely piloted aircraft, RPAs): areas used in, 154; armed drones, 134; bases for, 140; bodies and, 1; as bodily transformations, 141; children killed by, 131; cockpits, design of, 141–142; as guardian angels, 147; surveillance video from, 146; use in targeted killings, 152
Duara, Nigel, 128
Dubois, Page, 60
Duffield, Mark, 171
Durand, Robert, 72–73
Durbin, Richard, 71
Duvall, Raymond, 36

Edkins, Jenny, 23–24, 96
Edmonson, John, 49
Elshtain, Jean Bethke, 33, 39, 98, 100, 147, 158, 179, 184

INDEX [239]

Embodied subjects: fundamental aspects of, 122–123; as posthuman, 138, 196; in RtoP, 176; vulnerability of, 47–49
Embodiment: AI and AL as, 139; bomb's eye view and, 144–148; contemporary feminist theorizing on, 2; feminist theory on, 7–8, 11, 17, 41; nature of, 135; need for dynamic model of, 11; as performative, 123; posthuman view of, 138–139; in security assemblages, 105–106; sexed embodiment, 41; of subjects in IR, implications of, 6. *See also* Bodies; Posthuman embodiment; Precision warfare
Enemy combatants, 50, 56, 152. *See also* Targeted assassinations
Enhanced interrogation techniques, 49, 62, 64, 202. *See also* Torture
Enloe, Cynthia, 37
Entous, Adam, 146, 155, 160
Epstein, Charlotte, 66, 106, 108
Ethics: bodily vulnerability and, 186, 188; Butler on, 172–173; responsibility and, 189
Ettlinger, Nancy, 47, 201
Eurodac, 108
Europe, security procedures in, 108
European racial superiority, 118
Evans, Brad, 170, 176
Exceptionality, politics of, 50
Expert knowledge, for risk management, 27–28
Explosive bodies. *See* Suicide bombing
Extrajudicial killings (summary executions, targeted assassinations), 152–155
Exum, Andrew, 159
The eye, equation of, with the mind, 144–145

Faces, Levinasian, 185–186
Facial micro-expressions, 109, 111
Failed states, 183
False confessions, 57
FAST (The Future Attribute Screening Technology, Protect Hostile Intent), 109–110, 113
Fausto-Sterling, Anne, 119
Fearon, James, 35

Federal Bureau of Investigation (FBI), investigation of abortion clinic bombings, 208 $n3$ (ch.2)
Feldman, Allen, 65–66
Female suicide bombers, 13–14, 97–102, 209$n7$
Feminist theorization: on bodies, 3; on bodies and politics, relationship of, 190; conclusions on, 203–204; cyborgs in, 137–138; on embodiment, 2, 7–8, 11, 17, 41, 44–45; power of, 2; sex/gender theory in, 51–52; on subjectivity and embodiment, 29
Feminist theorizations of violence in IR, 29–48; bodies, sex, and violence, 40–48; overview, 29–36; violence, gendering of, 36–40
Femmes fatales, 99
Ferguson, Kathy, 43
Fierke, K. M., 4, 65, 66
Fineman, Martha Albertson, 31
Finn, Peter, 57, 153
Finnemore, Martha, 172
Fishel, Stefanie, 86, 169, 182
Fleshmobs, 128–129, 130, 180
Fleshy bodies, 44, 45–46
Foot, Rosemary, 5
Force, 3–4. *See also* Violence
Forced sterilizations, 32
Force-feeding: of Bey, 77–78; conclusions on, 191, 192; as gendering form of violence, 75; Geneva Conventions, Common Article 3, and, 72; performative effects of, 75, 76–77; physicians on, 73–74; use of, at Guantánamo Bay, 49–50, 69–78. *See also* Hunger strikes; Torture
Foucault, Michel: on biomedical knowledge, 145; on biopower, 31, 199; on bodies, individualization of, 25–26; on bodies, machines, and power, 137; Butler, differences from, 46, 51–52; on disciplinary power, techniques of, 55; on discourse analysis, 37–38; on dissection, 112; feminist critiques of, 45; on gender, 37; on mobile space, 140; on power relations, 23–24; on racism, 154; on sovereign power, 52, 58, 60; on torture, 54; on vital massacres, 132; on wars, 26; works

cited, 12, 27, 40, 57, 65, 70, 86, 92, 105, 116, 137, 156, 170, 198
Fox, Ben, 71
Frank, Thomas, 110
Free subjects, of liberalism, 31
Frost, Samantha, 11, 45
Full-body scanners. *See* Body scanners
Fuster, Gloria Gonzalez, 114
The Future Attribute Screening Technology (FAST, Protect Hostile Intent), 109–110, 113

Gallant, Nicole, 33
Gambetta, Diego, 4
Gatens, Moira, 19, 43, 87
Gender: of bodies, 6–7; Butler on, 8, 117, 207n4; definition of, 33–34; as discourse/discursive structure, 38–39; feminist theory on, 34–36; gendered binaries, 38; gender markers (M or F), 118–119, 120–121, 210n9; gender neutral bodies, 122; gender norms, 118, 160; gender performativity, 10–11, 51–52; gender presentation, match to, 116; gender violence, 33; immutability of, 116; instability of, as marker of identity, 123; intelligible, 117; non-conformity as security threat, 121–122; performances of, 125; presentation of, match to sexed embodiment, 116; as property of the state, 193; as separate from theorization of gender, 42–43; sex/gender system, 34, 51–52; state agencies' determination of, 119–120, 121; subjectivity and, 29; theorization of, as separate from sex, 42–43. *See also* Bodies, sex, and violence; Trans- and genderqueer people
Gendering: of bodies, as challenge to bodily informationalization, 122–123; of suicide bombers, 97–102; of violence, 36–40
Genderqueer: as term, 210n7. *See also* Trans- and genderqueer people
Gender Recognition Act (UK, 2004), 120
Geneva Conventions, Common Article 3, 56, 72
Genocide, military interventions against, 172

Gentry, Caron, 33, 97, 101
Germany, critics of security procedures in, 128
Ghailani, Ahmed Khalfan, 208n4
Gibbs, Raymond W., 142
Ginsburg, Mitchell, 93
GIRES, 120
Glanz, James, 57
Global Entry program, 108
God's eye vision of precision warfare, 160
God-tricks, 145, 146
Golden, Tim, 50, 72, 74, 137
Goldstein, Joshua S., 37
Gorgon Stare drone, 146
GPS-guided munitions, 145–146
Graham, Bradly, 153
Graham, Lindsay, 70
Grant, Jaime M., 121
Gray, Chris Hables, 143
Greece, ancient, torture in, 60
Greenwald, Glenn, 157
Gregory, Derek, 6, 140, 158, 161, 162
Grossman, Dave, 6
Grosz, Elizabeth: on the abject, 85; on prostheses, 142–143; works cited, 37, 45, 87, 88, 98, 196
Guantánamo Bay, 49–79: bodies of prisoners at, 5; conclusions on, 78–79, 191; deaths at, 208n2 (ch.2); deviant bodies in, 27; force-feeding and transformation of political status, 69–78; hunger strikes and bodies in pain, 65–69; images of bodies from, 1; overview, 12–13, 49–54; torture as practice of sovereign power, 59–65; torture as sovereignty, discipline, and biopower, 54–59
Guardian angels, drones as, 147
Guattari, Felix, 103
Gulf War (1991), 152
Gusterson, Hugh, 152

Hafez, Mohammed M., 4
El-Hage, Wadih, 208n5
Hall, Alexandra, 112, 115, 122
Hamdan v. Rumsfeld (2006), 56
Hannah, Matthew, 52
Hansen, Lene, 38, 188, 211n14
Haraway, Donna, 38, 86, 138, 144–145, 164–165

Harris, Harry, 72
Hasso, Frances S., 100
Hastings, Michael, 161
Hawkins, Robert J., 114
Hayles, N. Katherine: on embodiment and technology, 150; on enculturation of bodies, 142; on learning to type, 45; on posthuman subjects, 138–139; works cited, 105, 157, 196
Heaps of meat, bodies of suicide bombers as, 80, 93, 96, 97, 100, 193
Hekman, Susan, 45, 150
Herbert, Bob, 77
Heteronormativity, 117
Heterosexual matrix, 117, 122, 125
Hierarchical relations, 60, 84
High-tech militaries, 40. *See also* Technologies
Hijackers (from September 11, 2001 terrorist attacks), 96–97
Hobbes, Thomas, 18–19, 20, 31, 86
Hobbesian bodies, 18–19
Hoffman, Bruce, 81
Holder, Eric, 153
Homeland Security Department (DHS), 109, 121
Homines sacri (bare life), 23, 25, 42, 50, 162, 179, 192
Hooper, Charlotte, 37, 38, 40, 137
Horning, Kurt and Matthew, 96–97
Horn of Africa, Reaper drones in, 146
Horwitz, Sari, 153
Hostile Intent project, 210n8
Howell, Allison, 57, 76, 149
The human, 187
Human life, as sovereign, 168
Human rights, liberal norms of, 21
Humans, as fail-safes, 144
Human security, 4, 21, 168–170
Human subjects. *See* Subjects
Hunger strikers: bodies of, 5; conclusions on, 191, 192; as irrational, 75–76; strategic logic of, 72–73; subjectivity of, 70; suicide bombers, similarity to, 81; transformative power of bodies of, 194
Hunger strikes: as acts of war, 73, 75–76; at Guantánamo Bay, 49–50, 65–69. *See also* Force-feeding
Hussein, Saddam, and sons of, 152, 188

Hyndman, Jennifer, 163
Hyperarousal (in PTSD), 149

ICISS (International Commission on Intervention and State Sovereignty), 168, 169–170, 171
IDENT database, 108
Identities, 36, 108, 123
IDF (Israeli Defense Force) soldiers, 95
Idris, Wafa, 101
India, gender markers in, 210n10
Information gathering, torture as instrument of, 52–53, 54, 57–58
Infrastructural whiteness, 111
Inhumanity, subjects of, and mass violence, 184–188
Instability, 10, 11, 38–39, 46
Intellectual awareness (cognition), 142
Intelligibility, normative schemes of, 9
Intelligible genders, 117
International Commission on Intervention and State Sovereignty (ICISS), 168, 169–170, 171
International community, in RtoP, 177–178, 179, 182, 184
International political violence, IR's theorizing on, 3
International Relations (IR), 17–48; absence of bodies from, 40–41; biopolitics, security, and, 23–29; bodies in, 2–3, 79; bodies produced by, as productive of, 194; conclusions on, 190–191, 203–204; conventional, 11–12, 17; embodied subjects in, implications of, 6; feminist theorizations of embodiment in, 12; feminist theorizations of violence in, 29–48; political violence, international, theorizing on, 3; political violence, limitations of literature on, 4–5; political violence of, narrative of effects of suicide bombing on, 81–82; relation of bodies to, 1, 5; role of feminist theory in, 7; sovereignty, traditional theorization of, 170; subjects of, 18–23; violence in, 28; women, neglect of, 32–33. *See also* Guantánamo Bay
International Relations feminism, as reproductive of the subject "woman," 43–44

Intersex children, 119
Interstate wars, 18
Interventions, 151, 176
Invisible spectacles, 59
Invulnerable subjects, 177–178, 181
IR. *See* International Relations
Iran: travelers from, as security concern, 108
Iraq: deaths of civilians in, 159; drone surveillance of, 149; travelers from, as security concern, 108; UAVs used to kill in, 134
Israel: targeted killing in, 152; use of drones as weapons, 134. *See also* ZAKA
Israeli Defense Force (IDF) soldiers, 95
Israeli Institute of Forensic Science, 93, 96, 193

Jabri, Vivienne, 4, 28, 29
Jewish bodies, 93–95, 101, 193
Joint Task Force-Guantanamo, 55
Jordanova, Ludmilla, 127
Just bodies, 46, 176, 193, 199
Justice, care vs., 178
Justice Department: on detainment of prisoners, 57; on torture, 64; White Paper on anticipatory self-defense, 155, 161
Just war perspective, 157, 158
Just warriors, 147

Kahn, Paul W., 61
Kaldor, Mary, 169
Kantorowicz, Ernst, 178, 202
Karkazis, Katrina, 119
Keisling, Mara, 117
Kendall, Kate, 117
Kessler, Oliver, 105
Kilcullen, David, 159
Killability systems, 157–158
Killable bodies, 156, 158, 176, 193, 194
Kill chains, 139–140, 192, 211n4
Kings, sovereign power of, 178
Kinsella, Helen, 39, 160
Kirby, Vicki, 196
Kirkpatrick, David D., 70, 71
Knowles, Solange, 118
Koh, Harold, 161
Koo, Katrina Lee, 33
Krauthammer, Charles, 126

Kristeva, Julia: on abject as concept, 13; on abject bodies, 13, 82; interpretation of abjection, Butler's rejection of, 99; works cited, 84, 85, 92, 96, 193, 195

Lakoff, George, 87
Lalvani, Suren, 114
Lancet, open letter on force-feeding, 73
Landler, Mark, 50
Language, lack of, in torture victims, 60–61, 66
Laqueur, Thomas, 86
Laser-guided munitions, 145–146
Laustsen, Carsten Bagge, 114
Lawlessness, of Guantánamo Bay, 50
Lefebvre, Henri, 83–84
Legal analyses, in precision bombing targeting decisions, 211n4
Leonnig, Carol, 49
Leviathan, 18, 86
Levinas, 185–186
Lewis, Jeffrey, 156
Liberalism: autonomous subjects of, 31; bodies and violence in, 20–23, 135; free subjects of, 30; liberal discourses, vulnerability in, 31; liberal politics, biopower and, 24; liberal societies, 26, 135; liberal states, 138–139; liberal subjects and subjectivity, 22, 51; liberal tradition, on domestic violence, 32; pain in, 69; private vs. public spheres in, 30–31, 32
Libya: drone surveillance of, 149; NATO mission in, 168; travelers from, as security concern, 108; UAVs used in, 134
Life: as an information pattern, 156–157; biological vs. political qualified, 25; bodily truth and, 112–113
Lindlaw, Scott, 148, 149
Linking and differentiation, in formation of woman as subject, 38
Lived bodies, 68, 123, 130
Lives worth saving, 171, 172
Living dead, 176
Lloyd, Moya, 207n4
Lobo-Guerrero, Luis, 105
Locher, Birgit, 36, 38
Locke, John, 22, 31

Logic of abjection, 91
Logics of risk, 27
Loss, in representation, 188
Louk, Louis, 75
L3 Communications, 114
Luban, David, 53
Lyon, David, 107

MacKinnon, Catharine, 32
Magnet, Shoshana, 111, 128
Mahnken, Thomas, 140
Major powers, application of RtoP to, 171
Male bodies, 41, 86–88, 99
Mangum, Kevin, 146
Mapping, geographic vs. bodily, 158
Marked for death, as category, 10, 157, 158, 164
Martin, Matt J., 141, 142, 150, 156
Martin, Rachel, 148
Marx, Karl, 178
Masculine bodies, 137
Masculine-feminine/queer dichotomy, 41–42
Masculinity, 38, 40, 41–42. *See also* Men
Massacres, 176
Mass violence, responsibility to protect and, 177–184
Masters, Cristina, 29, 40, 44, 144, 147, 211*n*6
Material feminisms, 45
Materiality and materialization, 8, 45, 115–124, 124–129
Maternal bodies, 99
Matrix of war, 28–29
Mbembe, Achille, 176, 182
McCain, John, 77
McFarland, Stephen, 152
McKeown, Ryder, 5
McNay, Lois, 37, 45
Media, lack of reporting on human suffering of war, 187
Medical ethicists, 73–74
Medicalization, of torture techniques, 63–64
Melia, Michael, 73, 74
Men: bodies of, 41, 86–88, 99; in Locke's state of nature, 31. *See also* Gender; Masculinity

Menstrual blood, abjection and, 98–99
Mental patients, indefinite detention of, 74
Metadata analysis, by NSA, 157
Micro-expressions, facial, 109, 111
Milbank, Dana, 159
Miles, Steven H., 49, 64, 71
Militants (combatants), 151–152. *See also* Soldiers
Militaries, 37, 40, 41–42, 137, 151. *See also* Precision bombers; Precision warfare; Soldiers; Warfare and political violence
Militarized masculine bodies, 137
Military force, as focus of security studies, 3–4
Mill, John Stuart, 22
Miller, Greg, 156
Miller, Ruth A., 75
Milliken, Jennifer, 6
Millimeter wave scanners, 110
Minds, 35, 87, 142, 144–145
Mitchell, Luke, 72
Mobile space, 140
Moghadam, Assaf, 4
Mohamed, Binyam, 49, 67, 68, 186
Mohamed, Mohammed Ahmed, 211*n*13
Mohammad, Khalid Shaikh, 50, 62, 63
Mollica, Marcello, 4
Monstrous bodies, 116
Moon, Katherine H. S., 37
Moral responsibility, in war, 143–144
Morocco, CIA black sites in, 62
Mos Def (Yasiin Bey), 69, 77–78, 208*n*7
Mottet, Lisa A., 121
Moussaoui, Zacarias, 208*n*5
Muir, David, 155, 156
Muller, Benjamin, 105
Mulqueen, Tara, 108, 119
Muppidi, Himadeep, 174, 177, 212n13
Muscle memory, 45

Nakashima, Ellen, 146
Nakedness, 128–129
Nanji, Ayaz, 64
Nationalist discourses, women in, 101
National security, as center of analysis in security studies, 4
National Security Agency (NSA), 157

National Security Entry-Exit Registration (NSEER) program, 108
National security states, 25, 39
National Transgender Advocacy Coalition (NTAC), 116–117, 127
NATO, airstrikes on Afghanistan, 1
Natural bodies, 8–9, 19, 122
Nature versus culture, 45
Nayak, Meghana, 37
Nepal, gender markers in, 210n10
Neumayer, Eric, 33
New materialisms, 45
New York, changing gender markers in, 120
Nexus program, 108
Nicholl, David., 73
Nitkin, Karen, 111
Non-interference, sovereignty and, 169
Non-normative bodies. *See* Unnatural bodies
Nontraditional security threats, 169
Non-violence, 175
Norden Bombsight, 211n3
Normative bodies, 51. *See also* Unnatural bodies
Normative violence: Butler on, 47, 201–202; conclusions on, 200; description of, 9; drag as parody and, 124–125; ethical responsibilities and, 185; function of, 162; political violence, relationship to, 9; as producer of abject bodies, 174–177; RtoP and, 173
Norms, 46, 51, 85, 195
Norris, Margot, 159
Nossal, Kim Richard, 33
NSA (National Security Agency), 157
NSEER (National Security Entry-Exit Registration) program, 108

Obama, Barack: anticipatory self-defense, expansion of, 154–155; on civilian deaths in Pakistan, 159, 160; promise on closing Guantánamo Bay, failure to keep, 50, 62, 77; targeted killings by, 153, 154; targeting practices, defense of, 156; on torture, 49; trials for Guantánamo Bay prisoners, lack of, 56

Ohio, birth certificates, refusal to change, 120
Okin, Susan Moller, 30
Oliver, Kelly, 91, 97, 99
Orford, Anne, 37, 178
O'Rourke, Lindsey, 81, 97, 100
Ortega, Hernando, 141, 150
Other and otherness, 55, 85, 87–88, 186–187. *See also* Borders and boundaries
Owens, Patricia, 133

Pain, 20, 58, 60–61, 66–67. *See also* Bodies in pain
Pakistan: civilian deaths in, 159–160; deaths from drone strikes in, 134; drone surveillance of, 149; as state with ungoverned regions, 183; targeted killings in, 155
Palestinian female suicide bombers, 100–101
Panetta, Leon, 58, 154
Panopticon, 154, 156
Pape, Robert, 4, 5, 81
Parody, 10, 99–100, 124–125
Passive surveillance techniques, 109–110
Passports, 107
Pateman, Carole, 30, 87
Patterns of life, for targeted killings, 152, 156–158, 161
Pentagon, on civilian deaths, 159. *See also* Defense Department
Perfect bodies, 95
Performativity, 8, 10–11, 43–44, 46, 99–100
Peterson, V. Spike, 36, 38, 86
PGMs (precision-guided munitions), 133, 134, 145–146
Physicians, on force-feeding, 73
Physicians for Human Rights, 64, 73
Piiparinen, Touko, 182
Pin-Fat, Véronique, 23–24, 38, 39, 41, 42, 211n5
Pity, nature of, 187
Pitzke, Marc, 131
Plaw, Avery, 152, 160
Plumber, Thomas, 33
Poland, CIA black sites in, 62

INDEX [245]

Political violence, 4, 9, 18–19, 32–33. *See also* Warfare and political violence
Politics: bodies, relationship to, 192; bodily integrity and, 18; of bodily vulnerability, 202; of the body, feminist analysis of, 34; of exceptionality, 50; of female suicide bombers, 97; liberal theories of, feminist critique of, 30; political community, purposes of, 20; political distancing, 62; political order, biopolitical perspective on, 23; political self-sacrifice, 65; political speech, hunger strikes as, 73; political status, force-feeding and transformation of, 69–78; political subjectivity, visual capabilities as aspect of, 145; public sphere as subject of, 30. *See also* Biopolitics
Politics of abjection. *See* Suicide bombing
Population of organisms, citizens as, 170
Poss, James, 146
Posthuman bodies: conclusions on, 192, 194–197; nature of, 141; in precision warfare, 9, 15, 164; of soldiers, civilian bodies and, 163
Posthuman embodiment, 137–151; bomb's eye view and, 144–148; conclusions on, 196–197; Hayles on, 123; overview, 137–144; post-traumatic stress disorder and, 148–151
Poststructural feminists, on gender, 38
Post-traumatic stress disorder (PTSD), 149–151
Pouliot, Vincent, 203
Power: bodily performativity of power dynamics, 10–11; discipline and disciplinary power, 27, 54–55, 86; gender as signifier of, 36, 38, 39; as productive, 36; productive definition of, 23; social power, 3. *See also* Biopower; Sovereignty and sovereign power
Power, Matthew, 132, 141, 149
Precariousness, precarity vs., 174
Precarity, 47, 48, 174, 212n1 (concl.). *See also* Vulnerability
Pre-Check program, 108

Precision bombers: bodies of, 198; the bombed, relationship to, 14–15; disembodiment of, 135–136; invulnerability of, 134–135; as posthuman, 164; posthuman embodiment and, 196–197; production of bodies of, 137; prosthetic nature of, 150–151; sovereign power of, 164; transformative power of bodies of, 194
Precision-guided munitions (PGMs), 133, 134, 145–146
Precision warfare, 131–165; attractiveness of, 132–133; biopolitical warfare, 132–137; bodies that don't matter, 151–164; bodily instability in, 10; conclusions on, 164–165, 191–192; humans as source of code for, 138–139; justifications for, 28; overview, 14–15, 131–132; posthuman bodies and embodiment in, 9, 29, 137–151; precision bombing, 27, 152; representation in, 187–188; strategic studies on, 5–6; visual politics of, 144–148. *See also* Drones; Precision bombers
Predator drones, 140, 146, 156
Pregnant female bodies, 101
Press, Darryl, 5
Priest, Dana, 62
Prisoners of Guantánamo Bay: ambiguous legal place of, 56; as future danger, 57; protection of lives of, 59–60; sovereign power of, 68; transformation of political status of, 71; uncertain status of, 78; unlivability of, 175
Prison industrial complex, 78
Private spheres, public spheres vs., 30–31, 32
Procreation, suicide bombing as, 101, 102
Prostheses, 142–143
Protect Hostile Intent (The Future Attribute Screening Technology, FAST), 109–110, 113
Protector/protected dichotomy, 37, 39, 42, 100
Protevi, John, 74, 75

ProVision ATD (Automated Threat Detection) software, 113–114, 122
Prügl, Elisabeth, 36, 38
Psychological torture, 58
PTSD (post-traumatic stress disorder), 149–151
Puar, Jasbir, 123, 204
Public spheres, private spheres vs., 30–31, 32
Pugliese, Joseph, 107, 109, 111, 158

Quinlan, Karen, 75

Racialized bodies of surveillance, 123
Racism, Foucault on, 154
Raju, Mana, 70
Rankin, Susan, 119, 121
Rasmussen, Claire, 103
Rasmussen, Mikkel Vedby, 105
Rayashi, Reem Al, 91
Raytheon, 141–142
REAL ID law (2005), 118–119
Realism, bodies and violence in, 18–19
Reaper drones, 140, 146
Reason, liberal subject's possession of, 22
Recognition, body in pain as call for, 66, 67, 68–69
Reconstitution of bodies, 92–93
Reid, Richard, 108
Reid, Tim, 50, 72
Rejali, Darius, 57, 58, 63
Relationships, pain and, 66–67, 69
Remotely piloted aircraft (RPAs). See Drones
Representation, of suffering beings, 163–164, 187–188
Reprieve, 77
Resistance, 65–66, 123–129, 200
Resolution 1325 (UN, 2000), 33
Resolution 1973 (UN, 2011), 168
Responsibility to protect, 166–189; conclusions on, 197–198, 201; normative violence and, 174–177; overview, 15, 166–167; responsibility, restructuring of, 188–189; state sovereignty and, 21, 167–174; subjects of inhumanity and, 184–188; vulnerable bodies and, 177–184
Restraint chairs, for force-feeding, 71, 74

Resubjectification of bodies, 93–97
Richter-Montpetit, Melanie, 33
Rieff, David, 177
Right to life, 176
Risk and risk management, 27–28, 104–105, 111, 201
Ritual purification, suicide bombing and, 92, 93
Rivera-Fuentes, Consuela, 61
Rizzo, John, 161
Roberts, Michael, 4
Rodgers, Tara, 111, 128
Romania, CIA black sites in, 62
Rosch, Eleanor, 142
Rose, Nikolas, 24, 108
Rousseau, Jean-Jacques, 19
RPAs (remotely piloted aircraft). See Drones
RtoP (R2P). See Responsibility to protect
Rubin, Gayle, 34
Rumford, Chris, 107
Rumsfeld, Donald, 52, 57, 153
Runyan, Anne Sisson, 38
Russia, female suicide bombers in, numbers of, 209n7

Sacrifice, as abjection, 88
Sahnoun, Mohamed, 170, 176
Salamon, Gayle, 121, 123
Salter, Mark B., 106, 107, 109, 112
Sasser, Charles J., 141, 142, 150, 156
Savage, Charlie, 58
Savulesu, Jilian, 135
Scahill, Jeremy, 157
Scanners, 105. See also Body scanners
Scarry, Elaine, 60–61, 66, 75, 134–135, 149
Schelling, Thomas, 3–4
Schiavo, Terri, 75
Schogol, Jeff, 148
Schonhoff, Colleen M., 70
Scott, James C., 86, 105, 136
Scott, Joan Wallach, 33–34, 43
Screening Passengers by Observation Techniques (SPOT) program, 109, 111
Secure Flight program, 107–108, 118, 121–122
Securing bodies. See Airport security assemblages

Security: biopolitical practices of, 23, 197; bodily deviancy as threat to, 105; bodily sovereignty and, 24–25; Campbell on, 115; conclusions on, 198; contemporary drive of, 104; discourses of, violence in, 84; human security, 4, 21, 168–170; as knowledge, 104; in national security states, 25; in post–Cold War era, 107; production of bodies by, 112–113, 116; realist and liberal conceptions of, 23; in RtoP, 182; securitization of identity, 108; security practices, 15, 50–51, 85, 171; security regimes, bodies in, 104; subject of, as individualized human bodies, 25–26; threats to, traditional vs. nontraditional, 169. *See also* Biopolitics; Human security

Security scanners. *See* Body scanners

Security studies, 2, 3–4, 201

Seelye, Katharine Q., 52

Self-defense, rights of, 20

Self-formation, process of, 84–85

Self-identification of gender, 121

Self-preservation, 20

September 11, 2001 terrorist attacks, 96–97, 172, 183

Sex. *See* Bodies, sex, and violence; Gender

Sex/gender system, 34–35

Sexed embodiment, 41

Sexual assault, force-feeding as, 74–75

Sexual differences, erasure of, in body politic, 87

Shachtman, Noah, 144, 146, 147

Shah-i-Kot Valley, Afghanistan, drone killings in, 140

Shaler, Robert, 97

Shane, Scott, 50, 58, 154, 156, 159, 160

Shanley, Mary Lyndon, 30

Sharkey, Joe, 118

Sharkey, Noel, 141

Shepherd, Laura, 33, 37

Shildrick, Margrit, 88, 99, 101, 116

Shinko, Rosemary E., 69

Shklar, Judith, 20

Shue, Henry, 5, 52

SIM cards, 211n8

Singer, Peter W., 141, 144

Sjoberg, Laura, 33, 37, 38, 39, 97, 100, 101, 117, 179

Skin banks, 95

Slaves, torturing of, 60

Social hierarchies, torture as marking of, 60

Socially ecstatic structures, 199

Social relations, 3, 31, 34–35

Soldiers, 95, 137, 147, 211n6. *See also* Precision bombers

Somalia: drone surveillance of, 134, 146, 149; as failed state, 183

Somerville, Siobhan, 118

Sontag, Susan, 19

South Korea, body scanners in, 110

Sovereignty and sovereign power: abjection, bodies, and, 83–88; as bodily supplementation, 166; conclusions on, 202–203; exercise of logic of, at Guantánamo Bay, 52–53; incompleteness, 28; in liberalism vs. realism, 19, 20; nature of, 39–40, 83–84, 169; practices of violence and, 17; as responsibility, 170; RtoP and, 182, 184; sovereign states and sovereign men, 202–203; state sovereignty, 21, 83–84, 169, 182; torture as anxious practice of sovereign power, 59–65; torture as sovereignty, discipline, and biopower, 54–59; unchecked, liberalism on, 23. *See also* Responsibility to Protect

Spaces, of law and disorder, 83–84

Spade, Dean, 118–119, 120, 121

Spivak, Gayatri Chakrovarty, 89

SPOT (Screening Passengers by Observation Techniques) program, 109, 111

Spy blimps, 146–147

Sri Lanka, numbers of female suicide bombers in, 209n7

SSNP (Syrian Socialist National Party), 100–101

Stable bodies, 86

Stadler, Nurit, 93, 94, 95

State Department, on gender marker changes, 120, 210n11

States: abjection, borders and, 92–102; as bodies, 19, 86–87, 96; bodies and suicide bombing, relationship with,

88–89; failed states, 183; gendered bodies and, 87–88; gendering of, 39; good global citizenry for, 182; purposes of, 18; sex, ownership of, 119–120, 121; state sovereignty, 21, 83–84, 169, 182; structure of, 36; surveillance by, 107

Stealth technologies, for torture, 63

Stern, Maria, 38, 39, 41, 42, 43–44, 211n5

Stolberg, Sheryl Gay, 159

Stoler, Ann Laura, 118, 210n8

Stone, Sandy, 125

Stop and frisk policies, 126–127

Stories, about violence, gender in, 43–44

Strategic studies, on precision warfare, 5–6

Strategic visibility strategy, 127–128

Stress and duress torture techniques, 56

Strip searches, 115, 116

Stryker, Susan, 210n7

Subjects: biopolitical, 27–28; bodies, relationship to, 9, 22–23; boundedness of, 191; constructivism on, 35; embodiment of, 51, 195; Hobbesian bodies and, 18–19; incompleteness of, 180–181; of inhumanity, mass violence and, 184–188; of IR, 3; liberal assumptions of, violence in Guantánamo Bay and, 79; liberal subjects, 20–23, 30–32; precariousness of, 190; of precision warfare, 164; process of becoming, 9; in security studies, 2; separation from bodies, in violence, 44; sovereign, locus of, 173; of torture, 61; vulnerability and, 189. *See also* Bodies; Bodies, subjects, and violence in IR; Embodied subjects; Embodiment

Sudan: travelers from, as security concern, 108

Suicide bombers: abject bodies of, 88–92; description of, 1; effects of, 88; explosive bodies of, 14; female, 13–14, 97–102, 209n7; gendering of, 97–102; hunger strikers, similarity to, 81; motivations for, 208n2 (ch.3); posthuman embodiment and, 196–197; productivity of, 82; subjectivity of, 81–82; vulnerability of, 27

Suicide bombing, 80–103; abject body of the suicide bomber, 88–92; abjection, borders, and the state, 92–102; bodily instability in, 10; conclusions on, 102–103, 191, 194, 198; disruptive practices of, 28; as embodied practice, 194; overview, 13–14, 80–83; sovereignty, abjection, and bodies, 83–88

Summary executions (targeted assassinations, extrajudicial killings), 152–155

Supermax prison, 208n5

Supplementation, 68, 69, 79, 150–151, 166, 175–176

Supreme Court, US, *Hamdan v. Rumsfeld*, 56

Suskind, Ron, 64

Sylvan, David, 6

Sylvester, Christine, 34, 41, 42, 43, 44, 204

Syria: travelers from, as security concern, 108

Syrian Socialist National Party (SSNP), 100–101

Taliban, 1, 152, 155, 184

Tanis, Justin, 121

Targeted assassinations (summary executions, extrajudicial killings), 152–155

Targeted bodies, 151–156

Technologies: bodies of technology, 137; humans as information processors in, 141; as masculine, 147; in security discourses, 104; violence of, 28. *See also* Airport security assemblages; Drones; Posthuman bodies

Technostrategic discourse, 41

Telephony data, NSA analysis of, 157

Tennessee, birth certificates, refusal to change, 120

Terrell, Ellen, 125–126

Territories, ordered, of the state, 83–84

Terrorism Watch List, 108

Terrorist organizations, 90

Terrorists: bodies of, as bodies of information, 156; cross-dressers as potential, 121; discourse of formlessness and, 90; production of, 75–76, 192; rationalities of, 81 (*See also* Suicide bombing; War on terror); as social type, 55, 56; targeted killings of, 152–153. *See also* Suicide bombers
Thakur, Ramesh, 169
Thomas, Evan, 57
Thomas, Ward, 151
Thompson, Evan, 142
Ticking-time-bomb scenario, 52–53
Tickner, J. Ann, 33, 36, 38, 39, 43, 179
Tiedemann, Katherine, 159
Torah, corporeal nature of, 94–95
Torpey, John, 107
Torture: bodily instability in, 10; conclusions on, 191; definition of, 202; euphemism for, 62; Foucault on, 54; invisibility of, 59; IR literature on, 5; justifications for, 28; limits to, 13; McCain on, 77; nature of, 9; as not torture, 175; as practice of sovereign power, 59–65; precision warfare as akin to, 135; as sovereignty, discipline, and biopower, 54–59; state-sponsored, 20; techniques of, 63. *See also* Force-feeding; Hunger strikes
Towns, Ann, 86
Traditional security threats, 169
Trans-, as term, 210n7
Trans- and genderqueer people: airports as place of insecurity for, 118; at airport security, 9; bodily truth and, 116; body scanners and, 115; gender markers, requirements for changing, 119–121; lived embodiment of, 123; medical interventions for, 121, 127; problematic bodies of, 14; as security threats, 121–122, 123; strategic visibility strategy for, 127–128; unnatural (anomalous) bodies of, 106, 116; violence to, at airport security assemblages, 125
Transgender, as term, 210n7
Transportation Security Administration (TSA), 114, 116, 124, 126, 209n2, 210n5
Trapped bare life, 74, 75
Travelers: bodies of, 106; Canada Passenger Protect program, 209n2; National Security Entry-Exit Registration (NSEER) program, 108; US VISIT (United States Visitor and Immigration Status Indicator Technology) program, 108. *See also* Airport security assemblages; Body scanners
Tronto, Joan, 31
Truth, bodies as ultimate sign of, 116, 125, 129
Turkey, numbers of female suicide bombers in, 209n7
Tynor, John, 126

UAVs (unmanned aerial vehicles). *See* Drones
Ungoverned regions, states with, 183
Ungrievable life, 162–163
Unintelligible life, 162
Unintended dead, 151
United Kingdom: Gender Recognition Act (2004), 120; use of drones as weapons, 134
United Nations: adoption of RtoP, 168; Security Council Resolution 1325 (2000), 33; Security Council Resolution 1973 (2011), 168
United Nations Development Programme, 21
United States: anticipatory self-defense doctrine, 154–155; birth certificates, amending of, 120; border security, multilayered strategy for, 107–108; citizens, transformation of political status of, 76; on civilian deaths in Pakistan, 159–160; computing industry, military influence on, 139; on force-feeding, 69; force-feeding by, 71, 78; National Security Entry-Exit Registration (NSEER) program, 108; precision warfare, controversies over, 161–162; prison industrial complex, 78; sovereign power, exercise of, 60; as subject, 9/11 terrorist attacks as injury to, 172; summary executions by, 152; torture by, 54, 61–62; use of drones as weapons, 134; Visitor and Immigration Status Indicator

Technology (US VISIT) program, 108. See also Guantánamo Bay; *names of specific departments*
Unknowable bodies, 158–164
Unknowns, production of, 161
Unmanned aerial vehicles (UAVs). See Drones
Unnatural bodies, 26–27, 51, 89, 90, 164–165
Unruly (deviant) bodies, 105, 106, 115–116, 121
Useful bodies, 52
US VISIT (United States Visitor and Immigration Status Indicator Technology) program, 108

Van Der Ploeg, Irma, 104, 108
Van Munster, Rens, 105
Varela, Franciso J., 142
Vaughan-Williams, Nick, 107
Vietnam War, body counts in, 159
Violence: acceptability of, in precision warfare, 162; bodies, relationship to, 6; bodies, sex, and, 40–48; conclusions on, 200–201, 202–204; contemporary, constitution of, 12; embodied subjects and, 190; gender in feminist theorizations of, 33–34; gendering of, 36–40; instability of meaning of, 25; legitimization of, 183; liberal interpretation of, 32–33; in liberalism, 20; liberal subjects and, 20–23; in modern politics, 18; nature of, 3; nature of bodies as objects of, 3; normative, 9, 174–177; as performative, 9, 29, 53, 190; persons as bodies and, 1–2; political violence, 4, 9, 18–19, 32–33; in precision warfare, 10; productivity of, 12, 36, 84, 200; protection from, 189; in realism, 18–19; rethinking of, 8; in security discourses, 84; subjectivity and bodies and, rethinking of, 7–11; of visual strip searches, 115. *See also* Airport security assemblages; Bodies, subjects, and violence in IR; Guantánamo Bay; Normative violence; Precision warfare; Suicide bombers; Torture; Vulnerability; Warfare and political violence
Violent bodies, 12
Violent exclusions, natural bodies and, 8–9
Virilio, Paul, 151
Virtual strip searches, 115, 116
Visibility, of sovereign and disciplinary power, 56
The visual, Deleuze on, 187
Visual capacities, of posthuman bodies, 144–148
Vital massacres, 132
Voyeuristic intimacy, 149
Vulnerability: conclusions on, 200–201; embodied relationality and, 173–174; ethics and, 186; mass violence and vulnerable bodies, 177–184; ontological nature of, 47; rethinking of, 8; in RtoP, 176; stigmatized subjects in, 31; of suicide bombers, 81. *See also* Precarity; Responsibility to Protect
Vulnerable bodies, 177–184, 209n3 (ch.3)

Waddell, Nicholas, 171
Waldby, Catherine, 19, 112, 113, 115, 196
Walker, R. B. J., 84, 107
Walls (border fences), 96
Walt, Stephen, 3
Walters, William, 107
Warden's dilemma, 65
Warfare and political violence: absence of bodies in discourse of, 4; bodies, influences on, 10; disembodied war, 132; Foucault on, 26; gendering of, 37; as generative force, 3; just war perspective, 157; legitimization of, 39; matrix of war, 28–29; moral responsibility in, 143–144. *See also* Precision warfare; War on terror
War-fighting assemblages, 141–142
War on terror: biopolitics as explanation for, 26; enemy in, 184–185; as never-ending, 76; precision warfare and, 154; prisoner deaths in, 64, risk management in, 105; security threats in, 107; targeted killings in, 152–153; use of torture in, 27, 52–53, 54. *See also* Guantánamo Bay; Terrorists

Warrick, Joby, 57
Wars. *See* Warfare and political violence
Washington, Wayne, 57
Washington Post, on CIA targeting procedures, 156
Waterboarding, 63
Weapons, automated, 143–144. *See also* Drones
Weber, Cynthia, 33, 83, 86
Weber, Patricia, 171
Weiner, Norbert, 139
Weiss, Meira, 95, 137
Wendt, Alexander, 3, 35
Werner, Wouter, 105
White, Josh, 72
White Paper, on anticipatory self-defense, 155, 161
Whitlock, Craig, 146
Whitworth, Sandra, 37
Wilchins, Riki, 119
Wilcox, Lauren, 147, 179, 203
Williams, Rudi, 70
Winkenwerder, William, 72
Winter, Stuart, 97
Women: bodies of, 86–88, 99; discourses of the bodies of, 34–35; exclusion from liberal subjectivity, 22; exclusion from political and public spheres, 30, 87, 98, 99; exclusion of violence in lives of, 37; experiences of, 42, 43; female suicide bombers, 13–14, 97–102, 209n7; in Locke's state of nature, 31; nature of, feminist challenges to discourses of, 30; objectification of, 35; in Pakistan, as non-combatants, 160; principal threats to, 32; sexed bodies of, 41. *See also* Female suicide bombers; Gender
World Medical Association, on force-feeding, 73
World Summit (2005), 168
World Trade Center (WTC), 96–97. *See also* September 11, 2001 terrorist attacks
World War II, bombing during, 151–152
Worthington, Andy, 57, 65
WTC Families for Proper Burial, 96–97
Wyden, Ron, 71

Yemen: drone surveillance of, 134, 146, 149; as state with ungoverned regions, 183
Yoo, John, 56, 64, 152
Young, Iris Marion: on borders, 84; on protector/protected dichotomy, 39; works cited, 22, 31, 37, 123, 179
Youngs, Gillian, 33
Yousef, Ramzi, 208n5
Yuval-Davis, Nira, 32, 101, 102

Zagorin, Adam, 72
ZAKA (Identifiers of Victims of Disaster), 82, 93–97, 193, 209n5, 209n6
Zalewski, Marysia, 43–44
Al-Zawahiri, Ayman, 152
Zehfuss, Maja, 133, 134
Zetter, Kim, 128
Ziarek, Ewa Plonowska, 25, 42
Žižek, Slavoj, 208n2 (ch.3)
Zubaydah, Abu, 63, 64
Zucchino, David, 141, 147, 149

Ingram Content Group UK Ltd.
Milton Keynes UK
UKHW022355130323
418540UK00004B/174